Race, Equality, and the Burdens of History

This book philosophically addresses problems of past racial discrimination in the United States. John Arthur examines the concepts of race and racism and discusses racial equality, poverty and race, reparations and affirmative action, and merit in ways that cut across the usual political lines. A former civil-rights plaintiff and professor at an historically black college in the South, Arthur draws on both personal experience and rigorous philosophical training in this account. His nuanced conclusions about the meaning of merit, the defects of affirmative action, the importance of apology, and the need for true equality illuminate one of America's most vexing problems and offer a way forward. His book is relevant to any society struggling with racial differences and past injustices.

John Arthur died of cancer in January 2007, after completing this book. He was professor of philosophy and Director of the Program in Philosophy, Politics and Law at Binghamton University, State University of New York. He is the author of *Words That Bind: Judicial Review and the Grounds of Modern Constitutional Theory*; *The Unfinished Constitution: Philosophy and Constitutional Practice*; and *Studying Philosophy: A Guide for the Perplexed*. Since 1979, Professor Arthur was the editor of one of the most widely used ethics anthologies in the United States, *Morality and Moral Controversies*, soon to be published in its 8th edition.

Race, Equality, and the Burdens of History

John Arthur

Binghamton University,
State University of New York

CAMBRIDGE
UNIVERSITY PRESS

CAMBRIDGE UNIVERSITY PRESS
Cambridge, New York, Melbourne, Madrid, Cape Town, Singapore, São Paulo, Delhi

Cambridge University Press
32 Avenue of the Americas, New York, NY 10013-2473, USA

www.cambridge.org
Information on this title: www.cambridge.org/9780521879378

First published 2007

Printed in the United States of America

A catalog record for this publication is available from the British Library.

Library of Congress Cataloging in Publication Data

Arthur, John, 1946–2007
Race, equality, and the burdens of history / John Arthur.
    p. cm.
Includes bibliographical references and index.
ISBN 978-0-521-87937-8 (hardback) – ISBN 978-0-521-70495-3 (pbk.)
1. Racism – United States. 2. Race discrimination – United States–History. 3. African
Americans – Civil rights. 4. African Americans – Economic conditions. 5. Poverty –
United States. 6. African Americans – Reparations. 7. Affirmative action programs –
United States. 8. Equality – United States. 9. Merit (Ethics) – Social aspects – United
States. 10. United States – Race relations.   I. Title.
E185.615.A79   2007
305.896'0973–dc22   2007000595

ISBN   978-0-521-87937-8 hardback
ISBN   978-0-521-70495-3 paperback

For Amy, who made this and so much more possible

Contents

Preface

This book has been many years in the making. My academic interest in racism and racial equality dates from graduate school at Vanderbilt University, where I minored in Afro-American studies (as we called it then) at neighboring Fisk University while working on my Ph.D. in philosophy. After completing my Ph.D., I also did an M.A. degree in sociology, writing a thesis on racial integration of higher education. I later taught for nearly a decade at historically black Tennessee State University in Nashville.

Faculty and students at Tennessee State worked in appalling conditions, often overcoming obstacles that nobody should have to put up with, while a few miles away predominantly white Middle Tennessee State University enjoyed far better facilities. In an attempt to redress this injustice and eliminate de facto segregation, another faculty member and I decided to organize a biracial group of faculty and students in order to go to Federal Court. Our suit accused the State of Tennessee of violating the Equal Protection Clause of the U.S. Constitution through its failure to desegregate its educational system and for its neglect of Tennessee State University. We eventually agreed to accept a settlement offer that brought new programs and millions of dollars to improve Tennessee State University as well as a new Desegregation Plan for the state's entire system of higher education. I decided to write a book about racial equality during those years, and I have worked on it intermittently ever since.

Various parts of this book have appeared in print as articles. Sections of Chapter 1 appeared in "Critical Race Theory: A Critique"[1] and in

---

[1] John Arthur, "Critical Race Theory: A Critique," in *Reflections: An Anthology of African-American Philosophy*, edited by James Montmarquet and William Hardy (Belmont CA: Wadsworth Pub. Co., 2000).

"Multiculturalism."[2] My discussion of institutional racism in Chapter 4 draws on "Institutional Racism and Equal Protection."[3] An earlier version of parts of Chapter 6 appeared in "Racism and Reparations."[4]

I have also presented earlier versions to colloquia at many universities. My discussion of affirmative action formed the basis of presentations at Balliol College, Oxford, and at George Mason University. The material on racial equality and strict scrutiny also benefited from comments in the Oxford Seminar on Law and Philosophy in the spring of 2003. Parts of my discussions of Critical Race Theory were presented to the Philosophy Triangle at Cambridge University and at Hamilton College. And, finally, I gave parts of Chapter 6, on reparations and apologies, in talks at the University of Reading and at Green Mountain College. Whenever possible, I have indicated my debts to individual commentators and critics in my footnotes.

An early draft of this book was completed while I was a Visiting Fellow at Balliol College, Oxford, and I want to thank Balliol College and its fellowship for the opportunity to spend the year 2002–2003 in their remarkably stimulating and congenial environment. Jerry Cohen, Joseph Raz, and Nicos Stavropoulos were especially generous and helpful during that year. Many other friends and colleagues also provided invaluable criticisms and suggestions. These include Charles Goodman, Christopher Knapp, Mel Leffler, Steve Scalet, Danny Shternfeld, Bill Throop, and Lisa Weil. I especially want to thank Phyllis Leffler and Amy Shapiro, who read and made valuable comments on earlier drafts of this book.

John Arthur
Binghamton, New York

[2] John Arthur, "Multiculturalism," in *The Oxford Handbook of Practical Ethics*, edited by Hugh LaFollette (Oxford: Oxford University Press, 2003), pp. 413–432.

[3] John Arthur, "Institutional Racism and Equal Protection," *American Philosophical Association Newsletter on Philosophy of Law*, Vol. 4, No. 1 (2004).

[4] John Arthur, "Racism and Reparations," in *Morality and Moral Controversies*, 6th ed., edited by John Arthur (Upper Saddle River NJ: Prentice Hall, 2002), pp. 534–550.

Introduction

SLAVERY, RACIAL SEGREGATION, AND RACISM LEFT A LARGE AND lasting legacy. They scarred American history, and they continue to frame our country's self-understanding. Only in the last half of the twentieth century did Americans, awakened to the enormity of the injustices of racial oppression, undertake serious reform of their political and social institutions. At no point in that long process did changes come easily or without controversy and, more often than not, violence. There have been changes, but it is far from agreed how much change has taken place, how far we have left to go, or what policies should now be pursued.

The organizing theme of this book is racism: its nature, consequences, and cures. But racism cannot be considered in isolation, and so each of the first four chapters addresses theoretical issues that are often in the background of discussions of racism. These include: the nature of racism and of institutional racism, the ideas of social construction and of race itself, the history and nature of slavery, and the meaning and importance of the ideal of racial equality. The last four chapters of this book focus on the problems of race and poverty together with affirmative action, reparations, and other proposals designed to promote racial justice and to reduce the burdens of a racist history. This book concludes with discussions of the importance and the challenges of providing equality of opportunity.

Chapter 1 examines the nature of racism. Charges of racism – individual and institutional – are familiar. Suggestions that the response (or really the lack of response) by the federal government to Hurricane Katrina's devastation of New Orleans, with its large African-American population, was evidence of racism were common. Racial profiling is also often thought to be racist because it relies on racial stereotypes.

1

Some have suggested that any institutional structure that produces significant racial disparities in income, education, or incarceration rates is racist, while some think that opposition to particular policies designed to reduce racial injustice, such as affirmative action or reparations, is itself indicative of racism.

Yet, despite this widespread usage of the term, there is little agreement in the scholarly literature or elsewhere about what racism is. Some writers have thought of it as an attitude; others claim that it includes beliefs, systems of oppression, or a combination of those. I argue that at its core racism is neither a belief nor an oppressive institutional structure (though it is often associated with both). Instead, it is an attitude of racial contempt. I then examine the connections between racism and religious bigotry, and racism and prejudice and explain what is wrong with racism and why we have particular reason to condemn racists. With that as background, we are then able to understand the meaning of institutional racism, as an interpretive concept. I conclude with a discussion of stereotyping and racial profiling, asking whether racial profiling is an instance of institutional racism, whether profiling can ever be justified, and how society should respond to those who might be harmed as a result of profiling.

Chapter 2 focuses on the debate about the social construction of race – a subject that can also bring charges of racism in its wake. Although it is commonly assumed these days that races are not natural groups but are socially constructed, it is not clear what that means, or even why it matters. After a discussion of the idea of social construction itself, I go on to weigh the evidence on both sides of the constructivist/anticonstructivist divide with respect to race. Social constructivists, I argue, are correct to emphasize that the concept of race as it has traditionally been used is in fact a social construction rather than a biological category as was often supposed. But although that is true, there is growing evidence that there exists another respect in which race (or something close to it) is a biological category. Recent work in population genetics as well as new medical research suggests that human beings belong to distinct "continental" population groups. One question, then, is whether such biological divisions, if they prove important, provide a scientific basis for the older idea that races are real. A further question is what would follow, if anything, from the discovery that "continental races" are not social constructs but instead natural categories.

Chapter 3 begins with a discussion of an institution that was rooted in racism and racial inequality: chattel slavery. What was slavery, precisely, and how did slavery in the United States fit in the larger world in which slavery was widely practiced? How was it linked to racism? To answer those questions, I look at the institution of slavery and at arguments offered by slavery's defenders. Rather than claiming that slaves were not persons, as is sometimes supposed, they argued that slaves were less than *equal* persons. Slaves were thought to have less moral standing. That view, however, was far from universally accepted, and even slaveowners such as Thomas Jefferson understood that slavery was incompatible with slaves' status as persons. The chapter concludes with a discussion of the different positions of Jefferson and John C. Calhoun over what equality meant and whether slaves were equal persons.

The meaning and implications of racial equality are the subjects of Chapter 4. I explore the ways that slavery and racial segregation violated the ideal of equality, the consequences of racism, and the methods the law should use to root out institutional racism. Some have thought that racial equality is a natural fact about human beings, while others contend that it is a moral ideal. I defend the second, moralized account, arguing that equality is linked with human dignity and in particular with persons' self-worth, self-respect, and self-esteem. Building on these ideas of racial equality and racism, I argue that courts are correct when they secure the ideal of racial equality by attacking institutional racism under the banner of the U.S. Constitution's Equal Protection Clause. The chapter concludes with an assessment of the pessimistic conclusion reached by some social scientists that racism is a natural, inevitable feature of the human psyche and of what that might mean to the prospects of achieving racial justice.

With these theoretical discussions of racism, race, slavery, and racial equality as background, the second half of this book weighs some of the more practical moral and policy issues associated with efforts to achieve racial equality and justice. One hard fact lies behind much of my discussion of racism and inequality: that African-Americans are disproportionately represented among the poorest people in the United States. How is that fact to be explained? The answers to that difficult and important question, I contend, are rooted in history. But it is not just the history of slavery and racial oppression, although that is part of the story. Efforts to fight poverty, ironically, have added to the burdens that racial oppression already placed on the shoulders of blacks.

Chapter 5 begins with a description of economic differences that are found among many cultural, racial, and ethnic groups. The authors of the controversial book *The Bell Curve* famously argued that intelligence explains economic differences and that genetics plays a significant role in explaining racial differences in I.Q. tests. Rejecting such explanations of racial differences, I go on to examine the possible causes of African-American poverty in some detail. Instead of one explanation, I argue that poverty arises from a complex web of many different factors. These include unemployment, economic shifts away from manufacturing jobs, family breakdown, and crime. But gaps in educational achievement also account for an important part of the economic disparity between blacks and other groups, raising the question of how those gaps can be explained. The answer is in part the result of culture. I conclude the chapter with a discussion of the fear of competition that has been fed by public policies and pronouncements emphasizing the "racially stacked deck" and the "shackles of history." The effect of this, against a background of rumors of inferiority, has been to encourage black pessimism, undermine self-respect, and ultimately contribute to the economic inequalities the policies had hoped to reduce.

In view of the continuing plight of poor blacks, it is sometimes said that society owes a debt to the descendants of slaves, and that compensation for historic oppression is long past due. Yet, arguments about how to respond to the historic injustices of slavery and racism often confuse two different questions. Therefore, I begin Chapter 6 by examining two forms of compensatory justice: restitution and reparations. *Restitution* refers to the demand that stolen or otherwise wrongly acquired property be returned to its rightful owner or his or her descendants. *Reparation,* on the other hand, is modeled on tort law and the requirement that those who intentionally or negligently wrong others are responsible for eliminating the lingering effects of their wrongful past actions. The discussion ranges over the *form(s)* that restitution and reparations might take, *who or what* might owe the debt, *to whom* it might be owed, and *why* the debt might be owed. I conclude that neither restitution nor reparations (as usually understood) is justified. Although some part of the problems confronting African-Americans today is in fact a legacy of slavery and racism, reparations would tend to exacerbate the underlying causes of economic inequalities.

The question of how to respond to historic injustices does not end there, however, since an apology may be owed even though reparations are rejected. Apologies are important, I argue, because they are public expressions of remorse. Apologies, therefore, have the potential to alter moral relationships among groups as well as individuals. But an apology demands more than simply uttering it if it is to be more than a sham.

The remaining chapters explore possible responses to slavery and racism, from affirmative action and the ideal of equality of opportunity to programs designed to promote equality. Opponents of affirmative action sometimes claim that positions should be allocated based on "merit" rather than race. Defenders of affirmative action sometimes take the opposite tack, claiming that merit is a "myth" that is used to exclude African-Americans from positions of influence and limit their prospects. The nature of merit and its importance are therefore the focus of Chapter 7. I begin by distinguishing merit from desert and then I argue that merit and qualifications are not myths, as some have suggested, though merit and qualifications do rely on the assumption that some people have traits that will enable them to perform various roles better than others. That said, however, merit is only one of many possible reasons for placing people in roles. I then examine why race can, in certain circumstances, be a qualification for a position.

Chapter 8 discusses affirmative action more broadly, together with related questions about equality of opportunity and how it might be secured. I first weigh a variety of arguments in support of affirmative action, including the importance of role models, the need to combat lingering racism, and the importance of diversity. While affirmative action has served important purposes in the past, I conclude that it has in important respects now outlived its usefulness. Affirmative action imposes other burdens on blacks as well, I argue. There is evidence that it adversely affects achievement levels in school, graduation rates, professional qualifications, and, ultimately, job performance. Another concern is the message it sends. Given our racially oppressive history and the rumors of inferiority it bred, affirmative action tends to undermine self-respect of blacks while eroding support among whites for other policies that would be of more benefit.

I conclude by addressing the issues that are important as we reflect on the positive implications of my arguments in this book. The first idea, of a valuable life, is in the background of the second idea, which is equality of opportunity. The first question is crucial because without some guidance about a valuable life, we may be at a loss as we begin to think about why equality of opportunity is important and even what we might hope to equalize. After discussing the nature of a valuable life, I then explore the meaning and the importance of a genuine commitment to seeing that all Americans – but especially African-Americans – are provided with an equal opportunity to achieve a valuable life. If taken seriously, I argue, such a commitment would be more demanding and costly than continuation of current policies. I also argue, however, that nothing less is required if the history of slavery and racial oppression is ever to be acknowledged and effectively addressed. I conclude with a brief discussion of some programs and proposals that might be expected to begin to improve the opportunities available to African-Americans.

I want to conclude this Introduction with some brief comments about the methods I rely on in this book. Some of the arguments are conceptual. Philosophers have traditionally seen the elucidation of concepts as among their tasks, and it is an important goal of this book. One source of conceptual disagreements is the fact that concepts are often normative: they carry with them an implicit political or moral judgment. If racial profiling is a form of "institutional racism," for instance, that alone implies there is reason to condemn it. Others argue in the opposite direction. If affirmative action is a racist practice, then, for that reason, it must be rejected. Merit is another concept that is the object of sustained disagreement. If we are to understand whether hiring and admissions should be based on merit, we need first to understand what merit is.

Although it is important to be as clear as possible about the concepts we use in discussing matters having to do with racism and race, I do not assume that concepts are unchanging realities existing outside history and human practices. Nor do I argue that the reasons given in support of particular ways of understanding concepts are politically and morally neutral. Though philosophers are not limited simply to describing how words are used by modern-day speakers of English, usage does provide a starting point in thinking about concepts and how they should be understood. But while usage is the beginning, it is not the end. Often arguments can be provided in favor of interpreting a concept one way or another where a concept is otherwise unclear. Some arguments may be based in natural or social sciences; others may be normative. In that way, accounts of concepts are not neutral. That said, however, there are still constraints on the choice between competing accounts of concepts. Some constraints are based on how the concept is used; other constraints may be of a scientific or normative nature.

My goal, then, is to elucidate core concepts like racism, race, racial equality, and merit – among others – in ways that shed light on our social world and guide our thinking as we consider practical questions about what should be done. Other philosophical themes of this book are even more explicitly practical and normative, focusing on what policies should be adopted. Historical, economic, and sociological disagreement can lie behind these policy disputes. But these disputes can also reflect disagreement or confusion about core concepts, so that both types of philosophical problems – the conceptual and the normative – are woven together along with more empirical and sociological issues. Because reasoning about normative and policy issues requires both clarification of concepts and moral argument, this book reaches beyond philosophy to other disciplines. Questions about the legitimacy of racial profiling, affirmative action, and reparations, and even the nature of race itself, cannot be answered without engaging the disciplines of economics, history, psychology, and biology.

What is the larger process of moral and political argument in which this book is engaged? The answer I favor is that we are seeking the correct "balance of reasons," where "reasons" simply means considerations in favor of something. Reasons apply to people's beliefs and to their actions. Reasons can apply to a person, whether or not they are recognized or appreciated. A person may have a reason to leave a dangerous building, for instance, whether or not the reason is appreciated. When we have decided on an answer to a moral or political question, we normally do so because we think the balance of reasons favors the course we have chosen. Yet, there is often something worthwhile to be said for the other side as well, which means we are left with having to balance competing reasons. There is nothing strange about this; we do it all the time in both our personal and public lives. While going through the deliberative process, we know that no algorithm exists that we can employ to calculate the right answer. We must simply do the best we can, identifying and weighing various reasons in light of the available arguments on all sides. Such a process is as familiar as it is difficult.

The conclusions I reach here often cut across the familiar divisions we have come to expect in books on racism and equality. For instance, some readers may embrace my conclusion that courts should be aggressive in attacking institutional racism, my defense of the constitutionality of affirmative action, my defense of an apology for slavery and my argument that race sometimes constitutes a form of merit. Those same people may well disagree with my (qualified) defense of racial profiling, my account of race as a natural category, my criticisms of affirmative action and of reparations, and my defense of equality of opportunity rather than equality of outcome. So I hope this book might help us move beyond the stale and often predictable positions that too often surround discussions of racism and racial equality.

1

Racism

FEW TOPICS PROVOKE MORE DISAGREEMENTS THAN ONES INVOLVING the extent and possible cures of racism, and a part of those disputes can be attributed to confusion in the concept of racism itself. William Julius Wilson, for example, writes that the word *racism* "has been used so indiscriminately, has so many different definitions, and is often relied on to cover up lack of information or knowledge of complex issues, that it frequently weakens rather than enhances arguments concerning race."[1] I agree with Wilson that confusion about racism (and other concepts) can be pernicious, making fruitful discussion of many issues more difficult and disagreements harder to recognize and assess. So the first step is to understand the concept of racism.

While there is no generally accepted understanding of racism, there is at least a general agreement that racism is in some way wrong or objectionable. But beyond that lies widespread controversy and often confusion. What, precisely, *is* racism? Is it fundamentally different from religious bigotry and other forms of prejudice, and if so how? And what, exactly, is wrong with racism? Is it a character defect, or does its evil lie in its consequences? Or is it both?

Some think racism refers to people's beliefs about the inferiority of another race; others see it as a feeling or an attitude; still others emphasize the public and institutional forms it can take – slavery, segregation, and other institutions that establish and reinforce racial oppression. Some understand racism to encompass all of those: attitudes, beliefs, and institutions. Another question that is often in the background of these discussions is who and what can be racist. Some have suggested

---

[1] William Julius Wilson, *The Truly Disadvantaged* (Chicago: University of Chicago Press, 1987), p. 12.

8

that racism is only possible in the context of domination, and that the victims of racial oppression cannot truly be racist if the objects of their racism are the oppressors. If racism is related to power and dominance, then it is not possible for those who are weak and racially oppressed to be racists themselves.

I will argue that the best conception of racism – one that helps explain the relationships among all these different features – is that, *at its core*, racism is an *attitude* people take toward other persons in virtue of their race. This understanding of racism is not only more consistent with our understanding of the concept than its competitors, but it also enables us to clarify a range of closely related issues. These include the links between racism, beliefs, and institutional oppression; who and what are racists; the relationship between racism and prejudice; and the nature of institutional racism, racist beliefs and stereotypes, and racial profiling.

Racism as a normative concept

The term "racism" first came into wide usage with the appearance in 1938 of the English translation of a book written in 1933–1934 in German by Magnus Hirchfeld titled *Racism*, in which Hirchfeld stressed the idea that racism was "grounded" in the belief in a "biological hierarchy" of races.[2] Others have agreed that beliefs are at the core of the concept of racism. Herbert Aptheker, for instance, writes that racism is the "belief in the inherent, immutable, and significant inferiority of an entire physically characterized people."[3] Richard Schaefer thinks that racism is inherent in the doctrine that "one racial group is superior [to another],"[4] and David Theo Goldberg writes that we can identify racists "on the basis of the kinds of beliefs they hold" and in particular beliefs that "ascribe racial characteristics of others which purportedly differ from their own. . . ."[5] Leonard Harris also thinks the "systematic denial of a population's humanity" is the "hallmark of racism."[6]

[2] Magnus Hirchfeld, *Racism*, translated by Eden Paul and Cedar Paul (London: Victor Golancz, Ltd., 1938).

[3] Herbert Aptheker, *Anti-Racism in U.S. History* (Westport CT: Greenwood Press, 1992), p. xiv.

[4] Richard Schaefer, *Racial and Ethnic Groups*, 4th ed. (Glenview: Scott Foresman, 1990), p. 27.

[5] David Theo Goldberg, "Racism and Rationality: The Need for a New Critique," *Philosophy of the Social Sciences*, Vol. 20, No. 2 (1990), pp. 317–348), reprinted in *Racism*, edited by Leonard Harris (Amherst NY: Humanity Books, 1999), p. 370.

[6] Leonard Harris, "What, Then, Is Racism?" in *Racism*, edited by Harris, p. 437.

Some have gone even further in linking racism to beliefs and ideas. Joe R. Feagin thinks those who accept racial stereotypes are racists. Feagin compares what he calls the *"stereotypes of contemporary racism . . .* [such as] myths of the dangerous black man" with the "racist fictions that underlay the Nazi Holocaust."[7] Eduardo Bonilla-Silva describes what he terms "color-blind racism." According to Bonilla-Silva, color-blind racism is inherent in liberalism and its commitment to "equality of opportunity," to economic liberalism understood as "choice," to "individualism," and to "meritocracy."[8] By "framing race-related issues in the language of liberalism" he thinks that

> whites can appear "reasonable" and even "moral" while opposing almost all practical approaches to deal with de facto racial inequality. . . . For instance the principle of equal opportunity . . . is invoked by whites today to oppose affirmative action policies because they supposedly represent "preferential treatment" of certain groups. . . . . Another example is regarding each person as an "individual" with "choices" and using this liberal principle as a justification for whites having the right of choosing to live in segregated neighborhoods.[9]

On this view, racism takes other forms as well, including "naturalization" (thinking that racial differences are natural) and "minimization" (believing that discrimination is no longer a central factor affecting minorities' life chances or "It's better now than in the past") and "cultural racism" (relying on culturally based arguments such as "blacks have too many babies").[10] The point is that anyone (or at least any "white") who thinks in those terms is evidencing "color-blind racism." These different elements go together to form a "racial ideology."[11]

Rather than focusing on beliefs, others suggest that racism's most salient feature is that it names what people *do* to each other, especially through institutions that lead to subjugation and inequalities in power. Blackwell's *Dictionary of Sociology* states that the "key test" of whether something is racist "lies in the consequences: if it supports race privilege, then it is by definition racist."[12] The Dictionary's examples of institutions of

[7] Joe R. Feagin, Hernan Vera, and Pinar Batur, *White Racism*, 2nd ed. (New York: Routledge, 2001), p. 24 (emphasis added).

[8] Eduardo Bonilla-Silva, *Racism without Racists: Color-Blind Racism and the Persistence of Racial Inequality in the United States* (Lanham MD: Rowman and Littlefield, 2003), pp. 28–32.

[9] Bonilla-Silva, *Racism without Racists*, p. 28.

[10] Bonilla-Silva, *Racism without Racists*, pp. 28–29 and Chapter 2, passim.

[11] Bonilla-Silva, *Racism without Racists*, p. 173.

[12] Allan G. Johnson, *Blackwell Dictionary of Sociology*, 2nd ed. (Malden MA: Blackwell Publishing Co., 2000), p. 249.

"race privilege" include "neighborhood schools" and "the right of people to sell their homes to whomever they wish." These are "racist in effect, even if they are not racist in intent."[13] Robert Mills also thinks that racism involves "structures and institutions" with the "power to discriminate,"[14] while Joseph Brandt claims that racism is "the power to enforce one's prejudice. . . . Racism is prejudice plus power."[15] Michael Harrington emphasizes the economic aspects of this structural perspective: racism, he thinks, is "an occupational hierarchy rooted in history and institutionalized in the labor market."[16]

Some incorporate these various elements into their understanding of racism. According to Michael Omin and Howard Winant, racism refers to any practice that "creates or reproduces structures of domination *based on* essentialist categories of race."[17] A recent legal case book designed to introduce law students to "Critical Race Theory"[18] relies on the views of Richard Delgado, who thinks there are two types of racism: procedural and substantive. *Procedural racism,* he says, is present when the government uses "rules that invalidate or handicap black claims." These include requirements of proof of intent to discriminate, limits on the type and pace of relief granted in civil rights cases, and limitations on attorneys' fees. It is racism, he writes, to "elevate equality of opportunity over equality of result."[19] The other form of racism identified by Delgado, besides procedural, is *substantive.* He writes that "[b]y substantive racism I mean *that which treats* blacks and other nonwhite persons as though they were actually inferior to whites."[20]

Naomi Zack also takes a broad view, agreeing with Delgado and other critical race theorists that racism encompasses beliefs, attitudes, and institutional practices. Racism, she writes, refers to a "multiplicity of morally blameworthy attitudes and dispositions" as well as "specific beliefs, emo-

---

[13] Johnson, *Blackwell Dictionary of Sociology,* 2nd ed., p. 249, citing David Wellman, *Portraits of White Racism* (New York: Cambridge University Press, 1993).

[14] Robert Miles, *Racism* (London: Routledge, 1989), p. 54.

[15] Joseph Brandt, *Dismantling Racism: The Continuing Challenge to White America* (Minneapolis: Augsburg Fortress, Publishers, 1991), p. 28.

[16] Michael Harrington, *The New American Poverty* (New York: Holt, Rinehart, and Winston, 1984), p. 140.

[17] Michael Omin and Howard Winant, *Racial Formation in the United States* (New York: Routledge, 1994), p. 71, emphasis added.

[18] Dorothy A. Brown, *Critical Race Theory: Cases, Materials, and Problems* (St. Paul MN: West Publishing, 2003).

[19] Brown, *Critical Race Theory: Cases, Materials, and Problems,* p. 4.

[20] Brown, *Critical Race Theory: Cases, Materials, and Problems,* p. 4.

tions and actions that instantiate them."[21] Lawrence Bloom writes that
"all forms of racism" can be related to one of two general themes or
"paradigms," namely, "inferiorization" and "antipathy."[22] By "inferiorization," he means treating certain groups as inferior to other groups "by
reason of their biological nature"; the term "antipathy," he says, "unequiv-
ocally encompasses racial bigotry, hostility and hatred."[23]

And finally, some writers seem not to agree even with themselves. *The
Penguin Dictionary of Philosophy* offers the following definition:

> *Racism The doctrine that ascribes to another race inferior or dangerous qualities. . . .
> Racists often regard the other race as morally, biologically, or intellectually inferior.
> But not always. Hostile sentiments against Jews, Chinese, etc. have sometimes arisen
> from fear of their supposed racial superiority in certain respects.*[24]

This definition is doubly interesting. The first suggestion is that racism is
a *doctrine* that another race is inferior or dangerous, which seems to imply
that racism is about beliefs; but we are also told that racists are people
who harbor "hostile *sentiments*" toward another race. Then, finally, the
writer suggests that racism is sometimes the belief that the other race –
the object of the racism – is in some respect *superior*.

Clearly there is little agreement about racism. A good place to begin
is to take a step back and look at an important feature of the concept
of racism that is perhaps less controversial. It is a feature many other
concepts share.

How people describe, and frame, a particular situation or an action
often shapes how they then evaluate what they are describing. When we
call an act "terrorism" or a policy "genocidal," for example, we do more
than neutrally describe the act or policy; we also imply that there is reason
to condemn it. This is an instance of a more general phenomenon in
which the evaluative conclusion – that we have reason to condemn (or
approve) a thing – is embedded in the concept itself. Such concepts
are normative ones; they bring with them an evaluation as well as a
description. It is no wonder, therefore, that such normative concepts
often engender moral and political struggles. Once we define a person
as a terrorist, we have committed ourselves normatively.

[21] Naomi Zack, "Race and Racial Discrimination," in *The Oxford Handbook of Practical Ethics*,
edited by Hugh LaFollette (Oxford: Oxford University Press, 2003), p. 248.
[22] Lawrence Blum, *"I'm not a Racist, but. . . ." The Moral Quandary of Race* (Ithaca: Cornell
University Press, 2002), p. 8.
[23] Blum, *"I'm not a Racist but. . . ."* p. 8.
[24] *The Penguin Dictionary of Philosophy*, edited by Thomas Mautner (London: Penguin,
2000), p. 468.

Because concepts sometimes have general normative judgments embedded in them, it is tempting to define a concept in a way that supports a normative conclusion. The U.S. Department of State, for example, explains that terrorist acts are ones done by "sub-national groups or sub-national agents." Taking that as part of the meaning of terrorism implies that *governments* cannot commit acts of terrorism – a conclusion that the Department of State would presumably endorse. If "terrorism" were to extend to a government's decision to use saturation bombing that causes the death of innocents, however, then the opposite conclusion would follow: that we have reason to condemn the bombing of Hiroshima and Dresden as acts of terror. Debates about the concept of terrorism have also confounded attempts at the United Nations to implement Security Council Resolution 1373 requiring states to "take the necessary steps to prevent the commission of terrorist acts" and "refrain from providing any support" to persons involved in them. The U.N. Security Council deadlocked over debates about whether Israel engages in "acts of terrorism" and has been unable to identify states that engage in terrorism.[25] One reason is the normative content of the concept of "terrorism."

Racism and racist are normative concepts in that same sense: whatever else these concepts mean, we have reason to condemn racism and racists. To say that a person's racism is something to be admired is not merely controversial; it suggests that the speaker does not understand the concept of racism. Like terrorists or perpetrators of genocide, racists suffer from a defect of some sort.

That fact – that racism is a normative concept – helps explain why there is so much controversy about the concept. As with terrorism, there is always the temptation to try to win arguments about race by building specific reasons why racism is worthy of condemnation directly into the meaning of racism. This can happen on all sides of the political spectrum.

Conservative philosopher Anthony Flew, for example, claims that racism, properly understood, is what he terms an "essentially intentional" action.[26] It is an act of "unjust discrimination" on the basis of race, and

---

[25] For a discussion of this history, see Anne Bayefsky, "U.N.Derwhelming Response: The U.N.'s Approach to Terrorism," *National Review Online*, September 24, 2004. http://www.nationalreview.com/comment/bayefsky200409240915.asp. Accessed on March 29, 2007. The same type of argument can be observed in the case of genocide, when Israeli policy is termed "genocide" against the Palestinians.

[26] Anthony Flew, *Thinking about Social Thinking* (Oxford: Blackwell, 1985), p. 10.

anybody who practices such discrimination is a racist.[27] Because Flew believes that race names merely superficial characteristics of persons such as skin color, he is able to conclude that race should be irrelevant for virtually all decisions, including hiring. Flew has therefore welded a controversial moral judgment about affirmative action to the normative concept of racism.

The same embedding strategy can also be used by people with opposing political views. If racism is tied to institutional power, as Blackwell's *Dictionary of Sociology* suggests, then it could follow that a (powerless) black who commits an explicitly racially motivated murder could not be a racist. This shows why the broader accounts of racism I mentioned have very different political implications from the narrower ones like Flew's. They not only deny Flew's attempt to equate racism and racial preferences, but they also suggest racism is pervasive and that institutions that do not result in equality of racial outcomes are, for that reason, racist.

What is unsatisfying about such broad characterizations, however, is that they are not so much wrong as unhelpful. To simply list a panoply of attitudes, beliefs, practices, institutions, and outcomes that have something to do with racism, without explaining how they are connected, does nothing to explain the relationships between the racism, the beliefs that Zack said "instantiate" it, and the practices like slavery and segregation that grow out of racism. Narrower ways of understanding racism are often flawed in another way, however, when they seek to make political headway by providing a narrow definition that rules out the possibility of institutional racism or the legitimacy of racial preferences.

What is racism?

Consider, first, the interesting comparison between racism and patriotism. To be patriotic means having an affirmative, positive attitude toward one's own country, people, or nation. Racism is also, I want to suggest, an attitude, but rather than being positive, it is negative. Furthermore, instead of a nation or its people, its object is members of a racial group. Racism is a negative attitude toward persons in virtue of their race. But what attitude, specifically? The answer I will defend is "racial contempt in the form of either hostility or indifference." Briefly, then, my central claim is that, at its core, racism is best understood as racial contempt in

---

[27] Quoted in Anthony Skillen, "Racism: Flew's Three Concepts of Racism," *Journal of Applied Philosophy*, Vol. 10 (1993), pp. 73–89.

the form of an *attitude of either hostility or indifference toward people's legitimate interests in virtue of their race.* Many of these ideas require explaining.

First, it is interesting that the U.S. Supreme Court suggested the distinction between overt hostility and indifference, and that both raise issues of prejudice. In a case dealing with discrimination against the handicapped, the Court stated that "Discrimination was perceived by Congress to be most often the product, not of *invidious animus,* but rather of *thoughtlessness and indifference* – of benign neglect."[28] The first form, *hostility* (what the Court termed "invidious animus") is most clear in the blind racial hatred of groups such as the Ku Klux Klan and neo-Nazi organizations. It is also present, if less clearly, in simple dislike of persons in virtue of their race. Racism often takes a second but sometimes more insidious form. More subtle than the hostility of a lynching or other overt expressions of racial hatred, indifference (or "thoughtlessness" and "benign neglect") toward persons in virtue of their race is also a type of racism. Imagine a person who sits idly by doing nothing while someone is being beaten. If the person would otherwise have helped, and the explanation of the refusal is indifference to the victim in virtue of race, then that too is a form of racism.

What, then, does it mean to say that the attitude of hostility or indifference exists "in virtue of" a person's race? One possibility is that the race of the person is thought to be a reason or justification for the hostility or indifference. But while that is often true, racism can also be present without the person's conscious belief. We need to look for a broader understanding of the relationship between the hostility or indifference and the other person's race. I want to suggest that the attitude of contempt exists "in virtue of" race whenever the race of the person figures into the *explanation* of the attitude. That explanation may, but need not, appeal to a conscious reason. Thus, a person need not believe that race is a reason that justifies hostility or indifference to exhibit racism. All that is required is that race of another figure in or be part of the explanation of the attitude of hostility or indifference. People may be hostile or indifferent to others for many different reasons, some of which are legitimate. Hostility might be present in virtue of one person having wronged another, for example, and it is at least theoretically possible that such hostility may be justified. That is not racism. But when hostility or indifference exists in virtue of the race of another person, and race is itself part of the explanation of the attitude, then that is racism.

[28] *Alexander v. Choate,* 469 U.S. 287, 295 (1985).

Racial indifference, if not overt hostility, can also be combined with other more positive attitudes. Consider what might be called a "paternalistic racist" whose attitudes mix concern in one context with indifference in others. Some slaveowners conceivably manifested complex attitudes of paternalistic affection (analogous perhaps to feelings of parents for children) while ignoring or denigrating the legitimate interests of slaves in freedom and self-respect. This mix may have produced a level of genuine concern rather than hatred or even racial hostility.[29] How common such "paternalistic racism" was is not important. The central claim here is only that racism is an attitude toward persons in virtue of their race, and that the attitude can take a variety of forms ranging from hatred and hostility to dislike and, finally, to indifference. It is therefore a mistake to equate racism with hatred. Racism is much broader and includes weaker forms of racial contempt. It can also coexist with some more positive attitudes.

This account of racism can be extended to sexism and various forms of ethnic bigotry. To be a sexist or a bigot is also to harbor contempt in the form of hostility or indifference toward persons in virtue of their sex, religion, or ethnicity. Whether anyone was a paternalistic racist may be doubted, but paternalistic sexism has been pervasive. John Stuart Mill saw this clearly when he pointed out that men not only insisted on dominating women economically and politically but also wanted their affection.[30] It is a mistake, then, to think that a man who feels affection for a woman cannot also manifest sexism toward her, just as a slaveowner could not claim to be free of racism on the grounds that he had genuine affection and concern for his slaves. Although it is impossible to hate what one loves, it is not uncommon to show indifference toward, or to fail to appreciate the interests of, those for whom we have otherwise positive feelings.

All of this leaves many questions open, including both the *causes* of racism and the *effects* it can have. The answer to each question varies from case to case. Racism's prevalence in one society might be the outgrowth of historical conditions such as severe social and economic problems combined with racial scapegoating by leaders. Or it might be a reaction to having been the subject of racial injustice and oppression by

---

[29] For a valuable discussion of how the institution of slavery in general ignored the legitimate interests of slaves, see Joshua Cohen, "The Arc of the Moral Universe," *Philosophy and Public Affairs*, Vol. 26, No. 2 (1997) pp. 91–134.

[30] John Stuart Mill (1869), *On the Subjection of Women*, edited by Elizabeth Rapaport (Indianapolis: Hacket Publishing Co., 1978).

another racial group. Racism's presence can also be explained in individual persons in different ways, including family background and social conditioning. Some have also thought that it is innate – a topic I will address in a later chapter.

We also know that racism can have a variety of effects on individuals and on institutions: it often leads to oppression and violence. It need not do so, however, and it is even possible that racism might have no effect on any other person. (Imagine a racist hermit living alone on some deserted island.) It is a mistake, then, to tie racism too closely to institutional oppression. While it often brings that oppression in its wake, racism can also, in theory, if not in fact, be completely benign in its effects.

I noted earlier that racism is a normative concept that carries with it an implicit negative judgment. It would be very strange, if not nonsensical, to praise a person for his racism or to suggest that in general racism is an attitude that is desirable or good. If racism is an attitude of hostility or indifference that is not *necessarily* linked to any action, as I am arguing, then how can its normative character be accounted for? Suppose (as is at least theoretically possible) that a person privately harbors hostility toward persons of another race, but that he has never done anything based on that hostility. Perhaps he has never met a person of that race, never lets the attitude be known, and never acts on his racism in ways that could harm anybody. By hypothesis, then, the racism has never resulted in his doing something wrong to another person. Nevertheless, the person is a racist. I am not suggesting, of course, that ordinary racism has no practical moral and practical implications. As I discuss in later chapters, and as the uniqueness of my example of apparently harmless racism suggests, racism is profoundly important morally. Racism has not only underwritten some of the worst injustices in human history, but it is also – I will argue – a further, unique moral harm when it is given the force of law. My point here is a conceptual one, that because racism is an attitude, and attitudes are not necessarily linked to actions, racism may not necessarily be linked to actions. The question then arises: why should even the harmless racist be faulted, or his racism condemned? If racism is an inherently normative concept, as I argue, we must look beyond its likely effects on actions for the basis on which to criticize it. But where?

The answer must be that the defect inherent in racism must rest with the attitude of hostility or indifference itself. Instead of thinking of racism as some form of *moral* defect for which the person should always be held responsible, we should instead see racism as an epistemological defect.

Even if it has no consequences, racial contempt in the form of racial hostility or indifference is defective because it is unjustified. And because of that fact, because of its inappropriateness, we have reason to condemn it even if it is otherwise harmless and the person who has it is blameless.

Attitudes can be defective in that epistemological sense because attitudes are "judgment sensitive."[31] Unjustified fear of falling off of a ladder, for instance, might be explained by a mistaken belief that the ladder is weakened, by some early childhood experience, or even – conceivably – by some sort of genetic disorder. So a rational appraisal that an attitude is defective does not depend on the attitude arising from a false belief, although unreasonable beliefs do often explain people's unjustified attitudes. Attitudes can be unjustified as a result of other, psychological factors as well. Whatever the particular explanation, however, the point is that attitudes can be either appropriate or inappropriate.

Indeed, the rational appraisal of attitudes is common. Phobias, for instance, are often clearly irrational – a fact that can be sometimes recognized even by the people who suffer from them. Cognitive psychotherapy is built on the premise that irrational attitudes can often be overcome if people can come to see that they are irrational. Positive attitudes can be irrational as well, for instance, when a person continues to feel affection for another despite overwhelming evidence that the affection is unwarranted.

This brings us back to racism. Many of the attitudes I have mentioned differ from racism in the sense that they have no inherent normative significance. When fear is present, for example, there is always a further question of whether the fear is appropriate or warranted. Fear is not necessarily bad. But racism is *always* a defect. The reason is that racism is always unwarranted. It is an attitude that is never justified. That fact – that it is an unjustified and, in that sense, inappropriate attitude – is what is wrong with racism. In the terminology I used earlier, the concept of racism "embeds" the conclusion that the attitude is defective.

That said, however, racism also differs in an important respect from the other *normative* concepts I mentioned, terrorism and genocide. Terrorism and genocide name actions – the embedded normative judgment is that there is reason to condemn the *actions*. Racism is different, however, because it does not name a category of actions but is instead an attitude. Racism is therefore defective in a different way, because the *attitude* of racial contempt is unjustified.

[31] T. M. Scanlon, *What We Owe Each Other* (Cambridge MA: Harvard University Press, 1998), pp. 18–22.

It might seem, however, that there must be more wrong with racism than its epistemological flaw. Surely, someone might object, racism represents a moral defect as well as an epistemic one. But is it true, that racism alone constitutes a moral defect? If so, what is the nature of the defect? There is no doubt that racism often leads people to do horrible things, and for that reason alone it is rational to be wary of racists and to condemn them morally when they commit racist actions. However, we can also imagine a "reluctant racist" whose upbringing or other experiences have made him a racist, but who deeply regrets that upbringing and the attitudes he has inherited. Suppose further that the racist person has done everything that could reasonably be expected to change those attitudes, yet failed. He simply cannot avoid his hostility as much as he regrets it. Although he is still a racist, it seems clear that it would be wrong to blame such a person. He is like a person who is born with an inclination to be violent, or a kleptomaniac who feels a strong desire to steal worthless junk. Indeed, there is reason to feel some sympathy for the person. Such a reluctant racist, were he to exist, has a heavier moral burden to bear than others who are more fortunate. But that does not mean the person is morally defective unless there is something that he has done that warrants moral condemnation. He is like someone who is instinctively cowardly but who overcomes his fears. A reluctant racist, if anything, might be admired for his ability to deal with problems ordinary people are lucky enough never to face. The core of racism and its normative force is therefore epistemic. Merely having the attitude is by itself not an indication of any defect other than the fact that the attitude is unjustified.

There is another dimension to the normative character of racism, however, besides the epistemological defect in the attitude itself. Although it is not always the case, as the example of the reluctant racist illustrates, in fact racists are often partly responsible for their own racist attitudes. That is because the past decisions we make, including the people we associate with and the habits we allow ourselves to form, shape our future attitudes. Attitudes are to an extent self-inflicted, which means we can be held at least partly responsible for them.[32] One researcher summarized the evidence about the role of choices this way:

---

[32] A nice example in literature is from the novel *Lonesome Dove*. Before he is hanged for murder and horse theft by his old friends Gus and Call, Jake Spoon says, "I ain't done nothing. I just fell in with these boys to get through the Territory." Call later tells Gus, "Well, I wish he hadn't got so careless about his company. It was that that cost him." Larry McMurtry, *Lonesome Dove* (New York: Simon and Schuster, 1985), pp. 641–642.

In predictable ways, people react to the things we do and say to them, and we react to the things they say and do. Over time these reactions change both them and us. . . . Consider the decision to associate with someone. In the absence of unexpected negative feedback, and sometimes even in the presence of it, deciding to spend time with someone is tantamount to a decision to like him and to develop sympathy for his interests. If his values were initially different from yours, a decision to spend time together is likely to diminish those initial differences. Our choices of associates, therefore, is at least in part a strategic choice about the kind of values we want to hold.[33]

Not only are we often partly responsible for our attitudes and feelings, but often we also criticize racists or others based on the fact that they have such attitudes.[34] Sometimes the criticism focuses on the fact that the person with the attitude was at fault for not being more conscientious in framing it. In his biography of Adolph Hitler, Allan Bullock writes that

Hitler's was a closed mind, violently rejecting any alternative view, refusing to criticize or allow others to criticize his assumptions. He read and listened not to learn, but to acquire information and find additional support for prejudices and opinions already in his mind.[35]

Assuming that this was an accurate description of Hitler's behavior and character, it adds something important to our picture of the nature of the man and what was wrong with him. There is an important respect in which Hitler deserves blame for his own racism: he acquired the racism as a result of his own decisions. Because racists do not take adequate care in the process of forming their beliefs and attitudes, it is fair to say that they deserve condemnation not just for having an unjustified attitude but also for their decisions that led to the formation of the attitude.

We often express this as a criticism of a person's character. We say Hitler lacked openmindedness and a commitment to truth, for instance, or perhaps intellectual courage. So not only do racists harbor unwarranted attitudes (and of course often commit horrible atrocities as a result), they *also* show defects of character – defects for which the racist is often blameworthy. Racist attitudes are therefore a sign of *two* different defects. The core is the fact that the person's attitude is unjustified. But

[33] Robert H. Frank, *What Price the Moral High Ground?* (Princeton: Princeton University Press, 2004), pp. 24–25.

[34] My discussion of these issues has benefitted from James Montmarquet, "Epistemic Virtue and Doxastic Responsibility," *American Philosophical Quarterly*, Vol. 29, No. 4 (October 1992), pp. 331–341.

[35] Allan Bullock, *Hitler: A Study in Tyranny* (New York: Harper and Row, 1962), p. 398. Quoted in Montmarquet, "Epistemic Virtue and Doxastic Responsibility."

racism is also usually an indication of a lack of intellectual virtues such as commitment to truth and openmindedness. Indeed the fact that racists typically lack valuable character traits is evidenced by the very presence of the racism.[36]

We no doubt all have some beliefs and attitudes that are unjustified, and it is also likely that we have them in part because we failed to be sufficiently attentive to truth in the ways I mentioned. But racism is different, for historical reasons. Racism is and has been a particularly dangerous attitude to have, and people therefore have a special responsibility to avoid it. It is not like unjustified hostility toward snakes or Harlequin novels, for which a person might be easily forgiven. Racism is dangerous.

I have argued racism is an epistemological defect, but, as I noted earlier, it might be thought a racist's character is defective in a moral sense.[37] I suggested that racism's normative content derives from various facts: that the attitude (of racial contempt) is always unjustified, that the racist will usually deserve blame for having the attitude, that the racist will (in normal cases) evidence serious character defects involving the formation of attitudes, and that history teaches that such a failure to form appropriate attitudes is especially dangerous in the case of racism. Is it not also the case, however, that the racist is *morally* defective merely because of the presence of the attitude? The suggestion, then, is that merely having racial contempt in the form of hostility or indifference is in itself reason to think a person is morally defective. If that is right, then racism is at its core not only an epistemic defect, as I am suggesting, but also a moral one. But is it right?

I think not. Imagine again our reluctant racist, and suppose further that while his early upbringing made him a racist, he knows that the attitudes are unjustified. Suppose further that he pays special attention to his attitudes in order never to act on his racism. He knows that decent people show equal concern for people regardless of race, and he is careful always to do so himself. That person is like individuals who are colorblind or lack depth perception and therefore must be especially careful when driving. Those people, like the racist I described, suffer from a handicap. For the racist, the handicap makes it more difficult to be just or fair to

[36] The defect is not, as I have emphasized, the mere *inclination* to be closed-minded or careless in forming beliefs but the fact that the racist acquired the attitude as a result of past failures in these areas. A person who is inclined to be careless does not deserve condemnation merely for the inclination, and indeed may even be especially praiseworthy for overcoming that inclination.

[37] I thank Christopher Knapp for pressing this point.

people of different races, let alone to befriend or love them. If the person succeeds in overcoming his racist attitude, as I imagined, then the right attitude for us to take is one of approbation. Although the handicap makes it more difficult to be just, it is not a moral defect.

I have said that racism is *unjustified* racial hostility or indifference, which raises the further question whether racial hostility could ever be justified. If racial hostility can sometimes be justified, and my account of racism is correct, then such hostility would not qualify as racism. This issue is related to one that I mentioned earlier in this chapter, whether victims of racial oppression can themselves be racist. If it is assumed, as it sometimes is, that racism is identical to *any* form of racial contempt, then victims of racial oppression could themselves be racist. But since racism is an *unjustified* attitude, that conclusion is not so clear cut. Indeed, those who think racial hatred on the part of a racially oppressed race is not racism may have just that thought in mind: that it is not racism because the hostility is justified. Is it possible, then, that racial hostility might be justified, and therefore not (on my account) genuine racism?

We do often think that hostility toward people in virtue of their membership in a *nonracial* group can be appropriate, for example, when people belong to a particularly vicious political party. But membership in those groups is voluntary, which suggests that the hostility toward persons who belong to such groups may depend on the fact that the members chose to join the group. Can we imagine cases where hostility directed at each individual member of a race might be justified? Suppose, in the manner of *Star Trek*, that a race of people arrives on Earth whose members all enjoy nothing more than torturing and oppressing other races – a trait that (I will assume) is inherent in the race itself. (This raises a variety of issues about the nature of race, which I take up shortly. But for now, assume that this possibility makes sense.) Assume, then, that it is part of their nature, as members of that race, to hate and oppress others. Hostility toward those persons seems justified, but it is also clear, I think, that such hostility is not what we think of as racism. *Justifiable* racial contempt directed at all members of a race, were it ever to exist, would not constitute racism. (This also confirms my earlier point, that racism's defect is epistemological. When an attitude is not defective in that way, it is not racism.)

If racism is understood as contempt for persons in virtue of their race, then what should be said about a situation in which hostility seems to be directed not at individual persons but at the group? I know a man who, when he was young, spent four years running from Nazis in

Europe and then spent time in German concentration camps. Take it for granted that he suffered unimaginable horrors during those years. Suppose also (although this part is not, in fact, true) that he is now hostile toward Germans as a group. Imagine that he hates to hear the German language spoken, refuses to visit Germany or purchase German-made products, and often speaks ill of "Germans." We can even imagine a person who sympathizes with individual members of the group, perhaps in part because they were unlucky enough to be born into it. Although (we are now supposing) the person does not manifest hostility toward every individual member of the group, there is nonetheless a group-based hostility directed toward the group. We might also imagine the same situation occurring with respect to a racial group, in which hostility is directed at the race itself, as distinct from any individual person.

If in fact it is possible to have such an attitude, and to distinguish a group from its members in that way, then it seems clear we have identified another form of racism. Anyone whose attitudes include unjustified hostility toward *a racial group* per se is also a racist, just as are people who are hostile toward *persons as members of a racial group.* The ordinary cases of racism will continue to be racial hostility directed at individuals in virtue of their race, and I will continue to use that terminology. But it is worth noting the existence of this second form of racial hostility as well.[38]

These distinctions shed important light on the question whether blacks or other members of oppressed groups can be racists. As I have emphasized, if hostility toward a racially oppressive group, qua group, were ever justified, then that hostility would not constitute racism. Whether or not such group-based hostility is justified, for instance by blacks against whites, is a further question. But that said, in the more usual case of hostility directed at all *individuals in virtue of* their race, the irrationality of the attitude seems clear enough. How could racial hostility toward an *individual* in virtue of race ever be justified, even if hostility at the group somehow could be justified? If it is not justified, then such an attitude is racism. It follows that those who claim that victims of racial oppression cannot be racists are mistaken; although if justified hostility were somehow directed at the group and not at individuals in virtue of their race, then the charge of racism would be mistaken. (I will have more to say about these issues, and especially racism and racial stereotypes, later in this chapter.)

---

[38] I will have more to say on this subject, and especially the responsibilities among groups, in Chapter 6 when I discuss compensatory justice and reparations.

Thus, oppressed persons may themselves be racists. It is possible, however, that those who think otherwise have something else in mind. Instead of thinking that racial contempt of oppressed groups is *justified*, perhaps the point is that in the circumstances the attitudes is *excusable*. It is important, then, to distinguish justifications from excuses. Self-defense is a *justification* for killing. Although, in general, the law forbids killing another person, self-defense is an exception and the law does not condemn killing *in those circumstances*. In that case, the law makes an exception due to the special circumstances. Excuses are different. Insanity, for instance, is an *excuse* but not a justification for killing another person. The idea is not that what was done was legally acceptable under the circumstances, but rather that the person should not be held responsible for the killing because of something about the person – in this case a mental disease. Or suppose I burn your chair. I might be justified if my only alternative was to freeze to death. If I burned it thinking it was mine, then that would be an excuse because (we are supposing) I had a mistaken belief.

In the case of a victim who harbors racial hostility or hatred of a racial oppressor, we can easily imagine that the person should be excused even though the racism is unjustified. "Given what he went through," we might think, "he just doesn't have it in him not to hate." That way of speaking suggests an excuse rather than a justification. Often excuses function not to completely exculpate or eliminate responsibility but to reduce it, which might also seem right in such cases. It may be too much to expect people to overcome past experiences. Racism is still racism, however, and it still embeds the normative conclusion that the racial hostility is unjustified.

I have been arguing that once we see that racism is a normative concept – an unjustified attitude of racial contempt in the form of hostility or indifference – then much more comes into focus. We see the normative character of racism to rest on two facts: the attitude is unwarranted, and the person who has the attitude (probably) acquired it as a result of failures in areas such as conscientiousness, open-mindedness, and commitment to truth. This account of racism has other important implications as well. First, it means that we can infer the presence of racism from a person's beliefs and actions. Just as we might explain a person running from a bear by his fear, we might explain a lynching or a murder by ascribing racism to the mob. There is nothing unusual or mysterious about this; we constantly seek to understand each other's motives, and noticing racism is just one of many instances of that.

But because racism is an attitude, it may be present without being evident to an outsider. A racist could resemble a spy who hides his true loyalties even from his closest friends and family. It would be wrong to say the person is not a racist merely because there have been no overt acts of violence or oppression, or even explicit statements of racial contempt.

Finally, as with other attitudes, it is also possible that the *causes* of racism are hidden – even from the person who has the attitude. Sometimes people may know they are afraid, for instance, without knowing what is causing it. They may even know that the fear is unjustified yet still not be able to understand it or shake it. It is, as we may say, "just a feeling." Racial hostility can show a similar pattern, in which people are aware of the presence of the attitude, yet are unaware of its causes. Or they might know of the causes, as my example of the young victim of the Nazis was, yet regret the attitude, thinking that it is unjustified.

We are now in a position to answer other related questions, such as who or what is a racist, and when some things such as jokes, words, and works of art are racist. Let's begin with the question of racist actions, which I have suggested are actions that are motivated, in part or whole, by racism. As I noted, there is a useful analogy between racism and patriotism, and there is a similar parallel between the concepts of a racist and a patriot. A patriot is a person who has settled attitudes that include patriotism, which we can think of as love of or affection for one's nation or people. The attitude is "settled" in the sense that it is not merely fleeting or temporary. A single instance of affection for one's nation does not usually make a patriot, any more than one day's work makes a person industrious, or one charitable act makes a person generous. A racist is, likewise, a person with a specific, relatively stable attitude, namely, the attitude of rac*ism*. That attitude explains why racists are people who have the tendency to do racist actions.

It follows from this that some people may appear to be racists because they do what appear to be racist actions but are not racists in fact. Imagine a person who is a member of the Ku Klux Klan. Under normal circumstances, we could infer that the person is, indeed, a racist. Joining such an organization is good evidence of racial contempt. But suppose we learn that in fact the person joined under duress, or is an FBI agent who has gone undercover to investigate the group's illegal activities, or is just curious about secret meetings. Then, of course, we would conclude that we had been mistaken and the person is not a racist, confirming my conclusion that racism is an attitude of racial contempt.

Other cases may be similar. Suppose a person believes, reasonably, that a situation is dire and the only solution is to impose some burden on a racial group. Perhaps only by California's segregating the races in prison can a very great evil be prevented, for example. Although such racial segregation could be taken as evidence that the warden is a racist, in this case, we might reach another conclusion. Internment of Japanese-Americans during World War II raises similar issues. It is often said that this was evidence that the authorities were racists, and that may well be the case. But, this is not necessarily true. *If* officials had good reason to believe that there was indeed a grave danger and that there was no plausible alternative to internment, *and if* they would have done the same thing to any other group in similar circumstances, then the charge that they were racists would be called into question. Everything depends, again, on their attitudes and what explains the action they took. If (however implausibly) their attitudes and beliefs were as I imagined, then officials would be exonerated of the charge of being racists.

There is one other type of case, however, which may seem more difficult.[39] Imagine a white restaurant owner living in the South in 1950, who has a sign saying "whites only" on the wall and who has joined the Klan. But suppose also that this person works hard to disguise that he is not, in fact, hostile or even indifferent to blacks. His sole motivation, we assume, is personal; he wants to stay in business. Is he not what might be termed an "opportunistic racist," despite his absence of any racist attitudes? There are two possibilities here. One is to say that he is not a racist, although he may be blameworthy for what he has done on other grounds. To condemn him as a racist would miss the point. His actions reflect other motives, besides racism. Suppose we learn that he really would behave in exactly the same way if a different racial or religious group was being mistreated by the community and his potential customers.[40] The natural conclusion is that this was not a racist, although the institutions in which he lived were. (I will discuss the nature of institutional racism later in this

---

[39] Thanks to Bat Ami Bar On and Bill Throop for helpful discussions of this problem.

[40] Charles Goodman suggested to me that this might explain the fact (assuming it is a fact) that legal segregation disappeared as quickly as it did in the South even in the absence of legal pressure. "Massive resistance" was not the rule. The explanation is that people were less racist than many had supposed, so that when it was possible to integrate public accommodations without paying a heavy price, many people happily did so. This account of the nature of racism, and of racists, explains the "moral cascade" by showing that people were less racist than was suggested by the social practices in which they had participated.

chapter.) While it is true that we normally infer that people are racists from what they do, and for that reason we associate racism with acts, the real meaning of racism is not actions but attitudes.

The alternative way of dealing with this is to say that we should call him a racist despite the absence of the attitudes of racism. If that alternative is accepted, however, then the concepts of racism and racist would pull apart, and not *always* be linked in the way I have described. A person could be a racist despite the absence of racism. That said, however, it would remain the case that the paradigm or core examples of racists are people whose attitudes include hostility or indifference toward persons in virtue of their race, leaving my central claim standing. It is still important not to tie racists to actions, however, since as I have emphasized, a person can, in theory, be a racist without participating in any racist institutions and without having performed any action that is motivated by racism. The link between racism and racist actions is an important one, because racism motivates action; but that is not to say that racism can not be distinguished from actions.

Another question, along a similar vein, is how this account of racism and racist things would explain all the various things – from single words to entire institutions – that we normally call racist. If being a racist involves having the attitude of racism, then how could something that cannot have an attitude – a word, for instance – rightly be called "racist"? Similarly, what sense can be made of the claim that things such as jokes and beliefs are racist, as well as institutions, laws, and social practices?

Suppose a black calls his black friend a "nigger." Although in this case it would be a mistake (I assume) to infer that the speaker is a racist, when we speak of a word as being racist we mean that it is a word that is normally used by *people who* are likely to be racists. Using such racist words is a *sign* of racism, like a storm cloud is a sign of impending rain. Words we describe as racist generally do show something about their user's racial attitudes, and often what they show is that the speaker is a racist – but not always. Words are deemed racist in that indirect sense because of the attitude that they normally reflect.

The same should be said of jokes and objects. When we say a joke is racist we mean that the joke is one that would *normally* indicate or express the attitude of racism. We are using the term in that same indirect, derivative sense as when we call a word racist. A similar point can be made about objects such as movies and books: when they are racist, the suggestion is that they are objects that normally signify racism on the part of the person who made or enjoyed them. Such charges can be mistaken, of course, and that is as it should be. Whether or not a book is racist depends in part on the interpretation of the book itself, and on the context in which the book was produced or made public.

If racism is best understood as racial contempt, then how is that attitude related to prejudice? What is prejudice? The answer is that although similar, the concept of prejudice has a broader, and slightly different, meaning than racism. Philosophers became interested in the concept of prejudice during the Enlightenment.[41] Prejudice began as a legal notion, but, in the hands of Kant, Condorcet, and others, it came to be understood more broadly – as something standing in the way of human progress and thought. Because prejudiced people lack experience with reality (at least with relation to issues they have "pre-judged"), beliefs that rest on prejudice were themselves thought to be dubious. Prejudice is in that sense a general, topic-neutral idea. One can be prejudiced about almost anything.

We must, however, make judgments about what it is rational to believe, often without any of the direct personal experience and information that supposedly marks the person who is without "prejudice." Much of what we know about how the natural world works, for example, we believe because we have read books or learned from experts. It would be wrong, however, to suggest that a person who has investigated a question carefully and reached a conclusion based on evidence is *prejudiced* only because the investigation relied on second-hand information from books or conversations rather than direct, first-hand observations. Prejudice often carries the suggestion of a mistake of some sort. But what sort of mistake, if not that the belief was formed without *direct* experience?

Suppose a person said of another, "His dislike of baseball is mere prejudice" or "Her refusal to take aspirin is based on prejudice, not fact." The suggestion in these cases is that the person's attitude or action is mistaken, if only in the sense that it would be different if the person had more information or were willing to act on information he does have. But that leaves open the question of whether or not *the person* is subject to criticism for not having gathered more information. Perhaps the person never had the opportunity to overcome the prejudice. It is also true, however, that when we say that a *person* is prejudiced, we refer not to any particular beliefs or attitudes but to the fact that the person is not, *in*

---

[41] My discussion of the origins of prejudice relies on Andreas Dorschel, *Rethinking Prejudice* (Aldershot UK: Ashgate, 2000).

general, up to normal standards of openmindedness. Racism is usually a form of prejudice in just that sense: it is an attitude that is grounded in beliefs formed on insufficient evidence, or beliefs that are held too firmly without adequate regard for other information that may call these beliefs into question. When racism manifests a character defect, as it often does, it is therefore showing itself as prejudice.

Sometimes, however, there is only a mild criticism implicit in the claim that a person has a prejudice. Suppose a friend admitted to having a "prejudice" against ranch-style houses and, asked to explain why, reported that she grew up in them and can't imagine living in one as an adult. The point of calling this preference a prejudice could be merely to emphasize that the dislike is a matter of personal taste and is not based on reasons. However, although the attitude might be considered, in that limited sense, to be defective, there is no suggestion of something defective about the person, unless we think, implausibly, that a person's likes and dislikes must always be based on reasons.

So while prejudices are contrasted with rational, well-informed beliefs and attitudes, and may sometimes indicate a person's failure to take adequate care in the formation of beliefs, it is nonetheless incorrect to think of prejudice, in general, as embedding an evaluative judgment of the person. We are all prejudiced at least in the sense that some of our attitudes, preferences, and beliefs did not all arise after careful consideration and weighing of available evidence. Prejudice, in that sense, is inevitable given constraints on time and information.

Racism is different. We owe it to people not to allow racism to flourish. It undermines our ability to fulfill duties to treat others fairly both in our individual interactions and in the context of politics. So while "prejudice" against ranch houses is a harmless matter of personal preference, racism is – as I have stressed – both an unjustified attitude *and* a dangerous one.

We began the discussion of racism by noting the wide variety of definitions of racism and the confusion that follows. Because racism is a normative concept, political argument sometimes takes the form of conceptual disagreements over racism. I argued that racism is best understood as a form of irrational contempt directed at persons in virtue of their race. It gains its normative force from its epistemological defects, though it is also accompanied by character defects and, therefore, moral defects as well. It is also a form of prejudice, I argued – a particularly dangerous and defective one.

Institutional racism as an interpretive concept

Given the account of racism I have defended, it might seem to follow that institutional racism is an incoherent concept. If racism is an internal, mental attitude of racial contempt, and if institutions are not the sorts of things that are capable of having attitudes, how can the concept of institutional racism make sense?

Unsurprisingly, perhaps, those who speak in terms of institutional racism often have different examples of it in mind as well as different definitions. Some emphasize outcome, and others emphasize intentions. Angela Davis describes the incarceration of a "disproportionate" percentage of African-Americans as "institutional racism."[42] James M. Jones defines institutional racism as "policies, practices and procedures that adversely affect some ethnic (or racial) group so that they will be unable to rise to the level of equality."[43] Following Davis's lead, he writes that although the "intent was probably not to increase the number of blacks and Hispanics incarcerated . . .those were in fact its consequences." Other examples of institutional racism he mentions include fewer banks in black neighborhoods; the distribution of jobs among professional, laboring, and management services; educational achievement; life expectancy and health.[44] Gertrude Ezorksy also thinks that institutional racism is present *whenever* there are racial differences in results, so that any institution that fosters or allows economic, social, or political benefits or disadvantages to vary according to race is racist.[45] That way of understanding institutional racism makes two claims: it denies that there must be any person in charge who is guilty of racism in order to condemn an institutional arrangement as racist, and also claims that institutional racism is present whenever distributions of valuable (or disvalued) goods is racially unequal.

Others, however, are skeptical of the idea of institutional racism completely, claiming it is incoherent just because it seems to improperly attribute attitudes and intentions to institutions rather than to persons. As I mentioned earlier, Anthony Flew, for example, thinks that racism is an "essentially intentional" action,[46] suggesting that institutions can

---

[42] Angela Davis, "Prisons, Reparations, and Resistance," in *The Angela Y. Davis Reader,* edited by Joy James (Malden MA: Blackwell Publishers, 1998), pp. 3–109.

[43] James M. Jones, *Prejudice and Racism,* 2nd ed. (New York: McGraw Hill, 1997), p. 438.

[44] Jones, *Prejudice and Racism,* pp. 440–464.

[45] For example, see Gertrude Ezorsky, *Racism and Justice: The Case for Affirmative Action* (Ithaca NY: Cornell University Press, 1991), p. 9.

[46] Flew, *Thinking about Social Thinking,* p. 10.

never be racist. An institution is not a person, he points out, and, therefore, it cannot have intentions.

The view of institutional racism I want to defend is based on my
understanding of racism in general. It also differs from both of those
approaches, although it is similar to how the writers who first coined
the term used it. In a 1960s book titled *Black Power*, Stokeley Carmichael
and Charles Hamilton begin with the claim that racism is the use of race
for purposes of "subordinating a racial group."[47] "Institutional" racism,
they concluded, involves acts by the "total white community against the
black community" and "relies on the active and pervasive operation of
anti-black attitudes."[48] Jorge L. A. Garcia also thinks that institutional
racism is linked to the actual attitudes of individual people. He writes
that "institutional racism exists when and insofar as an institution is racist
in the aims, plans, etc., that people give it, especially when their racism
informs its behavior. Institutional racism begins when racism extends
from the hearts of individual people to become institutionalized."[49]
For these writers, then, institutional racism is present when, but only
when, the people who set up or maintain the institutions are, in fact,
racists.

While I do not want to deny that some sense can be made of institutional racism in that way, by showing that the institutions are in fact
designed or run by racists, I believe that such an approach unreasonably
narrows the concept. Those who equate institutional racism with differences in outcome, on the other hand, see it too broadly. But what, then,
is the alternative?

One possibility, suggested by Charles R. Lawrence, III, is to appeal
to "unconscious" racism.[50] Instead of relying only on evidence of the
conscious motives of people who create and maintain institutions, according to this suggestion, we should also understand institutional racism as
an expression of the racist attitudes of which people are unaware. But
that would mean, in turn, that we can have no more confidence in the
existence of institutional racism than in the existence of unconscious
motives in general. Lawrence is therefore led, in exploring this line of

---

[47] Stokeley Carmichael and Charles Hamilton, *Black Power* (New York: Vintage, 1967), p. 3.
[48] Carmichael and Hamilton, *Black Power*, pp. 4–5.
[49] Jorge L. A. Garcia, "The Heart of Racism," *Journal of Social Philosophy*, Vol. 22, No. 1
(Spring 1996), reprinted in *Race and Racism*, edited by Bernard Boxill (Oxford: Oxford
University Press, 2001), p. 266.
[50] Charles R. Lawrence, III, "The Id, the Ego, and Equal Protection: Reckoning with
Unconscious Racism," *Stanford Law Review*, Vol. 39, No. 2 (January 1987), pp. 317–388.

thought, to a discussion of Freudian psychoanalytic theory and to the hypothesis that racism is found in the unconscious world of the "id."[51] But there is another, less-controversial approach to institutional racism available that does not rely on speculative psychological theories about the existence and nature of the human unconscious.

We should begin with the idea that it is common in law for institutions to be *treated for some purposes* as persons; they are in that sense "personified." We do that when we look for the intention of a legislative body to interpret a statute. We also do it when a corporation is legally liable for harms it has caused by its negligence. In both cases, we treat the institution, whether a legislature or corporation, *as if* it were a person and then hold it liable for violating its legal duties.[52] The question whether it was negligent is answered by first asking whether or not an actual person would be liable if he or she had done what it did. If the answer to that is yes, then the corporation is liable, and we are brought to the next question: damages. What should the corporation be required to pay, given that it was liable? The only issue is whether there would be negligence present on the (contrary to fact) assumption that a single individual had done what the institution did. There is nothing mysterious or even particularly controversial about that process. The corporation is not literally a person in the sense that you and I are – it was not born of woman, it feels no pain, and, most importantly, it need not literally have any beliefs or attitudes. The law does treat the corporation like a person for purposes of assessing its potential liability.[53]

Using that as a model, we can see how we might also charge an institution with being racist and thereby make sense of the concept of institutional racism. Rather than attributing hidden, unconscious motives to those who made decisions, as Lawrence recommends, we would treat the institution as if it were a person and interpret its actions in that light. The charge of institutional racism would then be settled by asking whether

---

[51] Lawrence, "The Id, the Ego, and Equal Protection: Reckoning with Unconscious Racism," pp. 331–336.

[52] On legislative intention see Tony Honore, "Interpretation," in *About Law: An Introduction* (Oxford: Clarendon Press, 1995); on personification of corporations, see Ronald Dworkin, *Law's Empire* (Cambridge MA: Harvard University Press, 1986), chapter IV.

[53] People also do sometime appear to have *moral attitudes* toward corporations, feeling resentment or anger when they are responsible for causing harms. Whether these attitudes are appropriate or reasonable is not an issue I address here because in the law the idea of treating an institution as a person for purposes of liability is familiar and generally not problematical.

if we were to assume that an action taken by an institution had been performed instead by a single person, would that person be a racist? In asking that, we are treating institutional racism as an *interpretive concept*. We first personify the institution, imagining what it has done to be the action of a single agent that can have attitudes, and then, with that assumption as background, we ask whether the institution's action is a reflection of racism, just as when we ask if the corporation was negligent. This view is therefore distinct from each of the others I have described. It does not (necessarily) mean that differential results signify racism, but neither is it skeptical of the concept in general. Nor does a finding of institutional racism depend on whether in fact the institution was created by racists or is currently run by them as Garcia and others claim, or by people motivated by unconscious racism as Lawrence suggests.

The claim that legally enforced segregation, for example, constituted institutional racism is an interpretive one. It means that the best interpretation of segregation laws is that they were the product of a racist government rather than, say, of a fair-minded, nonracist one. But because it is an interpretive claim that relies on personification, the charge of institutional racism does not require that legislators were *in fact* racists. Racists need not be present for institutional racism to flourish. So rather than understanding the charge literally and supposing that the institution has racist attitudes or saying that actual racists are in positions of power in the institution, we ask what motive would provide the best explanation were a person to do what the institution has done. (In Chapter 4, I use this idea, of institutional racism as an interpretive concept, to explore the ways that judges should interpret the U.S. Constitution's Equal Protection Clause.)

Racism and racial inferiority

Another important question that I have not yet considered is racial "inferiority." Indeed, some may feel reluctant to agree with my account of racism on the ground that it does not tie racism closely enough to the belief in racial inferiority. But what is the link between the racial contempt that is the hallmark of racism and beliefs in racial inferiority?

I agree that there is an important relationship between racism and the belief in racial inferiority. That link, however, is not as simple as it is usually supposed. The short answer is that beliefs in racial inferiority almost always accompany racism, although there can be exceptions. To see why, consider the history of anti-Semitism. Was it racism or some other form of religious, ethnic, or cultural bigotry?

Both racism and anti-Semitism are unjustified hostility or indifference to persons in virtue of their membership in a group. The question whether that attitude is racism or something else depends on how the person with the attitude understands the group that is the object of their contempt. Is being Jewish seen as belonging to a race or to a religion? In other words, the question whether anti-Semitism is racism depends on the person's beliefs about the nature of Jews as a group, and at different periods of history Jews have been seen as both a race and a religion.[54] In late Medieval Europe, anti-Semitism was often grounded in religion. Jews were thought capable of conversion to Christianity, and the differences between Jews and Christians were understood as growing out of culture and beliefs. That form of anti-Semitism was therefore no different, in principle, from anti-Catholic or anti-Muslim bigotry. It was grounded in religion and culture rather than race.

Everything changed, however, as being Jewish came to be seen by Christian anti-Semites not as a matter of holding different beliefs and cultural practices but as belonging to a race. That belief – that being Jewish was a natural, racial property of people rather than a cultural or religious difference – also has roots in medieval times. When Jews were understood biologically, as a natural group, anti-Semitism was transformed from religious bigotry and intolerance into racism.

This view of Jews as having an inherent nature distinct from others showed itself in the transition from the belief that Jews could be converted to Christianity to the view that they were unworthy of conversion. As ideas of a separate Jewish race emerged, Jews were increasingly portrayed with distinctive characteristics such as horns (which being natural features were inherited, not chosen) that marked them as associated with the devil. Later, in its Nazi variant, Jews were also portrayed as possessing distinctive physical features and as a lower form of biological life associated with rats and vermin.

That same belief in the *inherent* inferiority of a group has also been a feature of anti-African racism. It was reflected in the Arab world and its attitudes toward black Africans; blackness was thought to be inherited because of a Biblical curse visited on Ham and his descendants.[55] As I will discuss in Chapter 3, the idea of African inferiority took on deep

[54] My discussion of the roots of racism and anti-Semitism is indebted to George M. Fredrickson, *Racism* (Princeton: Princeton University Press, 2002).
[55] For a discussion of this history, see Bernard Lewis, *Race and Slavery in the Middle East* (New York: Oxford University Press, 1990).

roots in the United States, as part of the justification of slavery. Being of African descent was seen as a mark of inherited, natural inferiority – a form of taint. Race was regarded as a natural category into which people fall biologically as well as culturally. It was one thing to regard people as belonging to an inferior religious or cultural group; it was something different to regard Jews or Africans as members of an inferior race.

I have said that racism is unjustified hostility toward people *in virtue of their race*. We can now see how the reference to race matters. Like most persons, racists suppose that their attitudes are appropriate or justified. Thus, the racists' particular form of hostility normally rests on the belief that being a member of that race is a mark of some type of inferiority that makes a person worthy of the contemptuous attitudes. It would be odd for a racist to believe otherwise because that would imply that the racial contempt was without justification. (Obviously, the belief that there are natural differences need not be true. The point is that the racist *believes* it.) This, then, is a fundamental difference between racism and other forms of bigotry. Racists' attitudes of hatred or indifference rest on more than the accidents of history and culture. These attitudes are thought to be justified by the fact that the world is divided into races, that some races are inferior, and that such inferiority justifies the racist's attitude.

Such beliefs in racial inferiority can take different forms, but there are five major ones. Another race may be thought to be (1) *intellectually* inferior (naturally less able to understand complex problems or less artistically creative); (2) *morally* inferior (inherently less virtuous; less trustworthy, hard working, loyal); (3) *physically* inferior (less athletically gifted); (4) *aesthetically* inferior (less physically attractive); or (5) *emotionally* inferior (less mature or more childlike). While a racist need not believe the other race is inferior along all those dimensions, the five encompass the major types that history has seen. Each of the five is familiar from portrayals of Africans, Jews, Native Americans, and others.

It is clear as we consider the five forms that there is no bright line between beliefs in cultural and in racial inferiority. Ethnic, cultural, and religious hatred can flourish independent of any beliefs in race or racial inferiority. The key is whether the supposed "inferiority" is thought to be natural or is merely an accident of history. Hostility to groups based on linguistic, cultural, or religious differences is not racism. That said, however, it is also possible for a particular group trait to come to be regarded as natural or inherent rather than as an accident of history or culture. Whether or not the trait is *in fact* a natural one, if members of the group are believed to be a race, and membership in that natural group warrants contempt, then the attitude is racism rather than cultural bigotry or some other form of bigotry.[56]

So my first, positive claim about the relationship between racism and racial inferiority is that in addition to the attitude of contempt that comprises the core of racism, racists generally hold two beliefs. First, they believe that race is an important natural category dividing human beings. Second, they also believe that the objects of their hatred or indifference are in some sense inferior to others in virtue of their race. If a group that is the object of contempt is not seen in those racial terms, then the person is a cultural or religious bigot, perhaps, but not a racist.

That said, however, there is nonetheless an important conceptual point that should be made in the form of a qualification. I have emphasized that, in the usual case, racists believe both in the reality of race and also that their racial contempt is justified because of the inferiority of the racial group that is the object of their contempt. But while that has been true historically, and is no doubt true of most racists today, it is not *necessary* that racists believe in racial inferiority. Imagine what might be called an irrational racist, whose contempt is by his own admission not based on anything but his feelings. Or imagine someone whose contempt arises out of racial jealousy and the belief the race he hates is actually superior to others in some respect. Although the cases are no doubt unusual, such people are racists. Belief in racial inferiority is therefore not an essential feature of racism, as some have supposed.

Generalizations and stereotypes

Relying on generalizations about racial groups is controversial, often for good reason. Indeed some equate it with racism. Jennifer K. Hochschild, for example, points to the fact that one-third of whites agreed in a survey that "blacks are more violent than whites" as evidence that racism has

---

[56] We might also wonder why there is not a name for all the various other irrational attitudes people sometimes have. *Xenophobia* and *homophobia* are also examples of unjustified attitudes that suggest a moral defect as well as irrationality, but why only those? Perhaps the answer to my question, of why there is not always a name for irrational hostile attitudes, is that we name those forms of unjustified hostility that we know from history are dangerous, leaving other forms of unjustified hostility without a specific name. Whatever the truth about that, race-based hostility and indifference *is* a serious problem and racism names it.

not been eradicated.[57] Joe R. Feagin also criticizes whites for believing in racial stereotypes by their "fearful reaction" to black men because, as he points out, white criminals commit "most violent crime affecting whites."[58] Jorge L. A. Garcia describes a woman walking alone at night who crosses the street to avoid a group of black teenagers as someone who "indulges her prejudice."[59] Judith Lichtenberg thinks crossing a street under those circumstances would be racist unless the woman would respond the same way if the teenagers were white.[60]

David Theo Goldberg is explicit in claiming that truth is no defense against the charge of racism. He writes that a person would show himself to be a racist even if, learning that the chances are *in fact* much higher that a black has a criminal record than a white, he were to "construct from this a predictive estimation of his future experiences. . . ." Although a person who did that would meet what he terms the "strictest demands of rational agency," he is still racist because, according to Goldberg, racist beliefs do not "necessarily transgress criteria of rationality."[61] For Goldberg, then, racist beliefs can be rational; it is therefore sufficient to condemn a person as racist because the person generalizes about historically oppressed groups whether or not the stereotype is true.

But if I am right that racism is contempt for persons in the form of hostility or indifference in virtue of their race, then the issues are not nearly so simple. The problem is how best to *explain* people's beliefs when they generalize on the basis of race. Is the belief best explained by the facts and evidence, for example, or does the person's belief reflect attitudes of racism? To explore these issues, we should look briefly at the two underlying ideas of beliefs and of generalizations. First, what, more exactly, are beliefs? And second, how are generalizations different from racist attitudes?

One point should be acknowledged at the outset. As I will use the term, *generalizations* are beliefs about traits or characteristics of groups of people or things. Often their purpose is to make predictions, whether

[57] Jennifer L. Hochschild, "Race, Class, Power, and Equal Opportunity," in *Equal Opportunity*, edited by Norman E. Bowie (Boulder: Westview Press, 1988), p. 76.

[58] Joe R. Feagin, *Racist America* (New York: Routledge, 2000), reprinted in Boxill, *Race and Racism*, p. 114.

[59] Jorge L. A. Garcia, "The Heart of Racism," p. 281.

[60] Judith Lichtenberg, "Racism in the Head, Racism in the World," *Philosophy and Public Policy* (College Park MD: Newsletter of the Institute for Philosophy and Public Policy, 1992), p. 12.

[61] Goldberg, "Racism and Rationality," p. 377.

it is that small-town people are friendly, that Golden Retrievers are gen-
tle, or that Roman Catholics are anti-abortion. Given that the issue is
people's beliefs, I will assume that the meaning of a given generalization
is precise enough that it makes sense to speak of its being either true
or false. Yet, some generalizations and stereotypes might not qualify as
beliefs at all, if the content of the belief is not such that it is (broadly
speaking) either true or false. Thus, a claim that members of a group
are "lazy" or "intelligent" may require more specificity before it is even
possible to identify clearly what it might mean. Unless that further spec-
ification is given, we may not know how to assign a truth value to such
claims.[62]

Whether general or specific, we do not choose our beliefs like we
choose our socks. We acquire beliefs in many ways, and the process
is often more like digesting or blinking than choosing. A belief often
simply emerges, as a result of things that have happened to us and especially what we have seen, heard, or felt. A person might believe that his
friend is in the library because he saw him going in, or that it will not
rain today because the forecaster just said so, or he noticed the sky is
clear. Each of these beliefs is an attitude toward a proposition, and if
asked, people can usually give the reason why they believe what they
do. But it is misleading to say that people are given evidence and then
are entirely free to decide what to believe. (Other beliefs that we have
involving immediate experiences, such as your belief that you are reading now, or your belief that you now have a sore ankle, are even less
open to choice.) The point I want to emphasize is that we don't generally *decide* to accept the beliefs we have. We can, however, influence
our beliefs. We can decide to investigate a question further, or perhaps
to seek either corroborating or contradictory evidence by consulting
sources whose opinions we believe will encourage us to believe one thing
or another.[63] But even if we try to disprove one of our beliefs, we may not
succeed.

Nor is it *surprising* that beliefs are stable in that way, including beliefs
we reach about how things are in general. People could not survive
without the ability to generalize: it is both natural and rational for people to notice similarities and differences among the various elements in
their environment and then to lump them together into categories. Cats,

---

[62] Thanks to an anonymous reviewer for emphasizing that point.

[63] It was for that reason, as I suggested, that Hitler's racism may be more than just an
epistemic flaw. He was careless in his formation of his beliefs.

cattle, mice, and grizzly bears are linked together conceptually because they are animals and furry things, but we also separate them into additional categories that mark their size, whether we have them as pets, whether we can eat them, and, perhaps most importantly, whether they may want to eat us. The categories are also vague. Bears are clearly in the category of dangerous, but depending on its type and size, a cat may be dangerous or friendly.

Once we have categories like dangerous and edible, we naturally ask which other things belong to the different categories and, just as important, we can go on to invent new categories that allow common sense and science to progress. We learn that some animals are not only dangerous but are also mammals; that only some mammals hibernate; and that some animals reproduce without the aid of sex. The ability to make both obvious and subtle distinctions has great survival value for our species and grounds our capacity to understand our world. The process of categorizing the different parts of our environment is therefore essential to our understanding the world, and this process has also presumably played a part in evolution since humans who could not distinguish a dangerous bear from an edible deer could not have survived long enough to reproduce.

All of that is perhaps obvious, although the implications may not always be sufficiently appreciated. As people engage in predictive generalizing, they use what psychologists sometimes call "default assumptions."[64] Guns and bears are assumed to be dangerous generally, which means a particular bear or gun will be assumed to be dangerous as well. If we did not allow ourselves to generalize and instead investigated the truth of every belief each time out, we would have little chance to survive, let alone prosper. There is no reasonable alternative, throughout our lives, to acting on default assumptions. Generalizations are therefore sometimes nothing more than these more-or-less accurate assumptions that we sometimes cannot help but make in a world where information is imperfect and first-hand investigation almost always costly if not impossible.

That distinction, between warranted generalizations and unwarranted ones (including ones that may not be precise enough to qualify as factual at all) is indicated in language when we distinguish general beliefs from stereotypes. Naming a general belief a "stereotype" often indicates that there is something defective about the belief, and, in what follows, I

---

[64] Douglas Hofstadter, "Changes in Default Words and Images, Engendered by Rising Consciousness," in *Metamagical Themes* (New York: Basic Books, 1985), p. 136.

will distinguish between generalizations that are rational to believe and stereotypes.

Returning to the issue of racism, we see that because some generalizations are known to be true, it may not be reasonable to infer the existence of racism *merely* because people believe these generalizations. The reason is that the belief may be able to be explained by the available evidence for its truth in the absence of any evidence of racial contempt. For instance, those who claim that greater fear of black teens than of white teens indicates racism must confront the possibility that the belief is justified, and that the evidence explains the belief. In fact, recent figures show that blacks are not only more likely to be victims of violent crime, but they are also more likely to commit violent crimes. From 1976 to 2000, blacks committed 51 percent of all homicides in the United States, while whites committed 46 percent. Because blacks are only about 12 percent of the population, there were seven times more murders *per capita* committed by blacks than whites.[65] That means that a randomly chosen black teenager on the street was statistically 700 percent more likely to commit homicide than was a randomly chosen white teenager.

Given the truth of the generalization about crime and race, it is not true that only *racism* can explain the belief. Because racism and truth can be competitive explanations of the belief, we would need to look further in order to determine if the belief is evidence of racism. That is especially clear in cases where the usual assumptions are reversed. Suppose a black woman is walking alone in a white neighborhood known for its racist, antiblack attitudes. It seems clear it would be a mistake to accuse her of racism merely because she crossed the street to avoid a group of white teenagers. That would remain true even if most whites in the neighborhood were not dangerous or racists. It is not unreasonable, under the circumstances, for her to avoid the risk. The point is that there is evidence for the generalization of which she is aware, and it is prudent for her to act on the generalization. She may also hate whites, of course, but that is not a fair inference from her action alone.

Often there are competing explanations of beliefs about a group of people: the truth of the belief or the racist attitude. The crucial question is which attitude best explains the belief. Does the person hold the belief

[65] U.S. Government Bureau of Justice Statistics, "Homicide Trends in the U.S.: Trends by Race." http://www.ojp.usdoj.gov/bjs/homicide/race.htm. Accessed on November 12, 2002.

because it is true, or is the belief a reflection of racial hostility? Or is it both? I am not denying that racists may also harbor even justified beliefs, nor am I suggesting that it is always easy in individual cases to disentangle racism and sound generalizations. Whether the belief is best explained by the facts, or by racist attitudes, may not be able to be settled in any given instance.[66]

One further piece of evidence supporting the distinction between generalizations and racism is suggested by surveys of black attitudes. One survey done by the University of California concluded that *more blacks than whites* said blacks are "aggressive or violent."[67] Another study found that black landlords prefer renting to white rather than black tenants.[68] Such beliefs could easily reflect racism if found among whites, but it seems reasonable to think that the facts explain blacks' beliefs rather than racial contempt directed at their own race. Negative beliefs about other races are more likely to be explained by racism than similar beliefs about one's own race, of course, although it is possible to harbor unjustified racial contempt of one's own race. The point, again, is that a person who accepts a racial generalization for which there is evidence available, and acts on the assumption, is not *necessarily* a racist. Without evidence of racist attitudes the truth of the generalization may constitute a complete explanation of the belief.

It is also important in this connection to emphasize the distinction between a person who is justifiably fearful of persons who *happen to be* of a particular race and a racist who holds people in contempt *in virtue of* their race. I argued that for racists, race is thought to be a natural category: racial contempt is thought to be justified by the natural inferiority of persons of that race. Merely believing racial generalizations is importantly different. The nonracists I am describing have beliefs based on sociological, or other, facts about persons that just happen to correlate with the person's race. This, however, means that their fear is not directed at the person *in virtue of their race*. For them, race is only a marker – an indication – of something else. Like wearing a Swastika or belonging to the KKK, racial appearance is merely a predictor (and we are assuming for the moment a reasonably good one) that the person is more likely

---

[66] I am grateful to a reviewer for pressing the importance of this point, which I explore further in the following paragraphs.

[67] Thernstrom and Thernstrom, *America in Black and White: One Nation, Indivisible* (New York: Simon & Schuster, 1997), p. 141.

[68] William Tucker, *The Excluded Americans: Homelessness and Housing Policies* (Washington DC: Regnery Gateway, 1990), p. 92.

to have the attitude than other persons. The crucial point is that the attitude is not directed at the person in virtue of their race in the relevant sense. If the person is not a racist, then it is not the other person's race, understood to be a natural trait, which is the basis of the attitude. The fear is explained only indirectly by race, since race is merely a marker. The fearful person may feel no contempt for persons based on race itself, and may even be of the same race as the person feared. For racists, on the other hand, the racial attitudes include contempt for persons in virtue of their race itself, understood as a natural trait.

None of that is to deny the important truth that a mark of racism is often the easy acceptance of stereotypes and the inclination to overgeneralize. My point is that the question whether a person is a racist cannot be settled *merely* by pointing out that the person accepts a generalization, but neither can a person be acquitted merely because the generalization has merit. My point is that the two questions – of believing generalizations and racism – are, in principle, distinct.

It is also important, finally, to note that reasonable generalizations as well as unjustified stereotypes can both severely disadvantage groups who suffer under them. Housing is a good example. Even if it is, in fact, somewhat more likely that a member of one group will be a less reliable tenant, general acceptance by landlords of that generalization can result in serious harm to the many members of the group who would make reliable tenants. For that reason, antidiscrimination laws can be important not only to counteract racism and stereotypes but also to limit the harmful effects of even sound generalizations.

That said, antidiscrimination laws that attack *justified* generalizations can be difficult to enforce. Because information is neither free nor easily acquired, it is sometimes more efficient for landlords and others to rely on generalizations than to expend the resources needed to judge individual cases. Unless everyone is forced to ignore such generalizations, those who accept the added costs may find themselves at a competitive disadvantage when forced to compete with those who rely on them. In those cases, antidiscrimination laws function like antipollution regulations. Companies that do not pollute would be at a disadvantage competing with those who do pollute, all else being equal. The best solution is for everyone to be required to bear the added cost of avoiding harmful pollution. Similarly, laws forbidding discrimination in housing or employment can therefore reduce the damage to minority groups of both accurate generalizations and unwarranted stereotypes. These laws force everyone to gather relevant information, such as credit scores, rather than relying on the shortcut of race as a surrogate for some other trait.

Racial profiling

Racial profiling is often a difficult and deeply controversial issue, whether done by individuals or institutions. It involves generalizations, and sometimes the cost of avoiding the generalization can be great. On the other hand, racial profiling is frequently cited as an example of institutional racism.

One reason that is given to reject profiling is that it relies on unjustified racial stereotypes. But the argument against profiling does not end there, because racial profiling might be condemned for other reasons. Racial profiling not only relies on what may be unjustified stereotypes but also imposes burdens on persons because of their membership in a racial or ethnic group. The burdens themselves may sometimes be relatively minor – taking more time than others to get through screening at airports, for instance – or the burdens can be significant and quite time consuming, for example, when people are continually pulled over for traffic violations. Thus, profiling can have a cumulative effect, when people are subjected to repeated instances. It is also true that the large majority of people who must bear the burdens of profiling are perfectly innocent.

The fact that the burden falls disproportionately on a racial group is not sufficient to show that when profiling becomes policy it is institutional racism. For that, we must choose between competing explanations of the policy. One explanation is institutional racism, but the other is a suspicion that, in fact, justifies imposing the burden on this or any other group. We also cannot rule out institutional racism merely because no official has expressed racist attitudes. The question, as always, is interpretive. Which motive would we be justified in attributing to a legislative or other body that has adopted a policy of racial profiling: racism, or justified concern for the well-being of everyone?

Airport security is a good example of profiling. Called Computer Assisted Passenger Prescreening System, or CAPPS, the screening policy takes into account nationality along with how the ticket was purchased, the clothes the passenger is wearing, travel history, and even books the passenger bought at the airport. The goal is to use an algorithm-based computer program to calculate the probabilities that specific passengers are terrorists.

Complaints about the CAPPS profiling system, lodged by the Council of American-Islamic Relations about profiling Arabs and Muslims, led to a review by the Justice Department Civil Rights division to determine if the CAPPS program was discriminatory. Interestingly, the complaints had declined from twenty-nine in 1977 to none in 2000, but since the destruction of the World Trade Center, the Council has reported increased complaints and widespread profiling. In the wake of 9/11, airlines initiated new, more "aggressive measures for passenger profiling."[69] Blacks have also long complained about racial profiling by police, store owners, and others. Representative John Conyers, who sponsored a bill to ban racial profiling before 9/11, has said he now equates "driving while black" and "flying while Arab."[70]

Yet, despite the controversies, profiling in general is widely practiced and generally accepted in many contexts. Police often develop profiles as part of their effort to identify criminals, a practice that provided the centerpiece of the popular movie *Silence of the Lambs*. Profiling is also used extensively by the Internal Revenue Service in deciding which tax returns to audit. Rather than auditing returns at random, the IRS has developed a profile that it applies to each tax return. It uses the profile to assign a numerical score, and on the basis of that score it decides which people are most likely to have underpaid their taxes. The factors that are used in the IRS profile are secret, but some of them are widely known (and announced to taxpayers by professionals who prepare returns for clients). Taxpayers who deduct home-office expenses are more likely to be audited, for example, as are people like taxi drivers and restaurant waiters who deal in cash for a living. Unusually large charitable contributions can also increase the likelihood of an audit. Profiling for drugs at airports is another example, as passengers are screened based on factors like whether they paid cash for a ticket, traveled without luggage, and recently flew to or from certain destinations where drugs are produced. The real issue, then, is not whether to profile in general, but whether there is reason to reject *racial* profiling in particular.

Racial profiling can be done in either of two ways: officially, as a matter of public policy, or unofficially by police or other officials charged with law enforcement. The racism often inherent in unofficial, lawless acts of profiling by racist police finds few defenders. There are also two ways that officially sanctioned profiling can be institutionally racist, although

[69] *The Wall Street Journal*, October 23, 2001, p. 1.
[70] *The Wall Street Journal*, October 24, 2001, p. 22.

again, neither raises serious issues of morality or public policy. First, if it is done when there is little or no evidence that the generalization on which it relies is justified, then the best explanation of the policy is likely to be institutional racism. Second, institutional racism can be evident in profiling via its implementation. Rude and offensive language, unnecessary physical violence, and unwarranted body cavity searches often indicate failure of institutional oversight and are evidence of institutional racism.

Few if any would defend those cases of profiling, and they are not the heart of the moral and policy issues swirling around racial profiling. Even the most ardent proponents of racial profiling need not tolerate, let alone approve, profiling that is based on unsound statistical evidence or that is implemented in the racist fashion I have described. The difficult cases occur when racial or ethnic appearance may be among the useful features of a successful profiling procedure. Airplane terrorists, for example, are thought more likely to be males with a Middle Eastern appearance and background.[71] The interesting question, then, is what should be done when excluding race from the profile will have costs, either in the form of greater resources being required for the same amount of security, or of less security. Is it always racist to use a racial profile?

Some have suggested that it is racist merely because it harms people based on their race. Annabelle Lever, for example, writes that the

> harms of racial profiling will be hard to justify, even if we consider only the embarrassment, humiliation, inconvenience and distrust that it occasions. For what it is to suffer racism is, in part, to suffer such harms as an ordinary part of daily life, and to suffer them simply because one is black, rather than white.[72]

If that is right that it is racist to impose harms merely because of one's race, then it may seem that profiling is indeed racist. But it is not always true that the harm is inflicted "simply because one is black" in the sense that the policy is explained by racial hostility and indifference. When profiling is legitimate, as I am suggesting it can sometimes be, then there is a justification for the profiling that *distinguishes it* from cases where a group is made to suffer merely because of race. For example, affirmative action policies giving preference to people "because they are black" can

---

[71] Frederick Schauer, *Profiles, Probabilities and Stereotypes* (Cambridge MA: Harvard University Press, 2003), p. 181.

[72] Annabelle Lever, "Why Racial Profiling Is Hard to Justify: A Response to Risse and Zeckhauser," *Philosophy and Public Affairs*, Vol. 33, No. 1 (Winter 2005), p. 106.

be said to "harm" other groups "merely because" they are white or Asian. But it would be mistaken, I believe, to call such policies racist. For the same reason, it is also a mistake to think that racial profiling must, of necessity, be racist.

Suppose, first, by analogy, that there is good evidence that bald men carry a dangerous virus in significantly higher proportions than the population as a whole, and that we have only a limited amount of vaccine to distribute. Second, suppose also that the vaccine runs a small chance of causing grave illness, and third, suppose that vaccinating bald men will protect everyone from the virus. Now the government has three options. It can (1) refuse to vaccinate anybody, (2) give the vaccine to a randomly selected proportion of the whole population without profiling or (3) choose to vaccinate only bald men. It is hard to see in such a case why vaccinating bald men would be objectionable. True, it imposes a burden on one discrete group (bald men), many of whom would not otherwise have been harmed, while allowing others who are not bald but who also carry the virus to avoid the burden. Nevertheless, the policy might make public health sense and, more importantly, would not show hostility or indifference toward bald men. Of course, it is unfortunate that the bald men must bear the burden of being vaccinated, but that is not evidence of hostility or indifference to the interests of bald men. It is based on the rational use of limited resources to protect public health. The "unfairness" of their having to bear the burden is, if anything, a kind of "cosmic" injustice or bad luck.

This analogy suggests that profiling should not be ruled out merely on the ground that it imposes burdens on groups in virtue of physical appearance. And if that is true for baldness, why is it not also true, at least in principle, for race? We do need to be especially careful when imposing burdens on groups that have been victims of racist institutions and racial oppression to be sure that racism plays no role in the decision. The possibility of racist motives should make everyone wary of too easy acceptance of racial profiling. But that is a different matter. Racial profiling need not be, in principle, racist. I want to conclude by looking at three different arguments against racial profiling on more practical grounds.

The first argument against racial profiling is developed by Frederick Schauer in a 2003 book.[73] Schauer begins with the observation that

---

[73] Schauer, *Profiles, Probabilities and Stereotypes*, pp. 186–190.

racial appearance is easy for officials to use. Blacks are relatively easy to identify. This greater salience of race compared to other characteristics in a terrorism profile, such as whether the person's travel originated in particular countries, used carry-on luggage, or paid for the ticket in cash, raises an important problem for racial profiling according to Schauer because racial profiling may be overused by those charged with implementing it. Because of their greater salience, in other words, race and physical appearance tend "to occupy more of the decision making space than their empirical role would support."[74]

The point of this argument, then, is not that racial profiling is unfair, racist, or even irrational in principle, but that it is *irrational as typically applied.* Therefore, this is a practical problem, although one that is not easily overcome. It is also an argument that defenders of profiling will need to answer, since it strikes at the heart of the reasons given *for* racial profiling – namely, that it is *more effective* to use race than to ignore it.

There are two problems with Schauer's argument, however. One is practical: instead of abandoning race profiling, we should train those who do the profiling so that they are able to compensate for the tendency to overuse race. We do not know, of course, how effective such training might be, but there seems to be no reason for thinking it would not help solve the problem. But there is also a less obvious and more important theoretical response to this criticism of profiling.

Assessing the value of race (as well as any other factor) as compared with other traits to use in profiling requires weighing three different factors: (1) the relative *predictive power* of the different factors (Schauer assumes that race passes that test and is useful predictively); (2) the *cost* of knowing that the factor is present (where cost includes not only economic costs, but noneconomic costs such as infringement of rights); and (3) the *reliability of the belief* that the factor is, in fact, present. The problem with Schauer's argument is that it ignores the last two, especially the reliability of the belief that the factor is present.

What I mean is this. The best predictor that a person will blow up an airplane would be that the person has the present intention, the means, and a developed plan to commit a specific terrorist act. If we could know that, other tests would soon be abandoned. While this would rank highest in predictive power (1), it nonetheless fails overall. First the

---

[74] Susan T. Fiske, "Stereotyping, Prejudice, and Discrimination," in *Handbook of Social Psychology,* edited by Daniel T. Gilbert, Susan T. Fiske, and Gardner Lendzey (New York: McGraw-Hill, 1998), p. 391.

cost of gathering such information about intentions, if it were possible, would be prohibitive. Learning about people's intentions would require substantial violations of privacy rights, for instance. More importantly, for our purposes, we have no reliable method to learn about people's present intentions. In assessing the overall value of any particular profiling factor we cannot ignore this last point. The fact that we have little evidence available to establish the existence of a present intent to commit a crime undermines its value despite the fact that such a factor, *if* we could learn it, would be better than all the others that we are forced to rely on.

Race is different in that respect, as Schaur has emphasized. The reliability of the belief that the factor is present undercuts Schauer's argument against the rationality of race profiling because the normal markers of "race," as the concept is usually understood, are obvious facts about people associated with skin color, hair texture, and facial construction.[75] Indeed, it is because racial appearance is the usual basis of racial identification that Schauer thinks it could easily be overused.

This last point does not show racial profiling is good policy, however, unless overuse of racial profiling could be overcome by training. But it does suggest a weakness in Schauer's argument on the ground that its salience means it will be overused relative to other factors.

The second argument against racial profiling is more troubling. Here the thought is that because racial profiling relies on generalization, racial profiling may reinforce *irrational* stereotypes because of what is, in effect, a feedback loop. In other words, stereotyping can create a self-fulfilling prophecy.[76] For example, suppose there is a belief among cab drivers that young black males are dangerous. Because that is believed (whether it is true or not is unimportant), it will make it more difficult for all young black males to get a taxi to stop, with the result that many will tend to take other forms of transportation. As that happens, however, the proportion of law-abiding blacks hailing cabs will decrease, leaving a still higher proportion of dishonest ones who rob cabs, thereby reinforcing

[75] As I discuss in Chapter 2, matters of racial identity are more complex than this paragraph suggests. There, I consider another, biologically grounded sense of "race" that is tied to the evolution of different populations. That conception of "race" is in important ways different from the ordinary one and is not as closely tied to appearance as the ordinary one that Schauer is relying on. Thanks to an anonymous reviewer for emphasizing this point.

[76] Glenn C. Loury, *The Anatomy of Racial Inequality* (Cambridge MA: Harvard University Press, 2002).

the original stereotype.[77] The practice of profiling resulted, ironically, in the generalization's greater accuracy.

Such cases can be multiplied endlessly. Teachers, for example, may expect black students to work less hard and do less well. If that causes teachers to spend less time with them, the result will be that they do less well and the stereotype is reinforced. Realtors may expect blacks to be willing to pay more for houses, with the result that the Realtor selling the home drives a harder bargain, the buyer pays the higher price, and the stereotype is strengthened once more. Racial stereotyping can result in a cycle in which the stereotype creates conditions in which the stereotype is strengthened.

Similar dangers occur with racial profiling. If police assume that a group is much more likely to be guilty, then two things may occur. First, the police may profile, with the result that they discover more criminals among the group being more heavily screened and the stereotype is confirmed. And, second, being constantly under suspicion may itself have an adverse and alienating impact on members of the group. The alienation itself may even create another feedback effect.

Although this is a potentially serious cost of racial profiling, it does not settle the issue. That would depend on how serious these costs are. The benefits of profiling might still outweigh its costs. That question can only be resolved by seeing how profiling might actually work in practice. But what is clear is that, because of the potential for overuse and feedback effects, profiling should be used only with great caution, and only after the costs and benefits have been carefully weighed in light of all the available evidence.

Finally, it may seem that I have ignored the most compelling reason to reject racial profiling. Racial profiling takes place in the United States against a background of slavery and racial oppression, and that background colors how profiling will be interpreted. Even if it is not in fact racist, it is likely to be seen by African-Americans and others that way. Racism has historically taken the form of beliefs in the inherent criminality of blacks, and it is easy to see racial profiling in that same light – as an expression of past, racist assumptions about the inherent inferiority and criminality of African-Americans. I will have more to say about the causes of crime and the issue of racial inferiority in Chapter 5, but for now I will focus only on the possibility that profiling will be (mistakenly) interpreted as racist even when it may not be. That is a powerful

[77] This example is Loury's. See Loury, *The Anatomy of Racial Inequality*, p. 30.

objection, and may be a good reason to reject profiling. How might it be addressed?

The first way – assuming profiling is rational and not in fact racist – is by political and other leaders making the reasons for it clear. Leaders should also be sure that those who implement profiling do it in ways that give no hint of disrespect, let alone of racism. Everyone who is held under suspicion, for whatever reason, is liable to be made to feel humiliated. Those who work as screeners at airports need to be respectful and courteous of everyone; those who use racial profiles need to be even more so. Police and other officials need to profile in ways that reduce potential alienation of groups being profiled and that do not suggest or imply that all members of the group are guilty. It should be done politely, and with respect for the dignity of the persons being questioned.

A second way that the misinterpretation of profiling as racist could be addressed is through public expressions of gratitude and appreciation. It is more difficult to treat a policy as racist (even if imposes a cost on one group) if society undertakes to compensate for the burdens it has imposed. What practical steps could be taken to express that gratitude and to lessen the burden on those who, we are assuming, are bearing a disproportionate burden? One suggestion is to treat profiling like we now do jury duty and military service, as a public service for which the rest of society owes a debt of gratitude. Former military personnel are not only treated with respect in speeches and in the media, but they are also given educational, health, and other benefits. Jurors also typically receive small monetary payments for each day of service, again as a sign of society's appreciation. In addition to encouraging respect and expressing gratitude, pay and benefits also serve as partial compensation for their time, effort, and, in the case of the military, the risks they took. Compensation to people who are profiled could do the same.

Racial profiling is therefore analogous to other forms of profiling that leads police to search a house for evidence of a crime. Such searches often damage the property of the (I will assume) innocent person who happened to fit the profile of the criminal. How should society, and the innocent person whose property was damaged, each respond? If the community responds appropriately, then there may be little ground for the individual's resentment. The goal of society's response should be recognition of the burden that the innocent person was made to bear. That can be accomplished, at least in part, by compensation for the damage and public recognition of the person's sacrifice.

As with other acts that benefit the public, the idea that those who are profiled have performed a public service could be encouraged in speeches by public officials and through public policy. Acknowledging the public service that people who have been profiled have given could also help engender public respect for those who are profiled, promote acceptance of the practice on the part of those who are asked, and provide some amount of compensation for the special burdens they shouldered.

One point bears special emphasis. Although, *in principle*, racial profiling is no different from other types of profiling, including of bald men, *in practice* it cannot be divorced from racism's history. The point, however, is not that racial profiling must be rejected, but rather that it should be done with special awareness of its danger and of its historical significance. Although, in fact, it says nothing about the integrity of any individual, when it is directed at a member of a racial group its meaning can easily be misinterpreted as institutional racism. It is vital, therefore, that it be used only when there is no viable alternative, that it be done with respect, and that the message accompanying it is that it is practiced without racial animus and with genuine regret at the costs it imposes on innocent victims.

2

Race

T HE SUBJECT OF THIS CHAPTER IS RACE, AND, IN PARTICULAR, the question of whether or not race is a social construction, a natural category, or both. The debate over the social construction of race is often ignored in works on racism and racial oppression, where it is simply taken for granted that race is a social construct. I think that is a mistake. Arguments over racism and racial equality often proceed as if we all understood what race is, whether it is socially constructed, and why it is important. Yet, this is not true: we do not agree what race is, let alone what significance it might play in our understanding of human life. Although evolutionary genetics has opened the door to the possibility that race is not merely a social construction, some devoutly assume that it is. Social construction even finds its way into *definitions* of race; many academics who write on racism and racial equality avoid considering the possible biological basis of race.[1] Yet, it is important to respond to racists who abuse arguments about racial differences to defend policies and practices that are incompatible with racial equality. As one African-American economist observed, "If decent people don't discuss human bio-diversity, we concede the turf to black and white racists."[2]

Is it racist to believe in races?

I have argued that racists believe in the reality of race; if they didn't, then their bigotry would take a different form than racism. But the converse does not follow – that all people who believe in races are racists. David

[1] For instance, *The Blackwell Dictionary of Sociology*, discussed in this chapter.
[2] Quoted in Jon Entine, "Why Race Matters in Sports." www.jonentine.com/reviews/aol_Why_/race_matters.htm.

52

Theo Goldberg claims not only that racism is "characterized" by beliefs about racial differences, but also that it does not matter whether the beliefs are rational. "Some racist beliefs," Goldberg writes, are "strongly rational, for they satisfy widely accepted formal criteria of rationality."[3] He then gives as an example of such rational beliefs that are nevertheless inherently racist Pierre ven der Berghe's work.[4] Ven der Berghe claims that human beings instinctively prefer their own kin, that racial differences serve as markers for kin, and that people are therefore instinctively inclined to make racial distinctions. The fact that this theory may be rational – it meets accepted standards of evidence and truth – is irrelevant, according to Goldberg. Such a belief is "racist expression"[5] simply because of its content, that is, because its author thinks racial differences are "natural, inevitable, and therefore unchangeable."[6] Naomi Zack takes a similar position, saying that it is "illegitimate" even to investigate the biological basis of race and that those who accept the biological basis of race often do so to secure the "preservation of white privilege" or the "preservation of [white] tradition."[7] Lawrence Blum similarly claims that belief in racial differences and in racial "inferiority" is a "*paradigm*" of racism.[8]

The depth of this hostility toward those who deny social constructionism and believe in racial differences was evident in reactions to a bestselling book by Charles Murray and Richard Hernstein, *The Bell Curve*. The book is mainly about the role of I.Q. scores in predicting economic success and social problems, ranging from crime and poverty to welfare dependency. But it was Chapter 13, the material on race and I.Q., that met with a firestorm of criticism. On that basis, the authors were often denounced as racists. One author spoke of the "repugnant invocation of 'scientific objectivity' in defense of his racist undertakings."[9] Tariq Modood even invented a name for this "new" racism: he called it "scientific

---

[3] Goldberg, "Racism and Rationality," p. 390.
[4] I discuss this work and its significance later in this book.
[5] Goldberg, "Racism and Rationality," p. 391.
[6] Goldberg, "Racism and Rationality," p. 370.
[7] Naomi Zack, "Race and Racial Discrimination," p. 259. She also mentions "non-white liberatory efforts" (by which I assume she means blacks who use illegitimate biological ideas of race as a tool of political struggle) as a third, illegitimate use of race. Whether such a use reflects racism, however, may be doubted.
[8] Blum, *"I'm Not a Racist But . . . ,"* p. 8.
[9] Louise M. Antony, "Quine as Feminist," in *A Mind of One's Own: Feminist Essays on Reason and Objectivity*, edited by Louise M. Antony and Charlotte Witt (Boulder: Westview Press, 1993), p. 217.

racism" because it is "based upon biological theories of superior and inferior races."[10] I will argue that Murray and Hernstein are mistaken. But are they also racists?

Although it is common to denounce anyone who suggests that racial differences may be real as being a racist, there are some notable exceptions whose commitment to racial progress and equality can hardly be questioned. Early abolitionists of both races, for instance, believed that there were intrinsic differences between blacks and whites. Blacks, it was often felt, were both more "spiritual" and less aggressive.[11] Another more recent example is Noam Chomsky, one of the most forceful leftist social critics on the scene. Yet, Chomsky asks, why should it be disturbing

> to discover that relative height or musical talent or rank in running the one-hundred-yard dash is in part genetically determined? Why should one have preconceptions one way or another about these questions, and how do the answers to them, whatever they may be, relate either to serious scientific issues (in the present state of our knowledge) or to social practice in a decent society?[12]

Other well-known philosophers have expressed similar views.[13] There are good philosophical reasons to reject claims that believing in race constitutes racism; to see why, it is necessary to return to issues that I discussed in Chapter 1 and say something more about the similarities and differences between beliefs and racism.

Like racism, beliefs are attitudes people can take. But instead of attitudes toward persons, beliefs are attitudes toward propositions.[14] To believe that it will rain this afternoon, for instance, is to have a particular attitude toward the proposition "It will rain this afternoon."[15] Beliefs show themselves in different ways, often depending on the nature of the proposition. A person who believes that it will rain, for example,

---

[10] Tariq Modood, "'Difference,' Cultural Racism and Anti-Racism," in *Race and Racism*, edited by Boxill, p. 238.

[11] Fredrickson, *Racism*, p. 154.

[12] Noam Chomsky, "Psychology and Ideology," in *For Reasons of State*, edited by Noam Chomsky (New York: Vintage Press, 1973), p. 363.

[13] See, for example, "Equality and Genetic Diversity," in Peter Singer, *Practical Ethics* (Cambridge UK: Cambridge University Press, 1995).

[14] Whether the belief *just is* those attitudes, or something else, such as a physiological state a person is in, is a question I leave aside here.

[15] A belief is an attitude toward a proposition rather than toward a sentence because the same belief can be expressed in many different sentences in English and in other languages. "It is likely to rain." and "Rain is probable." are only two of many examples of different sentences expressing the same proposition.

will presumably evidence that propositional attitude by saying things like "It's going to rain soon" when asked to make a prediction about the weather or by taking an umbrella when going outdoors.

So while beliefs and racism are both attitudes, they are directed at different objects: the object of a belief is a proposition, but the object of a racist's attitude is persons belonging to a racial group. That said, however, we can understand the claim that a belief is racist in the same, indirect sense that I argued we should understand the claim that a joke or word is racist. Calling a belief racist means that it is the sort of belief that is *typically* held by people who are, in fact, racists in the strict sense. If a belief (or word) is racist, we have (some) reason to believe the person who uttered it is probably a racist. But the "probably" is important because it may prove not to be the case. The question of racism always depends on the person's attitudes toward people, not toward propositions.

The same can be said of whole systems of beliefs, such as ideologies. The United Nations General Assembly adopted, then revoked a resolution claiming Zionism is a form of racism. What might that mean? Whether or not Zionism, Christianity, Islam, Nazism, or whatever is a *racist* ideology depends on whether it is a system of beliefs typically held by persons who are racists. Such claims about ideologies may or may not be true, but correctly interpreted they cannot be dismissed as conceptually confused. There is a gap between even racist beliefs and racist persons because the fact a person has a racist ideology only provides a reason to believe the person is racist – nothing more.

The *truth* of a charge that an ideology is racism could be confirmed in two ways. First, we could observe the people who subscribed to the ideology to see if, in fact, they were racists – if they evidenced racial contempt. And, second, we would think about the content of the ideology – what it says about different races – to see if some of its core beliefs are themselves the sorts of beliefs that we expect would indicate racism on the part of those who believe them. It, therefore, does not follow from what I have said, nor is it true, that beliefs in natural racial differences are *unrelated* to racism.[16] Like the utterance of specific words, beliefs may be a *sign* or indication of racism, and indeed some beliefs (or statements of belief) will almost surely indicate racism. Suppose a person were to

---

[16] It also does not follow – contrary to the claim I quoted earlier – that those who believe in another group's racial *superiority* harbor racism toward that supposedly "superior" group unless there is also reason to suspect racial hostility. Believing Jews are more intelligent than others does not constitute racism, even if Jews are thought of as a race and the greater intelligence is believed to be an inherited trait.

say, apparently sincerely, that "Niggers are stupid." Without more, there would be little doubt that the speaker was a racist. The word "nigger" is itself a strong indication of racial hostility. But even in this case, the claim of racism is an *inference* from the belief and the words used to express it, and it could prove false. We might learn the statement was uttered by a black coach to encourage a black player in his studies, for instance.

Beliefs in racial differences, and even claims of racial inferiority, must be interpreted in context, and not all contexts indicate racism. Take acting and singing, for instance: whites are in some respects "inferior" to blacks in the context of playing the roles of Othello or Martin Luther King. White men might also, other things being equal, be inferior at mentoring a troop of black Boy Scouts whose fathers are absent. Or suppose a person believes that Asians are inferior to whites and blacks in terms of ability to play basketball, but then goes on to explain that of course she knows this is not to say that all Asians are worse at basketball or that Asians should be denied opportunities to play on the same terms as others. We might even learn that the person who holds the belief is herself Asian. Researchers at historically black Howard University who are trying to understand why blacks are more vulnerable to hypertension and other diseases are not racists, despite the fact that they are assuming race is real, rather than socially constructed, and that blacks are "inferior" to Asians and Caucasians in their ability to resist some diseases.

None of that is to deny, however, that there are often very deep connections between people's racism and their beliefs about races. As I said, sometimes the best explanation of the belief *is* the fact that the person is a racist. So although it is always true that a racist believes in biological races, and it is also often true that a person who believes in the natural inferiority of another race is a racist, the fact that the person holds that or any other belief does not *constitute* racism. Yet, the idea persists, often strongly held, that there is something deeply wrong or immoral when people believe that races are real, or that races are "unequal" along some dimension. Why should that be? I can only offer a few speculations about why that attitude persists, though I will return to the issue of race and equality in the next two chapters.

The answer begins, I suspect, with a point that I have emphasized: racists believe races are real. So there may be a form of guilt by association. As one writer put it, if race were believed by people to represent a biological "classification system," then the result could be to "excuse if not justify" colonialism and racism.[17] If racists believe in race, then other people can inoculate themselves against the charge of racism by affirming that any differences that exist between racial groups are products of history and culture rather than natural. Another possible reason to deny that race is a natural category is the potential political or policy consequences of people's acceptance of racial differences. Natural differences might compete with other explanations of economic differences such as racial discrimination, so that equality could be threatened as the "default" position. That would make it more difficult to show that group differences in income, poverty, and incarceration rates can only be the result of social injustice and oppression.

None of that constitutes a defense of the *truth* of the idea that races do not exist, of course, but it may go some way to explain why the subject is so controversial and so little studied. Because the choice to study a subject and to put forward a conclusion can have grave moral and political consequences, studying natural racial differences might be wrong in the same way that some thought studying how to make nuclear weapons was wrong. Indeed, we often do think it is right to sacrifice truth to other values. For example, illegally acquired evidence is excluded from criminal trials and spouses are exempt from testifying against each other. We choose to ignore those sources of evidence, and possibly to sacrifice knowing the truth, in order to secure privacy, in the case of illegal searches, or to protect personal relationships in the case of spousal privileges. Could it be that some potential racial differences also belong to this category – of possible truths that we are better off not knowing and that it would therefore be wrong even to pursue?

I do not know how, ultimately, to answer that worry, except to say that while I share the concerns about the misuse of such information, I do not think censorship – whether by ourselves or by governments – is the remedy. As John Stuart Mill emphasized, we are better off in the long run as we make practical decisions if even false ideas are presented in the marketplace of ideas. There may be at least some truth to the claim, and, even if not, it may be useful to the truth to be tested. "He who knows only his own side about the case," said Mill, "knows little of that."[18]

---

[17] Linda Martin Alcoff, "Philosophy and Racial Identity," in *Philosophies of Race and Identity*, edited by Peter Osborne and Stella Stanford (London: Continuum, 2002), p. 15.

[18] John Stuart Mill, *On Liberty*, edited by Elizabeth Rapaport (Indianapolis: Hackett Publishing Co., 1978), p. 35.

History often confirms the importance of learning the truth if we are
to find solutions to problems. For instance, although it did not question
the social constructivist account of race, in 1965, an important study
of race was effectively censored with important consequences. In that
year, the United States Department of Labor published *The Negro Family:
The Case for Action* (also known as the *Moynihan Report*, named for U.S.
Senator Patrick Moynihan). It pointed out, among other distressing facts,
that 26 percent of negro children were born to unmarried women, and
that there were growing problems of welfare dependency, poor school
performance, and crime in the black community. The report met with
a chorus of hostile reactions from a variety of quarters. It was criticized
for blaming the victim, and its authors were vilified. As a result, the
problems it had described were forced off the political agenda, and
there was very little discussion of these issues for a generation. All the
while, the problems got worse. A generation after the *Moynihan Report*
was driven underground, its findings were widely recognized, and it is no
longer considered racist to acknowledge such differences.[19]

Trying to take the subject of the nature of race off the agenda is
also both futile and unwise. The fact that racists have abused the idea
of biological races is irrelevant to the truth of the matter, and ignoring
possible natural racial differences may lead researchers to ignore medical
or other advantages that would follow from a more realistic approach to
science and race. That said, the question still remains: Is race a social
construction? Many assume it is, and so we first need to consider more
carefully what social construction is and what is at stake in the debate.

The idea of social construction

Social constructivism has its roots in eighteenth-century British empiri-
cism and especially the idea that the mind is a white paper on which
"experience" of the environment writes whatever it wishes. In its broadest
sense, "social construction" is a modern expression of this centuries-old
idea, though it is also more. A lake, for instance, can be either natural or constructed, but buildings are always constructed. When we say
something is constructed, we mean its existence is *in some sense* optional

[19] One further concern leading people to deny the reality of race might be the belief
that acknowledging such differences could undermine the important ideal of racial
equality. The response to that will require careful attention to just what racial equality
requires and the grounds for claiming racial equality – both topics that will be taken up
in following chapters.

because constructed things are contingent on past decisions and actions. That means, in turn, that truth claims about objects that are constructed are dependent on those past choices and actions of construction, rather than independent of them. If water's being H_2O is a natural fact, for example, rather than being "socially constructed," then the statement that water is H_2O is true regardless of human actions, desires, or interests, and would have been true had humans never existed. On the other hand, if water's being H_2O were thought to be a social construct, then that truth would not have the same independent status.

If water, planets, and beaver dams are thought to be examples of natural things, then (again, staying with common sense) what would be a clear case of a socially constructed thing? The easiest examples come from rule-governed social practices, such as law and games: plaintiffs, motions for dismissal, and juries depend entirely on the existence of a legal system, just as strikeout, checkmate, and quarterback depend on the existence of games. None of those would exist without the institutions and rules in which they figure. We could imagine a piece of wood that looks like a rook or a person physically running across a line on a field independent of the games of chess and football; but they would not have any existence as a rook or a touchdown, independent of the practices, concepts, and rules in which they find meaning.

These commonsense distinctions suggest that social constructionism offers little that is either new or controversial. In fact, however, the idea has been used in ways that have seemed profound to some and shocking or silly to others. In his book, *The Social Construction of What?*, Ian Hacking (who is in many respects sympathetic with social constructivism in general) describes the "degeneration" of social construction from a liberating idea into one that is "both obscure and overused" and has left its defenders "smug, comfortable, and trendy in ways that have become merely orthodox."[20] Part of the problem is that the idea of social construction has become ubiquitous, as more and more things are said to be socially constructed. Examples include quarks, AIDS, illness, anorexia, masculinity, the feeble mind, and homosexual culture – to name only a small fraction of them.[21] Other things that have sometimes been thought

---

[20] Ian Hacking, *The Social Construction of What?* (Cambridge MA: Harvard University Press, 1999), p. vii. My discussion of social construction has benefited from Hacking's, especially his emphasis on the importance of "inevitability" in understanding social construction.
[21] Hacking managed to compile a list extending from A (authorship) to Z (Zulu Nationalism). Hacking, *The Social Construction of What?*, p. 1.

to be socially constructed include nature,[22] vital statistics,[23] facts,[24] minds and emotions,[25] reality,[26] and deafness.[27] Not to be outdone, two writers have even claimed the social construction of everything.[28]

But, of course, if everything is socially constructed, then it is natural to wonder: what is the point of saying so? If it is that we cannot know the world as it is "in itself," independent of human concepts or categories, then claiming that *race* is socially constructed would say nothing in particular about race at all, which cannot be what the social constructivist view of race is trying to get at. Because it is clear that some things do exist only because of social practices and rules (weddings, carburetors, and good chess moves come to mind) and others exist independently (I have mentioned water, planets, and beaver dams), what is the point of stretching the concept beyond the commonsense ideas I have described?

The answer is found in my earlier point: that a socially constructed thing is, for that reason, in some sense arbitrary. Had the social world been different, then this thing would also have been different or perhaps not exist at all. In that way, social constructivism invites inquiry into the assumptions behind those contingent social practices – assumptions that may be hidden from view. How did it come to be that women are seen as more emotional, that mental illness is treated differently from physical illness, that homosexuality is thought to be unnatural, and that the female body is regarded as suitable for ornaments? Social constructivism invites investigation into the social forces working behind the scene, shaping how investigations are conducted, which questions are asked, and the assumptions behind what may otherwise seem natural and inevitable.

Social constructivism, therefore, belongs to a long tradition, going back to Karl Marx and to what Karl Mannheim in the middle of the last

[22] Klaus Eder, *The Social Construction of Nature*, translated by Mark Ritter (London: Sage Publishing Co., 1996).

[23] George Neil Emery, *The Facts of Life: The Social Construction of Vital Statistics, Ontario, 1859–1952* (Montreal: McGill-Queens University Press, 1993).

[24] Bruno Latour and Steve Woolgar, *Laboratory Life: The Social Construction of Scientific Facts* (Beverly Hills: Sage Publishing Co., 1979).

[25] Jeff Coulter, *The Social Construction of Mind: Studies in Ethnomethodology and Linguistic Philosophy* (Totawa NJ: Rowman and Littlefield, 1979).

[26] Peter L. Berger and Thomas Luckmann, *The Social Construction of Reality: A Treatise in the Sociology of Knowledge* (Garden City NJ: Doubleday Pub. Co., 1966.)

[27] Gillian M. Hartley and Susan Gregory (eds.), *Constructing Deafness* (London: Pinter Publications, 1991).

[28] Berger and Luckmann, *The Social Construction of Reality*.

century termed "unmasking."[29] When Marx sought to explain law and religion, for example, he took neither at face value. Notions of justice and religious beliefs are best understood functionally, Marx thought, by reference to the role they play in maintaining the capitalist economic order and preventing conflict from undermining social stability.[30] By unmasking the social realities lying behind what may otherwise seem inevitable, the social contingency of the things is exposed. A claim that *property* is socially constructed, for example, also conveys the idea that there is nothing inevitable about property. The hope is that such unmasking will help undermine beliefs about "natural" rights to property. Mari Matsuda sees feminists and other "progressive scholars" such as critical race theorists as belonging in that tradition. All of those, she writes, work at "unmasking: unmasking a grab for power disguised as science, unmasking a justification for tyranny disguised as history, unmasking an assault on the poor disguised as law."[31]

This contingency of social constructions leads to another conclusion: that because the social construct sits in a particular historical and social context, what appear to be facts about the thing may be brought into question. And it could then follow that if something is a (mere) social construct, there is the possibility of change – of constructing it differently. Because it is not part of an objectively fixed, ahistorical nature, we (as societies) are collectively responsible for having constructed it. In that way, social construction has a reformist and critical tendency.

A final feature of social construction is more explicitly political. Articles and books written from this perspective generally share not just a critical perspective, but a *leftist* critical one. The authors of *Not in Our Genes*, for instance, are explicit in acknowledging what they see as a connection between their social constructivism and their politics. According to them, the essential "unity" of the "biological and the social" means that science "is an integral part of the struggle to create a just [i.e., socialist] society."[32] Because the human sciences are inherently social, the authors seem to

[29] Karl Mannheim, *Essays on the Sociology of Knowledge* (London: Routledge and Kegan Paul, 1952).

[30] For a discussion of functionalism and its role in Marx's thought, see G. A. Cohen, *Marx's Theory of History: A Defense, Expanded Edition* (Princeton: Princeton University Press, 1978, 2000).

[31] Mari J. Matsuda, "Voices of America: Accent, Antidiscrimination Law, and a Jurisprudence for the Last Reconstruction," *Yale Law Journal*, Vol. 100 (1991), pp. 1329, 1394.

[32] R. C. Lewontin, S. Rose, and L. J. Kamin, *Not in Our Genes* (New York: Pantheon, 1984), pp. ix, 76.

think the sciences are part of the authors' larger socialist project. But why *should* social construction be dominated by the left, rather than the middle or the right, of the political spectrum?

A partial answer is that because the plasticity of human nature is inherent in social constructionism, utopian-style reforms may seem more realistic. Human nature can be altered and people taught to be less selfish and more egalitarian, as advocates of "socialist man" have traditionally argued. Radically utopian, reformist ambitions are therefore less compatible with basic tenets of conservatives like Edmund Burke, Karl Popper, and Michael Oakshott who worry that radical changes based on utopian ideals will lead to disaster. For them, human nature is more fixed, and attempts to change it are doomed to (often disastrous) failure.

Although constructivism is often thought to be most friendly to those on the left, it is important to note that there are utopians on the extreme right as well. By definition, utopians are interested in radically remaking society, and both right and left could, in theory, claim the social constructivist mantel. It is easy to *imagine* a Neo-Nazi book titled *The Social Construction of Hitler* that aspires to "unmask" common attitudes about the evils of Nazism. Or, we could even *envision* a book titled *The Social Construction of the Holocaust* arguing that the Holocaust was the social creation of a Jewish media conspiracy. Like today's more leftist constructivist works, these too might seek to undermine their opponents' ideas by showing that they are not objectively true or rooted in any objective historical fact, but instead mirror the power of certain groups. So although constructivism does have a reformist tendency, the methodology of social constructivism can be separated from the conclusions that its followers typically accept. The nature of the reforms that are required is left open by social constructivism.

Social construction is often taken for granted, and those who challenge it may find themselves at the center of controversy. Harvard University's then-president, Lawrence Summers, got into hot water for suggesting in a speech that females may be naturally less good at higher mathematics than males.[33] One prominent scientist walked out. Others, including a prominent female geneticist, publicly defended the possibility that

---

[33] Lawrence H. Summers, "Remarks at National Bureau of Economic Research Conference on Diversifying the Science & Engineering Workforce," Cambridge, MA, January 14, 2005. http://www.president.harvard.edu/speeches/2005/nber.html. Accessed on March 29, 2007.

natural differences exist and should be investigated. Olivia Judson, from Imperial College London, wrote,

> I would love to know if the averages are the same but the underlying variation is different – with members of one sex tending to be either superb or dreadful at particular sorts of thinking while members of the other are pretty good but rarely exceptional. . . . I'm keen to know what sets men and women apart – and no longer afraid of what we may find.[34]

Summers nevertheless apologized for his remarks in a letter to alumni and later resigned, in part, some have suggested, as a result of this incident. Whatever the truth of this matter may be, it is clear that these were ideas many thought should not be put forth, especially by a university president. The reason, said his critics, is that such statements discourage talented women from studying math and science.

What is interesting about this affair and the often heated debates about social construction versus nature is that mixed with the controversy is the widespread acceptance of the idea that some sex differences are socially constructed, while others are not. All agree that many societies traditionally assigned women roles involving children and the home, and that men were expected to work outside the home. Such roles include informal socialization practices and legally sanctioned differences in the rights and responsibilities of the sexes. Women were encouraged to take only some jobs with others – often the most rewarding and powerful – reserved for men. Most egregiously, women have been and often still are relegated to second-class citizenship, denied voting rights, equal educational and employment opportunities, and the opportunity to participate in political life in general.

That said, however, there is another equally obvious and important respect in which sex is *not* a social construction. Natural sex differences mean that only females can have children, of course, and sex differences are also important in the diagnosis and treatment of diseases. Sex and age are two of the first questions doctors ask about patients. There are other contexts in which natural differences are taken for granted, beyond the obvious ones of childbearing and medicine. Few deny that males are naturally "superior" to females physically: men are, on average, bigger, faster, and stronger. The evidence for this is overwhelming, and it is present across a wide range of species. Human females are rarely able to

---

[34] Olivia Judson, "Different but (Probably) Equal," *New York Times*, January 23, 2005, p. WK 17.

compete on the same level with men in sports demanding size, speed, and strength, and social practices take account of that fact by providing separate sports competitions. And it is also generally accepted that sex differences in athletic ability imply nothing about how opportunities and resources should be distributed. These are further questions, involving a variety of moral and policy issues. Males are on average bigger, faster, and stronger than females, but, we think, so what?

The issue is, therefore, not about whether or not sex (or "gender") is a social construction; it clearly both is and is not. (That may explain why some have thought of using "sex" to refer to the natural, biological category and "gender" to refer to the differences that are not natural but that society encourages or requires in treatment of people of different sexes.) Yet, as the Summers controversy illustrated, in other contexts, challenges to social constructivism are met with hostility or worse. One of the most important legal challenges to campus speech codes involved a psychology teacher at the University of Michigan who was threatened with disciplinary action for suggesting in his class that there may be innate differences between males and females. According to university officials, presenting this idea was a form of sexual harassment because it created a "hostile environment" for his women students.[35] Why is it that these ideas remain so controversial?

One concern is that these ideas may undermine arguments for equal opportunities for women. But why would that happen? *Even if* females, on average, have fewer exceptionally high mathematical skills than males, that has nothing to do with the *opportunities* that should be afforded girls and women.

A different worry might be that talented girls could be less motivated to learn mathematics or engineering if it became widely accepted that boys are better at these subjects. But again, it is not clear that this would be the result. A girl who learns she has exceptional talent, might, for that reason, want to develop it instead of doing what other girls do. Letting people be who they are is one thing; making them conform to whatever is common among members of their sex is another.

One final issue in the background of arguments over social construc-tionism might be the most salient: if all differences are socially con-structed, then social injustices are easier to see and social criticism is easier to justify. If it is society rather than nature that is causing differ-ences in outcome, then equality of outcome seems the natural baseline.

---

[35] *Doe v. University of Michigan*, 721 F. Supp. 852 (E. D. Michigan, 1989).

And equality of outcome is a handy yardstick against which to measure the extent to which sexism remains a problem. As long as there are differences in the proportions of men and women in various positions, we could argue – as long as we remain social constructivists – that the system is tilted unfairly and sex-roles are being "assigned" by society. On the other hand, introducing the possibility that women *naturally* prefer some positions or endeavors to others or are on average more or less able to do some tasks would make it more difficult to measure the extent to which females are not being given the same opportunities as males. If women are naturally less inclined to play aggressive, competitive sports, then differences in levels of participation among college men and women cannot necessarily be attributed to discrimination against women.

Despite all the controversy, it is important to emphasize that we also accept that there are important ways in which sex differences *are* a social construction and other ways in which they *are not* a social construction. As I noted, that men are generally bigger, faster, and stronger is uncontroversial and is reflected in our social practices. The disagreements are over the boundaries between the socially constructed and the natural differences, with policies often hanging in the balance. All agree that girls and women should be treated fairly, though we do not necessarily all agree on what that entails. The dispute over social construction with respect to sex has, to that extent, been put in its place.

Social construction and race

Although the idea that human beings fall naturally into racial groups dates at least from the eighteenth century, the supposed significance of those racial differences has changed dramatically over time. Indeed, there has been a tendency to swing between emphasizing the idea that racial differences are hereditary and natural, on the one hand, and the view that race is biologically insignificant on the other hand. Broadly speaking, the constructivist and environmental view of race was predominant in the eighteenth century, and the naturalistic, anticonstructivist view came to dominate in the nineteenth century. The last half of the twentieth century, in turn, saw a resurgence of environmental, constructivist understanding.

The early social constructivist view of race reflected the idea, common in the eighteenth century, that hereditary differences among people mattered far less than their social circumstances, such as education, family, and other environmental factors. This constructivist idea was "enshrined in the radical bourgeois political programs under the influence of Locke's doctrine of the tabula rasa"[36] famously expressed as follows:

> [S]uppose the mind to be, as we say, white paper void of all characters, without any ideas. How comes it to be furnished? Whence comes it by that vast store which the busy and boundless fancy of man has painted on it with an almost endless variety? Whence has it all the materials of reason and knowledge? To this I answer, in word, from EXPERIENCE.[37]

Another prominent eighteenth-century philosopher, William Godwin, used the same metaphor. Children, he wrote, "are a sort of raw material" and their minds are "like a sheet of white paper."[38] This understanding of human beings as naturally similar – but made different as a result of political and social conditions – was also among the core beliefs of the French Revolution, and shared by thinkers as different as Thomas Hobbes and Jean-Jacques Rousseau. Although they took opposing views about whether humans are basically self-interested or good, the two at least agreed that there is a fundamental sameness of human beings.

Racial differences (in the nonconstructivist sense), therefore, took on a fairly minor role as "Eighteenth century geneticists tended to deprecate the power and permanence of racial differences."[39] What differences *were* observed among groups of people arose, it was assumed, from factors such as different diets, natural environments, and climates. This view won some acceptance in the United States as well, where race was often thought to derive ultimately from differences in people's natural environment. Many thought, for example, that white-skinned people could become black by sufficient exposure to sunlight. A story told of a former slave who, when he moved North, became white, prompted Benjamin Rush, at a meeting of the American Philosophical Society in 1797, to argue that black skin was not inherited.[40]

---

[36] *International Encyclopedia of the Social Sciences*, Vol. 13, edited by David L. Sills (New York: Macmillan Co., 1968), p. 265. My discussion of the history of race is indebted to this useful work.

[37] John Locke (1690), *An Essay Concerning Human Understanding* (New York: E. P. Dutton, 1947), Book II, Chapter 1, p. 26.

[38] Quoted in Thomas Sowell, *A Conflict of Visions: Ideological Origins of Political Struggles* (New York: Quill, 1987), p. 63.

[39] *International Encyclopedia of the Social Sciences*, p. 265.

[40] Thomas Gossett, *Race: The History of an Idea in America* (Dallas: Southern Methodist University Press, 1963); quoted in *International Encyclopedia of the Social Sciences*, p. 265.

This view, that natural, biological differences were relatively unimportant in understanding racial differences, changed significantly in the nineteenth century with the realization that huge expanses of time had transpired as human beings evolved. Racial differences are not merely transitory differences that emerge when a person is exposed to a new environment, but instead are the product of thousands of years of natural selection. The full title of Darwin's book reflected the significance of his discovery for the races of man: *The Origin of Species by Means of Natural Selection or the Preservation of Favoured Races in the Struggle for Life.* That huge time scale of the evolution of the races meant that race took on much greater importance in contrast to the assumptions of the earlier "egalitarian geneticists" that racial and cultural differences were linked. Race did not matter, on that assumption; such differences were, like suntans, relatively unimportant and transitory features of people. But as it became accepted that races were fixed features of human beings, new ways of thinking about race seemed inevitable.

This biological linking of natural selection, race, and culture was defended most famously by Herbert Spencer. (It was not Darwin but Spencer who first coined the phrase "survival of the fittest.") Emphasizing the importance of survival and self-interest in explaining the motivations of individuals, Spencer saw societies in much the same way that evolutionists saw species, as in a competitive struggle in which the ones most "fitted" to their environment survive and flourish, and those that are less fit wither or die. Respect for individual liberties, Spencer believed, was essential for the survival of a society. Spencer thought that biology and society were linked together, and survival of the fittest explained the progress of both. Over the huge expanse of time, there was "feedback" as biology and culture interacted over the generations.

These ideas were taken up by others as racial thinking was pushed further in an attempt to understand cultural differences. This naturalistic view of the races, which saw human beings as falling into evolved biological types, paralleled the work of botanists who sought to classify plants into their natural categories. Underlying much of this theorizing was the idea that biological differences among people determine cultural differences, and differences in civilizations could be understood as the natural creations of the different races.[41]

---

[41] For a useful discussion of this history, on which my discussion relies, see Michael Banton and Jonathan Harwood, *The Race Concept* (New York: Praeger, 1975).

A one-volume encyclopedia produced in the middle of the nine-teenth century, purporting to give the reader an overview of all there was worth knowing at the time, begins with a table dividing humans into the "Five Races of Man."[42] The five basic races were then each divided into different subgroups or "families." The five races it lists are: White/Aryan; Yellow/Mongolian; Black/Negro; Brown/Malay; and Red/American, and each is then described first in terms of various nat-ural or physical features (skull, face, skin, and hair) followed by cultural differences (ranging from intellectual and social characteristics to reli-gious differences). The authors admit, however, that there are other ways to categorize people. Some anthropologists had used six basic categories rather than five; another, whom they quote, thought that there were eleven races. But, the authors explained, they followed the categoriza-tion proposed by Blumenbach[43] and other anthropologists because they considered it to be the "most convenient."

Many anthropologists were willing to do more than merely describe superficial differences they saw, so that these racial differences were themselves sometimes explained in terms of angles of the bones of the face and cranial size.[44] The authors of that encyclopedia also offered normative judgments, reporting that whites had the highest grade of intellect, were the "most progressive," and had the greatest influence on the "affairs of mankind." Blacks were described as "rather imitative than intellectual, perhaps owing to lack of opportunity," exercising "no influence on the progress of humanity," and "marked by natural talent for music."[45] Other nineteenth-century racial theorists drew further conclusions, describing the "fragmentation" of the white race and claiming the superiority of the Aryan Anglo-Saxons over other whites, such as the Irish and Scottish Celts.[46]

These ideas of natural racial differences, combined with self-serving assessments of the value of different cultures, were picked up in the mid-twentieth century. Nazism employed racial theories in order to jus-tify genocide, mass murder, and war. Despite its associations with Nazism,

[42] Moses Folsom and J. D. O'Connor, *Treasuries of Science, History, and Culture* (Chicago: Moses Warren Pub. Co., 1879), p. 21.

[43] Johann Friedrich Blumenbach, *On the Natural Variety of Mankind* (1776).

[44] Banton and Harwood, *The Race Concept*, mention Charles Hamilton Smith, *The Natural History of the Human Species* (1848) as an example.

[45] Folson and O'Connor, *Treasuries*, p. 21.

[46] Matthew Frye Jackson, *Whiteness of a Different Color* (Cambridge MA: Harvard University Press, 1992), p. 38.

however, the idea that humans are naturally divided into racial groups survived for a few more decades, albeit shorn of its explicitly racist content. The 1968 edition of the intellectual lodestone, *Encyclopedia Britannica*, includes an article on the "Races of Mankind" that begins:

> Race as a biological concept in man and other animals refers to the taxonomic (classificatory) unit immediately below the species. Biologically, a race is a population or a group of populations distinct by virtue of genetic isolation and natural selection; in these terms a race is neither an artificial construct, a collection of individuals arbitrarily selected from a population, nor a religious grouping, linguistic division, or nationality.[47]

That same edition of the *Encyclopedia Britannica* goes on to say that the races "differ considerably" genetically, including differences in teeth, bones, blood types, facial hair, and scarring.[48] These racial differences are attributed to "evolutionary mechanisms working on isolated populations" leading to a "genetic constitution best fitted to the circumstances."[49]

As I discuss in Chapter 3, beliefs that there are natural races played a role in the philosophy of slavery and in later forms of racial oppression in the United States as well as in Europe.[50] But what is also not much in doubt is that although race may have served as a rationalization for slavery, the many anthropologists who studied race also thought race marked real distinctions among groups of people. Race, they thought, explained what they observed, which were very great differences not only in the physical appearance of people but also in their cultures. The extent to which those cultural differences are best explained by race as a *biological* concept is a further question, however, as Kant himself well knew. In fact, Kant reported that he was undecided about the causes of the differences he noticed among the races. The philosopher, he claimed, is "*at liberty to choose* whether he wishes to assume natural differences" or whether other races "should be regarded as equal in natural ability to all other inhabitants in the world."[51]

[47] *Encyclopedia Britannica*, Vol. 18 (Chicago: William Bentor Pub., 1969), p. 985.

[48] *Encyclopedia Britannica*, Vol. 18, p. 985.

[49] *Encyclopedia Britannica*, Vol. 18, p. 986.

[50] Others have gone further, suggesting that racism might have infected anthropologists' and philosophers' thinking in more subtle ways. One writer thinks that Kant's beliefs about race "belong in an 'intimate' way" to his philosophical theories that, on their face, have nothing whatsoever to do with race. Emmanuel Chukwudi Eze, "The Color of Reason," in *Postcolonial African Philosophy: A Critical Reader*, edited by Emmanuel Chukwudi Eze (Oxford: Blackwell, 1997), p. 129.

[51] Immanuel Kant, *Political Writings*, edited by Hans Reiss (Cambridge UK: Cambridge University Press, 1991), p. 217, emphasis added.

If this history of the different ideas about race shows anything, it is not that naturalistic accounts of race inevitably lead to racism but that such ideas of race can be abused. When these ideas are treated as if they are natural and not socially constructed, race has often been used to justify atrocities of the worst imaginable kind. People who think and write about the nature of race have been rightly wary of any suggestion that race is not socially constructed. It is hardly surprising that an early suggestion that race is a social construction came in 1950, in the shadow of Nazism, when a United Nations (UNESCO) panel of scientists defined race as a "social construction," adding that it is without any biological significance.[52] Half a century later, Linda Martin Alcoff wrote of the "emerging scientific consensus that race is a myth."[53] Indeed, that remains so much the orthodox view now that it has sometimes become part of the official definition of "race" used by academic organizations and dictionaries. The *Blackwell Dictionary of Sociology*'s entry on "Race," for example, adopts both the conceptual and the political components of the constructivist position: "Most sociologists (and biologists) dispute the idea that biological race is a meaningful concept. . . The consensus is that race exists as a socially constructed set of categories used primarily as a basis for social inequality and social oppression."[54] The American Psychological Association has also taken the official position that "race is a social construct" and that there is "danger" in the "conception of race as biological."[55]

But what view of race is the constructivist position meant to deny, exactly? Glenn Loury's answer is typical. He describes the "axiom" of social construction as follows:

> "Race" is a socially constructed mode of human categorization. That people use marks on the bodies of others to divide the field of human subjects into the subgroups we call "races" is a social convention for which no deeper justification in biological taxonomy is to be had.[56]

The central idea of race, says Loury, is that the groups "*we call* races" are selected as a matter of "social convention" rather than as part of biology. Louise B. Antony writes in a similar vein that " . . .race is not

[52] Sean Thomas, "Are Whites Cleverer Than Blacks?" *Spectator*, May 24, 2003, p. 26.

[53] Alcoff, "Philosophy and Racial Identity," p. 15.

[54] Allan G. Johnson, *Blackwell Dictionary of Sociology*, 2nd ed. (Malden MA: Blackwell, 2000), p. 249.

[55] Nicholas Wade, "Gene Study Identifies 5 Main Human Populations, Linking Them to Biology," *New York Times*, December 20, 2002, p. A. 37.

[56] Glenn C. Loury, *The Anatomy of Racial Inequality* (Cambridge MA: Harvard University Press, 2002), p. 5.

a biological kind, but a social kind. That is to say that while there may be a biological explanation for each of the characteristics that constitute racial criteria – skin color, hair texture, and the like – the selection of those characteristics as criteria of membership in some category is conventionally determined."[57] According to these writers, race's meaning and significance are no different in principle from the significance of a flag, a political office, or a rule of etiquette. Race matters *only* because societies give it meaning.

There is much truth – or, rather, many truths – in the constructivist view of race. In its broadest sense race is obviously a cultural and social idea. Winston Churchill sometimes spoke of the "American" race and of the "English-speaking race," for example. Prejudice against immigrants from Mexico, the Middle East, or Latin America is sometimes characterized as "racism" in the U.S., while in Great Britain the term can be used to refer to hostile attitudes toward foreign asylum seekers coming from Eastern Europe or even to English prejudice against the Scots and the Irish. A judge in England recently ruled that a soccer fan had violated laws against using "racially abusive language" when he referred to an opposing team's supporters as "pakis." Unlike "yank" or other innocuous terms, this one, said the judge, was a "racist" reference to people from the nation of Pakistan. What made it racist, according to that judge, was the fact that it expressed hostility toward the group. Nazis treated Jews as a race as well, of course, although viewed from the perspective of traditional racial categories they were overwhelmingly Caucasians like the Germans. Although Nazis used inherited physical appearance as a marker of being Jewish, in practice they relied mainly on cultural characteristics such as synagogue membership, last names, testimony of acquaintances, and circumcision to determine Jewish racial identity. One writer estimated that in determining whether an individual was Jewish, such cultural factors accounted for 85–90 percent of the evidence, while biological ones made up the rest.[58] In treating Jews as a race, then, Nazis simply assumed that members of that religious/cultural group also shared important naturally inherited characteristics.

If we take race in the broadest sense, and include cultural and linguistic groups, then obviously *in that sense* race is socially constructed.

[57] Louise B. Antony, "Quine as Feminist," in *A Mind of One's Own: Feminist Essays on Reason and Objectivity*, edited by Antony and Witt, p. 217.
[58] Pierre L. van Den Berghe, "Does Race Matter?" *Nations and Nationalism*, Vol. 1, No. 3 (1995) reprinted in *Race and Racism*, edited by Boxill, p. 109.

Differences marked by language, nationality, and culture are contingent on history, just as constructivists claim. In fact, the word "race" is used in any number of different ways, each of which is socially constructed. Sometimes, as we saw, it is used to refer to a group with a common heritage, as when Churchill spoke of the American and English-speaking "races." Other times, it refers simply to a group that is culturally or linguistically different from the majority, sometimes but not always identifiable by skin or hair color and other bodily features. Others speak of the "white" race as contrasted with "persons of color" as if there were basically two races. And insofar as race is used to mark people who are regarded as less valuable or worthy of respect, it serves as a justification of oppression and there can be no doubt that constructivism provides the right account. The social constructivist's account of race is therefore in some respects both true and important.

But what, then, of the other more familiar usage of race that also tracks biological and inherited differences such as skin color, hair texture, and facial features? Is race in *that* sense socially constructed, or is it natural? The constructivist answer is not to deny that superficial biological differences like skin color track racial categories; its claim is that those inherited characteristics do not matter. The real meaning and importance of race, said Alcoff, is as a social "convention" that does not correspond to "any *significant* biological category, and. . . no existing racial classifications correlate in useful ways to gene frequencies, clinical variations, or other significant human differences."[59] Or as another constructivist put it, there is nothing of "biological interest" in dividing people along such lines.[60] So although people do inherit characteristics associated with race like skin color, bone structure, and hair texture, the constructivist view is that those have no more biological importance than attached or unattached earlobes.

The reality of race

As we have seen, race, as commonly understood, is, in many important respects, a social construct. But that does not rule out the possibility that race is *also* a natural category. That is because it is possible

---

[59] Alcoff, "Philosophy and Racial Identity," p. 15 (emphasis added).

[60] K. Anthony Appiah, "Race, Culture, Identity," in *Color Conscious: The Political Morality of Race*, edited by K. Anthony Appiah and Amy Gutmann (Princeton: Princeton University Press, 1996), p. 72.

for something to be both real *and* for its meaning to be (in important respects) socially constructed. Consider the example of the sun.
Although different societies have "constructed" various religious and
other meanings for the sun, the sun is not *merely* a social construct. Whatever social constructions are put on it, the sun is also a relatively small
star comprised of hot gasses that is approximately 93 million miles from
Earth.[61]

The real issue concerning the natural account of race is about
explanation: does race figure in any important way in the biological
explanation of human beings and their nature? The question is therefore not whether race is a social construction – all agree that in important respects it is – but whether like sex/gender it is *both* a socially
constructed concept and a natural one. In that way, the question is
an empirical one, and it cannot be settled by social or philosophical
theorizing.

Recent research into human genetics and evolution suggests how race
(or something like it) may figure into human biology. The December
2002 issue of *Science* magazine describes work growing out of the Human
Genome Diversity Project: as a result of which, it is claimed, we now
know that human beings belong to different population groups or families. Based on 377 different DNA markers of the type that police use
in identifying suspects, the scientists "identified six main genetic clusters
[of humans]." The article went on to note that five of the six biological
categories "correspond to major geographic regions" of Africa, Eurasia
(Europe, the Middle East, and South Asia), East Asia, Melanesia, and
the Americas.[62] Although there were noticeable subgroups within the
five, which also could often be identified genetically, their results showed
genetic variations among the five population groups sufficient to identify
the ancestry of each human being. This could be done even though the
genetic differences represented only 3–5 percent of the genetic variation among people. Up to 95 percent of the variation was due to differences among individuals within the same population groups. Two other

---

[61] The claim that science is a "social construction" is irrelevant for purposes of this argument because those who think race is socially constructed claim that race is precisely *not*
a useful biological or scientific concept. Calling race a social construct, in other words, is
meant to contrast it with concepts that refer to natural, biological differences in people.
Also saying that science is a social construction would undermine the distinction that
defenders of race as a social construction ordinarily draw.

[62] Noah A. Rosenberg *et al.*, "Genetic Structure of Human Populations," *Science*, Vol. 298,
No. 5602 (2002), pp. 2381–2385.

researchers in an essay titled "Mapping Human History" summarized the situation this way:

> The DNA of modern humans contains a record of the travels and encounters of our ancestors. . . . By sampling genotypes from people across the globe, geneticists have reconstructed the major features of our history: our ancient African origin, migrations out of Africa, movements and settlements throughout Eurasia and Oceana, and peopling of the Americas. . . . statistical methods reveal genetic clusters of Africans, Eurasians, East Asians, Pacific Islanders, and [Native] Americans, corresponding to the major ancient human migrations.[63]

Although it was sometimes possible to divide these "genetic clusters" into geographical subgroups, it was not always the case. Another study that looked at southern Indians, for instance, concluded they have more in common with either Asians or Europeans than with others now living in the same geographical area. What is important, then, is that genetic differences can be used to trace the ancestry of all living humans, including ones who descend from more than one of the major continental groups.

The explanation for these biological differences is that each of the five groups acquired its own genetic pattern through inbreeding and natural selection.[64] Although the different population groups all originated in Africa, their evolutionary histories departed. One group of people slowly moved north from Africa into East Europe, and then split off into different groups that continued to migrate and change over generations, eventually evolving into genetically distinct groups of East Asians, Eurasians (including Europe, South Asia, and the Middle East), Native Americans, and the peoples of Oceana or Pacific Islanders. The "genetic differences that arose on each continent" did so, according to one report, after the "ancestral human population dispersed from its African homeland."[65] In that sense, these groups are like extended families that inbreed. The process of inbreeding in different environments explains the various physical differences we observe between stereotypical Africans, East Asians, and Caucasians – differences in skin color, hair, facial structure, and so forth.

---

[63] Mary-Claire King and Arno G. Motulsky, "Mapping Human History," *Science*, Vol. 298, No. 5602 (2002), p. 2342.

[64] Nicholas Wade, "The Palette of Humankind," *New York Times Science*, December 24, 2002, p. D. 3.

[65] Wade, "Gene Study Identifies 5 Main Human Populations, Linking Them To Geography," p. A. 37.

Assuming that these and other researchers are proven correct, and all humans belong to one of these groups, the next question is whether it is correct to refer to these groups as "races." The authors of the study avoided using the word "race," preferring instead to speak of "population ancestry" and "population groups." One anthropologist was also quoted as saying that these discoveries do not cast any doubt on his belief that there is no biological basis for making distinctions among races because this research was, as he put it, "driven by geography, not race."[66] But the fact that geography played the role it did does not settle the real question, which is whether or not there are important biological or other differences that result from the different geographical histories of these population groups and whether such groups should be thought of as separate races. The key questions, then, are first whether and in what respects such natural family groups are properly thought of as races, and second whether we can learn anything useful for science by dividing humans into those groups.

Looking to the first question, it seems evident that these groups do roughly correspond to or track the idea of race that is most commonly used in making ordinary racial distinctions. Four of the groups, East Asian, African, European, and Native American, match in broad outline the way people identify themselves racially as well as how they are racially identified by others. As we saw, many nineteenth-century anthropologists also divided the world into the "races of man" along roughly the same physical and geographic lines as these continental groups. The authors of the recent *Science* magazine study, although reluctant to call the groups races, stated that the genetic differences they identified "often correspond closely to predefined regional or population groups" and that they "have found that predefined [racial] labels were highly informative about membership in genetic clusters."[67] Even the United States government, in its census forms, divides people into roughly those five racial groups: white, black (or African-American), Asian, Native American, and Pacific Islander. The census forms add that a Hispanic person can be of "any race," again mirroring the evolutionary groupings.

---

[66] Wade, "Gene Study Identifies 5 Main Human Populations, Linking Them to Geography," p. A. 37.

[67] Rosenberg *et al.*, "Genetic Structure of Human Populations," pp. 5, 6.

An article discussing that same research in *Scientific American* titled "Does Race Exist?" posed the question explicitly, asking whether "dividing people by familiar racial definitions or by genetic similarities says anything useful." The answer, concluded the authors, is a "qualified" yes.[68] "Most people who describe themselves as African-Americans," they note, "have relatively recent ancestors from West Africa, and West Africans generally have polymorphism [genetic] frequencies that can be distinguished from those of Europeans, Asians and Native Americans."[69] A Stanford University geneticist concluded that in light of these and other studies "*race*, referring to geographically based ancestry, is a valid way of categorizing these differences" that have arisen among people living on different continents.[70] Another report summarized the significance of the findings with the observation that "Humankind falls into five continental groups – broadly equivalent to the common conception of races – when a computer is asked to sort DNA data from people from around the world into clusters."[71]

The second issue is not whether these "groups" track traditional racial categories – they plainly do – but whether or not membership in such continental racial groups matters biologically. The contructivist position, recall, is not that traditional racial markers like skin color and facial structure are socially constructed but rather that the *importance* of race is limited to whatever meaning societies happen to assign those trivial characteristics. The real issue is whether membership in these continental racial groups matters in some other ways than the social constructions that have been placed on skin color and other observable differences, or whether, as contructivists assume, there is nothing more to race than those superficial natural differences.

It is no answer to this question to point out that there are significant genetic differences *within* these large continental races; the fact that the groups can then be further subdivided does not prove the larger categories are unimportant or meaningless. Nor can the argument over

---

[68] Michael J. Bamshad and Steve E. Olson, "Does Race Exist?" *Scientific American*, December, 2003.

[69] Bamshad and Olson, "Does Race Exist?" p. 4.

[70] Nicholas Wade, "Race Is Seen as Real Guide to Track Roots of Disease," *New York Times*, July 30, 2002. http://nytimes.com/2002/07/30/healthe/genetics/30race.html. Accessed December 10, 2002 (emphasis added). The same article goes on to quote others who claim that race is "biologically meaningless." As I will argue, however, these others are referring to the socially constructed conception of race.

[71] Nicholas Wade, "The Palette of Humankind," p. D. 3.

constructionism be resolved by pointing out that humans, of every race, share something like 98 percent of the same genes. The issue is whether whatever differences that do exist among these groups are important to a scientific understanding of humans. Whether we call them races, continental races, or just major population groups that "correspond closely" to traditional racial categories is of no real consequence.

In thinking about the potential biological significance of continental races, it is interesting to note how the character of the discussion of racial differences has changed in recent decades. One place that this is most evident is in encyclopedias. A recent version of the *Encarta Encyclopedia* mirrors the idea of continental races. Race, it says, refers to

> the identification within a species of subpopulations whose members share with one another a greater degree of common inheritance than they share with individuals from other such subpopulations. The primary application of the concept of race is to subpopulations of the human species, and race is thus a term that ordinarily applies to groups of people. Applied to an individual, race refers to membership in a group, and not to aspects of the person's appearance, such as skin color. No two human beings, not even twins, are identical, and groups of human beings differ from one another in many biological characteristics. The proportions of traits and, to an extent, even the kinds of traits are differently distributed from one part of the world to another. In the past, when people traveled less and marriages were likely to be between neighbors, races tended to develop and be retained as geographic entities. Although some historic conceptions of race were thus based on geographic variation in physical traits such as skin color and hair form, such traits can accurately be used to ascribe a person to a race only insofar as they were inherited from ancestors belonging to the population in question[72]

So while acknowledging the evolutionary history of human "subpopulations," the article nonetheless says virtually nothing about the physical differences that might exist among such "subpopulations."

The older *Encyclopedia Britannica* entry, on the other hand, was more specific in describing the extent of the differences among the races. "The characteristics of most value to the scientific study of race," it concluded, are hereditary.

> Such genetic differences include size, shape, and cusp number of teeth; proportions and even densities of various bones; and configurations of the skull

---

[72] *Microsoft Encarta 98 Encyclopedia* entry on "Races, classification of." The most recent Encarta entry on "Race" does not endorse even the idea of "subpopulations," stating that "most scientists today reject the concept of biological race and instead see human biological variation as falling along a continuum." http://encarta.msn.com/text_761576599_1/Race.html. Accessed June 3, 2007.

and face. They include the form and abundance of head and body hair, the tendency toward male pattern baldness, and the number of sweat and sebaceous glands. Racial differences are obvious in palm prints and fingerprints; in the form of the eyelids, eyebrows, and nasal tip; in the thickness of the lips and in the amount of pigmentation of the gums. The tendency to form raised scars (keloids), the ability to fold the tongue and to taste phenylthiocarbamide and thiouracil also vary with race. Racial differences also exist in the frequencies of various blood groups, the haptoglobins, in abnormal hemoglobins, in sensitivity to numerous antimalarial drugs, and in resistance to various infections and parasitic diseases, especially malaria.[73]

The significance of biological differences is evidenced in recent medical research, which has pushed well beyond the familiar examples of sickle cell anemia and malaria. Many now believe race may be an important factor in understanding a wide range of diseases and treatments. The authors of the study describing the evolution of continental races speculated that the differences in the genetic structures of human populations may prove "relevant in various epidemiological contexts."

> As a result of variations in frequencies of both genetic and non-genetic risk factors, rates of disease and of such phenotypes as adverse drug response vary across populations. Further, information about a patient's population of origin might provide health-care practitioners with information about risk when direct causes of disease are unknown.[74]

According to another recent account, many research geneticists are now persuaded that "it is essential to take race and ethnicity into account to understand each group's specific pattern of disease and to ensure that everyone shares equally in the expected benefits of genomic medicine."[75]

Given the potential medical implications of race, one of the nation's premier black medical colleges is creating the world's largest repository of DNA for African-Americans. The stated goal of Howard University's program is to "find the genes that are involved in diseases that have a particularly high incidence among blacks."[76] In describing Howard's program, the journal *Science* quoted an evolutionary geneticist who observed that "genetic frequencies tend to vary based on the continent of origin. It doesn't make a lot of sense to say that *race* is irrelevant."[77]

---

[73] *Encyclopedia Britannica*, Vol. 18, p. 985.

[74] Rosenberg, et al., "Genetic Structure of Human Populations," pp. 5–6.

[75] Nicholas Wade, "Race Is Seen as Real Guide to Track Roots of Disease," *New York Times*, July 30, 2002. http://nytimes.com/2002/07/30/healthe/genetics/30race.html.

[76] "DNA Repository Will Aid Health Studies on Blacks," *International Herald Tribune*, May 28, 2003, p. 3.

[77] Jocelyn Kaiser, "African-American Population Biobank Proposed," *Science*, Vol. 300, No. 5625 (June 6, 2003), p. 1485. (Quoting Stephen Warren of Emory University.)

Genetic research is among the most important research areas in modern medicine, and racial differences are often an important component in that research. For example, one recent study identified a genetic variant associated with prostate cancer. The report said that the variant increases the risk of getting prostate cancer by 60 percent. It also noted that "the variant is carried by about 13 percent of men of European ancestry. . . . [but] among African-American the variant is twice as common. . . [and] could explain a significant part of the reason prostate cancer is more common in this population."[78] Other areas in which it has recently been suggested that race may be medically important include: AIDS;[79] asthma;[80] bone marrow density, fractures, and osteoperosis;[81] heart disease;[82] hormone levels;[83] general

---

[78] Nicholas Wade, "Scientists Discover Gene Linked to Higher Rates of Prostate Cancer," *New York Times*, May 5, 2006, p. A. 18.

[79] ". . . [T]he first AIDS vaccine ever to be tested in a large number of people has failed, overall, to protect them from infection. . . .However, the vaccine did seem to lower the infection rate significantly among African-Americans . . .," in "Landmark Trial, Vaccine for AIDS Failed to Work," *International Herald Tribune*, February 25, 2003. http://iht.com/cgi-gin/generic.cgi? Accessed on February 25, 2003.

[80] "The incidence of asthma in African-Americans is four to six times that among Caucasians, and it is of considerable public health concern. . . . [R]ecent scientific findings have strongly implicated genetic factors in the etiology of asthma. Identifying asthma-specific genes, polymorphic markers, and candidate gene loci in African-Americans can be the foundation of developing more specific ways of diagnosing asthma," in National Human Genome Center Developing Research Programs, "Gene-Environment Studies of Asthma among African Americans," Howard University. http://www.genomecenter.howard.edu/research_programs.htm#6. Accessed on June 12, 2003.

[81] "Racial differences in bone mineral density (BMD) appear to account in part for racial differences in the incidence of osteoporosis and fractures," in N. M. Wright *et al.*, "Growth Hormone Secretion and Bone Mineral Density in Prepubertal Black and White Boys," *Calcified Tissue International*, DOI: 10.1007/s00223-001-1068-0 (New York: Springer-Verlag New York, Inc., 2002).

[82] "[The Federal Food and Drug Administration] will consider whether BiDil should become the first drug intended for one racial group, in this case African-Americans. A study of 1,050 African-American heart failure patients showed that BiDil significantly reduced death and hospitalization. . . .[T]he drug, in combination with two generic drugs, worked better in African-Americans than whites." In "U.S. to Review Drug Intended for One Race. Maker Says Heart Pill Helps Black Patients," *New York Times*, June 13, 2005, p. A.1.

[83] "There seems to be a direct relationship between prostate cancer, hormone levels, and race. . . . Asians are in the group of lowest testosterone and, therefore, the lowest risk of prostate cancer. Caucasians fall in the middle risk group. Blacks are the highest testosterone levels and have about twice the incidence of prostate cancer as other groups." In "Patient's Platform – An Overview of

medicine's effectiveness;[84] obesity;[85] sickle cell anemia;[86] and tuberculosis.[87] Medicines' effectiveness is also an important area of study. Indeed,
"by one count at least twenty-nine medicines are more effective for one
race than another."[88]

It should also be noted, however, that some are urging caution in
using ordinary (often socially constructed) methods of identifying race
such as skin color and self-identification when prescribing medicines.
Medical geneticist Lynn Jorde, for example, has noted that "There are
[racial] differences on average. But there is so much overlap that you can
make serious [medical] mistakes if you try to infer something about an
individual patient based on his or her racial background. . . Using race
is crude and potentially misleading."[89]

What is clear, however, is that scientists are actively investigating these
issues and that many researchers believe that taking race into account
is important to medical research and practice. Writing in *Science* magazine, two researchers summarized these trends: "The current medical
literature increasingly includes studies exploring population differences
[including race] in disease incidence or in efficacy or adverse responses
to drug treatment."[90] Clearly, using some of the traditional indicators of
race can be misleading. And just as obviously, various social and cultural
differences are also important in understanding diseases. The point is

Prostate Cancer," http://www.prostateservices.com/patient_plantorm2.htm. Accessed
December 12, 2002.

[84] Sharon Begley, "Science Journal," *Wall Street Journal*, October 29, 2004, p. B. 1.

[85] "Study finds heavier black women outlive their thinner sisters. . . . I find that fascinating,"
said Dr. Robert Eckel, Chairman of the Council on Nutrition, Physical Activity and
Metabolism of the American Heart Association. Being overweight seems to actually be a
benefit for black women. In "Obesity Research Surprising," *Rocky Mountain News*, January
8, 2003.

[86] "A common mutation that causes sickle cell anemia is prevalent among Africans and
is thought to have originated among Bantu-speakers before the Bantu expansion
2,000 years ago." [Sickle cell is a disease that is far more prevalent among blacks.]
In "Race Is Seen as Real Guide to Track Roots of Disease," *New York Times*, July 30,
2002. http://nytimes.com/2002/07/30/healthe/genetics/30race.html. Accessed on
December 10, 2002.

[87] ". . . [U]nder the same social conditions, blacks are apparently infected more readily
by Mycobacterium tuberculosis than whites," Gwangpyo Ko, Kimberly M. Thompson,
and Edward A. Nardell, "Estimation of Tuberculosis Risk on a Commercial Airliner,"*New
England Journal of Medicine*, Vol. 322 (1990), p. 422.

[88] Begley, "Science Journal," *Wall Street Journal*, October 29, 2004, p. B. 1.

[89] Lynn Jorde as quoted in Begley, "Science Journal," p. B. 1.

[90] King and Motulsky, "Mapping Human History," *Science*, p. 2342.

that the strong constructivist position on race is under increasing pressure from both medicine and population genetics. Race seems to matter for medicine and for human history, and race may prove important in other ways as well, such as sports.[91]

That said, it is important to acknowledge the dangers of emphasizing the limits of social constructivism when thinking about race. Although the claim that race is a natural category gives no support for racism, its non-racist proponents have unpleasant company: racists also assume that races are real. There may be other dangers lurking in these ideas as well. In his review of Stephen Pinker's *The Blank Slate*, a book critical of social constructivism, Simon Blackburn put the point this way:

> [T]he natural thought [of those who emphasize genetic differences] is that if, say, crime is scripted in the genes, then there is no reason on that score to work for the equality of wealth and the eradication of poverty, because you will get crime anyhow. If mad jealousy or rape is an evolved strategy for unsuccessful males, then there is no reason to promote an atmosphere of respect for women, because you will get mad jealousy or rape anyhow.[92]

I will take up this style of argument in more detail in discussing racial equality, but offhand it is not at all clear *why* learning that some people (males, for instance) are more naturally aggressive should undermine efforts to reduce crimes or should excuse those who commit them. Nor is it clear that people would have less reason to be concerned about, or expend fewer resources to deal with, social problems that have a biological component. They may well spend more. Coming to understand the

---

[91] Sports is another area in which social construction is sometimes thought to be only part of the story. In an article in *Scientific American*, one reviewer of a recent work on the subject concluded that scientists "have identified physical attributes that are more common to West Africans and East Africans than to Europeans, ones that might provide an edge in sprint and endurance exercises. These include a lower percentage of body fat, a higher proportion of fast-twitch muscle fibers, a greater capillary-to-muscle fiber ratio, and a superior resistance to fatigue during high-intensity endurance activities that is associated with a higher muscle oxidative capacity and with lower plasma lactate accumulation." The article went on to say that "the verdict is still out as to whether natural talent or hard work and determination account primarily for athletic prowess. The most probable answer is that they are inextricably linked. Rather than nature or nurture, the answer most likely lies in an interaction between the two." Loretta DiPietro, "Tackling Race and Sports." Reviewing *Why black athletes dominate sports and why we're afraid to talk about it* by John Entine. *Scientific American*, May 21, 2000, pp. 112–114.

[92] Simon Blackburn, "Meet the Flintstones." Reviewing *The Blank Slate: The Modern Denial of Human Nature* by Steven Pinker. *New Republic Online*, Nov. 25, 2002. https://ssl.tnr.com/p/docsub.mhtml?i=20021125&s=blackburn112502. Accessed on July 8, 2003.

nature of a problem (including the fact that the problem may be difficult to address) does not justify inaction. It may lead people to seek different solutions to the problem, but knowing the real nature of problems is surely an important step in solving them.

Erroneous claims about natural racial differences have often been used in the service of the worst sort of abuses of rights and racial exploitation, including slavery. But, that said, it is also important to keep in mind that even if continental races are important to a full biological understanding of human beings, those differences would provide no support – *none* – for racism. Such a belief could not warrant the attitude of contempt toward persons in virtue of their race, which is what racism is.

What race is Tiger Woods?

When discussing the social construction of race, I noted that there are many ways of understanding races, ranging from Winston Churchill's idea of an "English speaking race" to ones that treat Eastern Europeans, Jews, and South Asians as if they were separate races. Most of those conceptions focused on skin color and other physical characteristics, though some had more to do with culture, dress, and language. Another feature of the commonly accepted, socially constructed view of race is illustrated by the phenomenon of racial "passing." The fact that a light-skinned person might "pass" for being "white" shows that the concept of race is not just about observable physical features but also about ancestry that is typically but not universally associated with skin color, hair, and facial features.[93] Now we have added into the mix the idea of continental races whose roots are in biology. What, then, should we conclude about the concept of race?

It seems clear that in fact there are two ideas traveling under the same banner. One is the socially constructed idea, by which is meant that society has made arbitrary distinctions among people when they are thought to belong to different racial groups. But it now appears that science is also discovering that the traditional racial divisions among human beings, sometimes called population groups or continental races, are not *mere* social constructions. Like the concept of the sun, then, race as a concept is both based in reality and socially constructed. The

---

[93] My discussion of racial taint and passing benefited from a paper by Richard Wasser-strom, "Racism, Sexism, and Preferential Treatment," *UCLA Law Review*, Vol. 24 (1977), pp. 581–622.

socially constructed concept of race and its biologically based relative
are not identical, though there is enough similarity to conclude that
biological races (understood as population groups) track fairly closely
what have been traditionally understood as races (though without the
socially constructed "baggage" of racial taint and inequality).

The question remains, then, whether the socially constructed concept
of race is worth keeping. That has proven to be a controversial question. Take the case of golfer Tiger Woods. Woods is half East Asian, a
quarter African, an eighth European, and an eighth Native American.
Yet, despite his occasional protests, he is widely referred to as black or
as an African-American. Similarly, in a *New York Times* op-ed article Bob
Herbert described 2008 Democratic presidential hopeful (then a candidate for the U.S. Senate from Illinois) Barack Obama as "African-
American" even though, as Herbert noted in the same article, Obama
has a "white" mother.[94]

It is often assumed that these two features of our current socially constructed view of race – appearance and ancestry – have been present
from the beginning. In the Jim Crow South, ancestry was thought so
important that "a single drop of Negro blood" defined a person as a
"Negro." This view, however, was not widely accepted during the slave
period. Virginia law, for example, provided that "Every person who has
one-fourth part or more of negro blood shall be deemed a mulatto,
and the word 'negro'. . . shall be construed to include mulatto."[95]
The only state that referred to all "negroes, mulattoes, and persons of
color" without specifying the degree of African blood required was South
Carolina, though even there the courts determined that the test was
whether there was a "visible mixture" along with the "reputation" of the
person.[96] That changed, however, after the Civil War when even "one
drop" of African ancestry became sufficient to define a person racially.
In 1911, the statutes of the state of Texas, for instance, defined "black"
as "any person with a drop of black blood."[97] In the case that eventually
led the Supreme Court to uphold legal segregation, *Plessy v. Ferguson*,
railroad officials had to have Plessy pointed out to them as "black" before
they could evict him from the segregated whites-only railroad car.

[94] Bob Herbert, "A Leap of Faith," *New York Times*, June 4, 2004, p. A. 20.
[95] Kenneth Stampp, *The Peculiar Institution: Slavery in the Ante-Bellum South* (New York: Vintage, 1956), p. 195.
[96] Helen Tunnicliff Catterall (ed.) *Judicial Cases*, II, pp. 358–359; quoted in Stampp, *The Peculiar Institution: Slavery in the Ante-Bellum South*, p. 195.
[97] Goldberg, "Racial Realism," p. 374.

Because continental races are not clear categories, race is not like an on/off switch as is sometimes assumed by traditional conceptions. It is a matter of degree how much one "belongs" to one or another race. In that sense, continental races are more like the relationships among colors. If we imagine a triangle with each vertex representing one of the three basic colors of red, yellow, and blue, then each point within the triangle would represent a different color that is constituted of a mixture of the three primary ones. Brown, which is made of equal parts of all three basic colors, would be in the center of the triangle. Some points would have only one color, some two, and some three – all in different ratios. Continental races therefore have nothing in common with the one-drop rule, or with racial taint. Any particular person might be any racial combination, making the question of which race they "really are" meaningless. On this model, Tiger Woods is less African-American than Asian. Furthermore, according to a recent study roughly 30 percent of Americans who consider themselves "white" have less than 90 percent European ancestry.[98] Similarly, the average African-American has nearly 20 percent Caucasian ancestry. About 10 percent of (again self-identified) blacks have over 50 percent white ancestry.[99] (Given that the number of interracial couples quadrupled between 1960 and 1990, these percentages are likely to become even larger.)

Interestingly, allowing people to identify themselves in surveys as "mixed race" has proven controversial. Part of the explanation of this resistance to the more accurate term "mixed race" may be political. But membership in a particular continental racial group is distinct from language, religion, values, and all the other markers of culture. Although there may be noticeable tendencies for some cultural differences to track continental racial groupings, that is nothing more than an historical coincidence. It has nothing to do with race itself. In a world where the concept of continental race replaced the socially constructed concept entirely, individuals could find it easier to emphasize some of their ancestral roots rather than others or to simply see themselves as mixed race.

Therefore, I in part agree and in part disagree with K. Anthony Appiah. Although he writes that he has "no problem with people who want to use

---

[98] Bamshad and Olson, "Does Race Exist?," p. 3. Studies are by Mark D. Shriver at Penn State University and Rick A. Kittles of Howard University, along with other researchers.

[99] Steve Sailer, "Analysis: White Prof Finds He's Not," Washington Politics and Policy Desk, United Press International. www.upi.com/StoryID=15042002-084051-5356r. Accessed on May 31, 2003. Interview with Mark D. Shriver at Penn State University.

the word 'race' in population genetics," nonetheless

> the fact is that in many plants and animals there are, in fact, local populations that are reproductively isolated from one another, different in clustered and biologically interesting ways, and still capable of interbreeding if brought artificially together; and biologists both before and after Darwin could have called these "races."[100]

He then adds, however, that "this doesn't happen in human beings" because most are racial "mixtures."[101] Yet, as I have stressed, there is evidence that his further claim that racial differences lack significance is wrong. Whether groups are called races, continental races, or population groups does not alter whatever medical or other biological significance membership in such groups might have. Parallels between continental racial groups and traditional racial categories would remain. Indeed, replacing the older, socially constructed idea of race with continental races opens the possibility that race may be useful scientifically, including in improving medical care. Also, racial categories would become more blurred, and the distinction between race and social identity more apparent, thereby opening up more possibilities for persons to shape their social identities. The fact that Tiger Woods is mixed race, biologically, says nothing about how he should define himself culturally, which groups he should join common cause with, or which social and political commitments he should pursue. Continental races also make no sense of racial taint. In those respects, emphasis on natural, continental races could be liberating.

Conceptual neutrality?

In Chapter 1, I defended an account of racism that sees it as an attitude of contempt directed at persons in virtue of their race. I also discussed the sense in which it is an epistemologically normative concept, and how that view of racism can be used to explain institutional racism. In this chapter, I argued that the widely accepted idea that race is a social construct is only partly true. I then provided an alternative account of race as biologically based. My views about both racism and race are at odds with much current scholarship. I contended, however, that the definitions match closely our

---

[100] Appiah, "Race, Culture, Identity," in *Color Conscious: The Political Morality of Race*, edited by K. Anthony Appiah and Amy Gutmann (Princton: Princton University Press, 1996), p. 73.
[101] Appiah, "Race, Culture, Identity," in *Color Conscious: The Political Morality of Race*, edited by Appiah and Gutmann, pp. 74, 75.

ordinary understanding. In concluding this chapter, I want to take a
step back from my accounts of racism and race to consider whether and
in what sense I was justified in suggesting that my explication of those
concepts is politically or morally neutral.

I said that my goal of defending a politically and morally concept of
racism was in contrast to some writers, like Anthony Flew, who defined
"racism" as "unjust discrimination" where that includes, he said, racial
preferences.[102] On the other hand, I did claim that racism in an inherently normative concept, which brings epistemic if not also moral condemnation in its wake. But unlike some of the writers I discussed, who
defined racism in ways that effectively condemn affirmative action as
racist, or others who defined as racist all institutions that produce different results in income, my account leaves those questions open. In that
sense it is morally and politically neutral. But that said, it is also worth
noting how my understanding of racism is not neutral in another sense.
It means, for instance, that, as I discussed in Chapter 1, racial profiling
is not necessarily racist. Since some assume that it must be racist, my
understanding of racism is, at least in that sense, not neutral.

A similar point may be made about different conceptions of race.
In contrast to my own goal of capturing the accepted meaning of race
while avoiding controversial moral issues, Sally Haslanger rejects ordinary
meanings and makes politics central to her definition of race. Rather than
trying to "explicate the ordinary concept" of race she asks "what cognitive
or practical tasks do [definitions of concepts] enable us to accomplish?
Are they effective tools to accomplish our (legitimate) purposes. . . ."[103]
The purpose of offering a definition of race, she says, includes the need
"to identify and explain persistent inequalities" among people of different colors, to "identify the effects of interlocking oppressions," and to
"aid anti-racist effort to empower critical social agents."[104] To achieve
those objectives, she writes, we should understand a race as a group
whose "members are socially positioned as subordinate or privileged,"
that is, they have features (e.g., skin color) that mark them as "appropriately occupying certain kinds of social positions that are in fact either

---

[102] Quoted in Anthony Skillen, "Racism: Flew's Three Concepts of Racism," pp. 73–89.
[103] Sally Haslanger, "Gender and Race: (What) Are they? (What) Do We Want Them To
Be?" *Nous*, Vol. 34, No. 1 (2000), p. 33.
[104] Haslanger, "Gender and Race: (What) Are they? (What) Do We Want Them To Be?"
p. 36.

subordinate or privileged."[105] "Race" for her therefore becomes a term of art. By definition then, any society that has a concept of race is one in which some groups are oppressed.

Haslanger thinks that this approach is useful because it provides "rhetorical advantages,"[106] and it is pretty clear why she thinks that. If a race is *by definition* an oppressed group, then any society that has a concept of "race" must be oppressive. As I noted, Haslinger is not alone in packing political ideas into definitions of racism and race.

I want to make two observations about that overtly political method of understanding concepts. The first is that it is inaccurate as a description of the ordinary concept. There is nothing conceptually impossible or even odd about saying that two or more races of people live in a society in which neither oppresses the other. Trying to abolish racial oppression is not like looking for a circular square or a married bachelor; races do not *by definition* exist only in societies marked by oppression.

Nor, second, is it clear that this (new) concept of race would be useful in understanding racial oppression. In ordinary life we easily make a distinction between the question of whether a group is a race, on the one hand, and how members of the group are and should be treated, on the other. Indeed, I would go further. Not only is it unnecessary to add "oppression" to our definition of race but we also encourage conceptual confusion by proposing what is in effect a stipulative definition. Nobody who questions whether racial oppression remains a grave problem will be persuaded otherwise by the claim that *by definition* "racial" groups are groups that are oppressed. Their response would instead be to deny that "races" exist in that sense of the term. All that is accomplished is confusion and uncertainty in the meaning of "race." Serious dialogue aimed at resolving issues is made harder, not easier, where there is no broad agreement on what concepts mean.

That is not to say, however, that my accounts of racism and of race are neutral in the broadest sense of lacking all political and moral consequences. In denying that racism is present *whenever* race is used as a basis for distributing jobs or positions, for instance, I allow for the possibility that affirmative action is not racist. That understanding also leaves open

---

[105] Haslanger, "Gender and Race: (What) Are they? (What) Do We Want Them To Be?" p. 44.
[106] Haslanger, "Gender and Race: (What) Are they? (What) Do We Want Them To Be?" p. 52.

the question whether racial profiling reflects racism, just as my understanding of race allows for races to exist in a society that is not racially
oppressive. So, I do not want to go so far as to suggest that my accounts of
racism and race have no moral or political consequences. Complete neu-
trality, I believe, is impossible. What I have tried to do, however, is to offer
an account of those concepts that matches accepted usage rather than
being designed to serve particular political purposes. Whether I have
succeeded in that is one issue. The political implication of my account,
assuming that it is correct, is another.

3

Slavery

S LAVERY, AND THE RACIAL OPPRESSION THAT FOLLOWED IN its wake, left a scar on American history whose consequences linger to this day. Before examining the policies designed to respond to that history, it will be helpful in this chapter to explore the history and nature of slavery itself. The institution was deeply controversial from the beginning of the United States, when debates over provisions to protect the African slave trade were among the most vitriolic of the constitutional convention. Those disagreements lasted as long as slavery did, eventually contributing to the bloodiest and most costly war in U.S. history. Not only were the contemporary arguments over the morality of slavery interesting in their own right, but they also provide important background to the following chapter on racial equality.

A brief history of slavery

Slavery has been a pervasive feature throughout most of human history, in almost all societies. Egyptians, Persians, Chinese, Israelites, Babylonians, Greeks, Romans, Russians, Native Americans, and Africans all practiced slavery. The word "slave" originated from the word "Slav" after Southern Europeans had enslaved so many Slavic people that the two ideas acquired the same meaning.[1] According to one historian, slavery has been "universal" in two senses: "Most settled societies incorporated the institution into their social structures, and few peoples in the world have not constituted a major source of slaves at one time or another."[2]

---

[1] *Oxford English Dictionary*, 2nd ed., Vol. 15 (1989), p. 665.
[2] David Eltis, "Europeans and the Rise and Fall of African Slavery in the Americas: An Interpretation," *American Historical Review*, Vol. 98, No. 5 (1993), p. 1400.

It existed in North and South America before Columbus as well as in Southern and Eastern Asia, Europe, and Africa. It predates both Christianity and Islam. Orlando Patterson concluded it is probable that there is "no group of people whose ancestors were not at one time slaves or slave holders."[3]

Slavery was not only commonplace, it was also largely uncontroversial for much of human history. The Ottoman Turks required the defeated Hungarians to provide one-tenth of their population as slaves every decade.[4] As late as the 1820s, six thousand Greeks were sent into slavery in Egypt.[5] There is "no evidence," wrote another historian, "that slavery came under serious attack in any part of the world before the eighteenth century."[6] If slavery in the United States was in fact a "peculiar institution," it is peculiar only in the sense that it was incompatible with the ideals of equality that the nation claimed to endorse.

African slavery flourished with the birth of Islam and the emergence of the great Arab civilizations, culminating in the Ottoman Empire. During the thousand years before 1600, from three to ten million Africans were bought by Muslim traders for sale or use in their own societies as slaves.[7] Spanish, Portuguese, and other European powers were also involved in African slavery prior to the British settlements in the New World. Many European powers, but especially Great Britain, Spain, and Portugal, then took a major role in the trade to America. Africans were also themselves sometimes active, enthusiastic participants in the slave trade, capturing and selling other Africans to the European and Arab slave traders. Africans saw themselves as members of different tribes, often making war on each other and capturing members of other groups who were then taken to ports and sold. When European powers stopped the slave trade, some African leaders strongly protested.

---

[3] Orlando Patterson, *Slavery and Social Death: A Comparative Study* (Cambridge MA: Harvard University Press, 1987), p. vii.

[4] John Balfour Kinross, *The Ottoman Centuries: The Rise and Fall of the Turkish Empire* (New York: William Morrow, 1977), p. 221.

[5] R. W. Beachey, *The Slave Trade in Eastern Africa* (New York: Harper and Row, 1976), p. 122.

[6] Martin A. Klein, "Introduction: Modern European Expansion and Traditional Servitude in Africa and Asia," in *Breaking the Chains: Slavery, Bondage, and Emancipation in Modern African and Asia*, edited by Martin A. Klein (Madison: University of Wisconsin Press, 1993), p. 14.

[7] Paul Lovejoy, *Transformations in Slavery: A History of Slavery in Africa* (Cambridge UK: Cambridge University Press, 2000), p. 25.

Before 1776, slavery existed in all of the British colonies that eventually became the United States, though those colonies were a relatively minor player in the slave trade to the Western Hemisphere. Only about 3 percent of the total number of Africans sold into slavery in the New World were brought to what is now the United States. More than 90 percent of slaves went to the Caribbean and to Central and South America. And slaveowning in North America was not unique to Southern whites, although they did own the vast majority of slaves. American Indian tribes also owned black slaves until after the end of the Civil War, despite U.S. Government orders that this stop.[8] Slaveowning tribes included Cherokees, Creeks, Chocktaws, and Seminoles.[9] By one count, 3,775 free blacks also owned slaves in 1830, out of a total free black population of 180,000.[10] African slavery was therefore very much a mutual undertaking among Arabs, North Americans, Europeans, and Africans, with Native Americans and others also participating, though to a much lesser extent.

Arab slavery differed in important ways from slavery in the Americas. Not only did many more slaves die while being taken to the Islamic world, but the death rates once they arrived were also much higher – so much so that very few slaves lived to adulthood. Slaves also had many fewer children in the Middle East and North Africa, in part because marriage and extramarital sex were forbidden.[11] Slaves in the Americas often lived in families (though without the benefit of legal marriages).

The first nation to make slavery illegal and to seek its abolition was Great Britain.[12] Great Britain was able to abolish slavery within the British Empire with compensation paid to slaveowners that amounted to approximately one-twentieth of its total national output.[13] Outside the Empire the British used other means, mainly military force, to blockade slave

---

[8] Theda Perdue, *Slavery and the Evolution of Cherokee Society* (Knoxville: University of Tennessee Press, 1988), pp. 38-39.

[9] Dinesh D'Souza, *The End of Racism: Principles for a Multiracial Society* (New York: Simon & Schuster, 1996), p. 75.

[10] Loren Schweninger, "Slaveholders, Black," in *Dictionary of Afro-American Slavery*, edited by Randall M. Miller and John David Smith (Westport CT: Greenwood Press, Inc., 1988), p. 665.

[11] Lewis, *Race and Slavery in the Middle East*, pp. 10, 84.

[12] *Somerset v. Stewart*, 1 Lofft 1 (1772); 12 Geo. 3 (1772) K. B. The argument rested on common law and on the ground that slavery is so "odious" and "immoral" that nothing can support it.

[13] Claudia Dale Goldin, "The Economics of Emancipation," *Journal of Economic History*, Vol. 33 (March 1973), p. 71.

ships coming from the West African coast. John Stuart Mill interpreted this as an act of principle rather than national self-interest. For a half century, he wrote, the British "have spent annual sums equal to the revenue of a small kingdom in blockading the Africa coast, for a cause in which we not only had no interest, but which was contrary to our pecuniary interest."[14] In the United States, beginning with Pennsylvania in 1780, various states passed statutes abolishing slavery while courts in other states interpreted constitutional guarantees of equality to prohibit slavery. The battle to abolish slavery was fought in the United States in the Civil War, but slavery continued in the rest of the world for a century, and continues in some places still. The end of slavery in the U.S. was not achieved without conflict, however, and there were also serious questions about how slaves were to be treated once freed. Were they to be allowed to vote, for example, and be treated in all other ways like equal citizens?

What is slavery?

Slavery can exist either legally, in the form of rights of slaveowners enforced by governments, or as an informal and even illegal social practice – for instance, when women are sold as "sex slaves." Slaves are normally denied the legal power to control their labor (where and for whom they work), to move and travel, to participate in political decision-making processes, and to create families and raise children. Nowhere in America were slaves legally allowed to marry, exercise authority over their children, or enforce contracts.

Every slave state had a slave code, which defined the rights and responsibilities of slaves as well as of their owners. Slave codes prescribed how slaves were to be disciplined and punished for violations of laws – especially insurrections. All codes required slaves to submit to both their owners and to whites in general. They also controlled slaves' movements. Slaves were, legally speaking, human property. States varied in how they treated this form of property. Some treated slaves more like personal property, while others looked at slaves more like real estate. Most often it was some combination of the two.[15]

---

[14] John Stuart Mill, "The Contest in America," *Collected Works of John Stuart Mill, Vol. XXI: Essays on Equality, Law, and Education,* edited by John M. Robinson (Toronto: University of Toronto Press, 1984), p. 127.

[15] Stampp, *The Peculiar Institution: Slavery in the Ante-Bellum South,* p. 197.

Slavery is therefore more than the absence of various rights, because it is possible for a government to deny a range of rights to some or all persons without thereby making them literally slaves. In the United States, slavery was a *property* relation between two persons. To be a slave meant that another person had property rights over the slave. But even in societies where a slave could not be sold, the central idea of property would remain. All private property rights provide individual citizens with powers over a thing, whether it is an object, an animal, or a person. Powers, in turn, are the ability to have one's own will dominate in the case of a conflict with another's will. When a conflict arises and one person has the legal right, then that person has recourse to the power of the state to secure his will. Property rights, in short, are the right to control whatever is owned, which usually, though not always, includes the right to sell. Making a person a slave gives owners power over their slaves. Slavery is therefore, at its roots, about power.

Frederick Douglass was correct when he described the slavemaster as a person "who claims and exercises a right of property in the person of a fellow man." Douglass went on to say that the "slave is a human being, divested of all rights. . . . He can own nothing, possess nothing, acquire nothing, but what must belong to another."[16] Yet, there is nothing inherent in the concept of ownership of property that makes the power of owners *limitless*. Owners of a painting, for instance, are sometimes not allowed to destroy it; owners of land may not be allowed to pollute it or exclude people who want to walk on a trail across it; owning livestock or a pet does not include the right to torture the animals; and owning an historic building may mean little more than the right to occupy and sell it. The fact that slaves were property therefore did not *necessarily* mean they had no rights, or that they were completely powerless. Were U.S. slaves *in fact* completely powerless? Were masters all-powerful?

Again, the picture is more complex than is sometimes supposed. Although owners were given vast powers over slaves, one right that owners did not have was the right to teach a slave to read and write. The rationale was captured when a religious publication asked, rhetorically, "Is there any real moral reason why we should incur the tremendous risk of having our wives slaughtered in consequence of our slaves being taught to read incendiary publications?"[17] Other limits on owners were

---

[16] Frederick Douglass, "The Meaning of Slavery," in *African Philosophy*, edited by Emmanuel Chukwudi Eze (Malden MA: Blackwell 1998), p. 375.

[17] Southern Presbyterian, quoted in Stampp, *The Peculiar Institution*, p. 208.

designed to benefit the slaves. All slave codes gave some protections to the physical person of a slave, although before the Revolution there were only minor penalties for killing a slave. That changed significantly after 1776, though, as always, the laws varied from state to state. The experience of North Carolina is illustrative. In 1774, a law was passed imposing a twelve-month imprisonment for the first time any person murders a slave. But the law was amended after the Revolution so that "if any person shall be guilty of wilfully and maliciously killing a slave" that person "shall upon the first conviction thereof be adjudged guilty of murder, and shall suffer the same punishment as if he had killed a free man." The legislature made an exception, however, for cases in which the slave died under "moderate correction."[18] Some slave codes limited the workday to fourteen or fifteen hours, and all codes provided penalties for working slaves on Sundays.[19]

Whatever legal rights slaves may have had, application of the law by judges was uneven, at best. The laws were enforced "now and then."[20] In *State v. Boon*, the Court held that the words of the statute, particularly "wilfully and maliciously killing a slave," were not sufficiently clear that it could be enforced.[21] In *State v. Hoover*, however, the North Carolina Court upheld a criminal conviction of a white for murdering his own slave.[22] One study found that in Alabama there were thirteen cases in which convictions were upheld on appeal for murder or attempted murder of a slave by a master during a 30-year period.[23]

Slavery was notoriously cruel in part because of the institution itself. Slaves could not be punished by imprisonment or fined because they already lacked liberty and the right to own property, meaning other forms of punishment needed to be used. The only treatise on slave law was written by a Southerner, Thomas R. R. Cobb. Cobb was a court reporter, professor of law in Athens, Georgia, and major contributor to the Confederate Constitution. Cobb's legal treatise on slavery makes

---

[18] *Laws of North Carolina*, Chapters III and IV, in *The Law of Freedom and Bondage: A Casebook*, edited by Paul Finkelman (New York: Oceana Publications, 1986), p. 201.

[19] Stampp, *The Peculiar Institution*, p. 218.

[20] Stampp, *The Peculiar Institution*, p. 217.

[21] *State v. Boon*, Taylor 246 (1801), in *The Law of Freedom and Bondage*, edited by Finkelman, p. 202.

[22] *State v. Hoover*, 4 Dev & Bat N.C. 365 (1839).

[23] A. E. Deir Nash, "A More Equitable Past? Southern Supreme Courts and the Protection of the Antebellum Negro," *North Carolina Law Review* Vol. 48 (1970), p. 197. Quoted in Lawrence M. Friedman, *A History of American Law* (New York: Simon and Schuster, 1973), p. 199, fn. 58.

clear that the condition of slavery "renders it impossible to inflict upon him the ordinary punishments," which means "he can be reached only through his body" (i.e., whipping). The general principle, he reported, is that "the master's right to enforce obedience and subordination on the part of the slave should, as far as possible, remain intact. [But] whatever goes beyond this, and from mere wantonness or revenge inflicts pain and suffering, especially unusual and inhuman punishments, is cruelty, and should be punished as such."[24]

Slave codes made it a crime to subject slaves to "cruel" punishment, although they did allow severe beatings. In Louisiana, the law against cruelty explicitly allowed "flogging, or striking with a whip, leather thong, switch or small stock, or putting in irons." In Mississippi, the punishment for perjury by a slave was to be nailed by the ear to a pillory for an hour, the ear cut off, and then the other ear nailed for an hour.[25] In another famous case in which an owner was charged with murder, *Souther v. Commonwealth*, the brutality of the beating was so horrendous that it helped move Harriet Beecher Stowe to write *Uncle Tom's Cabin*.[26] The owner received a sentence of 5 years in prison for the torture and murder of his slave.

Even the formal right not to be killed or cruelly tortured did not mean that such rights were respected in practice. By its very nature, slavery invites illegal as well as legal domination. Slaves had no right to sue on their own behalf, nor could slaves testify against their masters. In some states, a slave could not testify against any white person under any circumstances, allowing white criminals to go free when slave testimony could have led to a conviction.

That inability to instigate legal action in order to vindicate their rights is important in thinking about the power of slaves because it meant that whatever legal protections they supposedly enjoyed had to be enforced by others on their behalf, if at all. A slave's desire to prosecute a case could have no legal effect. In that sense, slaves were like livestock. Although they had (some) legal *protections*, along with a range of legal duties, they had no other legal status. The rights they had were therefore not a significant source of power for them; the legal powers rested with others – either

---

[24] Thomas R.R. Cobb, "An Inquiry into the Law of Negro Slavery," reprinted in *The Law of Freedom and Bondage*, edited by Finkelman, pp. 193, 195.

[25] Friedman, *A History of American Law*, p. 200.

[26] *Souther v. Commonwealth*, 7 Gratt. (Va.) 672 (1851).

the slave's master or those who might want to invoke the slave's rights on behalf of the slave.

This ambiguous status of slaves as holders of rights and as slaves is nicely illustrated by the law's treatment of mutual duties of masters and slaves. Alabama's legal code included a requirement that masters be "humane" to their slaves and that they provide slaves with adequate food, clothing, and healthcare, while at the same time defining slaves as property of their masters who must comply with masters' commands. Despite these supposed legal rights, however, Louisiana slaves owed their master and his family "a respect without bounds, and an absolute obedience." In *State v. Mann*, the judge went further, concluding that "the power of the master must be absolute, [in order] to render submission of the slave perfect."[27] That meant in practice that slaves were often subjected to cruelty and neglect – a fact that is most clearly illustrated in the many suits brought by owners against others for damaging their slave-property. A judge, in one case in which a slave had died after being loaned to another person, wrote that "the hirer of a slave should be taught . . . that more is required of him than to exact from the slave the greatest amount of service, with the least degree of attention to his comfort, health, or even life." Another owner sued when his slave was scarred due to severe beatings because the slave's "market value" was reduced.[28]

Given their very limited legal rights and the absence of the right to sue on their own behalf, combined with the fact that the law demanded nearly complete submission to the master's will, it might seem that slaves completely lacked all power. In *Slavery and Social Death: A Comparative Study*, Orlando Patterson links the fact that slavery is a relationship of power with honor and with what he terms "social death." Honor, according to Patterson, has three components: an internal feeling or sentiment, external conduct, and reputation.[29] Honor involves both how people see themselves and how they are seen by others, and it depends on people's ability to exercise control and to impose their will on the world. Those who lack the power to impose their will also lack the internal sense of their own will, as well as a social place and their acceptance by others. In an important sense, he concludes, slaves therefore *do not exist* as members of a community. To be a member means having a sense of one's own "position among one's fellow members, to feel the need to assert and

---

[27] *State v. Mann*, 2 Dev. (N. C.) 263 (1829).

[28] Catterall, *Judicial Cases* I, cited in Stampp, *The Peculiar Institution*, p. 204.

[29] Patterson, *Slavery and Social Death: A Comparative Study*, p. 79.

defend that position, and to feel a sense of satisfaction if that claimed position is accepted by others and a sense of shame if it is rejected."[30] In that way, according to Patterson, slaves are completely without power. They are socially "dead" (at least with respect to the white community and its legal system).

Although there is much truth in the idea of slavery as social death based on slaves' lack of legal power to defend their rights and their relative powerlessness vis-á-vis their masters, there are two problems with Patterson's claim. First, honor seems to be the wrong concept to use to describe what he has in mind. To say a person is "honorable" implies that the person has virtues such as trustworthiness and integrity. Honor has little to do with a person's feelings or sentiments and more to do with reputation. That subjective "sentiment" that Patterson thinks is one element of honor (along with conduct and reputation) is better captured by the concepts I discuss in Chapter 4 – self-respect and self-esteem.

This problem aside, the more important issue for present purposes is whether slavery was truly a condition of complete powerlessness and social death. As I have said, slaves lacked most rights and could not themselves assert in courts what rights they had. In one sense, then, we might say that they were "legally" dead because they could not use the legal system. But that is not the same as saying they had no *social* existence or that they had no *power*. While slaves did indeed lack all these legal rights, there are other ways in which slaves were able to exercise (limited) control over their own lives.

Slaves' power begins with the fact that they are persons.[31] As rational beings, they were not only held legally and morally accountable for their actions, but they were also able to threaten harm to others. Part of the power of slaves rested in that fact and in their capacity to resist. Slaves could run away, injure or kill their owner or his family, steal from their masters, lie, slow down work, damage tools, harm themselves, and kill or injure other slaves. Slaves could also resist in a more organized way such as by slave revolts and insurrections.

These were not idle threats. In the Southern states, slaves made up more than a third of the population; in some states more than half. The threat that slaves posed showed itself in many ways. Slave patrols were

[30] Patterson, *Slavery and Social Death: A Comparative Study*, p. 79.
[31] My discussion of slavery and the power of slaves is indebted to Cohen, "The Arc of the Moral Universe," p. 91.

regularly on the lookout for slaves who were traveling without permis-
sion. Insurrections were punishable by death, as was incitement to insur-
rection. Alabama even prescribed the death penalty for anyone whose
writing could *tend to* encourage slave rebellion. So it would be a mistake
to infer from the limited rights of slaves and the severity of legal sanctions
that slaves were entirely without power. Indeed, the brutality of slavery
can be seen as an indication of slaves' ability to exert limited power. The
possibility of resistance and rebellion gave slaves power not only because
of the harm they could do but also because the economic well-being
of the owners depended on the productivity of slaves. Slaves had to be
made to work, one way or another. One method was beatings, and the
severity of the beating testifies to the importance of making them work.
But economic necessity demanded that owners find other ways to motivate slaves besides threats of physical pain. Because it was inefficient if
not impossible to use *only* force to motivate slaves, owners and overseers
also employed positive incentives. These incentives included financial
rewards, autonomy and limited freedom, family security, and sometimes
manumission. Eugene Genovese quoted one overseer:

> Surely, if industrious for themselves, they will be so for their masters, and no
> Negro, with a well-stocked poultry house, a small crop advancing, a canoe
> partly finished, or a few tubs unsold, all of which he calculates soon to enjoy,
> will ever run away. In ten years I have lost by absconding, forty-seven days,
> out of nearly six hundred Negroes.[32]

The fact that slaves had some limited power can be appreciated by comparing slavery with a situation in which the dominating person needs
or wants nothing from the victim. Helpless victims of sadistic torturers,
for example, are in a condition of true, absolute powerlessness. They
have nothing the torturer wants, and there is no practical constraint on
the actions of the torturer. Some slaves no doubt suffered under similar
conditions, but most were in a different position. They had (limited)
power, which grew out of the few legal rights they enjoyed and, more
importantly, their economic importance to their owners.

The power of slaves also reflected their status as persons. Not only
were they legally responsible for what they did, but as rational beings
they were also able to act (or threaten to act) in ways that others often
had to accommodate in some way. One response was harsh beatings and

---

[32] Eugene Genovese, *Roll, Jordan, Roll* (New York: Pantheon, 1974), p. 539. Quoted in
Cohen, "The Arc of the Moral Universe," p. 105.

severe legal punishment. Yet, slaves' nature as rational beings and their economic utility were also sources of (limited) power. The fact they were rational human beings, and recognized as such, did not mean they were treated as equals in other ways – far from it.

Slavery and racism

Was American slavery a racist institution? I believe the answer is obvious – it was. The institution can be seen only as the product of hostility or indifference toward blacks on the basis of race. But some contemporary writers, most famously Dinesh D'Souza, have disputed what he terms that "conventional wisdom" about slavery. I want to begin by making clear why D'Souza is wrong. D'Souza's argument rests on two points that I already mentioned: that Africans had provided essential support in the slave trade, and that some blacks owned slaves.[33] Given the nature of racism, however, it is clear that neither of these undermines the idea that slavery was a racist institution. The fact that Africans participated in the slave trade says nothing about the racial attitudes of white slave owners. Even if Africans' willingness to sell members of other tribes into slavery somehow reflected a kind of prejudice on their part, that has nothing to do with slavery in the United States, and, in any case, prejudice against another tribe is different from racism. Nor is it relevant that a few free blacks owned slaves. The majority of those slaveholding blacks owned members of their own families, often because they lived in states where manumission was illegal.[34] And furthermore, the fact that a few blacks owned slaves provides no evidence about the attitudes of those who were largely responsible for creating and sustaining the practice.

It is also worth noting that slavery was very much a one-way street: although a (very) few blacks did own black slaves, nobody, white or black, owned a white slave. Indeed, even before slavery was formally established in Virginia, the colony prohibited free blacks from having white indentured servants.[35] In an 1832 case involving a white person who had been convicted of assaulting a black person, the judge observed

[33] Dinesh D'Souza, *The End of Racism*, p. 2.
[34] John Hope Franklin and Alfred A. Moss, Jr., *From Slavery to Freedom: A History of African Americans*, 7th ed. (New York: McGraw-Hill, 1994), pp. 156–157.
[35] "Noe Negroes nor Indians to Buy Christian Servants," Act V., Oct. 1670 in *The Statutes at Large: Being a Collection of All the Laws of Virginia, from the First Session of the Legislature, in the Year 1619*, edited by William Waller Kenning (New York: R. & W. & G. Bartow, 1823), p. 280.

that "By law, every negro is presumed to be a slave, the onus of proving his freedom . . . is cast upon him."[36] In another case, the Arkansas Supreme Court stated that slavery rested on "an inferiority of race" and therefore that the enslavement of a slave by a black lacked a "solid foundation."[37] Slave codes also spoke of free blacks as a denial of the fact that "nature's God intended the African for the status of slavery."[38]

Historically, slavery was often associated with war and conflict rather than racism. Victors would lay claim to the vanquished as slaves, and to have lost in battle was not necessarily to belong to a group that was thought inherently inferior or less valuable. Indeed, history records many instances where elites were forced into slavery. People also sometimes enslaved members of their own group. There have been "Arab slaves in the Middle East, Chinese slaves in China, Russian slaves in Russia, and Indian slaves on the Indian subcontinent. On the other side of the world, Scandinavians enslaved each other."[39] Before the sixteenth century "anyone, regardless of nation, religion, or race, might be a slave."[40] Even if racism had played no role in other slave societies, that would hardly show racism was not at the root of American slavery.

The international slave trade in Africans was indeed different from other slave systems, though the racism that was at its heart was not limited to Europeans. Arabs, too, had long justified African slavery in terms of racial inferiority.[41] Arabs notoriously preferred their own skin color to both the lighter shades they observed among the Greeks and the darker shades of Southern Africans. As one tenth-century Iraqi writer put it, "The Iraqis are neither half-baked dough nor burned crust."[42] Writing a century later, another author gave an even more explicitly racial account of the differences between Muslims and Africans. Living in a distinct climate in the South, he wrote, has resulted in the fact that Southern Africans do not have "self control and steadiness of mind," but, instead,

[36] *State v. Harden*, 2 Spears (S. C.) 151 (1832).
[37] Catterall, *Judicial Cases* cited in Stampp, *The Peculiar Institution*, p. 195.
[38] Stampp, *The Peculiar Institution*, p. 215.
[39] Paul Finkelman, "The Rise of the New Racism," *Yale Law and Policy Review*, Vol. 15, No. 1 (1996), p. 262.
[40] Carl N. Deglar, "The Irony of American Negro Slavery," in *Perspectives and Irony in American Negro Slavery*, edited by Harry P. Owens (Jackson: University of Mississippi Press, 1976), p. 19.
[41] See Lewis, *Race and Slavery in the Middle East*. My comments on Arab attitudes toward slavery owe much to Lewis's work.
[42] Lewis, *Race and Slavery in the Middle East*, p. 46.

they are often "overcome by fickleness, foolishness, and ignorance."[43] Another Arab writer expressed the thought that even an ape is more "teachable and more intelligent" than the black African; still another compared Africans with wild animals.[44] Orlando Patterson concludes that it is "appalling ignorance" to suggest Americans were alone in using race as a justification for slavery. "Throughout the Islamic world," he concludes, race was a "vital issue" in slavery.[45]

In North America, some Africans were not treated as slaves, although as I noted, being African usually created a presumption that a person was not free. In Virginia, for example, some Africans were originally brought as indentured servants rather than slaves.[46] Other early records suggest early Africans were given rights that were later lost. The *Minutes of the Council and General Court of Virginia* records an occasion in which a black was allowed to testify against a white in a court of law.[47] Soon, however, the laws of Virginia began to make sharp distinctions between blacks and whites. Though under English common law children, including bastards, had the status of their fathers, a statute passed in the Virginia House of Burgesses in 1662 required that "Negro women's children" were to serve according to "the condition of the mother." The preamble to the statute noted that "doubts" had arisen over whether the children of negro women were slave or free. Another law imposed double the fine on any white who "commits fornication" with a "negro man or woman."[48] However it had begun, by the middle of the seventeenth century, whites had come to make clear distinctions between blacks and whites, always to the detriment of blacks. People regularly spoke of "slaves" as contrasted with "whites." Blacks had come to be viewed as suitable for enslavement by whites.

As slavery grew, the ideological tensions and contradictions became more apparent. The American Revolutionary War had been fought, it was said, based on the self-evident truth that "all men are created equal" and are "endowed by their Creator with certain unalienable Rights." The Preamble to the U.S. Constitution speaks in similarly idealistic terms, of

[43] Lewis, *Race and Slavery in the Middle East*, pp. 47–48.
[44] Lewis, *Race and Slavery in the Middle East*, pp. 52, 53.
[45] Patterson, *Slavery and Social Death: A Comparative Study*, pp. 176, 193.
[46] Finkelman, "The Rise of the New Racism," p. 266.
[47] In re Sir Henry Maneringe (November 30, 1624), in *Minutes of the Council and General Court of Virginia, 1622–1632*, reprinted in *The Law of Freedom and Bondage*, edited by Finkelman, p. 10.
[48] Finkelman, "The Rise of the New Racism," p. 267.

its purpose as the creation of a "more perfect union" among "the people" and the establishment of "justice." Yet, as the Constitution was being debated, its prime architect, James Madison, wrote in one of the Federalist Papers that "The Federal Constitution decides with great propriety on the case of our slaves, when it views them in the mixt character of persons and of property. This is in fact their true character."[49] Indeed, the United States Constitution didn't just allow slavery, it facilitated it by assuring that fugitive slaves would be returned and that slavery would not be abolished for many years.

Despite its injustice, slavery was accepted in order to win agreement on the new Constitution. Although most delegates to the Constitutional Convention opposed slavery on moral grounds, many were also sympathetic to the economic loss and other problems that eliminating slavery would cause. Most important, Southern delegates refused to join the Union unless the right to own slaves was protected. Though it was assumed by many that it would die a natural death, slavery did not disappear. The advent of the cotton gin meant that slavery continued to be profitable in the South.

Pre-Civil War courts were reluctant to upset the constitutional compromises. For the first three decades of the nineteenth century, the free states and slave states worked together to reinforce the institution. With Nat Turner's rebellion and the growth of abolitionism in the 1830s, however, that compromise began to unravel.

Slavery presented troubling legal issues to courts charged with enforcing criminal and property laws. Some were of slight political consequence, for example whether slave states could jail free black sailors whose ships were unloading cargo in their ports.[50] At one point, abolitionists even took to sending mail to slaveholders and slaves, provoking a proposal in the Senate in 1836 making it unlawful for any postmaster knowingly to receive and mail any matter "touching the subject of slavery, directed to any person or post-office in any state where by the law thereof their circulation is prohibited."[51] The bill, however, was rejected. More serious conflicts arose over two other issues: the enforcement of fugitive-slave laws in nonslave states and the future of slavery in the territories and in new states. Debate raged over whether slavery was protected by the

---

[49] James Madison, "The Federalist Number 54," in Clinton Rossiter, *The Federalist Papers*, p. 337.
[50] *Elkison v. Deliesseline*, 8 Fed. Cas. 493 (No. 4366) (1823)(C.C.D.S.C.).
[51] Alfred H. Kelly, Winfred A. Harbison, and Herman Belz, *The American Constitution, Its Origins and Development*, 7th ed. (New York: W. W. Norton and Co., 1991), pp. 258–259.

Constitution, whether Congress could outlaw it, or whether the question should be left to the citizens of the territories.

Politically, the South was dominant. Eleven of the first fifteen presidents were Southerners, as were seventeen of twenty-eight Supreme Court justices and twenty-one of thirty-four speakers of the House. One critical legal case that reflected this Southern influence was *Prigg v. Pennsylvania*[52] (1842), in which the U.S. Supreme Court overturned a Pennsylvania law designed to prevent slaveholders from simply kidnaping people they claimed were runaway slaves. Such proslavery decisions stressed the importance of judicial restraint, the historical record of the constitutional convention, and the intent of the framers.

The most important slave case was, of course, *Scott v. Sandford* (1857), often called "Dred Scott."[53] In 1855, the debate over slavery in the territories had become ferocious; Kansas was even experiencing civil war between proslavery and antislavery forces. Dred Scott was a slave owned by John Emerson, a surgeon in the U.S. Army. Scott had been taken in 1834 by the Emerson family from Missouri to Illinois and then to the Wisconsin Territory, which was "free soil" under the Missouri Compromise. Emerson had died soon after his return to Missouri, and ownership of Scott was passed to John Sandford of New York. Twelve years later, in 1846, Scott sued Sandford, claiming that he was entitled to be regarded as free in virtue of having been taken to free territory. Scott lost in the lower court. In 1857, in the midst of the war in Kansas, he appealed to the Supreme Court. The case generated tremendous public interest, as proslavery judges on the Court insisted on trying to settle the slavery issue once and for all. The Court denied Scott his relief. The grounds were that Scott could not sue because he was not a citizen of the United States. Justice Taney, who wrote the opinion of the Court, set out the issues this way:

> The question is simply this: Can a negro, whose ancestors were imported into this country, and sold as slaves, become a member of the political community, formed and brought into existence by the Constitution of the United States, and as such become entitled to all the rights, and privileges, and immunities, guarantied by that instrument to the citizen, one of which rights is the privilege of suing in a court of the United States in the cases specified in the Constitution?

[52] *Prigg V. Pennsylvania*, 41 U.S. 539 (1842).
[53] *Scott v. Sandford*, 60 U.S. (19 How.) 393 (1857).

To answer that, Taney turned to the views of the "citizens of the several States when the Constitution was adopted."

> In the opinion of the court, the legislation and histories of the times, and the language used in the Declaration of Independence, show that neither the class of persons who had been imported as slaves, nor their descendants, whether they had become free or not, were then acknowledged as a part of the people, nor intended to be included in the general words used in that memorable instrument.

Taney also claimed the justification for slavery, accepted at the time, was the "inferiority" of the African race. This meant, he said, that slaves have "no rights." Negroes

> had for more than a century before been regarded as beings of an inferior order, and altogether unfit to associate with the white race, either in social or political relations, and so far inferior that they had no rights which the white man was bound to respect, and that the negro might justly and lawfully be reduced to slavery for his benefit. He was bought and sold, and treated as an ordinary article of merchandise and traffic whenever a profit could be made by it. This opinion was at that time fixed and universal in the civilized portion of the white race.

Taney then suggested that the Declaration of Independence did not mean what it said. Despite affirming the "self-evident" truth "that all men are created equal," if the Declaration were interpreted to include African slaves then

> the conduct of the distinguished men who framed the Declaration of Independence would have been utterly and flagrantly inconsistent with the principles they asserted, and instead of the sympathy of mankind to which they so confidently appealed, they would have deserved and received universal rebuke and reprobation. Yet the men who framed this declaration were great men – high in literary acquirements, high in their sense of honor, and incapable of asserting principles inconsistent with those on which they were acting.

The opinion concluded that "the right of property in a slave is distinctly and expressly affirmed in the Constitution" and "no word can be found in the Constitution which gives Congress a greater power over slave property [than over other property], or which entitles property of that kind to less protection than property of any other description." Taney further held that the "act of Congress which prohibited a citizen from holding and owning property of this kind in the territory of the United States north of the line therein mentioned is not warranted by the Constitution, and is therefore void," and further "that neither Dred Scott himself, nor any of his family were made free by being carried into this territory even if they had been carried there by the owner, with the intention of becoming a permanent resident."

This opinion is mistaken on a number of different fronts, and it is important to see why. It has been an ongoing source of confusion about the Constitutional basis of slavery and, more importantly, about the ideal of equality. It also showed a breathtaking level of judicial activism combined with its dubious legal claims.

Taney's key legal claims in the decision were, first, that slaves were not viewed by the framers as equals and were therefore not given any of the rights enjoyed by whites, including access to the courts. To decide otherwise, according to the Court, would mean that "the conduct [i.e., allowing slavery] of the distinguished men who framed the Declaration of Independence would have been utterly and flagrantly inconsistent with the principles they asserted." Second, Taney asserted that the right to own slaves was protected by the Constitution. The "right of property in a slave," he had said, "is distinctly and expressly affirmed in the Constitution."[54] Both claims are mistaken.

The first claim, that slaves lacked the right to sue in court because they were not citizens, was misguided. National citizenship automatically followed state citizenship, and state citizenship was not limited to those who enjoyed *equal* political and civil rights. Women and children were fully citizens but lacked many of the rights of adult males. There was therefore no need to assume, as Taney did, that only people with full and equal legal rights were citizens with the right to sue. Slaves did have some rights, and although they were certainly not treated as *equal* citizens, there is no reason to conclude as Taney had done that they were not citizens at all.

The second claim, that the Constitution protected the right to own slaves, is also mistaken. Although the Constitution did explicitly prohibit Congress from limiting the slave trade before 1808, that is not an endorsement of the practice. Indeed the dated limitation implicitly suggests the possibility of regulating it *after* that date. Nor is there any language in the Constitution denying the moral or legal equality or the citizenship of slaves, let alone requiring that they have no rights. Laws did give slaves rights, and, as I discuss in what follows, judges sometimes also what follows acknowledged the injustice of the laws they

---

[54] *Scott v. Sandford*, 60 U.S. 393, 410, 451.

were enforcing. Slavery was treated as a "creature of positive law only" that has "no support in natural law or justice."[55]

The experience of Africans in the New World was radically different from that of other immigrant groups. Brought as slaves, they were deprived of rights to own property, to pursue an education, to marry and raise children, to choose where to live and work, to protect their personal privacy, to control their sexuality, and to practice their religion. At the same time, it was impossible to justify their enslavement either as punishment of a vanquished enemy or as retribution for crimes. African slaves were brought to the New World merely because they were available, they were black, and they were useful. Racism was at the heart of African slavery virtually from the beginning.

In 1852, a former slave, Frederick Douglass, was asked to give a Fourth of July oration to his fellow citizens in Rochester, New York. After asking "Do you mean, citizens, to mock me, asking me to speak today?" Douglass famously said:

> What to the American slave is your fourth of July? I answer, a day that reveals to him more than all other days of the year, the gross injustice and cruelty to which he is the constant victim. To him your celebration is a sham; your boasted liberty an unholy license, your national greatness, swelling vanity; your sounds of rejoicing are empty and heartless; your denunciation of tyrants, brass-fronted impudence; your shouts of liberty and equality, hollow mockery; your prayers and hymns, your sermons and thanksgivings, with all your religious parade and solemnity, are to him mere bombast, fraud, deception, impiety, and hypocrisy – a thin veil to cover up crimes that would disgrace a nation of savages. There is not a nation of the earth guilty of practices more shocking and bloody than are the people of these United States at this very hour.[56]

Despite its evident injustice and its racism, slavery was not without its defenders. What is more surprising, perhaps, is how often the views of slavery's defenders are misunderstood. It is important to understand what those who supported slavery actually said, however, in order to appreciate what was wrong with their position and how slavery was, in fact, unjust.

[55] Herbert J. Storing, "Slavery and the Moral Foundations of the American Republic," in *Slavery and Its Consequences: The Constitution, Equality and Race*, edited by Robert A. Goldwin and Art Kaufman (Washington DC: American Enterprise Institute, 1988), p. 48.

[56] Frederick Douglass, "What to the Slave is the Fourth of July? An address delivered in Rochester, New York, on 5 July 1852," in *The Frederick Douglass Papers*, series 1, *Speeches, Debates, and Interviews*, vol. 2, 1847-1854, edited by John W. Blasingame and John R. McKivigan (New Haven: Yale University Press, 1982), p. 371.

The philosophy of slavery

Popular assumptions about the justification given for slavery are often erroneous. It is sometimes said, pointing to the three-fifths compromise in the U.S. Constitution, that the rationale for slavery rested on the idea that slaves were seen as less than fully persons. Charles Mills expresses this idea when he writes that "the peculiar status of a sub-person is that it is an entity which, because of phenotype, it seems (from, of course, the perspective of the categorizer) human in some respects but not in others. It is a human who . . . is not fully a person."[57] It is also sometimes suggested that to be a person and property are incompatible. But neither of those claims is true: slaves were not seen as "three-fifth" of persons, nor is being property inconsistent with personhood.

Contrary to popular belief, the Constitution did not deny the person-hood of slaves. Though it never actually mentions the words "slave" or "slavery," the Constitution makes three explicit references to the practice. But in every case, slaves are explicitly referred to as "persons." Requiring the return of fugitive slaves, for example, Article IV, Section 2 states that "no *person* legally held in service or labor" who escapes will be discharged, but instead must be "delivered up" to the party to whom the labor is due. The second reference, the banning of the importation of slaves in Article I, Section 9, refers to the "migration or importation of such *persons* as any of the states now existing shall think proper to admit," and says such trade cannot be prohibited by Congress before 1808.

Those who appeal to the three-fifths compromise in support of the idea that slaves were regarded as "three-fifths persons" also ignore the histor-ical meaning of the compromise itself. S*laveowners* had wanted slaves to be counted equally among the populations of the slave states for deter-mining representation in Congress, while the Northern states wanted them not counted at all. Three-fifths was a compromise about how much representation and political power the South would enjoy, not about the nature of slaves as persons. In fact, the three-fifths clause explicitly states that all free persons plus three-fifths of "all *other persons*" will determine the apportionment of representatives in Congress. The Constitution left no doubt that slaves were persons.

---

[57] Charles Mills, "Non-Cartesian Sums: Philosophy and the African-American Experience," *Teaching Philosophy*, Vol. 17, No. 3 (October, 1994), p. 228.

Slave codes and judicial opinions interpreting them also acknowledged slaves' status as persons. They did it in part when they held slaves responsible, morally and legally, for their actions. The law often spoke of the need to deter other slaves, which was also a clear sign that slaves were seen as rational agents. As one Tennessee judge wrote, "A slave is not in the condition of a horse. . . . he has mental capacities, and an important principle in his nature. . . . [slavery did not] extinguish his high-born nature nor deprive him of many rights which are inherent in man."[58] Slave practices also sometimes included manumission as incentives, a clear indication that slaves were understood to be not only rational beings but also motivated by a desire for the freedom to shape their own lives according to their own chosen aims.[59]

Finally, slaves' status as persons was acknowledged even by judges interpreting the slave codes. In the Mississippi case of *State v. Jones*, for example, the defendant claimed that slaves cannot have any rights. In response, the judge stated that just because individuals "have been deprived of many of their rights by society, it does not follow that they have been deprived of all their rights." A slave, he said, "is still a human being." The judge added that because murder is defined as taking the life of a human being, and a slave is a human being, killing a slave is murder. The Court went further still, however. It said that because a slave is a person, he "possesses all those rights, of which he is not deprived by the positive provisions of the law."[60] In other words, it is the positive law (in the form of statutes enacted by legislatures) that deprives slaves of the rights that all persons normally enjoy. Unless the law explicitly denies slaves a right enjoyed by others, the right is secure for the slave as well. The reason that the Court took that position again seems clear: unlike livestock, slaves are also persons. The justice of the positive law – whether or not it respects the *natural* rights of slaves – is a different matter from the *legal* rights that are granted, or denied, by the positive law.

Both the Constitution and slave law recognized that slaves were *both* property and persons. There is nothing *conceptually* wrong, or even odd, with the claim that a person is also, legally, property that can be controlled in all the ways that livestock can be controlled. But if slavery was not to be justified on the ground that slaves were not persons, then how was it defended?

---

[58] Catterall, *Judicial Cases*, cited in Stampp, *The Peculiar Institution*, p. 217.
[59] Joshua Cohen discusses these and related issues in "The Arc of the Moral Universe."
[60] *State v. Jones*, 1 Miss. 83 (1820).

As might be expected, the justifications of slavery took many forms. Some arguments were religious in nature. Not only did the Bible refuse to condemn slavery, but it was taken for granted as legitimate. Many Old Testament patriarchs from Abraham on owned slaves, and in the New Testament, Paul's letter to Philemon called for returning runaway slaves while other letters encouraged slaves to accept their status. Other arguments were practical. Some emphasized the profitability of slavery and the importance of cotton and other Southern crops to the economy. "Cotton," as Senator Hammond of South Carolina famously said, "is king."[61] Madison's notes on the debates over ratification of the Constitution echoed a similarly pragmatic tone on the part of delegates. Madison reported the following exchange between two delegates:

Mr. Rutledge: Religion and humanity had nothing to do with this question. Interest alone is the governing principle with nations. . . .

General Pinckney: South Carolina and Georgia cannot do without slaves. He contended that the importation of slaves would be for the interest of the whole union. The more slaves, the more produce to employ the carrying trade; The more consumption also, and the more revenue for the common treasury.[62]

There were other pragmatic considerations as well. In 1831, the Virginia legislature discussed a proposal to eliminate slavery by expatriation of blacks to Africa. The proposal failed, but in the debate Thomas R. Dew of the College of William and Mary described the costs of eliminating slavery. They included the economic effects of shifting to free labor, paying for slaves' passage, and compensating their owners. He then went on to suggest that "Any question must be answered by its circumstances, and if, as really is the case, we cannot get rid of slavery without producing a greater injury to both the masters and slaves, there is no rule of conscience or revealed law of God which can condemn us."[63]

[61] James Henry Hammond, *Congressional Globe*, 35th Congress, 1st session, March 6, 1858, p. 61.
[62] James Madison, "Notes on the Constitutional Convention," in *The Antifederalist Papers and the Constitutional Debates*, edited by Ralph Ketcham (New York: Signet Classics, 2003), pp. 161–163.
[63] "Review of the Debate in the Virginia Legislature," in *Slavery Defended: The Views of the Old South*, edited by Eric McKitrick (Englewood Cliffs NJ: Prentice Hall, 1963), p. 31. Quoted in Judith Baer, *Equality Under the Constitution: Reclaiming the Fourteenth Amendment* (Ithaca: Cornell University Press, 1983), p. 65.

Another argument purported to show that slavery was in the interests of slaves themselves. The Arkansas Supreme Court put the point succinctly: slavery's foundation, it said, was in "an inferiority of race."[64] Thomas R. R. Cobb, who was among slavery's most noted defenders, developed that argument in detail. If it can be shown, he wrote, that the "physical, intellectual, and moral development of the African race are promoted by a state of slavery, and their happiness secured to a greater extent than if left at liberty, then their enslavement is consistent with the law of nature."[65] Cobb appealed for support to no less a figure than St. Thomas Aquinas, whom he quotes as saying: "This man is a slave, absolutely speaking, . . . not by any natural cause, but by reason of the benefits which are produced; for it is more beneficial to this one to be governed by one who has more wisdom."[66] Defenders of slavery often compared slavery with the authority of parents over children. Just as it would not serve the interest of children and lunatics to be set free to compete with sane adults, wrote lawyer, author, and ardent defender of slavery George Fitzhugh, so too would it be bad for slaves to be freed.[67] Indeed, said Fitzhugh, slavery is commonplace in society. Criminals, children, the insane, and those serving in the military are all slaves in varying degrees.

The underlying assumption that these writers used to support this claim is the natural inferiority of the negro to whites. The negro race, wrote Fitzhugh, "is inferior to the white race, and living in their midst, they would be far outstripped or outwitted in the chase of free competition."[68] Cobb and others identified three respects in which Africans are naturally suited to be slaves, despite the fact that "we recognize in the negro a man, endowed with reason, will, and accountability." First, Cobb wrote, the negro is physically suited to endure heat and also has a physical nature that is a "natural preparation for strength and endurance."[69] Cobb also believed that slavery was justified by mental differences. The "mental inferiority of the Negro," he wrote, "has often been asserted and

---

[64] Catterall (ed.), *Judicial Cases* p. 215. Quoted in Stampp, *The Peculiar Institution*, p. 195. It was for that reason that many in the South objected to blacks owning slaves.

[65] Thomas R. R. Cobb, "An Inquiry into the Law of Negro Slavery" (1858), in *Defending Slavery: Proslavery Thought in the Old South*, edited by Paul Finkelman (Boston: Bedford/St. Martins, 2003), p. 147.

[66] Cobb, "An Inquiry into the Law of Negro Slavery," p. 146.

[67] George Fitzhugh, "Sociology for the South: Or the Failure of Free Society" (1854), reprinted in *Defending Slavery: Proslavery Thought in the Old South*, edited by Finkelman, p. 187.

[68] Fitzhugh, "Sociology for the South: Or the Failure of Free Society," p. 190.

[69] Cobb, "An Inquiry into the Law of Negro Slavery," p. 148.

never successfully refuted. . . . We deal with him as we find him, and according to the measure of his capacity, it is our duty to cultivate and improve him."[70]

The basis of this claim of intellectual inferiority fell into two broad categories: historic and scientific. History demonstrated Africans' intellectual inferiority because "they have never comprehended what they have learned, or retained a civilization taught them by contact with more refined nations, as soon as that contact had ceased." Nor, said Cobb, have Africans at any time "formed great political states, nor commenced a self-evolving civilization. . . . The history of Africa is too well known to require of us an argument or an extended notice, to show, that left to themselves the negro races would never arrive at any high degree of civilization."[71] Senator John C. Calhoun of South Carolina made a similar point in a famous speech attacking antislavery petitions sent to the Senate by abolitionists. Never before, he said, "has the black race of Central Africa, from the dawn of history to the present day, attained a condition so civilized and so improved, not only physically, but morally and intellectually."[72]

Intellectual inferiority was also thought to be supported by scientific studies. Writers went to great length in their attempts to establish their claim, quoting scientists who both supported and opposed slavery. Some pointed to physiological differences, including brain size. Most prominent among these "scientists" was a physician from New Orleans named Samuel Cartwright, whose medical practice focused on slaves. He found racial differences in bile, blood, bones, nerves, spinal marrow, brain, eyes, liver, and humors, among others.[73] Cobb's summary of the effects of these physiological differences is typical. The prominent intellectual defect, he wrote, is

a want of judgment. He forms no definite idea of effects from causes. He cannot comprehend, so as to execute the simplest orders unless they refresh his memory as to some previous knowledge. He is imitative, sometimes eminently so, but his mind is never inventive. The imitative faculty makes the negro a good musician, yet he never originates a single air.[74]

[70] Cobb, "An Inquiry into the Law of Negro Slavery," p. 149.
[71] Cobb, "An Inquiry into the Law of Negro Slavery," pp. 149, 154.
[72] John C. Calhoun, "Speech on the Reception of Abolition Petitions, Delivered in the Senate, February 6th, 1837," in *Slavery Defended: The Views of the Old South*, edited by McKitrick, p. 13.
[73] Samuel A. Cartwright, M. D., "Report on the Diseases and Physical Peculiarities of the Negro Race," *New Orleans Medical and Surgical Journal*, Vol. 7 (May 1851), p. 691.
[74] Cobb, "An Inquiry into the Law of Negro Slavery," p. 152.

In addition to physical nature and intellectual inferiority, Cobb and other slave defenders saw what they took to be a third difference in the races: the moral inferiority of blacks. Although they are not "malicious" and are inclined to "forgive and forget the past," blacks, Cobb claimed, are more indolent, thievish, and lascivious than whites.[75] Indeed, said Cobb, the "debasement" of their moral character has even led some to doubt the negro's "humanity."[76]

Tied to the supposed suitability for work and natural inferiority was another argument that was commonly made in support of slavery. It pointed to the advantages slaves enjoyed over both free blacks and free whites in the North. Census figures, it was widely claimed, showed that black slaves reproduced at the same level as whites and at a higher rate than free blacks. The 1850 Census was also quoted by Cobb and others to show that slaves had a greater life expectancy than free blacks in the North. Other indices supposedly pointing to the advantages of slavery over freedom for blacks included lower proportions of blindness and insanity and higher levels of knowledge and intelligence.

Not only were slaves advantaged over free blacks, but they were also said to be in some respects better off even than the free laborers in the North. In "The Mudsill Speech" before the U.S. Senate, James Henry Hammond of South Carolina argued that all successful societies, free or slaveowning, require a class of people to perform the "menial duties." Such people need little intellect or skill, though they do need "vigor, docility and fidelity." What distinguishes the South from the North is that in the South, slaves do the menial work, while in free societies it is done by manual laborers who are "essentially slaves." The difference between the South and the North, said Hammond, is that

> our slaves are hired for life and well compensated; there is no starvation, no begging, no want of employment among our people, and not too much employment either. Yours are hired by the day, not cared for, and scantily compensated, which may be proved in the most painful manner, at any hour in any street in any of your large towns. Why, you meet more beggars in one day, in any single street of the city of New York, than you would meet in a lifetime in the whole South. . . . Your [slaves] are white, of your own race; you are brothers of one blood. They are your equals in natural endowment of intellect, and they feel galled by their degradation.[77]

[75] Cobb, "An Inquiry into the Law of Negro Slavery," pp. 153–155.

[76] Cobb, "An Inquiry into the Law of Negro Slavery," p. 152.

[77] James Henry Hammond, "Speech on the Admission of Kansas, under the Lecompton Constitution, Delivered in the Senate of the United States, March 4, 1858," in *Defending Slavery: Proslavery Thought in the Old South*, edited by Finkelman, pp. 86–87.

Hammond went on to predict that in the North, the class of wage slaves would use their political power to overthrow the government and society and destroy Northerners' property. "How would you like it," he asked, "for us to send lecturers and agitators North, to teach these people this, to aid in combining, and to lead them?"[78]

Among the most striking documents of the period is an 1853 work by Edmund Ruffin titled *The Political Economy of Slavery.*[79] Ruffin sought an economic explanation of why wage laborers were worse off than slaves. If slavery were better for laborers than freedom, he asked, why has slavery not continued everywhere? The answer is found in the operation of capitalism.

> [S]harp want, hunger, and cold, are more effective incentives to labor than the slaveowner's whip, even if its use is not restrained by any feeling of justice or mercy. But under such conditions of free labor, domestic or individual slavery could not exist. For whenever want and competition shall reduce the wages of free labor, then it will be more profitable for the slave-owner and employer to hire free labor (both cheapened and driven by hunger and misery) than to maintain slaves, and compel their labor less effectually and at greater expense. Under such conditions slaves would be readily emancipated by masters to whom they had become burdensome.[80]

The reason that slavery must disappear is the self-interest of the ruling class.

> Soon, under the operating influence of self-interest alone on the master class, domestic slavery would come to an end of itself – give place to the far more stringent and oppressive rule of want as a compeller of labor, and be substituted by class slavery, or the absolute subjection of the whole class of laborers to the whole class of employers – or of labor to capital.[81]

Slaveowners thus looked not just to census figures and other historical records to show why slavery served the interests of slaves; they also provided economic theories to explain why free laborers suffered greater hardship.

---

[78] Hammond, "Speech on the Admission of Kansas," in *Defending Slavery: Proslavery Thought in the Old South*, edited by Finkelman, p. 88.

[79] Edmund Ruffin, "The Political Economy of Slavery; or, the Institution Considered in Regard to Its Influence on Public Wealth and the General Welfare" (1853), in *Defending Slavery: Proslavery Thought in the Old South*, edited by Finkelman, pp. 61–76.

[80] Ruffin, "The Political Economy of Slavery; or, the Institution Considered in Regard to Its Influence on Public Wealth and the General Welfare," p. 67.

[81] Ruffin, "The Political Economy of Slavery; or, the Institution Considered in Regard to Its Influence on Public Wealth and the General Welfare," p. 67.

Cobb concludes his treatise on slave law with the observation that "a state of bondage, so far from doing violence to the law of his nature, develops and perfects it; and in a state of nature he enjoys the greatest amount of happiness, and arrives at the greatest degree of perfection of which his nature is capable."[82] Fitzhugh said, in a similar vein, that "The Southerner is the negro's friend, his only friend. Let no meddling abolitionist, no refined philosophy, dissolve this friendship."[83]

History and science have disproven the core assumptions of the defenders of slavery, of course, but there remains an important issue that is far from settled: the ideal of racial equality. What does it mean? What does it entail? Before taking up those issues directly, in Chapter 4, I want to conclude my discussion of slavery and its history by asking how the defenders and critics of slavery understood the Declaration of Independence and its famous claim that "all men are created equal." Some denied equality altogether – others sought ways to exclude Africans from being considered "equal persons." Still others, including Thomas Jefferson, understood that equality and slavery were deeply incompatible, though Jefferson nonetheless thought abolition would make a bad situation even worse.

"All men are created equal"

Reconciling the founders' ideal of equality and their support of slavery was never easy. Defenders of slavery had various options. One was to deny that blacks were "men" in the relevant sense. One slaveholder claimed to believe all men are "free and equal as the Declaration of Independence holds they are . . . But all *men*; niggers and monkeys ain't."[84] Others argued that the Declaration referred not to all men but instead only to "citizens" or the "governing race."[85]

Another option was to attack the ideal of equality itself. This was common; both George Fitzhugh and John C. Calhoun took that approach. Fitzhugh described the founding principles of the United

---

[82] Cobb, "An Inquiry into the Law of Negro Slavery," p. 156.

[83] Fitzhugh, "Sociology for the South: Or the Failure of Free Society," p. 196.

[84] Quoted in James Oaks, *The Ruling Race: A History of American Slaveholders* (New York: Knopf, 1982), p. 143 (emphasis added).

[85] Alexander Stephens, quoted in Oaks, *The Ruling Race: A History of American Slaveholders*, p. 143.

States as "professedly false" and the Declaration as "fallacious."[86] Calhoun agreed. "It is a great and dangerous error," he wrote;

> to suppose that all people are equally entitled to liberty. . . . These great and dangerous errors have had their origin in the prevalent opinion that all men are born free and equal; [an idea] than which nothing can be more unfounded and false. It rests upon the assumption of a fact, which is contrary to universal observation, in whatever light it may be regarded.[87]

Calhoun did not regard slaves as equals entitled to basic rights, and he saw no contradiction between the commitments to justice and equality, on one hand, and slavery on the other. Slaves were not, in the appropriate sense, suitable candidates for equal citizenship because although persons, they were not *equals*.

Yet, that position, while familiar among many of slavery's defenders, was not the only possibility. Many others, including some Southern slaveholders, regarded slavery as deeply unjust and incompatible with the ideals of the Declaration. A Maryland delegate to the constitutional convention, Luther Martin, described the slave trade and the three-fifths compromise as a "solemn mockery of, and insult to that God whose protection we had then implored. . . . [it is] the only branch of commerce which is unjustifiable in its nature, and contrary to the rights of mankind."[88] Abigail Adams said, in a letter to her husband John, that slavery involved "daily robbing and plundering from those who have as good a right to freedom as we have,"[89] while George Mason of Virginia condemned it for its effect on the economy and on the slaveowners themselves: "[E]very master of slaves is born a petty tyrant." They bring the "judgment of heaven on a Country" since by "an inevitable chain of causes and effects providence punishes national sins, by national calamities."[90] One constitutional historian summarized the typical view of the framers this way. They saw slavery, he wrote, as "an evil to be tolerated, allowed to enter the Constitution only by the back door, grudgingly, unacknowledged, on

---

[86] Fitzhugh, *Sociology for the South: Or the Failure of Free Society* quoted in Paul Finkelman, "The Centrality of the Peculiar Institution in American Legal Development," *Chicago-Kent Law Review*, Vol. 68 (1993), pp. 1021–1022.

[87] Calhoun, "A Disquisition on Government," pp. 55–57.

[88] Quoted in David Brion Davis, *The Problem of Slavery in the Age of Revolution, 1770–1823* (New York: Oxford University Press, 1975), p. 323.

[89] Quoted in William M. Wiecek, *The Sources of Antislavery Constitutionalism in America: 1760-1848* (Ithaca: Cornell University Press, 1977), p. 64.

[90] Quoted in Derrick A. Bell, Jr., *And We Are Not Saved: The Elusive Quest for Racial Justice* (New York: Basic Books, 1987), p. 38.

the presumption that the house would be truly fit to live in only when it was gone, and that it would ultimately be gone."[91]

Thomas Jefferson seems to have taken a similar view of the situation. There is good evidence that Jefferson did not believe slavery was just. Writing about slavery in his autobiography, he famously confessed that because of slavery "I tremble for my country when I reflect that God is just; that his justice cannot sleep forever."[92] In his original draft of the Declaration of Independence, Jefferson had also accused King George of waging a "cruel war against human nature itself, violating its most sacred rights of life and liberty, in the persons of a distant people who never offended him, captivating and carrying them into slavery in another hemisphere."[93] (Those words were removed during debates over the Declaration's adoption.) In his draft of the Virginia Constitution, Jefferson also sought to reduce and eventually eliminate slavery in his own state.

But like many others Jefferson also feared the consequences of the abolition of slavery. The potential for racial conflict and race war that would emerge from the hatred the institution had engendered on both sides made slavery's continuation a necessary evil, Jefferson concluded. Slavery had produced

> deep rooted prejudices entertained by the whites; ten thousand recollec-
> tions, by the blacks, of injuries they have sustained; new provocations; the
> real distinctions which nature has made, and many other circumstances, will
> divide us into parties, and produce convulsions which will probably never
> end but in the extermination of one race by the other.[94]

Jefferson went on to explain that his efforts in the legislature to push for emancipation had failed because "the public mind would not hear of the proposition." Yet, he nonetheless saw abolition as inevitable. "Nothing is more certainly written in the book of fate than that these people are to be free."[95]

Jefferson was pessimistic about the future; he saw grave dangers in continuing slavery and yet no good way to end it. So although denying

[91] Storing, "Slavery and the Moral Foundations of the American Republic," p. 55.
[92] Thomas Jefferson, "Autobiography," in *The Life and Selected Writings of Thomas Jefferson*, edited by Adrienne Koch and William Peden (New York: Modern Library, 1944), p. 51.
[93] Thomas Jefferson, "Autobiography," in *The Writings of Thomas Jefferson*, edited by Merrill D. Peterson (New York: Library of America, 1984), p. 22.
[94] Jefferson, "Notes on the State of Virginia (1871–82)," in *Writings*, p. 264.
[95] Jefferson, "Autobiography," in *Writings*, p. 44.

the justice of slavery, Jefferson nonetheless also opposed abolition in favor of repatriation back to Africa. (Jefferson did not free his own slaves even on his death and fought against policies encouraging manumission.) Jefferson's view was also not unique. His fellow Virginian, John Randolph, opposed both abolitionists and slavery. Randolph described slavery as a "cancer" that must not be "tampered with by quacks, who never saw the disease." Race war threatened the "life-blood of the little ones, which are lying in their cradles . . . and not the white ones only, for shall not we too kill?"[96]

Like Calhoun after him, Jefferson believed that blacks, as a group, were intellectually inferior to whites. He wrote that "comparing [blacks] by their faculties of memory, reason, and imagination, it appears to me, that in memory they are equal to the whites; in reason much inferior . . . and that in imagination they are dull, tasteless, and anomalous."[97] Yet while he believed that the races were not equal in intellectual capacities, he did not welcome that possibility. "No body wishes more than I do to see such proofs as you exhibit," he wrote in a letter to Benjamin Banneker, "that nature has given to our black brethren talents equal to those of the other colors of men, and that the appearance of want in them is owing merely to the degraded condition of their existence, both in Africa and America."[98]

But the fact that Jefferson believed there were significant racial differences between Africans and Europeans did not mean, for him, that Africans were not "created equal." In speaking of the significance of the racial differences he thought existed, Jefferson wrote that

Whatever be [Africans'] degree of talent, it is no measure of their rights. Because Sir Isaac Newton was superior to others in understanding, he was not therefore lord of the person or property of others.[99]

This passage captures both the reason Jefferson thought all persons are equal and the reason he did not think that intellectual differences undermined that belief.

It is often assumed that Jefferson's primary intellectual debt was to John Locke. In fact there is good evidence that his real sympathies lay elsewhere. Although Locke's influence before 1776 was significant, it

[96] Henry Mayer, *All on Fire: William Lloyd Garrison and the Abolition of Slavery* (New York: St. Martin's Press, 1998), p. 176.
[97] Jefferson, "Notes on the State of Virginia (1781–1782)," in *Writings*, p. 206.
[98] Jefferson, "Letter to Benjamin Banneker August 30, 1791," in *Writings*, p. 982.
[99] Jefferson, "Letter to Henri Gregoire February 25, 1806," in *Writings*, p. 1202.

was also largely limited to his essay on religious toleration and his views on the nature of knowledge and the mind.[100] Much more important for Jefferson, and for the intellectual climate in general, was the "moral sense" theory of Francis Hutcheson, David Hume, and Adam Smith – all leading figures in the Scottish Enlightenment.[101] Indeed, the influence of the Scotish philosophers was pervasive. During the last years of the colonial period, America had "gone to school" with the Scots.[102] Hutcheson's famous work, *A System of Moral Philosophy*, had a huge influence on Hume, Smith, and others, and was the most widely used textbook in American colleges. Bentham thought that the moral sense theory was unchallenged throughout Europe as well.

In 1760, Jefferson began a four-year course of study at the College of William and Mary, which was founded by a Scot and was a stronghold of the moral sense theory. Jefferson's teacher was William Small, who had a huge influence on Jefferson. He used the same approach as had Smith and Hutcheson in Scotland. In his autobiography, Jefferson wrote of Small that "It was my great good fortune, and was probably what fixed the destinies of my life," that he was able to learn from Small "my first views of the expansion of science, and of the system of things in which we are placed."[103] Jefferson remained in Williamsburg for three years after graduating and was close friends with two friends of Small. Jefferson's writings, including the Declaration of Independence, clearly show the influence of the moral sense theorists who had been his teachers and from whom he had learned moral theory.

Hutcheson, Hume, Smith, and the other moral sense theorists shared the belief that morality rests not on reason but on sentiment or feeling. When people see that others are suffering or in joy, it is natural to respond in similar fashion. When people see benevolent acts, they also take delight, just as they respond negatively to evil ones. Morality is therefore not based on our own interests but instead on the natural feelings people have toward others. "We must at last acknowledge," writes Hume,

---

[100] My discussion of the intellectual influences on Jefferson is indebted to Garry Wills's *Inventing America: Jefferson's Declaration of Independence* (Garden City NJ: Doubleday and Company, 1978).

[101] Francis Hutcheson, *An Inquiry Into the Origin of Our Ideas of Beauty and Virtue* (1725) and *A System of Moral Philosophy* (1755); David Hume, *Treatise of Human Nature* (1740) and *Enquiry Concerning the Principles of Morals* (1751); and Adam Smith, *A Theory of Moral Sentiments* (1759).

[102] Wills, *Inventing America*, p. 176.

[103] Jefferson, *Autobiography*, quoted in Wills, *Inventing America*, p. 167.

that crime or immorality is not a particular fact or relation [of ideas] which can be the object of understanding, but arises entirely from the sentiment of disapprobation, which by the structure of human nature, we unavoidably feel on the apprehension of barbarity or treachery.[104]

Moral sense theorists described the perspective of morality as that of an "impartial spectator" in order to distinguish it from other points of view. "The notion of morals implies," said Hume,

> some sentiment common to all mankind, which recommends the same object to general approbation . . . When he bestows on any man the [moral] epithets of vicious or odious or depraved, he then . . . expresses sentiments in which he expects all his audience are to concur with him. He must here, therefore, depart from his private and particular situation, and must choose a point of view common to him with others.[105]

Hume summarized that common perspective as "whatever mental action or quality gives to a spectator." In the case of virtue, it is a "pleasing sentiment of approbation," and in the case of vice "the contrary."[106]

Reasoning, then, plays a different and in one respect subsidiary role in morals. Although it is "no motive for action," it does "direct" the impulse for action (which, in the case of morality, is the moral sense) "by showing us the means of attaining happiness and avoiding misery."[107] When we find ourselves moved by sympathy, reason can guide us in deciding how best to reduce the misery for which we feel sympathy. Reasoning is instrumentally important if we are to achieve our ends, though the ends derive from our feelings and our moral ends from natural feelings that we share with all other human beings. Hutcheson emphasized the same point, in explaining why opinions differ over moral matters. "Almost all our diversities in moral sentiments," he writes,

> arise from opposite conclusions of reason about the effects of actions upon the public or the affections from which they flowed. The moral sense seems ever to approve and condemn uniformly the same immediate objects, the same affections and dispositions, though we reason very differently about the actions which evidence certain dispositions or their contraries.[108]

---

[104] David Hume (1751), *An Enquiry Concerning the Principles of Morals*, in David Hume, *Enquiries Concerning the Human Understanding and Concerning the Principles of Morals*, edited by L. A. Selby-Bigge, 2nd ed. (Oxford: Clarendon Press, 1902), Appendix I, pp. 292–293.

[105] Hume, *An Enquiry Concerning the Principles of Morals*, p. 272.

[106] Hume, *An Enquiry Concerning the Principles of Morals*, p. 289.

[107] Hume, *An Enquiry Concerning the Principles of Morals*, p. 294.

[108] Hutcheson, *A System of Moral Philosophy* (1755), quoted in Wills, *Inventing America*, p. 212.

Jefferson often summarized his own moral views in strikingly similar terms. Not only did he explicitly refer to the "moral sense," but he also thought that good acts

> give us pleasure, but how happens it that they give us pleasure? Because nature hath implanted in our breasts a love of others, a sense of duty to them, a moral instinct, in short, which prompts us irresistibly to feel and succor their distress.[109]

Moral sense theory often employed the metaphor of the heart as an expression of the moral sense, a sense that was universally shared. Hutcheson, for example, wrote that "the sense of everyone's heart, and the common natural principles, show that each one has these perfect rights; nor without maintaining them can there be any social life. Sense is not unique to Europeans but is universal."[110] Jefferson spoke in similar terms, emphasizing sentiment over reason. Morals, he wrote, "are too essential to the happiness of man to be risked on the uncertain combinations of the head. [Nature] laid their foundation therefore in sentiment, not in science. That [morals] she gave to all, as necessary to all; this [rationality] to a few only, as sufficing with the few."[111]

Although he doubted the intellectual equality of Africans as a group, Jefferson did not doubt their "hearts."

> Whether further observation will or will not verify the conjecture that nature has been less bountiful to them in endowments of the head, I believe that in those of the heart she will be found to have done them justice ... we find among [African slaves] numerous instances of the most rigid integrity, and as many as among their better instructed masters of benevolence, gratitude, and unshaken fidelity.[112]

The virtues of benevolence, gratitude, and fidelity were not randomly chosen by Jefferson, much less selected as befitting "slave" morality. They are exactly the virtues that Hutcheson emphasized as central to the moral sense. So when Jefferson lists those virtues, "he is listing the cardinal virtues of moral sense theory, the central manifestations of man's highest faculty."[113] Jefferson also makes clear that the "disposition to theft with

---

[109] Wills, *Inventing America*, p. 206.
[110] Hutcheson, *A Short Introduction to Moral Philosophy* (1747), p. 143. Quoted in Wills, *Inventing America*, p. 224.
[111] Jefferson, *Papers*, Vol. 20, p. 250. Quoted in Wills, *Inventing America*, p. 187.
[112] Jefferson, *Notes*, p. 143. Quoted in Wills, *Inventing America*, p. 224.
[113] Wills, *Inventing America*, p. 226.

which [slaves] have been branded must be ascribed to their situation [of being enslaved], and not to any depravity of the moral sense."[114]

Thomas Jefferson's views of equality and slavery were complex and conflicted. He believed slavery was deeply unjust but opposed its elimination on the ground that it would lead to race war. Like Calhoun, he believed (or at least suspected) that Africans were racially inferior in various ways. But unlike Calhoun, who called equality a "dangerous error,"[115] Jefferson affirmed the moral equality of slaves. The reason was that they had the same moral sense that, he believed, was the basis of equality of all persons. The key difference between the views of Jefferson and Calhoun was therefore not over the personhood of slaves, as is sometimes supposed based on the three-fifths compromise. The real disagreement was over what equality consisted in and who is entitled to being treated as an equal.

[114] Jefferson, *Notes*, p. 142. Quoted in Wills, *Inventing America*, p. 226.
[115] Calhoun, "A Disquisition on Government," p. 55 (emphasis added).

4

Racial Equality

UNLIKE IN EARLIER CENTURIES, TODAY RACIAL EQUALITY IS *in some sense* widely accepted. But whatever consensus may exist at that abstract level evaporates when questions are raised about either its meaning or what it requires in practice. Besides disagreement about the idea of equality itself, other disputes about racial equality arise over what equality requires of government or society in general. What would a society that has achieved genuine racial equality look like? Some claim, for example, that racial equality is denied as long as there are significant differences in how racial groups fare economically or in any other important respect.

Although this chapter's primary focus is on the nature of racial equality, the discussion spills over into other related philosophical issues, including the value of persons and the ideal of social justice. My argument builds on the previous discussion of racism by linking the idea of institutional racism to the Equal Protection Clause of the Fourteenth Amendment to the U.S. Constitution. That clause, I argue, relies on an understanding of equality and the equal value of persons, and it seeks to put that understanding into practice by eliminating institutional racism. In that way, the earlier discussion of the nature of racism as racial contempt sheds light on a range of moral and legal puzzles. I conclude with a discussion of the pessimistic idea that because racism is inevitable, racial equality may be impossible.

The equal value of persons

While racial equality was historically controversial, few today would deny that in some sense all persons, including members of all races, are equal. But what, more precisely, does that claim mean? And is it justified?

Anthropologist Stephen J. Gould defends racial equality by questioning those who believe in racial differences in I.Q. scores of blacks and whites. Equality, he said, is a "contingent fact of history" and is not given a priori. In reality, he says, racial equality "just worked out that way. A hundred different and plausible scenarios for human history would have yielded other results (and moral dilemmas) of enormous magnitude. They just didn't happen."[1] But is Gould right, that racial equality is based on racial similarity and that it therefore depends on an accident of evolution? Or is racial equality something different entirely, as Jefferson supposed? I will return to Jefferson's conception shortly, but I first want to consider the views of philosophers in the utilitarian tradition, notably Jeremy Bentham,[2] and more recently Peter Singer,[3] who have a different approach to equality from Gould and others. Although they are not skeptical about equality as an ideal, they do question approaches that focus on natural rights. For them, equality is a moral ideal, which insists that actions and institutions give equal weight, or equal "consideration," to the interests of all beings who have interests.[4]

This interest-based understanding of equality would have important implications. First, because equality is simply the moral ideal of equal consideration of interests, Bentham and Singer both argue that it would follow that the interests of *all beings*, not just of persons, should be given equal consideration. An interest in avoiding pain, for instance, is of equal moral importance whether the pain is suffered by an animal or a baby. Because the interests are equal, they make the same moral demands on us.[5] Human beings are not inherently more valuable than other animals[6] because the foundation of their value is their interests, which Singer understands as the capacity for "enjoyment."[7]

---

[1] Stephen J. Gould, "Human Equality is a Contingent Fact of History," *Natural History*, Vol. 93, No. 11 (November 1984), pp. 26–27.

[2] Jeremy Bentham, *An Introduction to the Principles of Morals and Legislation* (1789).

[3] Peter Singer, *Practical Ethics* (2nd ed.) (Cambridge UK: Cambridge University Press, 1993).

[4] Singer, *Practical Ethics*, p. 18.

[5] The fact that humans may suffer emotionally at the thought of being killed can provide a reason to treat them differently from nonhuman animals that cannot suffer in that way, but it is only that fact about what people find unpleasant that justifies treating persons differently.

[6] Singer, *Practical Ethics*, p. 83; see also Peter Singer, "All Animals Are Equal," in *Animal Liberation* (New York: Avon Books, 1975), pp. 1–26.

[7] Singer, *Practical Ethics*, p. 7.

Second, and in contrast to Gould, who thinks racial equality is the idea that there are no important racial differences, this interest-based conception of equality is a purely moral idea. The truth of equality, on this conception, does not depend on there being no racial differences, for instance, in intelligence.[8] What is important for racial equality is that all persons, regardless of race, have interests that should be taken equally into account, not that they are similar in other ways. Indeed, any being with interests is entitled to have its interests weighed equally with any other equally important interests, regardless of the nature of the being. The utilitarian conception of equality questions the idea that humans are uniquely valuable since many different species of beings, besides humans, have interests.

Is either of these two ideas of equality right? When thinking about the utilitarian idea and contrasting it with Gould's approach, it is important not to confuse the *idea* that persons are of equal moral *value* with the *worth* of different persons. People differ in many ways and among these differences is their moral worth. Some people are more truthful; others are more courageous, generous, fair, or trustworthy. In that sense, they are better or more worthy people: they are more virtuous. They are, in that way, not equals of others. The idea of the equal *value* of persons, on the other hand, does not deny that some persons are more morally worthy than others. But then, on what basis might it be thought all persons, despite their different moral worth, have equal value?

As we saw in Chapter 3, Thomas Jefferson and the moral sense theorists held that the human capacity for sympathy and natural inclination to feel concern for the well-being of others provide the ground for moral and racial equality. But it is not clear that the moral sense, so understood, is enough. As utilitarians often emphasize, humans share many interests with lower animals, including interests that reflect our capacity to feel pain and pleasure. Many lower animals also are capable of sympathy and caring for others in their group. Nor are humans unique in their ability to pursue ends efficiently and rationally. Although rationality in other animals is more limited, they do often evidence it as well as benevolence. Witness problem-solving in chimpanzees and the family cohesion of elephants. Nor, finally, is it clear why having sympathetic feelings, even if it were unique to persons, should be the basis for claims that humans are uniquely and equally valuable.

[8] Singer, *Practical Ethics*, pp. 23–28.

So what might it mean to say that people are uniquely valuable? In thinking about this question of what makes persons or other things valuable, it is useful to begin with the idea of valuing a thing. When we say that a person *values* something, I will assume, we mean that the person has a positive or *pro-attitude* towards the thing. Signs of that fact, that a person values something, could be that the person wants to experience it, to spend time with it, or perhaps merely to contemplate it. Now if that is what it is to value something, what is involved in the idea that a thing (or a person) is *valuable?*

It may be tempting to think that something is valuable whenever it is valued, or perhaps whenever it is valued by a person. And indeed, one sense of "having value" just is having a price: being a valuable object in that sense means that people are willing to pay something for it. But that is not always what we mean when we say that, in fact, a thing has value. We often distinguish the question whether something is valued by a person or groups from whether it is, in fact, valuable. So we need to understand what it is for a thing to *have value* independent of whatever price it may have and whether or not people, in fact, value it.

Returning to the main issues, then, the answer to the question of what is valuable or has value depends on its being worthy of valuing. In other words, do people *have reason* to value it in virtue of properties or characteristics the thing has? Just as a person may have a reason to *do* something without being aware of the reason (e.g., to leave a building that is on fire), so too is it possible for there to be a reason for people to value something without their actually valuing it. When there is such a *reason* to value something, the thing is, *in fact*, valuable.

The reverse can also be true, because it is possible that a person might value something when it is, in fact, not valuable. Suppose someone cares deeply at every moment of the day, to know the exact time, down to the second, and spends most of every day watching a clock. Assuming the activity is not otherwise valuable (as a source of enjoyment, for instance), it seems clear that such knowledge is not something the person has *reason* to value and the activity is therefore not, in fact, valuable. Whether or not a person values something without good reason can often be controversial. My point is not that we always know or agree about the reasons to value things but rather that such reasons can exist and, in addition, that persons may be mistaken about whether the reasons do, in fact, exist.

We next need to make the familiar distinction between something having *instrumental* value, in the sense that it is valuable only as a means to something else, and its being valued in itself, that is, its having an *intrinsic or inherent* value. We normally value money, for example, not because of what it is intrinsically but because it is an instrument to get other things. Hedonists think that the only things that are intrinsically valuable are pleasant experiences, while what is inherently disvaluable are painful or unpleasant ones. Accepting that would have several consequences. It would mean not only that the only thing that is valued in itself is experiences. It would also mean that all pleasant experiences, including the joy of seeing others suffer, of dominating others, and of committing injustices, are not only valuable but equal in value with other comparably enjoyable experiences. Others take a broader view in this ancient debate about intrinsic value, and include on the list many different types of things. These can range from relationships like friendship and love to knowledge, play, aesthetic experiences, and sometimes life itself. But in looking at human beings and what they value, it does seem an oversimplification to suppose that only one thing is valued by humans. A normal life includes many different pursuits, and to insist they are arranged in some sort of hierarchy with one single value at the base seems arbitrary. I will therefore assume that persons normally value many different things and that these are not reducible to any single valued thing.

If we have a reason to value something instrumentally, then the reason makes essential reference to something else that we have reason to value in itself. All of this leaves open the question whether the reasons we have for valuing something intrinsically must ultimately make reference to human interests or needs. Or is it possible for there to be a reason to value something that is independent of any contribution it might make to human life? Although I won't defend it here, I see no reason to think that the reasons people have for valuing things must necessarily be limited in that way, to those things that might at some time become valuable to a person. Environmentalists, for instance, sometimes argue that species, ecosystems, or wilderness are inherently valuable independent of any contribution they might make to human lives. Nor is it clear that a beautiful object is valuable merely because of its potential to be valuable for persons. When thinking about what is valuable, not just valued, a bit of humility seems to be in order. Even if we were to agree that what is valuable is what an ideally rational, fully informed person would value, there is still a gap between what any actual persons might eventually come to value and what that (imagined) ideally rational person would value.

With that in mind, we return to the central questions of why persons have intrinsic value and whether the value of persons is, in some sense, equal. The issue is about reasons. Because the value of anything, including a person, does not depend on the value *attributed or given to it* by actual persons, it is possible for a person (or members of a racial group) to be valuable, yet not, in fact, be valued by other persons. But what sort of reason might there be for valuing persons intrinsically, for themselves? And how might they also be equally valuable?

People have many different properties. Besides being furless mammals, we have a range of capacities including sight, hearing, and movement. Persons also have the capacity for pleasant and painful experiences, as the utilitarians stressed. But it is not at all clear, and it indeed seems implausible to think that merely having the capacities to see, hear, and so forth in themselves gives a person value. According to utilitarians, even the capacity to have enjoyable experiences is not, in itself, valuable. Instead, it is the *actual experience* of pleasure that is valuable. Nor are the capacities I mentioned unique to persons, which means they cannot provide the reason to value persons over other creatures. So, if we think persons do have a special or "inherent" value that other animals lack (and that such a property makes us "equal"), the characteristic in virtue of which this is so must be different from the capacities people share with lower animals.

A familiar starting point to look for such a characteristic is found in the work of various Enlightenment figures (as well as in the *United Nations Declaration of Human Rights*). It is the inherent "dignity" of all persons. Critics of the moral sense theory, including Samuel Clark[9] and Immanuel Kant,[10] put greater emphasis on reason and especially its motivating role than did Hume, Hutcheson, and other moral sense theorists. Duty and morality, the critics believed, must ultimately be independent of human feelings or sympathy if morality's objectivity is to be secured. Reason's role, they argued, goes beyond enabling people to understand the consequences of their actions in the natural world. Reason also enables people to deliberate about their sentiments themselves, asking which ones are valuable. Critics thought reason can function in another way

[9] Samuel Clarke, *A Discourse Concerning the Unchangeable Obligations of Natural Religion and the Truth and Certainty of the Christian Revelation* (1706).
[10] Immanuel Kant, *Groundwork for the Metaphysic of Morals* (1785) and *Critique of Practical Reason* (1788).

as well, by motivating people to act in accordance with moral principles. Those moral powers are sometimes referred to as the "autonomy"
of persons, putting clear emphasis on the rational, deliberative powers.
Might autonomy then provide the basis for the claim that persons are
uniquely and equally valuable? And what, more particularly, is meant by
autonomy?

It is helpful in thinking about these capacities of persons to begin
with the fact that people often act intentionally, and not just by instinct.
Besides blinking an eye or yelping when injured, persons have the ability
to form and then execute (follow through on) a plan. To intend to do
anything, whether to marry or to rob a bank, requires formulating and
adopting a plan of action in the future. Intentions are therefore complex
intellectual accomplishments which differ from mere desires. We might
desire to own a new car, for instance, but without more we have not
yet formed the intention to own one. The capacity to act intentionally
therefore brings in its wake a capacity to reason.

In forming our intentions, we rely on our ability to assess reasons and
then to act in accord with them. We can therefore respond to reasons
both in the formation of our plans and in the process of their execution.
Suppose a person decides to buy a new car, then decides which car to buy
and where to buy it. Reasoning will play a role in formulating the plan
as well as later on, in the execution of the plan. More information about
the plan and its possible consequences can lead to modifications or even
abandonment of the plan.

Persons are therefore able to form and revise their intentions, based
on their ability to reason. What, then, is a capacity to reason? In the most
abstract sense, the capacity to reason is the capacity to understand that
something is a reason. And reasons are simply considerations in favor of
(or opposed to) beliefs and actions.[11] The fact that a car has no battery
is a reason – a consideration – in favor of believing it will not start; clouds
of a certain sort are a reason to believe it will rain. In addition to the
capacity to reason about the workings of the natural world, persons also
have the capacity to understand what it is rational to *do*. We understand,
for example, the fact that it may rain is a consideration in favor of taking
an umbrella, and the fact Bill made a promise is a reason for Bill to repay
the debt.

This leads us back to where we began. Rationality in the realm of actions
takes two forms, as those examples illustrate. One is instrumental, that

[11] Scanlon, *What We Owe Each Other*, p. 18.

is, reasoning about what it would be *prudent* to do. This was emphasized by the moral sense theorists. But, as rationalists emphasized, persons can also reason morally about moral principles and about their obligations and responsibilities to others as well as about the sorts of things that are worthwhile or valuable to pursue or preserve.[12] Exercising one or both of those capacities to reason forms the background of acting intentionally.

The capacities of persons to reason about what is valuable and about our duties to each other are normally assumed in our relations with people. When we give or seek advice about what to do or when we make demands on others that they respect our rights or treat others fairly, we assume they have the capacity to understand the reasons we give. This assumption – that others are rational beings – is confirmed by the fact that we do not reason with pets and small children. It is senseless to explain to an infant why he has reason to take medicine even though it tastes bad or why she should not hit her brother, or to explain to a dog why it should not chew a slipper. Having the capacity to identify and weigh such reasons is a condition of a person's being a moral agent. Without it we would be unable to act morally, that is, to decide how we ought to treat each other and how to direct our own lives toward valuable ends.[13]

This autonomy also brings the capacity to assess other people in a more global sense – not just their actions but their character and their lives generally. We often feel resentment at the actions of others, and sometimes may even conclude that others are not living decent, successful lives. More ominously, perhaps, we also have the capacity to assess *our own* actions and pursuits: "Was it wrong what I did?" and "Is what I am now pursuing really worthwhile?" are thoughts that lower animals are incapable of having. We can also ask whether or not we have talents or perseverance to achieve our goals, assuming they are worth pursuing: "Am I up to the challenge I have set for myself, or will I fail?" is again a familiar thought that autonomous beings can have and lower animals

---

[12] For Hume, reasoning is, strictly speaking, limited to enabling us to understand the natural world, though that knowledge does influence our sentiments and thereby our actions. For rationalists, the power of reason extends to providing motivations. But, in both cases, the capacity of reason is integral to morality.

[13] It is also what Rawls termed the "capacity for moral personality," which, for him, is a sufficient condition for being entitled to equal justice. The idea has a specific meaning in Rawls's book because he interprets it to refer to the ability to act in accord with rules chosen in the original position. John Rawls, *A Theory of Justice (Revised Edition)*, (Cambridge MA: Harvard University Press, 1999), p. 442.

cannot have. So, along with the capacity to reason, and to act intentionally, come these further capacities to assess the worth of others' actions
and pursuits as well as the actions and pursuits of ourselves. (I will have
more to say about the personal and political importance of these capacities later in this chapter.)

Autonomy, then, is how we might understand what makes people
uniquely and equally valuable. It is the source of our dignity, as persons.
But what justifies the idea that people's autonomy makes them uniquely
valuable?

The answer is that those who possess autonomy are able to form intentions and to make claims or demands on others, supported by reasons.
And because of that capacity, the claims that we can make should be
considered. This arises from the nature of reason itself.[14] That capacity
to assert moral claims, and especially rights, grows out of people's ability
to reason. Reasoning itself – recognized by other rational beings – is
enough. No other authority or power is needed. Reasoning beings can
both make moral demands and understand the moral demands others
make on them. The range and variety of the moral claims we make is
wide. They take such forms as insisting that our rights or legitimate interests be respected, that we are treated fairly, or that others treat us as they
would want to be treated themselves. Merely having the capacity to make
such claims on others is itself the reason to value beings that have the
capacity and to take them into moral account. Autonomous beings are
therefore unique in the sense that they are able to make claims on each
other, which in turn gives such beings value and gives others reason to
treat them with respect, as moral beings with rights.

Joel Feinberg put the point in terms of claiming rights against others.
He imagines a world in which there are no rights at all, asking how it
would differ from ours. Having rights, he concludes,

> enables us to "stand up like men," to look others in the eye, and to feel
> in some fundamental way the equal of anyone. To think of oneself as the
> holder of rights is not to be unduly but properly proud, to have that minimal
> self-respect that is necessary to be worthy of the love and esteem of others.
> Indeed, respect for others (this is an intriguing idea) may simply be respect
> for their rights, so that there cannot be the one without the other; and what

---

[14] My discussion of autonomy and rights is indebted to Joel Feinberg, "The Nature and
Value of Rights," *Journal of Value Inquiry*, Vol. 4 (Winter 1970) reprinted in *Rights*, edited
by David Lyons (Belmont CA: Wadsworth Pub. Co., 1979).

is called "human dignity" may simply be the recognizable capacity to assert claims.[15]

The fact that we in fact do value autonomy is further confirmed by the attitudes we take toward its loss. Destruction of the capacity to deliberate rationally, for instance through disease, is understood as a very grave loss, even if the person who loses it does not suffer pain or mental anguish. Indeed, there is an important sense in which diseases that destroy people's reasoning ability destroy *them*, as a moral person. As Socrates famously noted long ago, few would willingly choose to become a pig, even if that life were otherwise satisfying.

Without their autonomy, humans would also be unable to take responsibility for their actions, which is yet another reason why it is valued. Loss of autonomy would mean that there could be no genuine moral courage or other virtues, and no moral praise or blame. When we praise a dog for its courage, we do so only metaphorically. The dog was simply "trained" to run into the burning building, or it did it from some instinct. But when a person does a courageous act at great personal risk, something good has happened that would not have occurred if we had sent in a robot or even a dog. Appreciating the risk (which the dog cannot do), the person chose to go in. Autonomy is the precondition of responsibility and therefore of moral goodness. It is the basis of the unique value of persons.

But what then is the relevance of this for the second component of equality: the idea that all persons are of *equal* value? Even if possessing autonomy is a reason to value persons, what reason is there for thinking we should value equally all those who possess it? We do value persons for different reasons, and we may value some more than others. Some scientists make huge contributions while others accomplish much less. Some lives can be more or less wasted. We might even think (at least in the case of world-historical figures like Hitler and Stalin) that some lives were on balance best not lived at all. We clearly do have reason to value people differently, for their different and often unequal contributions, for their character traits, and even for their natural talents. Why does this not also apply to people's autonomy, given that some people have a greater capacity for reasoning than others? Does this therefore undermine the idea that all autonomous persons are of equal value?

[15] Feinberg, "The Nature and Value of Rights," p. 87.

To understand why it does not, we first need to distinguish a "range property"[16] from a spectral one. Many properties present a spectrum, so that we can say of a color that it is "more red than another color" or of a person that she is taller than her friend. But range properties are different. Consider, for example, the property of being within the jurisdiction of a state. It does not matter for purposes of jurisdiction if a house is near the border or sits in the exact center of a state. Both houses are equally under the jurisdiction of the state, subject to the same tax and other laws.

I suggest that autonomy works the same way, as a range property rather than a spectral one. Once a threshold has been reached, a being is autonomous and treated as an equal to all others. The fact that one person has a more highly developed capacity to reason is irrelevant for purposes of thinking about autonomy, just as being further away from a border is irrelevant to citizenship. That is not to say, however, that the underlying ability to reason cannot also be viewed as a spectral property, and in the case of children or retarded adults who have limited capacities to reason. While autonomy develops over time, once it is acquired to a sufficient extent we treat it as a range property.[17] Autonomy is different from other properties in another respect. It is only a *capacity* that persons have, which means it is a further question how it is used. Two people may both have the *capacity* to swim, for example, although one swims more often or swims better than the other. Having a capacity to do something is distinct from doing it better, or worse, than another person. So, as long as a person has the capacity to reason to a sufficient extent, that person is of equal value. Being worse at using reason to make decisions about what should be done or what is worthwhile to pursue does not make a person less than a moral equal since it is consistent with the equal value of persons that persons differ in *how much* of the capacity they possess above the minimum.

So, having autonomy (or perhaps the potential to become autonomous) makes persons uniquely and equally valuable. It also gives us a reason to treat autonomous persons differently from other beings: we must recognize them as equals. They, like all other autonomous beings, are capable of making moral claims on others, and with that comes

---

[16] Rawls, *A Theory of Justice, Revised Edition*, p. 444.

[17] Thanks to Amy Shapiro for pressing this point, although I am uncertain if she would find my answer satisfactory.

obligations of others to respect their claims. We do share with lower animals the ability to feel pain, of course, which means we have reason to avoid doing things to animals that cause pain. But it does not follow from this, nor is it true, that persons and animals are of equal value. Joining the universe of beings who deserve *some* level of moral consideration is not the same as joining a universe of beings who have equal value.

Borderline cases of autonomy do exist, however, and dealing with them poses difficult moral dilemmas. Severely retarded persons who cannot understand even simple reasons to act and form intentions lack autonomy, but other cases will be more difficult. If children in general are provided free public education, it would be wrong to deny a retarded person whatever education may be suitable for her to develop her capacities for autonomy. On the other hand, denying such a person the opportunity to participate with others in the community's political life by voting, for instance, would not seem unreasonable if the person lacks the requisite capacities to understand the world and to reason about the community's political decisions. Indeed, without a basic grasp of the political process it is not clear even whether it would make sense to speak of that person "voting" rather than merely pulling a lever. Voting assumes a capacity to understand and act intentionally based on relevant reasons. Denying others the right to sign contracts due to their diminished capacities may also be reasonable. The law may also excuse such persons from criminal sanctions on the ground that they cannot appreciate the nature of their actions.

Children are in a somewhat similar position, although the fact they have the *potential* to become fully rational, moral equals in the future is a reason to treat them differently in other respects. Although children are afforded few of the political rights reserved for rational adults (voting, free speech, privacy, and many other civil liberties are not guaranteed them), they do have other rights including the right to an education. This again seems the right approach. We need to respect people who are now or will in the future be autonomous.[18] As they become more rational and therefore more capable of exercising those rights, they are entitled to do so and to participate as equals in the political system.

---

[18] The fact that fetuses have the potential to become autonomous, valuable persons is often what makes the abortion issue difficult. (The fact that if a fetus is to be aborted, then it is *not now* a being who will become an autonomous person may also be relevant, although it may also seem to beg the question.)

What must governments do, then, if they are to respect the equal and unique value of persons? The answer begins with the ideal of justice, though I will argue that the story does not end there. Racial equality is a different ideal from justice, and its meaning extends beyond providing basic rights and opportunities. I will argue that it is best understood in terms of avoiding institutional racism, which imposes a particular burden on its victims. We begin, however, with justice.

Justice and equality

John Rawls famously begins *A Theory of Justice* with the statement that justice is "the first virtue of social institutions, as truth is of a system of thought. Just as a theory must be rejected, however elegant, if it is false, so too an institution should be reformed or rejected if it is unjust, however efficient or popular."[19] The aspect of justice on which Rawls focuses is the "basic structure" of society, by which he means the institutions that significantly influence people's life prospects by defining their rights, opportunities, and the distribution of economic and other goods. These major institutions include its constitution and laws, markets, private property, and the family.[20] As an ideal, justice is achieved with the protection of basic rights and liberties and the securing of whatever economic or other opportunities and advantages are morally required.[21]

The rights and liberties that should be protected fall into two broad categories, private and public. Private rights are ones that citizens have against each other, for example, the right not to be killed, injured, or robbed. But justice also imposes limits on government itself, and what it can do to its citizens. People should enjoy the right to speak their minds on important matters without fear of unreasonable government censorship, for instance, as well as to practice their religions and live their lives without unwarranted intrusions into their privacy.[22] Another group of public rights provides for self-government, such as voting and

[19] Rawls, *A Theory of Justice, Revised Edition*, p. 3.
[20] Rawls, *A Theory of Justice, Revised Edition*, p. 6.
[21] I mean to take no position here on what justice specifically demands but only to say that the ideal of justice refers to the correct or best answer to the question of which rights should be respected and how economic goods and opportunities should be distributed.
[22] I add "unreasonable" and "unjustified" here to emphasize the fact that the limits and scope of these rights can be controversial. I also assume, however, that we agree there are at least some reasonable limits that should be imposed on governments. Where the line is to be drawn in controversial cases is not my concern here.

running for office as well as the array of procedural rights associated with the criminal process.

The second subdivision within the realm of justice, besides public and private rights, is distributive justice. This ideal refers to the responsibility of government in the provision of educational and other opportunities and the distribution of wealth and income. Most people think, for example, that government should provide everybody with a chance for a decent education, and also see that those who cannot work are provided for. Others think distributive justice demands much more.[23]

These, then, are the main requirements travelling under the banner of justice: private rights, individual rights against governmental interference, self-government rights, and the correct distribution of educational, economic, and other advantages. Justice demands that government protect those basic rights and opportunities, and therefore governments cannot, consistent with justice, deny them either to *everybody* or to any *individual or group*. Either denial is defective on the ground of justice.

Besides protecting the rights and opportunities that justice requires, governments also provide "optional" goods ranging from water and public health to parks, roads, subsidies for industries and the arts, defense contracts, and much more. Provision of such goods and opportunities, although often important to the individuals or groups who get them, is optional in the sense that it is outside the scope of justice. Citizens do not have a *preexisting right* to parks, water systems, farm subsidies, or government contracts. A government that refuses to provide some of them may be unwise, inefficient, or imprudent, but it is not acting unjustly – as it would be if it failed to protect fundamental liberties and opportunities.

That is not to say, however, that the fact that these are optional goods from the perspective of justice means that they can be provided in any way government chooses. Depending on how they are distributed, a government could violate *equality* in its provision of optional goods such as farm subsidies, tax deductions, or public roads. If it provides farm subsidies or tax advantages only to whites, for instance, that would infringe equality without denying anything that people are entitled to receive on grounds of justice. While justice does not demand that people receive subsidies, equality insists that if government does provide them, it must do so in a certain way: but in what way?

---

[23] I will have more to say about these issues in Chapter 8, particularly the ideal of equality of opportunity.

Equality is used in a variety of different ways, and it is important not to confuse them. First, there is a familiar distinction between formal equality and substantive or outcome equality. Formal equality is the abstract requirement that persons should be treated similarly unless there is a relevant difference between them. *Substantive or outcome equality* demands equality of results along some specific dimension, for instance, rights, happiness, resources, welfare, or income.

A third type of equality, which cuts across the distinction between formal and outcome equality, is *procedural* equality. Procedural equality requires equal access to a practice governed by rules.[24] Sports and other games are examples of such processes, as are criminal trials and competitive elections. The ideal of *equality* in the context of procedures assumes a two-step process in which the procedure is first set up, and then it is run. Objections can be raised to the process at each stage. A person may think that the rules and procedures are not fair or that they were not followed. The point to emphasize, however, is that equality applies *only* in those two contexts, not to the outcome. If the rules and procedures are fair (perhaps only in the sense that they were freely accepted) and then followed, equality is silent about who should win or lose.

Political rights like voting and running for office belong in this category, as do truly competitive economic markets and civil liberties like speech, conscience, and privacy. The equal right to a fair trial is also a procedural right. Procedural equality is achieved, or not, independent of the result of the process: two defendants may be treated as equals but only one go free; two competitors may have had equal access to markets though one succeed; two candidates can have an equal opportunity to run for office but only one wins.

Disputes over educational opportunities and economic distribution often combine elements of both procedural and outcome equality. Once an educational structure is in place, for example, one that provides everyone with equal resources, even the most dedicated egalitarian would probably not insist that the outcome must be identical. To dictate ahead who will be valedictorian and who will be at the bottom of the class would not be consistent with the ideal of procedural equality because this ideal, unlike outcome equality, has no independent test for what the results of the procedure should be beyond the requirement that the procedure be open and fair.

---

[24] It is therefore what is often described as "pure" procedural justice.

People often emphasize different forms of equality in different contexts. But there is also room for disagreement within each form – about which differences are relevant in the context of formal equality, which outcomes should be substantively the same, and when someone is not being given an equal chance to participate in a fair procedure. Libertarians affirm outcome equality in the context of rights to contract, speech, and religion but deny that government should seek any form of outcome equality in the economic realm. Similarly, although the procedural right to criticize governmental policies is widely accepted as part of the electoral process, it is not agreed that this right includes the right to spend large amounts of one's own or others' resources to get elected. The distinctions I have described among formal, outcome, and procedural equality are not meant to resolve those problems but instead to identify various ideas of equality. The question remains of how to understand the ideal of racial equality. Is it a type of formal, outcome, or procedural equality? Or is it something different?

Segregation and racial contempt

I want to pursue those questions by bringing together the threads of my discussions of racism and of institutional racism. *Institutional racism* can take many forms. In the case of slavery, these included violation of private rights, failure to respect civil liberties, denial of political rights, refusal to provide educational opportunities, and much more. But however important those rights and opportunities were, their denial did not exhaust the harms of institutional racism, whether in the context of slavery or in its less egregious forms.

Suppose a legal system respects all the rights and provides for all the economic and other advantages required by justice for all races and, further, that its distribution of what I have termed "optional goods" is also consistent with the principles of equality. But now suppose that legal system also requires complete racial segregation of all its major institutions, including its educational systems, transportation facilities, and public accommodations – all the way down to its drinking fountains and bathrooms. Assume also that the separate systems are all of equal quality. It maintains, in other words, what is from the perspective of *justice* entirely equal but completely separate racial spheres. All of this, we must also imagine, is done by a scrupulously democratic political system. Both races accept the arrangement and there is no political advantage to belonging to either race.

What is wrong with such a system, if anything? *By hypothesis*, it directly
violates neither justice nor equality in the distribution of rights, opportunities, or other goods. Yet, I want to argue, the harms of such a system
are immense, not only to the affected group but to society at large.
The starting point is recognition of the fact that such a system could –
depending on the context – express public contempt for one of those
racial groups. Whether it in fact expresses such contempt depends on the
message of that segregation, that is, on how the laws and their meaning
will be interpreted. This possibility is clearly illustrated in the infamous
nineteenth-century case of *Plessy v. Ferguson* (1896).[25]

The Fourteenth Amendment, passed after the Civil War, gave explicit
expression to the ideal of equality and its requirement that states not
deprive any person of the "equal protection" of the laws.[26] Initially, courts
that interpreted the Equal Protection Clause of the Fourteenth Amendment actually obstructed congressional efforts to help newly freed slaves.
In an 1875 case, for example, the Court held that Congress lacked the
power to pass laws making it illegal for states to refuse to let blacks vote,[27]
and, in 1883, the Court invalidated public accommodation provisions in
the 1875 Civil Rights Act.[28] At the same time that the Court was weakening the Civil War amendments, the political power of those who had
fought for Reconstruction was also fading. In its place emerged southern Radicals committed to removing federal troops from the South and
to segregating, disenfranchising, and weakening the newly freed slaves.
"Jim Crow" laws were passed throughout the South, designed to protect that white supremacy. Those laws won Supreme Court approval in
Plessy, which upheld a Louisiana statute requiring segregated railroad
cars. Importantly, the law as written did not explicitly violate principles
of justice; it required provision of "equal but separate" facilities to the
"white and colored races." Homer Adolph Plessy was prosecuted under
the law when he refused to give up his seat to a white person.

Justice Brown wrote the opinion of the Court in *Plessy*. He concluded
that enforced "separation of the races" neither "violates the privileges
or immunities of the colored man, deprives him of his property without
due process of law, nor denies him the equal protection of the laws,

[25] *Plessy v. Ferguson*, 163 U.S. 537.
[26] It also promises citizenship to all persons "born or naturalized in the United States" and
provides that states should not deprive persons of "life, liberty, or property without due
process of law."
[27] *United States v. Reese*, 92 U.S. 214 (1875).
[28] *Civil Rights Cases*, 109 U.S. 3 (1882).

within the meaning of the Fourteenth Amendment." He gave essentially two reasons for this. At first, he suggested that "the statute of Louisiana is a reasonable regulation" because the Court must recognize "a large discretion on the part of the legislature" which is "at liberty to act with reference to the established usages, customs and traditions of the people, and with a view to the promotion of their comfort, and the preservation of the public peace and good order." But then he added that

> We consider the underlying fallacy of the plaintiff's argument to consist in the assumption that the enforced separation of the two races stamps the colored race with a badge of inferiority. If this be so, it is not by reason of anything found in the act, but solely because the colored race chooses to put that construction upon it. . . . If one race be inferior to the other socially, the Constitution of the United States cannot put them upon the same plane.[29]

If blacks feel that legally enforced segregation stamps them with a "badge of inferiority," the Court claimed, it is only because blacks choose to interpret it that way. Nobody, said the Court, is being wronged by segregation, as long as justice is secured and equal – though segregated – facilities are provided.[30] In his dissenting opinion, Justice Harlan (himself a Southerner) took a very different view from Justice Brown and the majority. He wrote that,

> [I]n view of the Constitution, in the eye of the law, there is in this country no superior, dominant, ruling class of citizens. There is no caste here. Our Constitution is color-blind, and neither knows nor tolerates classes among citizens. In respect of civil rights, all citizens are equal before the law. The humblest is the peer of the most powerful. The law regards man as man, and takes no account of his surroundings or of his color when his civil rights as guaranteed by the supreme law of the land are involved.

Harlan then asked:

> What can more certainly arouse race hate, what more certainly create and perpetuate a feeling of distrust between these races, than state enactments, which, in fact, proceed on the ground that colored citizens are so inferior and degraded that they cannot be allowed to sit in public coaches occupied by white citizens?. . . . [This law is] a badge of servitude wholly inconsistent

---

[29] *Plessy v. Ferguson*, 163 U.S. 537.

[30] One response is to deny that, in fact, separate but equal facilities and opportunities were, or could ever realistically be, equal. That response has a great deal of merit, but my goal here is to address the harder question I have identified, of why, even if equal justice, rights, and opportunities were achieved, segregation would *still* be objectionable.

with the civil freedom and the equality before the law established by the Constitution.[31]

Harlan believed that expressions of racial contempt deny equal protection of the law, and that segregation constituted a "badge of servitude" that assumed blacks were "inferior and degraded." The message of that law, according to Harlan, was racial contempt; the effect was humiliation and social stigmatization.

Other Supreme Court decisions reflect Harlan's position. Even before *Plessy*, the Supreme Court had described the exclusion of blacks from juries as "implying inferiority" and as "practically a brand on [blacks]."[32] When it eventually overturned legally mandated segregation in *Brown v. Board of Education*, the Court again emphasized the fact that segregation "generates a feeling of inferiority as to [blacks'] status in the community."[33]

On the other hand, we do often expect people to overlook others' prejudices as long as the prejudice does no harm. People don't have to like each other, we might think; the real question is always whether or not rights are violated. Indeed, expressions of racial or ethnic hatred by private persons are even protected by the Constitution on the ground that such speech does not harm its objects unless done in a face-to-face or threatening manner. Why not say the same thing in cases of racial segregation, as Justice Brown had suggested should be done in his *Plessy* opinion?[34]

Consider the case of segregated bathrooms: why do separate toilets for men and women not express contempt for either sex, while racially segregated ones do? The answer seems to be that we interpret sexually segregated bathrooms to express the reasonable desire of people for privacy. Knowing that these are the attitudes of the majority, expressed in law, even a person who does not happen to share those attitudes (say, a devoted member of a nudist colony) would find nothing about the sexual segregation of toilets denigrating. The situation is different, however, with race. Here, there is no reasonable explanation of laws mandating racial segregation except that they were an expression of contempt for the minority race. Like rules requiring Jews to wear special insignias,

---

[31] *Plessy v. Ferguson*, 163 U.S.at 559, 560, 562.

[32] *Strauder v. West Virginia*, 100 U.S. 303, 308 (1880).

[33] *Brown v. Board of Education*, 347 U.S. 483, 494 (1954).

[34] See John Arthur, "Stick and Stones," in *Practical Ethics*, 2nd ed., edited by Hugh LaFollette (Oxford: Blackwell Publishing, 2002), pp. 356–364.

these laws were a sign that members of a racial group were less valuable than others. The laws carried a message of impurity and inferiority.

This is important because, in addition to all of the possible inequalities associated with justice and optional goods, a social and legal system can express institutional racism in at least two other ways. First, it can require "badges" of inferiority such as wearing a yellow star. Laws and customs can also convey such messages by demanding various forms of public deference to other groups such as stepping aside on the street, not making eye contact, or using differential forms of public address. And second, even laws that are facially neutral and do not impose special burdens on any group, or even single them out for different treatment from others, can nevertheless convey contempt. My earlier account of institutional racism indicates how this works, since the judgment that a law expresses racial contempt is an interpretive judgment, focusing on institutional motivations. Laws express racial contempt when it is reasonable to understand them as *motivated by racism*, that is, as a public expression by the law-making institution of unwarranted racial hostility or indifference. To appreciate why such expressions of contempt constitute a distinct harm, and how it can conflict with the ideal of equality, we need to look once again at the basis of racial equality and dignity.

Self-respect and self-esteem

The equality of persons, I have argued, is grounded in the capacity of persons to deliberate rationally. This shared capacity enables persons to make claims on each other and is the source of their unique and equal value. But the deliberative capacity of persons to reflect on their own worth includes the capacity to *criticize* themselves, so that our sense of our own worth does not rest solely on our value as autonomous beings. That is because there is no guarantee that our lives are, in fact, successful. What we do with our autonomy – what life we lead – is also vitally important to us, along with the ability to reflect itself. Besides having a sense of our own worth as autonomous beings with the capacity to deliberate, we need to add a second attitude people can take toward themselves, which focuses on what we do with that capacity.[35]

---

[35] Although I differ in important ways from each of them, my discussion of self-respect and self-esteem has benefited from John Deigh, "Shame and Self-Esteem," *Ethics*, Vol. 93, No. 2 (January 1983), pp. 225–245; Thomas Scanlon, *The Difficulty of Tolerance* (Cambridge UK: Cambridge University Press, 2003); and Joseph Raz, "The Duties of Well-Being,"

We can begin with John Rawls's conception of self-respect, which he argues has two components.[36] One is the sense that our goals are valuable and worth pursuing, and the second is the sense that we have a reasonable prospect of achieving those (valuable) ends. To lack either of those, he claims, is to feel shame, either at our commitments or at our abilities. Self-respect, in short, is confidence and pride in what we value and who we are.

In thinking about self-respect, it is important to note that although Rawls thinks of it as a "primary good" that it is rational for all to want, there is a sense in which that is not the case. Self-respect is not something *everyone deserves*, in part because people's pursuits may not be valuable and worth seeking. A person whose goal is to dominate and humiliate others, for instance, should take no pride in himself for his ambitions or for his success in achieving them; nor should someone who enjoys inflicting (or seeing) cruelty and suffering. Or consider a drug addict whose life is dominated by the pursuit of cocaine and the high it brings, or a person who never strives or works hard at anything and who never undertakes any challenges. None of these have reason to feel self-respect. To be a genuine good, self-respect must be earned; it is a good only for those whose pursuits are in fact worthwhile. The same may be said for the second component. Confidence in one's ability to achieve an end is good for persons in general, but not when it is without any basis in fact. Nobody is advantaged by a deeply unrealistic sense of what can be accomplished or a grossly inflated self-confidence. Self-respect is therefore not, as Rawls suggests, a good for all persons. Although people may want it for its ability to help them pursue their goals, the goals must themselves be worthwhile for self-respect to be of genuine value. In that way, self-respect rides piggyback on the worth of the pursuits that it helps achieve.

There is another problem with Rawls's view. Besides the two aspects of self-respect Rawls identified – the sense that our pursuits are worthy and confidence that our abilities are sufficient – there is another attitude that is closely related to self-respect that can also be a source of shame. Imagine a girl whose grandparents came from the Old World and who feels ashamed in front of her teachers and friends when the grandparents

---

Ethics in the Public Domain: Essays in the Morality of Law and Politics (Oxford: Oxford University Press, 1994).

[36] Rawls, *A Theory of Justice, Revised Edition*, pp. 386–391. Rawls, however, understands shame too narrowly to concern only self-respect. As I argue, shame includes the feeling of lack-of-worth based on group identity, in which case what is really at stake is self-esteem and not just self-respect.

arrive at school to pick her up in their old clothes and speaking with thick accents.[37] It may be the case that she was merely embarrassed by the presence of her grandparents, wishing they had not come that day. But the feeling might cut more deeply than mere embarrassment at one event, reaching to her sense of herself as a member of that family and a descendant of that ethnic group. If that is her attitude toward herself, then her shame is not reflected in either of the two dimensions of self-respect. The child may continue to affirm her pursuits as valuable and have confidence in her abilities and talents. It is who she is, *qua member of a group with which she identifies,* that is at issue. Her shame is tied to her identity rather than to her goals or her abilities.

If this is right, then it follows that shame is broader than Rawls supposed: people can feel ashamed or unworthy based *either* on the lack of self-respect (the sense that their goals are unworthy or they have limited prospects for success in achieving them) *or* on the basis of their identification with a group. I will refer to that second sense of shame as lack of *self-esteem,* to contrast it with self-respect. Given what was said about dignity and autonomy of persons, we now have three related attitudes which I will refer to as self-worth (grounded in people's dignity and autonomy), self-respect (grounded in the sense that one's ends are worthy and confidence in the ability to achieve them), and self-esteem (the sense of acceptance if not pride in one's identity as a member of a group). The opposite of all three of these, I will say, is self-loathing.

I have said that self-worth based on dignity is always a good and that self-respect is a good unless it is based on the false assumption that one's pursuits are worthwhile or an entirely unrealistic assessment of one's abilities. What about self-esteem? Is it a universal good, whenever it is present? The answer to this is the same as for self-respect: pride in one's group is a good unless for some reason the group is unworthy and the pride therefore misplaced. A Nazi's self-esteem is not a good for the Nazi, unless we think false pride is itself valuable, and I can see no reason to think that. But assuming that there is nothing about the group that justifies condemning it, shame is unwarranted and self-esteem is a good.

I am not suggesting, however, that everyone is better off if they identify with a racial, religious, or ethnic group, though it is difficult to imagine people whose identity is not tied up with some group such as a family. Nor does self-esteem reflect an overall claim of group superiority. There

---

[37] As happened to someone I know when she was a young child.

is nothing wrong with feelings of pride in the accomplishments of one's racial, religious, ethnic, or other group whether it is demonstrated in the Black Pride Movement, in a sense of intellectual accomplishment among Jews, or in books about *How the Irish Saved Civilization.*[38] Different groups will have different strengths, and pride need not carry the connotation that other groups lack their own distinctive strengths as well. That said, however, there is also the potential that too heavy emphasis on group identity can lead to political disunity, separatism, and a self-defeating rejection of what is valuable about other cultures.[39]

The harms flowing from self-loathing (of whatever form) can be grave both to individuals and, when widespread, to society as a whole. Avoiding self-loathing is important to individuals primarily because of its effect on their lives. Successful lives depend on people's ability to achieve worthwhile ends, and unless it is excessive, self-respect is an important *asset* people have as they pursue those ends and exercise their powers of reason. Doubts about either the value of one's pursuits or one's capacities can diminish or destroy motivation. Without a sense that our pursuits are worthy and our prospects of success decent, we often find it difficult to put forth a sustained effort. That explains why self-respect is so important.

Society and law do not literally dispense self-respect or self-esteem, although they do influence both by showing people respect and esteem or, on the other hand, by treating them in ways that convey lack of respect or esteem for people. Living in a society where people of a certain type – whether it is a race, gender, sexual orientation, ethnicity, religion, color, or culture – are publicly typed as unworthy or less valuable than others encourages feelings of insecurity and alienation and undermines self-esteem as well. The depth of that damage will vary, of course, depending on the group's vulnerability to outside influences and on its own ability to support and affirm its members in the face of such assaults. Justice Thurgood Marshall, who was himself a product of segregation, explained why segregation has these effects. "Members of minority groups often respond to segregation and prejudice," he wrote, "by attempting to disassociate themselves from the group, even to the point of adopting the majority's negative attitude towards the minority."[40]

[38] Thomas Cahill, *How the Irish Saved Civilization* (New York: Random House, 1995).

[39] Arthur M. Schlesinger, Jr., *The Disuniting of America: Reflections on a Multicultural Society* (New York: W. W. Norton Co., 1992).

[40] *Castaneda v. Partida*, 430 U.S. 482, 503 (1977).

Besides harming *individuals* in the ways I have described, such expressions of contempt undermine social and political stability.[41] A stable political and legal system is one that by its nature is able to generate its own support. An unstable system creates conflict or in some other way tends to undermine support and allegiance to it. Two important sources of that stability are feelings of strong identification with institutions of government and attitudes of mutual concern for fellow citizens. By expressing racial contempt, institutional racism undermines solidarity in both respects. It makes identification by the victim group with the government and the law much more difficult to sustain, and it undermines their sense of community with other members of the society. The reason for this is clear: people tend to care about what they believe serves their own good. Institutions and practices that promote people's self-worth, self-respect, and self-esteem generate support and even affection; those that convey contempt are often themselves held in contempt. These attitudes then tend to encourage political instability.

Living in a society marked by public expressions of racial contempt also undermines stability because of its affects on the attitudes of people who are not, themselves, objects of the public contempt. When the law treats racial or other groups with contempt, it is easy for others to suppose contempt is the appropriate attitude to take toward the despised groups. Perhaps there is something about the group that makes it worthy of contempt. When that attitude takes hold, it weakens the larger population's ability or inclination to appreciate the problems faced by the victim group and often makes it more difficult to secure basic rights for those victims of institutional racism.[42]

It is important to note, finally, that because feelings of contempt depend on how laws and other social practices are interpreted, there can be disagreements over which institutional arrangements in fact express institutional racism. One group may think a law does not express racial contempt while another sees it differently. Since the harms that flow from contempt depend on how the group that is the object of the contempt

---

[41] For a discussion of the ways just institutions are also stable, as well as of stability itself, see Rawls, *A Theory of Justice, Revised Edition*, pp. 386–388 and 434–441. My own thoughts benefited from Rawls's work on the subject.

[42] It does not follow, however, nor is it true, that it is always wrong for society to express contempt. Criminal laws arguably do just that, without evidencing any form of institutionalized prejudice against those convicted of crimes. The reason these expressions of contempt are acceptable is that the condemnation is generally thought a reasonable response to what the criminal has done.

receives it, it is important to pay special attention to representatives of that group's perspective. Nonetheless, institutional racism is not present merely because a procedure results in inequalities of outcomes. Nor do legally mandated differences in treatment necessarily indicate institutional racism. As I noted, there are circumstances in which racial segregation might be interpreted differently than it was in *Brown*. And it would be even more absurd to describe laws providing for pregnancy benefits as evidencing institutional sexism because they benefit only women.

Slavery, and then *de jure* racial segregation, violated both equality and justice, though my focus here has been on equality. Slavery and other forms of racial oppression were unjust because they denied a whole range of rights and opportunities that governments should provide to everyone. Legally sanctioned segregation also caused further harms. When a government stigmatizes some members as inherently less valuable and worthy, it again denies equality in various senses. First, it treats some persons differently from others when there is no relevant difference. Second, it produces outcome inequalities indirectly, by reducing group members' sense of self-respect and self-esteem. And third, its attacks on self-respect and self-esteem can go even further, undermining the background social conditions required to work toward justice and to maintain political stability.

Institutional racism and the United States Constitution

Even slavery's most ardent defenders acknowledged that African slaves were persons, as the Constitution itself affirmed, while abolitionists and even some defenders of slavery also acknowledged that they were equals, entitled to the rights, opportunities, and public respect that flows from that status. Yet, slavery's end did not eliminate institutional racism. It continued long after the Civil War and the enactment of the Fourteenth Amendment to the U.S. Constitution with its promise that states would not deny anyone the "equal protection" of the law.

Some writers are skeptical that the search for legal equality holds promise of racial progress. Derrick Bell, for instance, urges blacks to accept "racial realism," "cast off the burden of equality ideology," and reject the "long-sought goal of equality under law."[43] Bell goes on to say,

---

[43] Derrick Bell, "Racial Realism," in *Critical Race Theory: The Key Writings that Formed The Movement*, edited by Kimberle Crenshaw, et al. (New York: New Press, 1995), p. 308 (1992).

however, that, having rejected the legal ideal of equality, we must nevertheless "maintain the struggle against racism."[44] But why suppose that the legal ideal of equality is not an ally in the fight against racism? I will argue that, correctly interpreted, it is a powerful ally.

Like other legal provisions, the Equal Protection Clause is neither self-interpreting nor self-enforcing. How then should a court use the Equal Protection Clause if it is committed to racial equality?[45] I will argue that the answer is found in the idea I developed in Chapter 1 that institutional racism is an "interpretive" concept. The purpose of the Equal Protection clause is to eliminate institutional racism.

If I am correct, and racism is an attitude of racial contempt, that might lead a skeptic to wonder how it is possible for a court to rule that a statute is unconstitutional based on institutional racism. Wouldn't that require the court to determine the motives of a legislature? Legislative bodies are not persons, after all, but collections of persons with different motives. A legislature, it may seem, cannot have a single motive. The simple answer is that institutional racism does not understand the motives of a legislature as residing in a single legislative "mind." Instead, institutional racism personifies the legislature by treating it as if it were a single person and then constructs its motives. But still, the skeptic might wonder how such a process might proceed, because its object is not the discovery of the motive of any actual person. What then are the raw materials courts use to judge the motives of a legislature? And how are the motives put together to reach a judgment about the attitudes behind legislation?

It is helpful to begin not with judicial review and racism, but with ordinary examples of statutory interpretation where it is common for judges to resolve disputes about the meaning of a law in light of the intention of legislators. One way that courts often try to do that is by looking at the legislative history, including statements of the authors and supporters of a piece of legislation as well as reports of committees from which the legislation emerged. Suppose, for example, there is a rule banning all "vehicles" from a park, and the question arises whether bicycles and motorcycles are included in that ban. If the committee that held the hearings on the rule focused on the problem of noise in parks, for example, and legislators offering the bill explained its purpose in

[44] Bell, "Racial Realism," p. 308.
[45] My discussion of these issues, especially the role of the Court in "policing" the democratic process, has benefited from John Hart Ely's *Democracy and Distrust: A Theory of Judicial Review* (Cambridge MA: Harvard University Press, 1980).

those same terms, then a court would reasonably infer that the intention of the legislature was to ban noisy vehicles – motorcycles – but not bicycles. But suppose, on the other hand, that the record of the hearings and legislative debates about the statute showed the problem the legislators sought to address was not noise, but the fact that pedestrians had been injured by bicycle and motorcycle riders. Then the court would reach a different conclusion about the intention of the legislature and decide that both motorcycles and bicycles are vehicles.

One reason it is important that judges follow the intention of a legislature is respect for democratically made decisions. Because legislators are elected, and often run on platforms that reflect the values and goals that, they claim, will guide them as lawmakers, it is right for unelected judges to defer to the intention of the legislators when deciding how to interpret the laws. But legislators also have another basis to claim authority that judges lack, besides the fact that they were elected to make these decisions. Legislative bodies pass laws after consultation with various interested groups, and often after extensive legislative hearings. When they pass a law, legislators therefore, and as a rule, have far more information than courts are capable of gathering when interpreting it. Deferring to the intention of the legislators makes sense not just out of respect for democracy but also on grounds of greater expertise.

Legislative intention is also used in determining the *constitutionality* of a law. When the Supreme Court rejected the constitutionality of a mandatory prayer or moment of silence in school, it did so on the ground that the legislature's aim was the unconstitutional one of establishing religion. "I have little doubt," wrote Justice O'Connor, "that our courts are capable of distinguishing a sham secular purpose from a sincere one."[46] *Racial* motivation is also used as a test for constitutionality of laws. When Alabama passed a law disenfranchising people convicted of a specific list of felonies and misdemeanors, the Supreme Court struck down the law on the grounds that is was motivated by a desire to discriminate against blacks by picking out crimes that blacks were believed particularly likely to commit.[47] The Court again emphasized the importance of motive when it explained that it would strike down a law if the motive of the legislature was to restrict offensive speech, even if the stated purpose was merely to

[46] *Wallace v. Jaffree*, 472 U.S. 38, 75 (1985).
[47] *Hunter v. Underwood*, 471 U.S. 222 (1985).

regulate against public "nuisance" and not to censor based on content.[48] But my real favorite (if only because of the legislators' audacity) is *Grosjean v. American Press Company*. This case tested the constitutionality of a Louisiana law requiring newspapers with a circulation above 20,000 to pay a 2-percent sales tax.[49] On its face, there seemed to be nothing wrong with a law that taxes the largest, and therefore presumably the wealthiest, newspapers. But relying on the legislative history, the Supreme Court concluded otherwise. The statute's constitutional flaw, said the Court, was that lawmakers were motivated by the desire to silence criticism of the Louisiana political establishment. It was "a deliberate and calculated device in the guise of a tax to limit the circulation of information. . . ."[50] The Court reached this conclusion in part because when introducing the bill, its legislative sponsors described it as a "tax on lying," and expressed regret that they could not find a way to exempt the one large paper that had supported Huey Long's political machine. "We tried to find a way to exempt the *Lake Charles American Press* from the advertising tax, but did not think we could do it," reported Governor Allen.[51] Although a tax on newspapers is not unconstitutional per se, reasoned the Court, one motivated by the desire to silence political enemies clearly is.

Existing legal practice often constructs legislative intentions, using the materials of the language of the statute, statements of lawmakers and others, and the apparent effects of the law. The process is a familiar one. But the story is more complicated in the case of institutional racism and the Equal Protection Clause. There, I want to argue, the Court's goal is similar but not identical to statutory interpretation. Instead of the intention of the legislature in passing the statute, the problem is to identify the legislature's motive. Does the statute reflect institutional racism?

It should be noted that I do not mean to suggest by these remarks that intentions and attitudes (such as racism) are identical, though they are relevantly similar. The difference is that intentions are goals and purposes, while racism, I have argued, names a particular attitude people sometimes have toward other persons in virtue of their membership in a racial group. Despite that difference, both are motives that can figure in the explanation of actions. When we ask: "Why did he do that?" we might

---

[48] *Arcara v. Cloud Books, Inc.*, 478 U.S. 697 (1986).

[49] *Grosjean v. American Press Co.*, 297 U.S. 233 (1936).

[50] *Grosjean v. American Press Co.*, 297 U.S. at 251.

[51] Record, *Grosjean*, p. 43. Quoted in Ely, *Democracy and Distrust*, p. 144.

hear in response either: "He wanted to show he cares" (an intention) or "He loves her" (an attitude). There is nothing surprising, then, in the idea that judges would look for racism as well as intentions. The problem is the same – to treat the legislature as if it were a single person and then judge whether racism figures in the explanation of the law's enactment. For this, however, the court has developed a more complex analytical structure.

The story begins with the Supreme Court doctrine of "strict scrutiny." As background, in the nineteenth and early twentieth century, the Supreme Court was widely criticized for striking down economic regulations by states and by the federal government during the New Deal, such as minimum wage and protections of unions, on the ground that the laws violated liberty of contract. As the Court retreated from this "Lochner Era"[52] of libertarian activism and began instead to uphold such laws, it was unclear to many how its new, more modest role would be defined. The Constitution protects a wide range of rights, including freedom of religion and speech, due process, and many others that are explicitly included in the Bill of Rights. But what role should the Court play beyond securing those basic rights?

The course the Court was to adopt was suggested in a well-known footnote to *Carolene Products*,[53] a 1938 case in which the Supreme Court case upheld the constitutionality of a federal statute prohibiting interstate shipment of "filled" milk (i.e., skim milk with vegetable oils added to increase the fat content). Although the particular case was relatively unimportant, Footnote Four, written by Justice Stone, charted a new course for judicial review that also sheds light on the role of judicial review in eliminating institutional racism.

In the first part of the footnote, Justice Stone suggested that, in the future, any legislation that *"restricts those political processes* which can ordinarily be expected to bring about repeal of undesirable legislation, is to be subjected to more exacting judicial scrutiny."[54] The idea was that although it is not the Court's primary responsibility to oversee state and federal legislatures' regulation of the economy or health and safety, it

---

[52] Named for *Lochner v. New York*, 198 U.S. 45 (1905). In the name of liberty of contract, *Lochner* overturned a New York law limiting the number of hours bakers could work.

[53] *United States v. Carolene Products*, 304 U.S. 144 (1938).

[54] *United States v. Carolene Products*, 304 U.S. at 152–153, emphasis added.

remained for the Supreme Court to insure that the political process functions democratically.[55]

Among the most obvious failures of democratic process are restrictions on voting and free speech, and the Court took an active role in both areas.[56] Besides protecting basic rights and the democratic processes, however, Footnote Four also suggested that in the future the Court would review "statutes directed at particular religious . . .or national . . .or racial minorities." The Court would do this review, he continued, by asking whether the laws reflect "*prejudice* against discrete and insular minorities" (emphasis added). If such prejudice is found, he concluded, then that would itself be evidence of a defect in "those political processes ordinarily to be relied upon to protect minorities."[57] Those words were written in 1938, at a time when the United States was beginning to confront the realities of Nazism but still had done little to make good on the promise to blacks made after the Civil War that no state shall deny its people "equal protection of the laws."

After Stone's *Carolene Products* opinion, the Court took its first, halting steps to address problems of racism and prejudice as it developed the doctrine of strict scrutiny. A key case, *Korematsu v. United States*, involved the U.S. military's World War II policy of interning Japanese-Americans living on the West Coast. Although the Court upheld the law on grounds of national security, it adopted what has now become the standard methodology used by the Court in Equal Protection cases. It held that laws directed at a racial group are "immediately suspect," and subject to "strict judicial scrutiny" by the Court. Although public necessity "may sometimes justify the existence of such restrictions" (as it did in *Korematsu*), concluded the Court, "racial antagonism never can." [58] The difficulty, of course, is how to identify "racial antagonism."

The Court's answer is provided in two stages. The first step is to identify groups that are in need of special judicial protection against the majority ("suspect classifications" or "suspect categories" in the Court's

---

[55] For a discussion of the concept of democracy and its defects, see John Arthur, *Words That Bind: Judicial Review and the Grounds of Modern Constitutional Theory* (Boulder: Westview Press, 1992), chapter 2.

[56] Important voting cases include *Carrington v. Rash*, 380 U.S. 89 (1965); *Dunn v. Blumstein*, 405 U.S. 330 (1972); *Kramer v. Union Free School District*, 395 U.S. 621 (1969); and *Reynolds v. Simms*, 377 U.S. 533 (1964). Major cases involving free speech were *Brandenburg v. Ohio*, 395 U.S. 444 (1969) and *New York Times v. Sullivan*, 376 U.S. 254 (1964).

[57] *U.S. v. Carolene Products*, 304 U.S. at 152, footnote 4.

[58] *Korematsu v. United States*, 323 U.S. 214, 216 (1944).

terminology). Racial groups, and especially African-Americans, are obvious examples, such as Japanese-Americans in *Korematsu*. How are such groups to be identified as needing special judicial protection? Stone's suggestion that such groups may best be identified by focusing on their discreteness and insularity, although helpful, is only a rough start. He was no doubt thinking of African-Americans and perhaps also Eastern European Jews, both of whom were fairly easy to distinguish from others and were relatively isolated. There is no reason to think that the only potential victims of racial antagonism would be members of a group that are segregated from the rest, or even easily identified. Distinguishing the groups that trigger strict scrutiny, therefore, cannot be done without an understanding of both history and the current political scene.

Once it is clear that the law has an adverse impact on a suspect category of persons, "strict scrutiny" is triggered. This means that the law in question must pass two tests if it is to survive constitutional challenge. To pass the first test, the purpose of the law must not only be a legitimate one for the government to be pursuing, but it must also be a (relatively) important goal. To pass the second test, the law must be narrowly tailored to fit that objective. This means that if the objective could have been reasonably accomplished without disadvantaging a racial minority, then the law or regulation is again struck down. The law cannot, in other words, be overbroad, in the sense that the costs it imposes on a suspect class are unnecessarily high, given the significance of the goal the law is meant to serve.

By going through that analytical process, strict scrutiny enables judges to identify laws that reflect prejudice. Without such "searching judicial scrutiny into the justification" for a law, Justice Sandra Day O'Connor wrote, "there is simply no way of determining what classifications are 'benign' and what classifications are, in fact, motivated by illegitimate notions of racial inferiority or simple racial politics."[59]

Beginning in the middle of the last century, the Warren Court applied strict scrutiny analysis to a range of laws disadvantaging African-Americans, and it did so in just the way, and for the reasons, I have described: as an effort to root out institutional racism understood as an interpretive concept. The most famous case was *Brown v. Board of Education*, which declared legally segregated public schools to be a denial of

---

[59] *City of Richmond v. J. A. Croson Company*, 488 U.S. 469, 493 (1989).

the equal protection of the laws guaranteed in the Fourteenth Amendment.[60] Subsequent cases struck down laws mandating segregation of other types of public facilities, and in 1967 the Court finally overturned a Virginia statute outlawing interracial marriage.[61] Each of these laws manifested institutional racism in the form of indifference or, more often, explicit contempt for persons based on their race. Because of the contempt that the racism lying behind the laws expressed, their harm was of a special sort, different from the harm caused by laws that *merely* provided poorer facilities or denied basic rights. Separate but equal cannot, said the Court, ever be consistent with equal protection.

This process of applying strict scrutiny analysis as a means of "smoking out" prejudice and racism shows that the Equal Protection Clause forbids institutional racism (and also confirms that my account of racism fits with judicial practice). Strict scrutiny is the analytical structure the Court uses to determine the motivation behind the law.[62] It is a device of construction that is neither simple nor uncontroversial. To call an institution racist is to personify it by treating it as if it were a single person who enacted a law. The question is then asked whether we would reasonably conclude that an action taken by that body was motivated by racism.

It is helpful to compare the process of constructing the intention of a legislative body with the interpretation of other things that represent the collective actions of many people, such as a play or movie. As with all interpretation, including interpretation of others' words, we begin by assuming the object we are interpreting serves a purpose or goal. We can do this despite the fact that we know that a movie, for example, is the product of many writers, producers, actors, and editors all working together in an environment where no single person is completely responsible for all aspects of the finished product. Similarly, although judges know that there was no single legislator whose motives they are interpreting, they, too, treat the statute or regulation as if it were the decision of a single person. Justice O'Connor hinted at this idea – that the motive of the legislature is a construction based on its "personification" – in a case striking down the school prayer/moment of silence requirement. "The relevant issue," she wrote, "is whether an objective observer, acquainted with the text, legislative history, and implementation of the statute, would

---

[60] *Brown v. Board of Education*, 347 U.S. 483 (1954).

[61] *Loving v. Virginia*, 388 U.S. 1 (1967).

[62] Thanks to participants in the Oxford University Seminar in Legal Theory, Trinity Term 2003, and especially to Nicos Stavropoulos for useful comments.

perceive it as a state endorsement of prayer in public schools."[63] In posing the question that way and asking if an "objective observer" would, hypothetically, perceive the action as "endorsement," she is not (necessarily) claiming that any individual lawmaker intended to endorse religion. Nor is she assuming that there is a separate legislative "mind" with its own motives.

The problem posed by strict scrutiny of racial motives is similar. It is to construct the motive by asking whether the act of passing the law, taken by the legislature as a whole, is *reasonably interpreted* as motivated by racism. Statements by legislators expressing their motives, especially ones who wrote and supported the law, are relevant but are not necessarily conclusive. The ultimate motive is constructed out of all the relevant raw material, including the statements of legislators, the language of the statute, the historical circumstances of its passage, the purposes it apparently serves, and the alternatives that were available. Just as explicitly stated racist motives of one or more lawmakers are not *necessary* to establish institutional racism, neither are they *sufficient* to do so. There may be many other lawmakers who voted for the law for different reasons. But more importantly, the key question is how to interpret their collective action, not the motive of persons. That interpretation of the state's action – passing the statute – is not reducible to any legislator's *actual* psychological state, although evidence of racist attitudes of members can sometimes be decisive and is always relevant.

Laws and regulations have different effects on different groups, and Equal Protection does not demand that laws must never disproportionately harm an historically disadvantaged racial or other group. Regulations requiring that firefighters be able to carry substantial amounts of weight have a disproportionate effect on women, while university admissions criteria like grades and test scores can also affect racial and ethnic groups differently. Or to take a harder case, suppose a restaurant decided to ban beards on waiters, and that this ban disproportionately harms blacks, who more frequently than others suffer from a skin disease that makes shaving difficult.[64] Based on those facts alone, none of those laws is inconsistent with Equal Protection. Merely showing disparate impact is insufficient, standing alone, to justify the charge of institutional racism. The Equal Protection Clause does not demand outcome equality.

[63] *Wallace v. Jaffree*, 472 U.S. 38, 76 (1985).
[64] I owe this example to Paul Bou-Habib.

On the other hand, we also know that racism can be unconscious as well as conscious, and we may find on closer examination that members of a legislative body were moved by attitudes that were hidden even from legislators themselves. The difficulties that can arise in constructing legislative intentions is nicely illustrated in the well known 1976 Supreme Court decision of *Washington v. Davis*.[65] The issue in *Davis* was the constitutionality of a test that the District of Columbia police department used to assess applicants for jobs. "Test 21" had been designed by the U.S. Civil Service Commission to evaluate verbal ability, vocabulary, and reading comprehension. Black applicants scored significantly lower on the test, so that fewer blacks were able to enter the police training program. The question that the Justices faced, as explained by Justice White, grew out of the fact that the "central purpose" of the Equal Protection Clause is the "prevention of official conduct discriminating on the basis of race." He then added, again consistent with my institutional racism account of equality, that "such an invidious discriminatory purpose, if it exists, must be inferred from all the relevant facts" and that among the most important will be any "unequal burden that a law places on a minority." However, White emphasized that "disproportionate impact" on a racial minority is insufficient to prove racism. There is nothing in the Constitution that prevents the government of Washington, DC from "seeking modestly to upgrade the communicative abilities of its employees rather than to be satisfied with some lower level of competence, particularly where the job requires special ability to communicate orally and in writing." The test was held constitutional even though fewer blacks than whites passed it.

But it does not follow that the enterprise of analyzing what motivated the legislature to pass a law is futile. Nor does it follow that judges should set aside their convictions when confronted by those who disagree. As I have stressed throughout, it is always possible for skeptics to raise doubts by demanding further justifications. But until skeptics provide a better solution to the problems, their skepticism remains beside the point. The fact there is no algorithm that we can use to calculate the motives of a legislature does not imply that all positions are equally reasonable.

The application of strict scrutiny may have surprising implications, cutting across familiar political divisions. For instance, race per se is not a suspect classification. Strict scrutiny is triggered only if there is reason to believe that racism explains the action of the legislature, and

[65] *Washington v. Davis*, 426 U.S. 229 (1976).

many laws that refer to race do not even suggest racism. Why would a legislature made predominantly of one race pass a law that is motivated by racism against itself, for example? That clearly implies there is no Equal Protection basis on which to criticize affirmative action policies benefiting a minority. Whatever the merits of such policies, it is difficult to see how *preferences* for African-Americans, or any other minority in admission and hiring, might be motivated by racism.[66] Strict scrutiny should not be triggered by racial classifications alone.

Although it has traditionally treated race in general as a suspect classification, the Supreme Court indicated recently that it is rethinking that position, albeit not explicitly. In *Grutter v. Bollinger*, the Court upheld the University of Michigan Law School's affirmative action program. It said that "not every decision influenced by race is equally objectionable" and that the purpose of strict scrutiny is still to examine "the importance and the sincerity of the reasons advanced by the government decision maker for use of race in that particular context."[67] Although the Court did not *say* that it was not subjecting the University to strict scrutiny, it said it was giving "deference to the University's academic decisions," adding that "good faith on the part of a university is presumed absent a showing to the contrary."[68] But, of course, "deference" is the logical opposite of strict scrutiny. With this decision the Court has in effect rejected its long-standing position that race always triggers strict scrutiny.

Furthermore, those who support affirmative action policies often also support aggressive legal efforts to use busing and other tools to force desegregation of schools, even when the segregation results from housing patterns and not from legally mandated segregation. On my understanding of Equal Protection, however, segregated schools are not unconstitutional unless there is reason to believe they resulted from institutional racism. De facto school segregation that grows out of nondiscriminatory housing patterns, for instance, does not offend the Equal Protection Clause. Significant numbers of blacks have recently been reported to be moving into the new Hunters Brooke subdivision near Washington, DC, for instance, where houses start at $400,000.[69] A resulting majority-black school would not be the product of institutional racism. Other cases of segregated housing will be more difficult to assess, of course,

---

[66] I discuss both the advantages and the costs of affirmative action policies in Chapter 8.

[67] *Grutter v. Bollinger*, 539 U.S. 306, 327 (2003).

[68] *Gruttner v. Bollinger*, 539 U.S. at 328, 330.

[69] "Federal Jury Indicts 5 in Subdivision Fires in Maryland," *New York Times*, January 4, 2006, p. A. 15.

and may suggest private violations of antidiscrimination laws if not also government infringement of Equal Protection.

Institutional racism produces great harms, including when it travelled under the banner of "separate but equal." Understood as an "interpretive" concept, I argued that it is similar to individual acts of racism: both are expressions of racial contempt. I also argued that the traditional judicial doctrine of strict scrutiny is designed to "smoke out" institutional racism by examining the motives of a legislature in passing laws that result in racial differences in outcomes. Understanding racism and institutional racism in this way throws light not just on those subjects but also on the idea of equal protection found in the U.S. Constitution. The Equal Protection Clause asks courts to be aggressive where institutional racism may be present but restrained when it is absent.[70]

Is racism natural?

I want to end this chapter by considering the pessimistic thought that equality is impossible and that racism is a natural feature of the human psyche. Perhaps the most influential defender of the idea that racism is natural is Pierre L. van den Berghe, who argues that humans instinctively sort people according to race, distinguishing members of their own race from the "other." Not only do humans tend to distinguish levels of *kinship*, but they also tend to behave either nicely or nastily toward others in accordance with racial differences. The more people look like relatives, the more humans instinctively care about them. "The biological basis for nepotism," writes van den Berghe, "has now been firmly established in hundreds of social species of both vertebrates and invertebrates. Indeed, nepotism is one of the main mechanisms of sociality in all known social organisms."[71]

This is explained by evolution. In the prehistoric world, where small groups of hunter/gatherers wandered and occasionally met each other, and where it was common to respond to outsiders violently, it was important to learn to identify members of one's own group. That became instinctive in some, who were then able to survive and reproduce, producing future generations with the same ability and the same instinct to favor those who look like themselves.

---

[70] Unless, of course, other fundamental rights are at stake.

[71] Van den Berghe, "Does Race Matter?" Reprinted in Boxill, *Race and Racism*, p. 104.

This is relevant to race, according to van den Berghe, because humans (and other animals) focus on differences that are easily observable, including skin pigmentation, facial features, and hair. Looking across a field, he points out, it is difficult to distinguish between two Europeans but much easier to tell an African or Asian from a European.

Some people have also suggested there is further evidence for the idea that race consciousness is natural. Lawrence Hirchfeld is a psychologist who studies the behavior of young children, and his studies suggest that children show an early, strong tendency to sort out people according to their race.[72] The extent of most people's racial consciousness is also suggested by the "Implicit Association Test." This online test was developed by psychologists Mahzarin Banaji and Anthony Greenwald and has been taken by thousands of people.[73] The test has consistently shown that nearly three out of four whites and Asians, including those who describe themselves as without racial bias, have negative associations with images of blacks. The test measures how quickly people are able to identify positive and negative ideas like evil, love, and failure with photographs of black and white faces, and the results show that the ability to make the association quickly depends on race. More recent work suggests that the parts of the brain that are active when people experience fear and anger are also more active when people see images of blacks, which perhaps explains the differences that the test has uncovered. Interestingly, however, that heightened activity is not present when faces of familiar and friendly faces, such as comedian Bill Cosby, are shown, suggesting that the reactions may be learned rather than innate. Like many other aspects involving human psychology and race, the extent of human's natural tendency to perceive racial differences and to feel differently toward different races is very much unsettled.

It is worth emphasizing that these attitudes of fellow-feeling toward one's own group and hostility toward outsiders might attach to *any* significant difference in appearance, which means that such attitudes need not be limited to natural differences typically associated with race. People might pay attention to cultural and social differences, such as body scarring, size, physical bearing, or even dress and other markers of cultural differences. The most that can be said is that if these results are

---

[72] Lawrence Hirschfeld, *Race in the Making: Cognition, Culture, and the Child's Construction of Human Kinds* (Cambridge MA: MIT Press, 1996). It should be noted that Hirschfeld emphasizes both the biological and the social factors that contribute to this tendency.
[73] See http://www.projectimplicit.net/. Accessed on March 8, 2007.

true, phenotypical differences in skin color, facial structure, and the like are among the differences that people instinctively notice: race, in that sense, naturally matters to people.

Of course, there is no sense in which these findings, even if they prove true, either excuse or justify racism or racial inequality. People have all kinds of desires and instincts, some of which are nice while others are not, but having a desire to prefer people who look like us, even a strong desire, is not a compulsion. In principle, even the strongest desires do not compel or force people to act, as if they were being swept away by water currents they cannot resist. Nor would such natural race consciousness – if it existed – serve as a *justification* for racial contempt. Having discovered a strong desire in ourselves to do something, it is still always possible to raise the question: shall I act on that desire?

The implication of such research, insofar as it might prove true, is that we may be up against a more serious challenge than is sometimes supposed as we attempt to eradicate racism and promote racial equality. That conclusion is a far cry, however, from the fatalistic view that nothing can be done to reduce racism, let alone the conclusion that because it is "natural" it must be justified. There is nothing in the explanation of racism that would justify it.

Indeed, racism is not an insoluble problem, whatever its origins. We already have on hand a variety of resources to address it. If we are worried about racism, we have available two different strategies, one procedural and one cognitive. Racism among jurors is a familiar example. We can make certain that the jury is racially balanced, for example, to produce the best chance for a fair trial. Outside the context of law, we also often use procedures that insure racial anonymity, for instance, as well as making provisions for reviewing decisions. Besides such procedural remedies, we might also try to address the problem cognitively, by making people aware of their attitudes. Schools and other institutions have worked hard in recent years to reduce or eliminate racist attitudes.

These two weapons, procedural and cognitive, suggest that even if the pessimists are correct and the fight against racism is a fight against our own natural instincts, it is not a lost cause. Perhaps there are limits, if these researchers are right, to how fair or impartial individual people can be. But we may at least hope that social practices, institutions, and laws will be developed that significantly reduce racism and promote racial equality.

5

Poverty and Race

"IN SPITE OF DRAMATIC CIVIL RIGHTS MOVEMENTS AND PERIODIC victories in the legislatures," writes law professor Derrick Bell, "black Americans by no means are equal to whites. . . . The reality is that blacks still suffer disproportionately higher rates of poverty, joblessness, and insufficient health care than other ethnic populations in the United States."[1] Bell is right: in 1990 poverty among blacks was roughly three times that of poverty among whites, and the average family income of native-born U.S. whites, $35,975, compares with $20,209 for African-Americans.[2] Figures in the most recent census changed little, with 22.1 percent of African-Americans still living in poverty.[3]

The official U.S. government definition of poverty dates back to 1960. It is simply the cost of feeding a family multiplied by three. For a family of four, in 2006, it was just over $19,000 per year. Many think that the definition is an inadequate measure of economic well-being, although their reasons differ. Some emphasize that it ignores other benefits, such as food stamps, tax credits, and housing subsidies. Others stress that it ignores costs such as childcare and transportation to work, as well as the wide variations in cost of living due to housing costs, for example. The question on which I want to focus is not how to define poverty, however, but how to explain differences in poverty rates among groups, in particular between blacks and others. Whatever the problems with the

---

[1] Bell, "Racial Realism," in *Critical Race Theory*, edited by Crenshaw, et al., pp. 302, 308.

[2] Thernstrom and Thernstrom, *America in Black and White*, p. 542. Figures from the U.S. Bureau of Census (1990).

[3] Joseph Dalaker, U.S. Bureau of Census, Current Population Reports, Series P60–214, *Poverty in the United States: 2000* (Washington DC: U.S. Government Printing Office, 2001), p. 4.

definition, it is clear that living in poverty means living on a very meager income.

Many point to contemporary racism and racial oppression as the explanation. In a book titled *White Racism*, the authors assert that most white Americans living today have "absorbed racist attitudes" and that "racist views are a normal part of being an American."[4] Though less open and blatant than in the past, racism is said to have subtly embedded itself in institutions that continue to disadvantages blacks.[5]

It is also sometimes assumed that racism's effects (whether contemporary, historic, or both) are measured by those racial disparities in income or other goods. Indeed, the explanation of all inequality is racism. Kimberle Crenshaw, for example, claims that differences in income, employment, and other measures of well-being represent "black subordination . . . and the effects of racial oppression."[6] She terms this the "expansive" view of racial equality, which she describes as "equality as a result."[7]

But is the reason that poverty is not addressed that whites are afflicted with a subtle form of racism? There is reason to doubt that conclusion. Poverty is not a problem faced exclusively, or even mainly, by blacks. Twelve percent of all American households are officially defined as below the poverty line. Although there is a higher *rate* of poverty among blacks, the majority of those in poverty are white. If the failure to eliminate poverty shows unjustified indifference, it is indifference toward *poor people in general* and is not racism unless people are mistaken about the racial make-up of those in poverty. The argument also assumes that poverty can be readily eliminated, without damaging side-effects. Some argue that poverty programs have made the situation worse by encouraging other social ills. Others think redistributive taxation is inefficient or unjust, and would oppose welfare transfers for those reasons.[8] As I will argue, the causes of poverty are immensely complex, and the idea that we have a

---

[4] Feagin, Vera, and Batur, *White Racism*, p. 236.

[5] See, for example, Charles R. Lawrence, III, "The Id, the Ego, and Equal Protection: Reckoning with Unconscious Racism," p. 317. See also Derrick A. Bell, Jr., *And We Are Not Saved: The Elusive Quest for Racial Justice* (New York: Basic Books, 1987).

[6] Kimberle Crenshaw, "Race, Reform, and Retrenchment: Transformation and Legitimation in Antidiscrimination Law," in *Critical Race Theory*, edited by Crenshaw, et al., p. 105.

[7] Crenshaw, "Race, Reform, and Retrenchment," in *Critical Race Theory*, edited by Crenshaw, et al., p. 105.

[8] Robert Nozick, *Anarchy, State, and Utopia* (New York: Basic Books, 1974), is perhaps the best known philosopher who defends this position. Many others including public officials and some black intellectuals do so as well. Thomas Sowell, *The Vision of the*

solution available and all that is needed is to implement it, while we all wish it were true, is not.

Recent data suggest that people who oppose antipoverty and similiar government programs do so not because they are racists but because they believe that the solutions will not work or should be rejected for some other reason. According to the authors of one study,

> if the opposition to efforts to improve the social and economic position of blacks through government action consisted only, or even primarily, of bigots, the problem of race would be far less pervasive than it is. . . . Thinking of the problem of race politics as a problem of prejudice trivializes the difficulties because most people who oppose more government spending on behalf of blacks are not bigots.[9]

Clearly we need to understand the nature and causes of the problems we face before we can effectively address them. To do that, I want to look first at economic disparities among groups defined by race and by other criteria. If current racism is not at the root of black poverty, then what can explain it?

Economic inequality and groups

Significant economic differences can be found among many different cultural and ethnic groups. The figures are striking. Recently the median family income of Americans of Japanese and Chinese descent was $52,728 and $56,762, respectively – far *above* the $35,974 figure for whites. There is also a wide variation among white ethnic groups: Hispanics of Cuban decent earn more than whites in general ($37,452), and Greek-Americans do much better than Irish-Americans.[10] In 1970,

---

Anointed: Self-Congratulation as a Basis for Social Policy (New York: Basic Books, 1995) is an example of the latter.

[9] Paul M. Sniderman and Thomas Piazza, *The Scar of Race* (Cambridge MA: Harvard University Press, 1993), p. 105.

[10] Thernstrom and Thernstrom, *America in Black and White*, p. 542. Figures from the U.S. Bureau of Census (1990).

Jewish families earned 172 percent of the average income for all American families,[11] and in 1988 the per capita income of Jews had grown to almost twice that of non-Jews.[12]

One reason for these differences in income levels is reflected in the occupations people typically pursue. One study found that 40 percent of the pilots in the Czarist Russian army were ethnically German, despite the fact that Germans comprised only 1 percent of the population of Russia. Similarly, "Jews have predominated in the manufacturing of clothing in medieval Spain, the Ottoman Empire, Argentina, the United States, and other countries."[13] Another study concluded that similar patterns are present in all societies. They universally "exhibit a tendency for ethnic groups to engage in different occupations, have different levels (and often different types) of education, receive different incomes, and occupy a different place in the social hierarchy."[14]

Education also helps explain poverty among blacks. Although blacks do now graduate from high school in levels approaching whites (83.7 percent),[15] less than 13 percent of African-Americans complete college. Almost twice as many whites, roughly 25 percent, have a college degree.[16] According to another study, titled "The Big Payoff," over a lifetime, black college graduates can expect to earn $850,000 more than blacks who did not graduate from high school and $1,700,000 more if they have a graduate or professional degree.[17] So while it is true, as Orlando Patterson put it, that a six-fold increase [since 1940] in college completion that leaves

[11] Daniel Farber and Suzanna Sherry, *Beyond All Reason: The Radical Assault on Truth in American Law* (New York: Oxford University Press, 1997), p. 56 (quotes 1970 Census data).

[12] Seymour Martin Lipset and Earl Raab, *Jews and the New American Scene* (Cambridge MA: Harvard University Press, 1995), p. 26.

[13] Thomas Sowell, *Affirmative Action around the World: An Empirical Study* (New Haven: Yale University Press, 2004), p. 7.

[14] Myron Weiner, "The Pursuit of Ethnic Inequalities Through Preferential Policies: A Comparative Public Policy Perspective," in *Independence to Statehood: Managing Ethnic Conflict in Five African and Asian States*, edited by Robert B. Goldmann and A. Jeyaratnam Wilson (London: Francis Pinter, 1984), p. 64.

[15] Phillip Kaufman, Martha Naomi Alt, and Christopher D. Chapman, National Center for Educational Statistics, *Dropout Rates in the United States, 2000*, NCES 2002–114 (Washington DC: U.S. Department of Education, 2001), p. 20.

[16] Orlando Patterson, "The Paradox of Integration," *New Republic*, November 6, 1995. Reprinted in *Color Class Identity: The New Politics of Race*, edited by John Arthur and Amy Shapiro (Boulder: Westview Press, 1996), p. 27.

[17] Jennifer Cheeseman Day and Eric C. Newburger, *The Big Payoff: Educational Attainment and Synthetic Estimates of Work-Life Earnings, Current Population Reports*, P23–210 (Washington DC: U.S. Census Bureau, 2002).

African-Americans "among the most educated persons in the world, with median years of schooling and college completion rates higher than those of most West Europeans is nothing to sniff at,"[18] educational disparities remain an important factor in understanding economic differences between blacks and others.

Although graduation rates and vocational choices are important, there are other important factors. One is that even people working in the same general profession or job, with the same level of education, often pursue paths that lead to different income levels. One business school or law school graduate might go to work for a large corporation with a big salary while another works to lessen innercity poverty, for example. Blacks (and women) who are employed as college professors tend to be in the humanities and social sciences while white males are often found in higher paying areas like engineering, math, science, and business.[19] Still another contributing factor that helps explain group-based economic differences is age: people who are between the ages of 45 and 54 earn 47 percent more than people aged 25 to 34. When the average age of different groups varies, the average income will naturally follow suit. Jews are, on average, older than most other groups in the workforce, including blacks, which explains part of the difference in earnings between those two groups.

Marital status and gender are other factors. As long ago as 1981, black married couples with a college education actually earned slightly *more* than white married couples with the same education. Similarly, female black college graduates earn as much as white female college grads.[20] Yet, black males, on the other hand, earn on average only 77 percent of comparably educated white males.[21] This is especially true in the case of native-born African-Americans. How, then, are we to understand those and other racial disparities?

---

[18] Patterson, "The Paradox of Integration," p. 67.

[19] Men earn more than 90 percent of the Ph.D. degrees in engineering, for example, and more than 80 percent in the natural sciences. In economics, the proportion of men to women is 9:1. Figures taken from statistics in the *Chronicle of Higher Education*, quoted in Sowell, *The Vision of the Anointed*, pp. 39–40.

[20] Jonathan Jacobson, et al., U.S. Department of Education, National Center for Educational Statistics, *Educational Achievement and Black-White Inequality*, NCES 2001–061 (Washington DC: U.S. Government Printing Office, 2001), p. 17.

[21] U.S. Bureau of Census, *Current Population Reports: March 1995* (Washington DC: Government Printing Office, 1996), table 9. Quoted in Thernstrom and Thernstrom, *America in Black and White*, p. 445.

One explanation of the causes of racial differences was made famous by the book *The Bell Curve*. In it, Richard Hernstein and Charles Murray argue that genetic differences in the I.Q.s of people of different races explain economic success. That argument is controversial, and for good reason. No decent person wants it to be true. I will term the idea that there are natural, racial differences in I.Q. the "repugnant hypothesis."[22]

Race and I.Q.: The repugnant hypothesis

Although it comprised only part of *The Bell Curve*, which dealt generally with the importance of I.Q. in explaining poverty, unemployment, crime, and other social problems, the repugnant hypothesis dominated discussion and reviews of the book. It also gave it a degree of infamy. The authors begin by stressing the fact that I.Q. scores help explain poverty in general, independent of race. For example, single white women with I.Q. scores in the bottom 20 percent have a 70 percent chance of being poor, while single white women with high I.Q.s have only about a 10 percent possibility of poverty. White women with an I.Q. in the bottom 20 percent also constitute 55 percent of those who go on welfare within a year of the birth of their first child, while those in the top 20 percent of I.Q. account for only 1 percent of those on welfare.[23]

It is also widely accepted that African-Americans score, on average, approximately 15 points, or one standard deviation, below whites and Asians on I.Q. tests. The same results occur on other similar tests, such as the Scholastic Aptitude Test (SAT).[24] The average white student scores higher than 84 percent of black students, while the average black student scores higher than only 16 percent of white students.[25] (Asians score higher than whites on mathematical tests but not verbal tests.)[26] This racial difference is also not accounted for by economic or other obvious

[22] Adapting a phrase from Derek Parfit, *Reasons and Persons* (Oxford: Oxford University Press, 1984). Parfit speaks of the "repugnant conclusion."
[23] Figures in this paragraph are from various sources, quoted in Richard J. Herrnstein and Charles Murray, *The Bell Curve: Intelligence and Class Structure in American Life* (New York: Free Press, 1994), pp. 138, 149, 194, 198.
[24] It is disputed whether all of the differences in I.Q. scores can be explained by environmental factors or whether, as *The Bell Curve* claimed, some of the difference is natural. Although I will have something to say about that issue, in any case the dispute is not relevant here unless lower I.Q. scores can somehow themselves be traced to past racism. Given the variety of different, competing explanations of I.Q. scores, in addition to genetic/racial ones, I will argue, that possibility seems unlikely.
[25] Hernstein and Murray, *The Bell Curve*, p. 269.
[26] Hernstein and Murray, *The Bell Curve*, pp. 272–275.

166

differences. Although in all groups, I.Q. scores rise as incomes rise, the racial differences in the scores do not diminish substantially. Relatively wealthy black students score lower than poor white students, and black students from families with relatively high incomes also score lower on I.Q. tests than poorer Asians.[27]

I.Q. also matters within racial groups. The differences in annual incomes between blacks and whites *with similar I.Q.s* is small; just over $500 per worker. The real question, then, is not whether there are racial differences in I.Q. or whether I.Q. differences account for some of the income differences. Both of those are accepted. The issue is how to explain the I.Q. differences.

The repugnant hypothesis claims that the reason for the differences in I.Q. scores is rooted in genetic differences between races. Those who defend the hypothesis emphasize the importance of genes in explaining I.Q. in general. Identical twins raised in different families have very similar I.Q. scores – much more similar than they have with their adopted brothers and sisters raised in the same family. Siblings who are not identical twins but were also raised apart show a less significant correlation in I.Q. than identical twins (approximately 0.4), while half-siblings, who share even less genetic material, show still less correlation. These studies suggest that between 0.75 and 0.80 of intelligence is inheritable, while 0.25 or less of the variance in I.Q. scores can be attributable to environmental factors.[28]

To test the question whether observed racial differences in scores can be explained by genetics, researchers have looked at the I.Q. differences in transracial adoptions. The Minnesota Transracial Adoption Study, for example, compared the I.Q. scores of black and white children raised by white middle-class families. For African-American high school-age children the mean I.Q. was 89, while white children raised in the same families had a mean I.Q. of 105.[29]

Although that suggests, to some, a race-based genetic explanation, it leaves open the possibility that environmental factors are at work even in those families. Skeptics of the repugnant hypothesis point to other

[27] Leonard Ramist and Solomon Arbeiter, *Profiles, College-Bound Seniors, 1985* (New York: College Entrance Examination Board, 1986), pp. 27, 37, 47, 57.

[28] T. J. Bouchard, et al., "Sources of Human Psychological Differences: The Minnesota Study of Twins Reared Apart," *Science*, Vol. 250 (October 1990), pp. 223–228.

[29] R. A. Weinberg, S. Scarr, and I. D. Waldman, "The Minnesota Transracial Adoption Study: A Follow-up of IQ Test Performance at Adolescence," *Intelligence*, Vol. 16 (1992), pp. 117–135.

studies, including one showing that after World War II, no significant difference was found between the I.Q.s of children fathered by black and white American soldiers in Germany.[30] Still other skeptics emphasize the "Flynn effect" – the fact that I.Q. scores have been rising for many years. In Holland, for example, they have risen by 21 points; the top 10 percent of Britons in the late nineteenth century had I.Q. scores putting them in the bottom 5 percent of Britons born in 1967.[31] The U.S. racial gap in I.Q. tests and similar tests also narrowed between 1965 and 1992, although the gap remains large and has widened since 1992. There is much disagreement about why it closed, and why it opened again.[32] Some explain part of the racial gap by what is termed "stereotype threat." There is evidence that when blacks are told a test is for intelligence, they do less well than when they are told it is for some other purpose.[33]

Opponents of a genetic explanation of racial differences also emphasize how complex the relationship is between environmental factors and genetic capacities. It is possible, for instance, that an inherited trait unrelated to I.Q. could affect a person's environment so that, due to that other trait, I.Q. is lower. By analogy, imagine a society in which all redhaired girls are repeatedly hit on the head when young. Red-haired girls could develop lower I.Q.s as a result, and the lower I.Q. would, strictly speaking, be "heritable" (in the sense that it tracks family lines) because their hair color was biologically determined. The point, however, is that the environmental fact that red-haired girls were hit on the head is an integral part of the explanation. Red hair alone would not explain the I.Q. differences.

It has also been suggested that genetic determinism is a "false picture" that has now been replaced by a more "interactionist" view envisaging a complex relationship between genes and the environment. Myopia (nearsightedness) is an example. Myopia occurs in people who live in an environment that allows people to read, but it also afflicts only people who have a particular gene. That means that in a society where nobody

[30] John Loehlin, Gardner Lindzey, and J. N. Spuhler, *Race Differences in Intelligence* (San Francisco: W. H. Freeman Co., 1975), p. 183.

[31] James Flynn, "I.Q. Trends over Time: Intelligence, Race, and Meritocracy," in *Meritocracy and Economic Inequality*, edited by Kenneth Arrow, Samuel Bowles, and Steven Durlauf (Princeton: Princeton University Press, 2000), p. 40, figure 3.2

[32] David Grissmer, Ann Flanagan, and Stephanie Williamson, "Why Did The Black-White Score Gap Narrow in the 1970s and 1980s?" in Christopher Jencks and Meredith Phillips, *The Black-White Test Score Gap* (Washington DC: Brookings Institution Press, 1998), pp. 182–226, concluding there is no "coherent story" to explain what has happened.

[33] I discuss stereotype threat in more detail later in this chapter.

reads (or does other things requiring close work), the gene is irrelevant. It also means that as reading becomes more socially important and more common, the gene becomes increasingly important in explaining differences in humans. This complex relationship is typical; genes are more like a "mechanism of human nature than a cause of it."[34] That means, in turn, that whatever genetic differences might exist are not natural capacities themselves but more capacities to develop capacities. Environmental factors take whatever natural capacities or abilities people have, and then shape them. In that sense, genes provide us with the potential to develop capacities, such as athletic and intellectual abilities, but they are not themselves those developed capacities.

There is also the possibility of feedback loops. A genetic difference, such as being naturally aggressive, could itself have an effect on a person's environment, making parents and teachers respond differently, for instance. But then those different responses, in the person's environment, might in turn have an effect on aggressiveness. If that happens, is the subsequent aggressiveness genetic or environmental? The answer, it seems, is both, and it can be difficult if not impossible to distinguish how much each is contributing.[35]

It is fair to say that the literature on race and I.Q. reveals both uncertainty and disagreement. The American Psychological Association suggested as much in a recent report of its *Task Force on Intelligence* titled, appropriately perhaps, "Stalking the Wild Taboo." After describing the differences in I.Q. scores among different racial groups, the authors state that psychologists do not yet know whether the causes of the I.Q. differences among races are environmental, biological, or a combination of the two, and conclude that there is no solid evidence to support the genetic explanation.[36] Everyone agrees that I.Q. differences are influenced by people's environment in many different and not well understood ways. People actually inherit from their parents a capacity to develop a capacity; whether or not it is developed depends on environmental factors.

What is most important, however, is how little would follow from the repugnant hypothesis even if it were to prove true. There are many different types of intelligence, and a high I.Q. score likely refers only to

[34] Matt Ridley, "Genes Are So Liberating," *New Scientist*, May 17, 2003, pp. 38–39.

[35] For an excellent discussion of these and other objections to *The Bell Curve*, see Ned Block, "How Heritability Misleads about Race," *Cognition*, Vol. 56 (1995), pp. 99–128.

[36] "Stalking the Wild Taboo. Intelligence: Knowns and Unknowns," Report of a Task Force of the Board of Scientific Affairs of the American Psychological Association, August 1995. http://lrainc.com/swtaboo/taboos/apa_01.html. Accessed on March 10, 2007.

one type. It is perfectly reasonable, for example, to think of the ability to understand people's attitudes and feelings as social intelligence, in which case high-I.Q. intelligence might even be tied to lower forms of this other type of intelligence. Indeed, Howard Gardner has famously suggested that there are at least seven different types of intelligence, including linguistic, mathematical, musical, spatial, and interpersonal. So one question is whether, and in what ways, these abilities overlap. Another question is what I.Q. tests actually measure, among the various forms of intelligence.[37] Still another is potential biases in tests.

What is also completely clear, and bears repeating, is that the repugnant hypothesis does not undermine the ideal of equality or the equal value of persons, any more than the hypothesis that blacks are naturally more gifted at sports would. I argued in Chapter 4 that racial equality rests on human dignity, which is a range concept. Greater intelligence gives no one greater moral standing among persons. Equality flows from humans' capacities to act intentionally and to reason. But that said, if we assume that neither white racism nor genetic differences explain race-based differences in income and poverty levels, then what does explain them? We need a fresh start.

Explaining African-American poverty

To put the discussion in context, we should first note the *overall* progress of African-Americans in recent decades, which is in some respects very impressive. The proportion of blacks who have attended college went up from about 15 percent in 1965 to nearly 50 percent in 1995, while at the same time the percentage graduating from college doubled, from less than 7 percent to more than 15 percent.[38] That is against a background of remarkable economic progress in general as well. In 1940, almost half of the white population lived in poverty, twice the rate of blacks today. According to the most recent census, almost half of all African-Americans

---

[37] A website run by Indiana University's cognitive science program describes some of the issues surrounding the nature of human intelligence. Plucker, J. A. (Ed.). (2003). Human intelligence: Historical influences, current controversies, teaching resources. http://www.indiana.edu/~intell. Accessed on March 10, 2007. See also "Jeopardy Millionaire Is Smart, But Is He a Genius?" *New York Times,* July 18, 2004, p. 5.

[38] Thomas Snyder and Linda Shafer, U.S. Department of Education, *Youth Indicators 1996: Trends in the Well-Being of American Youth* (Washington DC: U.S. Government Printing Office, 1996), p. 70.

describe themselves as middle class, while in 2000 nearly a third of blacks lived in a household that earned above $50,000.[39]

That said, however, it is also true that the average black family earns less than two-thirds as much as the average white family. The rate of poverty among blacks is still roughly three times that of whites. That tells us very little, however, until we look more closely. There was a very significant decline in black poverty from 1940, when it was an appalling 87 percent, to a still high, but much reduced, 47 percent in 1960. By 1970, it had reached 30 percent. Then the significant progress of the previous decades virtually stopped: poverty among blacks has declined only slightly since the 1970s.[40] The central problem is therefore not how to explain black poverty, but how to explain the lack of progress in eliminating it since the 1970s, and the answer is anything but simple.

First, in the United States, poverty is not usually permanent. Fifty percent of the people who are poor in one year will not be poor the next, and only 8 percent of the poor are poor for more than three years. That means less than 2 percent of Americans are poor for 3 or more years, although some who get out of poverty fall back in during later years.[41] The idea that there is a huge group of people who are permanently poor is therefore wrong.

Poverty is also a relative term. In some ways, people in poverty today are better off than people who were not in poverty a few decades ago. Increased productivity has made goods vastly cheaper and of higher quality for everyone. Houses are larger and cars are much better. Electrical appliances, such as air conditioners and televisions, are widely available today, and huge advances in health care have increased life expectancy for all groups. Some of these improvements have trickled down to the poor. According to the Census Bureau, 92 percent of the poor own color televisions, a large majority own both a microwave and washer (virtually all own a stove and refrigerator), and about half have air conditioning (compared with 75 percent of nonpoor). The poor in the United States also own more dishwashers and microwaves than the nonpoor in many

---

[39] U.S. Census Bureau, *Black Population in the United States: March 2000*, Series PPL-142 (Washington DC: U.S. Government Printing Office, 2001), table 15.

[40] Census and other figures from Thernstrom and Thernstrom, *American in Black and White*, p. 233.

[41] Data from *Panel Study of Income Dynamics*, quoted in *Inequality by Design: Cracking the Myth of the Bell Curve*, edited by Claude Fischer et al. (Princeton: Princeton University Press, 1966), p. 96.

European countries. Surprisingly, more than 40 percent own their own homes, and 70 percent of those have no mortgage.[42]

Although interesting, those figures can also be misleading. They do suggest that the lives of many of the poor are not as hard as in previous generations, but they ignore some of the deepest problems facing large numbers of poor people, including poor blacks. Those urban poor face a world not just of economic poverty but also of high rates of violent and nonviolent crime, high rates of unemployment and drug addiction, and a significant breakdown of the two-parent family structure. Income levels and consumer goods do not capture the nature and depth of the problem.

With that as background, I now turn to the causes of poverty. One of the most important writers on the subject of black poverty is the economist William Julius Wilson. Wilson argues that to understand poverty one must pay close attention to changes in labor markets and, in particular, to the fact that large numbers of relatively well-paying unskilled blue-collar jobs disappeared or moved abroad during the period when the black "underclass" emerged in the cities. Those manufacturing jobs were replaced either by jobs requiring more education and other skills or by relatively low-paying service jobs. The effects of this economic shift, he points out, were felt disproportionately by African-Americans.[43] Some lost jobs altogether; others were forced into the lower-paying ones.[44] But why were the effects of this economic shift particularly harmful to blacks? For that we need to look at other changes.

Among the factors that contribute to poverty *for all groups* is the proportion of children born to single women. In 1992, more than half (57 percent) of all African-American children lived with only one parent, and more than 7 percent lived with none.[45] By 1995, 70 percent of all black births were out of wedlock.[46] The result is that today, only 37 percent of black children live with both parents, compared with 81 percent of

[42] Bureau of Labor Statistics, quoted in Larry Elder, *The Ten Things You Can't Say in America* (New York: St. Martin's Press, 2000), pp. 213–214.

[43] Wilson, *The Truly Disadvantaged*, and William Julius Wilson, *When Work Disappears: The World of the New Urban Poor* (New York: Random House, 1996).

[44] Economic shifts that have occurred in recent decades have not just been limited to shifts away from manufacturing, as I discuss later in this chapter. These have also involved, crucially, changes in the *qualifications* for the jobs.

[45] U.S. Bureau of the Census, *Current Population Reports*, Series P-20, No. 468, (Washington DC: U.S. Government Printing Office, 1992), p. 27.

[46] Thernstrom and Thernstrom, *America in Black and White*, p. 237. (Figures are from various sources.)

Asian-Americans, 77 percent of whites, and 65 percent of Hispanics.[47] The implication of that on poverty among blacks is tremendous. The vast majority of poor black children, 85 percent, live in families without a father present.[48]

The impact of single-parent families on poverty cuts across race and ethnicity. As of 2004, 42 percent of all children in families headed by a female of any race with no husband present are poor, compared with only 9 percent of children in married-couple families.[49] Set that alongside the decline of the black family and the picture becomes clearer. The income for female-headed black families is barely over one-third of the income of black married couples.[50] That means, in turn, that the majority (62 percent) of black children living with only their mother are poor, while only 13 percent of black children living with both parents are poor. Indeed, the poverty level for married black couples was actually *lower* as of 1992 than the poverty rate for married white couples.[51] Marital status swamps race as an explanation of poverty.

These marriage figures are related to what Wilson terms the "marriage eligible" males, and leads back to unemployment and the larger economic shifts that have occurred. The percentage of employed black men, especially younger men, declined significantly beginning in the 1960s and continued. By 1992, more than half of blacks had never been married, compared with only 21 percent of whites.[52] Such statistics, writes Williams, "reveal a long-term decline in the proportion of black men, and particularly young black men, who are in a position to support a family."[53]

Why were (and are) so many not able or willing to find jobs that enable them to marry and support a family? During the Great Depression, when unemployment was also high and wages for blacks were half those of whites, marriage rates did not fall more rapidly among blacks than

[47] Abigail Thernstrom and Stephan Thernstrom, *No Excuses: Closing the Racial Gap in Learning* (New York: Simon and Schuster, 2003), p. 31.

[48] Thernstrom and Thernstrom, *America in Black and White*, pp. 236–237. (Figures are from various sources.)

[49] http://childstats.gov/americaschildren/eco.asp. Accessed on March 11, 2007.

[50] Thernstrom and Thernstrom, *America in Black and White*, p. 241. (Figures are from various sources).

[51] U.S. Bureau of Census, *Current Population Reports*, Series P-23, No. 181 (Washington DC: U.S. Government Printing Office, 1992), p. 32.

[52] U.S. Bureau of the Census, *Current Population Reports*, Series P-20, No. 468, p. vi.

[53] Wilson, *The Truly Disadvantaged*, p. 83.

whites.[54] Nor is it clear why innercity blacks today would be less inclined to marry than other immigrants living in the same neighborhoods.[55] The question remains, then, why marriage and family stopped being an option for so many young black males.

Part of the explanation may be in the increase in incarceration rates, which many think is at least partly due to the war on drugs. As crack cocaine came to be seen as a social scourge, states imposed strict penalties for possession as well as sale of illegal drugs. The effects of these laws fell disproportionately on blacks and have contributed to the fact that so many young African-American males are in jail rather than employed and married. Today, four times as many people are in jail as 30 years ago, and, as I will discuss, many of those are black. Yet, the increased rate of incarceration, although it did fall disproportionately on blacks, is not the reason for economic inequality. In a recent study of punishment and its effect on inequality, sociologist Bruce Western concluded that although the growth in prisons and incarceration often did split up families and make employment more difficult, it cannot explain "the unemployment and female-headed households. Unemployment and broken homes are as much a cause of imprisonment as a consequence." He concludes that "the prison boom is not the main cause of [economic] inequality between blacks and whites in America."[56] Nonetheless, the fact remains that nonviolent drug crimes represent a factor that explains why blacks are either in prison or are convicted criminals, which in itself raises serious questions about whether such laws should be changed.

Another part of the explanation of these crime figures may be institutional racism in the system. In a U.S. Justice Department review of recent studies of the role of race in the juvenile justice system, the researchers noted that two-thirds of those studies concluded there was a "race effect" at some stage in the juvenile justice process. The effects of race, the researchers concluded "may be felt at various decision points, they may be direct or indirect, and they may accumulate as youth continue through the system."[57] For instance, although there is evidence that drug use does

---

[54] Robert I. Lerman, "Employment Opportunities of Young Men and Family Formation," *American Journal of Economics*, Vol. 79 (1989), pp. 62–66.

[55] Wilson, *When Work Disappears*, p. 105.

[56] Bruce Western, *Punishment and Inequality in America* (Princeton: Princeton University Press, 2005), p. 7. Western also suggests, implausibly in my view, that the growth in prisons was at least partly due to working class whites' "anxieties and resentment" (p. 4) over the activism associated with the Civil Rights movement.

[57] Carl Pope and William Feyerherm, *Minorities and the Juvenile Justice System: Research Summary*, (Washington DC: Office of Juvenile Justice and Delinquency Prevention, U.S.

not vary significantly between white youth and black youth, blacks are both arrested and jailed more often for drug offenses than white youth.[58]

Yet, nonviolent drug convictions are far from the whole story. Between 1960 and 1995, the rate of *violent* crimes committed in the United States per 100,000 people went from 161 to 685, and black males contributed disproportionately to that increase. Although they comprise only 12 percent of the U.S. population, black males committed more than half of the murders in the last quarter of the twentieth century. Much of the violent crime occurred within the black community itself. Black men today are murdered at seven times the rate of white men, and black women are murdered at five times the rate of white women. Those figures, combined with the strict drug laws, mean that by some estimates from a quarter to up to a third of all black males in the United States are in jail, on probation, or in some other way under the control of the criminal justice system.[59]

Interestingly, though, when various socioeconomic factors such as family breakdown and poverty are considered, the racial differences in crime rates tend to diminish or disappear. The explanation of the higher crime rate has to do not with race but with the nature of the communities in which people, and especially young people, live. The proportion of poor black youth who live in high-poverty and high-crime communities where marriage has declined doubled between 1970 and 1990; it is those differences in the environment in which juveniles live that explain the differential crime rates between races.[60]

First, the relationship between crime and economic decline is itself complex. While it is often noted that unemployment and poverty contribute to crime, the relationship also goes the other way. High crime rates contribute to poverty and economic decline in a community. This

Department of Justice, 1995), quoted in Justice Policy Institute, *Crime, Race and Juvenile Justice Policy in Perspective*, October 3, 2005. http://justicepolicy.org/article.php?id=545. Accessed on May 4, 2006.

[58] C. Puzzanchera, T. Finnegan, and Wei Kang, "Easy Access to Juvenile Populations" and Melissa Sickman, T. J. Sladky, and Wei Kang, "Census of Juveniles in Residential Placement Databook." http://www.ojjdp.ncjrs.org/ojstatbb/cjrp/ in "Crime in the United States, 2001" (Washington DC: Justice Department, F.B.I. Publications) in *Crime, Race and Juvenile Justice Policy in Perspective*.

[59] Thernstrom and Thernstrom, *America in Black and White*, pp. 250, 281. (Figures are from various sources.)

[60] F. Peeples and R. Loeber, "Do Individual Factors and Neighborhood Context Explain Ethnic Differences in Juvenile Delinquency?" *Journal of Quantitative Criminology*, Vol. 10, No. 2 (1994), pp. 141–157.

is important because we are looking for an explanation of why poverty among blacks did not continue to decline in the 1970s, as it had done for the previous decades. Black crime exploded *not* during the 1930s and early 1940s, when poverty was rampant, but instead began to increase in the 1960s at the end of a period of sustained economic progress among blacks.

Second, crime makes it more difficult for those convicted of crimes to get jobs when they return to society, a problem that is aggravated by racial stereotyping and by reluctance to hire young black males, in general.[61] In the 1991 *National Survey on Race*, 52 percent of whites agreed with the statement that "blacks are aggressive or violent," but an even larger percentage of blacks, 59 percent, also agreed. About twice as many blacks as whites also agreed with the statement that "blacks are irresponsible."[62] A study of fast food restaurants in Harlem concluded that employers preferred not to hire blacks.

A third, economic effect of crime is that crime increases the cost (and danger) of doing business in a community, reducing economic activity and increasing the cost of living. Fourth, high crime rates can affect the wealth in a community by lowering the value of homes and businesses. This is especially important for African-Americans since home ownership has traditionally been the major source of wealth and a stepping-stone for families into the middle class. Fifth, and finally, high rates of crime can lower the quality of education in a neighborhood by discouraging good teachers from working there and making classrooms less conducive to learning. In those ways, crime is both an effect *and a cause* of economic inequality and poverty.

Another important part of this complex picture of poverty and its causes, in addition to shifts in jobs and the economy, marriage break-down, and crime, is educational achievement. Educational achievement is especially important in light of the dramatic shifts in the labor market. The decline in U.S. manufacturing jobs that Wilson described has continued into the twenty-first century, with the emergence of China and other developing countries as major sources of manufactured goods. According to one recent report, the actual percentage of Americans now employed in manufacturing is 10 percent.[63] But even that figure

---

[61] *Gratz v. Bollinger*, 539 U.S. 244 (2003), Justice Ginsburg dissenting.

[62] Sniderman and Piazza, *The Scar of Race*, p. 45.

[63] "Industrial Metamorphosis," *Economist*, October 1, 2005, pp. 69–71. The discussion in this and the next paragraph are based on figures from that article.

is misleading when the nature of the manufacturing jobs that remain is considered. Many of those employed in the manufacturing sector today are highly skilled, working in financial planning, product design, marketing, and distribution. So if we look at the number of relatively *unskilled* workers who work in traditional manufacturing jobs where people make things that "you can drop on your toe" the total is only half – roughly 5 percent of the U.S. workforce. That figure contrasts with 1970, when 25 percent of the workforce was in manufacturing There has been a sharp decline in manufacturing in general, especially in relatively unskilled factory employment.

None of this is likely to be stopped. As economies develop and become more efficient, there is a natural tendency for them to move away from manufacturing jobs that require lower levels of skill to service jobs that often require more skills. There are two reasons for this. First, it is easier to make efficiency gains in manufacturing than in service. Machines can build cars and toasters, but it is more difficult to use machines to replace service workers in McDonalds, in automotive design, or in computer programming. Second, as economies develop, people tend to shift consumption away from manufactured goods to services. Consumers can use only so many refrigerators and cars, but consumption possibilities of services are almost endless.

What all of this means is that there is an ever-increasing association in societies between educational achievement and economic success. Many of the jobs that are available in the U.S. economy, and will be available in the future, require high levels of educational achievement. As I noted earlier in this chapter, the good news is that growing percentages of African-Americans are attending and graduating from educational institutions. Yet, years spent in school and even graduation rates do not tell the whole story. *What* is learned is also important. Evidence shows that those persons with higher skills do better than those who lack those skills *even among those with similar years of education.* And when we look beneath the surface at what is actually learned, we notice significant racial differences.

The major tool for assessing learning outcomes, the U.S. Department of Education's *National Assessment of Educational Progress,* shows significant gaps in the skills and knowledge levels of black and white students at the same grade levels. In math, for instance, black high school seniors in 2000 performed on average below the level of white eighth graders. Similarly, almost 70 percent of black twelfth graders were below the "basic" level of math, compared with 20 percent of Asian-Americans and about 26 percent of whites. In reading, there was a 4-year gap, with black high school seniors performing at the eighth-grade level of whites. Similar figures apply for science. Even in reading, more than 40 percent of blacks have not achieved a basic level compared with 18 percent of whites.[64] A national survey of adult literacy revealed a similar pattern. It showed that black *college* graduates and white *high school* graduates were roughly equal in reading ability.[65] Significant racial disparities also exist on SAT achievement tests: blacks average 524 on the History and English SAT II while the national average is 736.[66]

Those differences in educational achievement (not merely years in attendance) are another important part of the economic picture. One study of the wages of black males from 26–33 years old found a significant racial gap in earnings when only the years of schooling that had been completed were considered. But when the researchers also included how well the men did on tests measuring skills in reading and mathematics, the difference in income between blacks and whites vanished. Indeed, blacks actually earned slightly more than whites with the same skills.[67] Another study that looked at men and women separately concluded that black women actually "earn 5 percent *more* per hour than white women with the same AFQT [Armed Forces Qualifying Test] score."[68] Although black males earned 9 percent less than comparably skilled whites, even that difference, they determined, was based on the fact that blacks on average start out working later in life and, therefore, have less job experience when they apply.[69] Differences in earnings of white and black males who work on salaries is explained, the researchers reported, by the fact that blacks work significantly fewer hours and weeks than whites. The point is again that "skills are important determinants of

[64] U.S. Department of Eduction, *National Assessment for Educational Progress*, cited in Thernstrom and Thernstrom, *No Excuses*, pp. 13, 15. Figures are for tests given between 1998 and 2001.

[65] Irwin S. Kirsch, et al., *Adult Literacy in America: A First Look at the Results of the National Adult Literacy Survey*, National Center for Education Statistics (Washington DC: U.S. Government Printing Office, 1993), p. 36.

[66] "Bilingual Students Use Language Tests To Get a Leg Up on College Admissions," *Wall Street Journal*, June 26, 2001, p. 1.

[67] George Farkas and Kevin Vicknair, "Appropriate Tests of Racial Wage Discrimination require Controls for Cognitive Skills," *American Sociological Review*, Vol. 61 (August 1996), pp. 557–560. Cited in Thernstrom and Thernstrom, *No Excuses*, p. 39. Other studies reach the same conclusions, they report.

[68] William Johnson and Derek Neal, "Basic Skills and the Black-White Earnings Gap," in *The Black-White Test Score Gap*, edited by Jencks and Phillips, p. 482.

[69] Johnson and Neal, "Basic Skills and the Black-White Earnings Gap," p. 495.

wages and earnings. Skill differences explain a substantial part of the wage and earning variation among blacks, among whites, and between blacks and whites."[70] Education and skill differences are important in explaining poverty rates as well as economic differences in general.

If we reject the repugnant hypotheses, as I argued we should, then how are we to explain these racial differences in educational achievement and its close effect on lower earnings? Is there anything about the cultural environment and historical experience of African-Americans that can help account for educational achievement? If Asians and other groups were able to adapt relatively well to changing economic circumstances, why weren't African-Americans? To get a fix on the problem, I will describe the cultural factors that influence educational (and therefore economic) success in all groups; then I will look specifically at African-American culture to see how it may have played a role in the problems I have been describing.

Educational achievement and culture

As I have noted, educational achievement is lower for children of single parents than for children raised by two adults. This remains true *even when income levels are the same.*[71] Part of the reason is presumably the young age of many of the females who head such households. Teenage parents are often themselves high school dropouts who may lack the skills, maturity, and information necessary to be a good parent. But cultural differences clearly also play an important role in explaining educational achievement.[72]

---

[70] Johnson and Neal, "Basic Skills and the Black-White Earnings Gap," p. 494.

[71] Thernstrom and Thernstrom, *America in Black and White*, p. 358.

[72] As Orlando Patterson notes ("Taking Culture Seriously: A Framework and Afro-American Illustration," in *Culture Matters: How Values Shape Human Progress*, edited by Lawrence E. Harrison and Samuel P. Huntington [New York: Basic Books, 2000], pp. 204–207), there is irony in the way that those suggesting the importance of cultural differences between blacks and others have been treated. On one hand, it is common to argue that cultural differences play a central role in explaining the different I.Q. scores of blacks and other groups by pointing out difference in the "socialization" of children in black and white families, so that children in white families have an advantage in I.Q. tests. These ideas can win easy acceptance while in other contexts those pressing the importance of cultural differences are sometimes thought to be "racist," for example, if cultural differences are offered as explanations of joblessness, unemployment, and crime. There cultural explanations are seen to be "blaming the victim" and are replaced by explanations favoring racial discrimination on the part of employers and police, biases in test like the SAT, and the like.

Few question the fact that families impart different cultural values and beliefs to their children. Some families stress the importance of religious faithfulness or wealth, while others might encourage artistic creativity, intellectual accomplishment, philanthropy, sports competition, political power, or social acclaim. Some children are read to from the time they are infants, while others are left to watch television; some are encouraged or even required to excel in school, others in athletics, in art, or in nothing at all.

But families do not exist in isolation; they are part of larger cultural groups. Indeed, Orlando Patterson thinks culture should be *defined* in terms of the values that are transmitted between generations. Culture, he writes, is "a repertoire of socially transmitted and intra-generationally generated ideas about how to live and make judgments, both in general terms and in regard to specific domains of life."[73]

The importance and the pervasiveness of culture was nicely summarized by Simon Blackburn. "The trick," he wrote,

> is to remember that facts about culture are not facts about some cloudy super-organism, some transcendental spirit of the age hovering around in hyperspace. They are summaries of facts about ourselves and our interactions. What they summarize is the very, very important part of our environment that concerns our interactions with other people. Those interactions shape the way we speak, but also the way we hope and fear and take pride and feel shame. They summarize what we imitate and emulate and eventually what we grow to be.[74]

One striking example of the important role of culture can be seen among Jews. Although they are less than 3 percent of the U.S. population, that group accounts for approximately 25 percent of law school faculty members. American Jews have also received 40 Nobel Prizes in science and economics.[75] In Hungary, half of the lawyers were Jews in 1920, although they were only 6 percent of the population. Similar patterns emerge in commerce, where Jews made up more than half the merchants before World War II in Hungary and owned 80 percent of the retail clothing

[73] Orlando Patterson, "Taking Culture Seriously," in *Culture Matters*, edited by Harris and Huntington, p. 208.

[74] Simon Blackburn, "Meet the Flintstones," reviewing *The Blank Slate: The Modern Denial of Human Nature* by Stephen Pinker. *New Republic Online*, November 25, 2002. http://www.tnr.com/docprint.mhtml?i=20021125&s=blackburn112502. Accessed on July 8, 2003.

[75] Farber and Sherry, *Beyond All Reason: The Radical Assault on Truth in American Law*, p. 58.

businesses in New York.[76] Various factors have been suggested to explain these figures, ranging from the advantages of belonging to a tight-knit family, the ability to trust other members of the community, and the value placed on education. The number of lawyers and law professors may also be related to the strong emphasis Jewish culture and religious practices place on law, language, and interpretation, as well as on the value of learning and scholarship in general.

The importance of the connections between culture and educational achievement are illustrated by an account of a black high school student reported in the *New York Times*. It shows the effects of culture in schools, and in particular, its effect on black children who criticize students who work hard as "acting white." Insulated from his normal environment, a student had done very well in a demanding summer course in math. But when he returned to his school, he failed a far easier class. In school, he said, we were all "lackadaisical." "One third of our school," he reported,

> was failing three or more classes. The pressure from my friends was mostly to chill and, like, do what you want to do. People were not doing their work, just coming to school for fun, coming to school high, just playing sports. It's hard to come in and really do work when everybody is just chillin' and playin' around.[77]

The reporter concluded that "the cultural pressure to behave in ways that are detrimental and even destructive goes well beyond the classroom. Several boys told me about their desire to gain experience as street hustlers so they can someday cash in as 'authentic gansta rap stars.'"[78]

The same phenomenon, of black children and young adults placing a low value on educational achievement and hard work, was suggested in several more systematic studies. In their book *Crime and Human Nature*, Richard Hernstein and James Q. Wilson describe a study of ghetto boys. It revealed that every one of the boys interviewed

> had been employed at one time, but the turnover was very high. When asked why they left the job, they typically answered that they found it "monotonous or low paying" . . . Being able to "make it" while avoiding the "work game" is a strong, pervasive and consistent goal.[79]

---

[76] Figures from Thomas Sowell, *Black Rednecks and White Liberals* (San Francisco: Encounter Books, 2005), p. 84.

[77] Bob Herbert, "Leaving Behind a Culture of Ignorance and Poverty," *New York Times*, July 11, 2003, p. 1.

[78] Herbert, "Leaving Behind a Culture of Ignorance and Poverty," p. 1.

[79] Richard Hernstein and James Q. Wilson, *Crime and Human Nature* (New York: Simon and Schuster, 1985), pp. 304, 335.

Other researchers have found similar behavior and attitudes.[80]

The potential importance of such attitudes is brought into sharp relief if we compare the situation of Asian-Americans. Historic prejudice against Asians has been widely documented. Indeed, Gunnar Myrdal wrote, in his study of race, that in America, "The Negroes are set apart, together with other colored people, principally the Chinese and Japanese." Although he thought the social disabilities of recent white immigrants are "temporary," he also believed the disabilities of blacks and Asians were "permanent."[81] Yet, he was wrong. Although they make up only about 4 percent of the population, Asian-Americans comprise a far higher proportion of the students at the nation's elite universities: 27 percent of the 2000–2001 freshman class at MIT, 25 percent at Stanford, and 15–17 percent at Harvard, Brown, and Yale. In 1999, Asian-Americans comprised 11 percent of the people who scored in the top of the SAT I in verbal reasoning and 25 percent of the top in mathematical reasoning.[82]

In 2001, some 16,000 Asian-American students scored above 700 on the mathematical portion of the SAT examination, compared with fewer than 700 African-Americans, even though Asians were far fewer as a proportion of the population.[83] These differences in scores are not explained by income differences: Asian-American students from lower economic strata score higher than students from upper-income black families.[84] Asian-Americans are also much more likely to graduate from college and to enter into professions such as medicine and law.

An important part of the explanation of Asians' educational success is cultural. A survey of 20,000 high school students concluded that Asian-American students cut classes less than other groups, paid more attention in classes, and placed a higher priority on education. They also spent more time studying and less time at part-time jobs, extracurricular activities, and socializing. The author concluded that Asian students "outscored other groups by a wide margin" in the priority they place on education.[85]

[80] See, for example, Edward Banfield, *The Unheavenly City Revisited* (Boston: Little Brown, 1974).

[81] Gunnar Myrdal, *The American Dilemma: The Negro Problem and American Democracy* (New York: Harper and Row, 1944), pp. 53–54, 667.

[82] Figures from Thernstrom and Thernstrom, *No Excuses*, pp. 85–87.

[83] Figures from the College Board, quoted in Sowell, *Black Rednecks and White Liberals*, p. 226.

[84] Figures from the College Board, quoted in Sowell, *Black Rednecks and White Liberals*, p. 227.

[85] Laurence Sternberg, *Beyond the Classroom: Why School Reform Has Failed and What Parents Need to Do* (New York: Simon and Schuster, 1996), p. 87.

The importance of family and culture for all groups was confirmed in a study by the College Board's National Task Force on Minority High Achievement, *Reaching the Top.* It concluded that educational achievement is greatly affected by "cultural attributes" found in the "home, community and school," and in particular the amount of emphasis placed on "diligence, thoroughness, and self-discipline."[86]

Cultural differences in parenting practices, especially as they relate to education, are also striking. Black children, for example, watch significantly more television than other groups. Two to three times as many blacks as whites say they watch television or videos for 5 or more hours a day.[87] But differences are deeper than television. Home environment in general was the subject of a recent study that looked at "cognitive stimulation" of children by parents. The study used as a measure the "HOME" test (Home Observation for Measurement of the Environment). This test measures a range of factors including the number of children's books in the home; how often a parent reads to the child; the effort put forth to teach children the alphabet, numbers, and colors; and a range of other factors. The study also noted differences in emotional support, such as expressions of affection, attention to questions, and presence of (nonphysical) discipline. There were, the study concluded, significant differences between blacks and whites in cognitive stimulation.[88] Two researchers summarized the importance of these results, with the observation that "changes in parenting practices might do more to reduce the black-white test score gap than changes in parents' educational achievement or income."[89]

Another study using the same HOME test found that parenting practices affect not just educational achievement but also help explain the black–white gap in I.Q. scores.[90] That same conclusion is also suggested by a study of black children who were adopted – some by black families and others by white families. The conclusion was that the children

[86] College Board, *Reaching the Top: A report of the National Task Force on Minority High Achievement* (New York: College Board Publications, 1999), pp. 7–18.
[87] U.S. Department of Education, *National Assessment of Educational Progress,* (1998) and (2000). Figures quoted in Thernstrom and Thernstrom, *No Excuses,* p. 142.
[88] These results are described in Meredith Phillips, et al. "Family Background, Parenting Practices, and the Black-White Test Score Gap," in *The Black-White Test Score Gap,* edited by Jencks and Phillips, pp. 126–129.
[89] *The Black-White Test Score Gap,* edited by Jencks and Phillips, p. 46.
[90] Phillips, et al. "Family Background, Parenting Practices, and the Black-White Test Score Gap," in *The Black-White Test Score Gap,* edited by Jencks and Phillips, pp. 103–145.

who were raised in white families had significantly higher I.Q. scores (13 points) than ones raised in black families.[91]

These cultural differences in parenting practices are further confirmed by studies of students' attitudes. A study by Roslyn Mickelson found that black children are "less hopeful than whites." Although they "subscribe to mainstream values as much as do whites," they "behave in ways that show less commitment to mainstream success."[92] Other studies have also noted differences in attitudes of students toward school work. Black students who said they were "working as hard as they could almost every day" reported they did an average of just 3.9 hours of homework per week, compared with 5.4 hours for whites and 7.5 hours for Asian-Americans who also said they were working hard.[93] Black children are also significantly less likely to complete their homework[94] and almost twice as many black students as whites report that they do not understand very well what they had been told to read.[95] Teachers in schools with a high proportion of minority students reported with much greater frequency, that learning was damaged by student behavior and that lack of respect for teachers was common among students.[96]

These results carry over to college as well, where black students get lower grades than others who have similar academic credentials. The authors of one study summarized their findings this way:

[A]t every level of SAT score, blacks earn lower grades than their white counter-parts, and this remains true after controlling (at least crudely) for other variables, including high school grades and socioeconomic status.

---

[91] Elsie G. J. Moore, "Family Socialization and the I.Q. Test Performance of Traditionally and Transracially Adopted Black Children," *Developmental Psychology*, Vol. 22 (1986), pp. 317–326.

[92] Ronald Ferguson, "Teachers' Expectations and the Test Score Gap," in *The Black-White Test Score Gap*, edited by Jencks and Phillips, pp. 292–294 [discussing a study by Roslyn A. Mickelson, "The Attitude-Achievement Paradox Among Black Adolescents," *Sociology of Education*, Vol. 63 (1990)].

[93] Figures from the National Educational Longitudinal Study, 1990, quoted in Thernstrom and Thernstrom, *No Excuses*, p. 145.

[94] U.S. Department of Education, National Assessment of Educational Progress, (1998) and (2000). Figures quoted in Thernstrom and Thernstrom, *No Excuses*, pp. 91–93.

[95] Ronald F. Ferguson, "Responses from Middle School, Junior High, and High School Students in Districts of the Minority Student Achievement Network," John F. Kennedy School of Government, Harvard University, November 18, 2002, reported in Thernstrom and Thernstrom, *No Excuses*, p. 22.

[96] Jennifer Part, "Deciding Factors," *Education Week*, January 9, 2003, pp. 17–18, describing results of the *U.S. Department of Education School and Staffing Survey*, 1999–2000.

Most sobering of all, the performance gap is greatest for the black students with the highest SATs.[97]

Only 19 percent of blacks earned grades above what would have been predicted for white students with the same high school grades and SAT scores.[98] These results have been confirmed by other studies, including those cited in *The Shape of the River*, a much-discussed book by William Bowen and Derek Bok defending affirmative action. According to the authors,

> The average rank in class for black students is appreciably lower than the average rank of white students within each SAT interval. . . . It is a strong indication of a troubling phenomenon often called "underperformance." Black students with the same SAT scores as whites tend to earn lower grades.[99]

There is another, especially perverse effect of cultural differences on students' performance. Evidence suggests that the explanation of the lower expectations teachers have of many black students is based on past behavior of individual students rather than on the student's race. A study of 1,664 sixth graders and their teachers indicated that what causes low teacher expectations are such factors as a student's past performance on test and grades, level of effort, time spent doing homework, and self-perception of ability. Race per se was not a factor because black students who had similar levels on these measures as whites were expected by teachers to perform as well as whites.[100] The study also found that low expectations by teachers in October by itself had an impact on students' performance in tests in May.[101]

---

[97] Fredrick E. Vars and William G. Bowen, "Scholastic Aptitude Test Scores, Race, and Academic Performance at Selective Colleges and Universities," in *The Black-White Test Score Gap*, edited by Jencks and Phillips, p. 458.

[98] Vars and Bowen, "Scholastic Aptitude Test Scores, Race, and Academic Performance at Selective Colleges and Universities," in *The Black-White Test Score Gap*, edited by Jencks and Phillips, p. 466.

[99] William G. Bowen and Derek Bok, *The Shape of the River* (Princeton: Princeton University Press, 1998), p. 77.

[100] Lee Jussim, Jacquelynne Eccles, and Stephanie Madon, "Social Perception, Social Stereotypes, and Teacher Expectations: Accuracy and the Quest for the Powerful Self-fulfilling Prophecy," *Advances in Experimental Social Psychology*, Vol. 28 (1999), pp. 350–351.

[101] Jussim, Eccles, and Madon, "Social Perception, Social Stereotypes, and Teacher Expectations: Accuracy and the Quest for the Powerful Self-fulfilling Prophecy," pp. 308–311. It is unclear how to explain those differences, though they may be due to differences in students' desire to please teachers as against parents (black children put more emphasis on teachers' approval). That might in turn be accounted for by the fact that black parents tend to convey less commitment to education or less confidence that their children can succeed in competition with white children.

It is hard to avoid the conclusion that learning is affected by differences in attitudes of parents toward childrearing, including teaching young children to read and other skills, restricting television, and placing a high value on education. Similarly, the attitudes of students toward education and toward other students who work hard also play a part in lowering black educational achievement. Nobel Laureate and economist James Heckman summarized the situation this way:

> The most important influences on young children's development are family, home and immediate social circle. Social scientists have found measurable differences in the quality of these that may account for black-white gaps in skills that affect school and job performance. Young black children are exposed to much lower levels of cognitive and emotional stimulation than white children, even in families with comparable income, education, and I.Q. They watch more TV, read fewer books, and converse and go on educational outings with their families less often. They are more likely to be raised in homes without fathers, family mealtimes or fixed routines.[102]

How, then, might these cultural differences be explained? It is often assumed that they follow from racial oppression and slavery. Abigail and Stephen Thernstrom, for example, write that the

> "cultural inheritance" of African Americans today is the product of a very long history of racial oppression – centuries of slavery followed by disenfranchisement, legally mandated segregation, and subordination in the Jim Crow South and intense racial prejudice in the north. . . . It was very difficult [after emancipation] to get much education, and when they entered the world of work, determination in school paid off very little. Most jobs that required the skills that were learned in school were closed to black people.[103]

Nigerian anthropologist John Ogbu has suggested another way in which history accounts for poor educational achievement and other problems. Ogbu also emphasizes that blacks were originally brought to North America involuntarily and in chains, and then forced into a slave and eventually a caste system. That history, according to Obgu, leads black youth to rebel against the system in self-destructive ways. School is seen as a "white" institution, and students "define certain forms of behaviours, events, symbols,

---

[102] James B. Heckman and Amy L. Wax, "Home Alone," *Wall Street Journal,* January 23, 2004, p. A. 14.
[103] Thernstrom and Thernstrom, *No Excuses,* p. 121.

and meanings as inappropriate for them because these are characteristic of their oppressors."[104]

It is difficult to know how much weight to put on such historical explanations, although I will assume they should be taken into account. It is not clear why history hampers black males so much more than black females, for example. The explanation also ignores the fact that black progress was significant for an extended period, and came to a halt only in the last third of the twentieth century. With respect to marriage rates and single-parent households, for example, the evidence suggests that blacks were actually married at a higher rate than whites throughout the period from 1890 to 1940 (the question had not been asked in an earlier census).[105] Indeed, in 1950, 72 percent of all black men and 81 percent of all black women were married.[106] The same pattern holds for higher crime rates, which also emerged later and in ways that cannot easily be explained by the history of slavery and racial oppression.

So while I do not want to deny that this history was part of the story, other less familiar explanations of cultural differences are also on the table. Thomas Sowell, for example, has suggested that the explanation of the cultural problems faced by African-Americans lies in the fact that many Southern blacks actually inherited the culture of Southern whites. They adopted what he calls the "redneck" culture.[107]

The story begins with the origins of white Southern redneck culture itself and the Europeans who immigrated to the American South in the seventeenth and eighteenth centuries. Although the English who settled in Massachusetts and elsewhere in the northeast, were drawn largely from central and southern England, those who immigrated to the American South were mainly from the relatively unsettled areas of the Scottish highlands, the border between Scotland and England, and Ulster County in Ireland. These people from the "Celtic fringe" brought very different attitudes than those of the other, Northern immigrants.

[104] John Ogbu, "Racial Stratification in the United States: Why Inequality Persists," *Teachers College Record*, Vol. 96, No. 2 (1994), p. 154.

[105] Henry Walker, "Black-White Differences in Marriage and Family Patterns," *Feminism, Children and the New Families*, edited by Sanford M. Dornbusch and Myra H. Strober (New York: Guilford Press, 1988), p. 91.

[106] Thomas Sowell, *Ethnic America: A History* (New York: Basic Books, 1981), p. 92.

[107] Sowell, *Black Rednecks and White Liberals*, chapter 1. Sowell relies on various historians, but principally Grady McWhiney, *Cracker Culture: Celtic Ways in the Old South* (Tuscaloosa: University of Alabama Press, 1988).

The original "Celtic fringe" settlers in the South came from a much wilder, less-civilized world than other European immigrants. In general, said one historian, they were "disorderly inhabitants of a deeply disordered land."[108] The cultural attitudes that these people brought were characterized by

> an aversion to work, proneness to violence, neglect of education, sexual promiscuity, improvidence, drunkenness, lack of entrepreneurship, reckless searches for excitement, lively music and dance, and a style of religious oratory marked by strident rhetoric, unbridled emotions, and flamboyant imagery.[109]

The evidence for this in the United States goes back to the earliest days. Differing attitudes toward work were noted early in the nineteenth century by Alexis de Tocqueville[110] and even by Southerners themselves. Robert E. Lee, for example, said that "Our people are opposed to work. Our troops, officers, community and press. All ridicule and resist it."[111] Dueling was much more common in the old South, and crime rates were higher. As for education, census figures show that in 1850 less than 1 percent of Northern whites were illiterate compared to 20 percent of Southern whites.[112] Whitney thinks that this culture lingers in the South, which explains why large parts of the South are still characterized by higher rates of crime, poor educational achievement and saving habits, casual attitudes toward sex, and lack of interest in work.[113]

This history also explains contemporary problems blacks face in cities in the North, according to this theory, because most of the immigrants to those cities came from the deep South, where the redneck culture was strong among both blacks and whites. Southern blacks had often adopted the "redneck" cultural attitudes of the Southern whites among whom they lived.

Redneck culture contrasted sharply with the culture of the Northern locals, both black and white. Before the massive migrations of Southern

---

[108] David Hackett Fischer, *Albion's Seed: Four British Folkways in America* (New York: Oxford University Press, 1989), p. 630. Quoted in Sowell, *Black Rednecks and White Liberals*, p. 5.

[109] Sowell, *Black Rednecks and White Liberals*, p. 6.

[110] Alexis de Tocqueville (1835), *Democracy in America* (New York: Alfred A Knopf, 1945), pp. 362–363.

[111] Robert E. Lee, *Lee's Dispatches*, edited by Douglas Southall Freeman (New York: G. P. Putnam's Sons, 1957), p. 8. Quoted in Sowell, *Black Rednecks and White Liberals*, p. 18.

[112] Whitney, *Cracker Culture*, p. 196.

[113] Whitney, *Cracker Culture*, passim.

blacks to the North and West, blacks there were a small but relatively successful minority. Southern blacks were seen differently. One Northern
black newspaper at the time even described the newly arriving Southern
black immigrants as "vulgar, rowdy, unwashed, and criminal."[114] Violent
crime rates among Southern blacks who moved to Philadelphia were five
times higher than among blacks born there.[115] The same differences
appeared in educational achievement. A study of students attending
black colleges concluded that the "superiority of freshmen from northern schools over those from the southern schools was found to persist
throughout the colleges."[116] W. E. B. DuBois summarized his rather harsh
view of many Southern blacks as wasting "thousands of dollars" annually
in "amusements, miscellaneous ornaments and gewgaws. The Negro has
much to learn of the Jew and the Italian, as to living within his means
and saving every penny from excessive and wasteful expenditures."[117]

More recently, one of the most influential African-American political
figures of the twentieth century, Ralph Bunche, also noted that white
Southerners share many characteristics with blacks. Southern whites
"often carry a 'chip on the shoulder'; they indulge freely in self-
commiseration; they rather typically and in real Negro fashion try to
overcome a feeling of inferiority by exhibitionism, raucousness in dress,
and exaggerated self-assertion."[118] In *An American Dilemma*, Myrdal noted
similarities between the attitudes of Southern whites and blacks. He
described both groups as having a "low level of efficiency, reliability,
ambition, and morals" as well as a "devil-may-care" view of the world
in which crime is "not so reprehensible."[119] Even black religious "emo-
tionalism" was, said Myrdal, "borrowed from and sanctioned by behavior
among whites."[120]

What are we to make of this explanation of cultural differences? First,
it does have the virtue of explaining the differences in attitudes between
Northern and Southern blacks – a difference that is left mysterious by
those who speak only of their common history of slavery and oppression.

[114] Sowell, *Black Rednecks and White Liberals*, p. 47.
[115] E. Franklin Frazier, *The Negro in the United States*, Revised Editor (New York: Macmillan
    Co., 1957), p. 643, citing a 1940 study analyzing incarceration rates back to 1906.
[116] Frazier, *The Negro in the United States*, p. 484.
[117] W. E. B. DuBois (1899), *The Philadelphia Negro: A Social Study* (New York: Schocken Books,
    1970), p. 178.
[118] Quoted in Myrdal, *An American Dilemma*, p. 962.
[119] Myrdal, *An American Dilemma*, pp. 208, 959.
[120] Myrdal, *An American Dilemma*, p. 962.

But like the emphasis on slavery and oppression, this argument also leaves unexplained why the very significant progress that had been made by blacks (including many with those same Southern roots) occurred and then came to a virtual standstill in the 1970s. I do not want to deny that history, whether in the form of oppression or of contact with redneck culture, is part of the explanation of the cultural patterns I have been describing. But I want to suggest another explanation as well. Its origins are in the philosophy of slavery and its ideology, which blacks internalized as fear of racial inferiority. I will begin, however, with recent research focusing on the self-concept of African-Americans.

"Rumors of inferiority"

In 1992, Claude Steele published a study which was meant to call into question the conclusion of *The Bell Curve*, that racial differences explain the lower I.Q. scores of African-Americans.[121] In his study, Steele gave black Stanford University students tests of verbal ability. Sometimes he would say that the test was a measure of intellectual ability tied to race, but other times he did not mention race at all. Later studies varied the test and the information given before the test, so that sometimes students were told only that the test was a measure of ability, with no explicit reference to race. What Steele discovered is that mentioning either their race or that the test was a measure of intellectual abililty tended to reduce African-American students' performance on the tests. Steele concluded that "making African-Americans more conscious of negative stereotypes about their intellectual ability as a group can depress their test performance relative to whites."[122] This conclusion was supported by the fact that students who had their racial stereotypes "activated" also scored higher on a test measuring anxiety. Students who heard mention of intelligence or race were less able to complete the test on time, spending more time on questions than white students who were not suffering "stereotype threat." Steele also noted in his studies that whites are affected when they are told they are competing with Asians.

But I want to emphasize another implication of Steele's study besides relative test scores. Behind the fact that a stereotype threat lowers scores is the question of *why* it affects black students particularly. The answer

---

[121] Claude Steele, "Race and the Schooling of Black America," *Atlantic Monthly*, April 1992.
[122] Claude M. Steele and Joshua Aronson, "Stereotype Threat and the Test Performance of Academically Successful African Americans," in *The Black-White Test Score Gap*, edited by Jencks and Phillips, p. 422.

was suggested in a report from the "Committee of Policy for Racial Justice." The Committee, which was headed by Sara Lawrence Lightfoot and included other noted black intellectuals, concluded that part of the problem facing blacks is a "myth of intellectual inferiority, perhaps genetically based." That myth, the report concluded, "props up an inequitable social hierarchy with blacks disproportionately represented at the bottom."[123]

Writing in the *New Republic* in 1985, two psychologists had been even more explicit about the myth and its importance in understanding black attitudes. They began by describing the "deteriorating" situation facing blacks, in terms that are similar to the account I have given. Though the evidence was less clear then, the authors emphasized the importance of academic underachievement and low scores on SAT tests as well as reading and math scores for all blacks. The reason for the underachievement, they concluded, is persistent "rumors of inferiority" that had taken hold among blacks. Their two "hypotheses" were first that "black performance problems are caused in large part by a tendency to avoid intellectual competition," and second that "this tendency is a psychological phenomenon that rises when the larger society projects an image of black intellectual inferiority and when that image is internalized by black people."[124]

Although only a "hypothesis" 20 years ago, based on the experience of two psychologists, we now have evidence that rumors of inferiority are indeed a part of the problem. Not only does this help explain why stereotype threat has the effect it does on blacks, but it also explains why whites sometimes do less well when competing with Asians. In each case, there is reason to think that the affected group has "internalized" rumors of inferiority. This internalization can also help explain the attitudes of parents and students toward academics. As we have seen, there is evidence from studies of parenting practices, children's behavior, and work habits, and the attitudes of black students toward those among them who do well that blacks do indeed "avoid intellectual competition."

---

[123] Committee on Policy for Racial Justice, quoted in Scott L. Miller, *An American Imperative: Accelerating Minority Educational Advancement* (New Haven: Yale University Press, 1995), p. 203. I know from my own experience that others who teach African-American students share that concern. In their book the authors wrote that they are "concerned that the popularization of *The Bell Curve* has demoralized our minority students, reinforced nagging self-doubts, and worsened the problems." (*Inequality by Design*, edited by Fischer, et al., p. 198.) I agree that this is a worry, though I believe there is much more to be said about those "nagging self-doubts." Rumors of inferiority may also help explain the ferocious reaction against *The Bell Curve*, although there are other possible explanations.

[124] Jeff Howard and Ray Hammond, "Rumors of Inferiority: The Hidden Obstacles to Black Success," *New Republic*, September 9, 1985.

In their study of the "acting white" phenomenon, Fordham and Ogbu concluded that the problem of poor academic achievement

> arose partly because white Americans traditionally refused to acknowledge that black Americans are capable of intellectual development, and partly because black Americans subsequently began to doubt their own intellectual ability, began to define academic success as white people's prerogative, and began to discourage their peers, perhaps unconsciously, from emulating white people in academic striving, i.e., from "acting white."[125]

As always with such issues, it is difficult to know with any precision just how much weight to put on this explanation of the cultural differences that lead to poor educational achievement. But it does seem clear that educational achievement is an important part of economic success, that cultural differences are a significant element in causing the achievement gap, and that rumors of inferiority contribute to academic underachievement.

The racist history of slavery, reinforced by the insistence on black inferiority, provided fertile ground for rumors of inferiority. As is often noted, African-Americans' fear of racial inferiority can be seen as a legacy of slavery and racial oppression, which were premised on such beliefs. But relatively ancient history is not the whole story. What has not been noticed is the effect of more recent events that have also tended to reinforce the rumors of inferiority. Powerful messages have been sent more recently about the inability of blacks to succeed, often by those who hope to aid the fight against poverty and racial equality. Those messages began, perhaps not surprisingly, in the 1960s.

In one of the most important and oft-quoted statements of his presidency, Lyndon Johnson explained the reasoning behind his Great Society program. He stated that, "You do not take a person who, for years, has been hobbled by chains and liberate him, bring him to the starting line of a race and then say, 'you are free to compete with all the others' and still justly believe that you have been completely fair." Johnson went on to add that it is not enough "just to open the gates of opportunity." What is required, he concluded, is "equality as a fact and as a result."[126] To achieve such equality, he proposed, and Congress passed, a variety of

---

[125] Signithia Fordham and John U. Ogbu, "Black Students' School Success: Coping with the Burden of 'Acting White,'" *Urban Review*, Vol. 18, No. 3 (1986), p. 177.

[126] Lyndon B. Johnson, Commencement Address at Howard University, "To Fulfill These Rights," June 4, 1965. Available at http://www.lbjlib.utexas.edu/johnson /archives.hom/speeches.hom/650604.asp. Accessed on March 25, 2007.

new and expanded welfare programs, all with the objective of overcoming the "hobbling" of African-Americans that resulted from slavery and historic oppression.

Johnson's message, that history has crippled African-Americans, resonated widely. Indeed, the idea that blacks cannot expect to compete as equals is still widely expressed. Recently, Supreme Court Justice Ruth Bader Ginsburg described the continuing effects of the shackles of history in her defense of Michigan Law School's policy giving preferences to blacks in admissions. "We are not far distant," she wrote, "from an overtly discriminatory past, and the effects of centuries of law-sanctioned inequality remain painfully evident in our communities and schools. In the wake of a system of racial caste only recently ended, large disparities endure."[127] The effects of that past, she concluded, show up in "large disparities" in blacks' abilities to succeed in college and on the job market.

The same theme, that African-Americans cannot compete with other groups, takes other forms. It is the dominant chord of much sympathetic scholarship about race. In an especially influential article, Derrick Bell describes what he terms "racial realism." Black people, according to Bell,

> will never gain full equality in this country. Even those herculean efforts we hail as successful will produce no more than temporary "peaks of progress," the short-lived victories that slide into irrelevance as racial patters adapt in ways that maintain white dominance. We must acknowledge . . . the permanence of our subordinate status.[128]

Hoping for no more than "short-lived victories that slide into irrelevance," Bell concludes that "The racial realism we must seek is simply a hard-eyed view of racism as it is and our subordinate role in it."[129] Law professor Kimberle Crenshaw mirrors that pessimism in another widely known article. She asserts (again with no real evidence) both that "virulent white race consciousness" plays an "important, perhaps crucial role" in the problems facing blacks, and that the "material conditions of the majority of Blacks" are "deteriorating day to day."[130]

---

[127] *Gratz v. Bollinger*, 539 U.S at 273 (Justice Ginsburg dissenting).
[128] Derrick Bell, "Racial Realism," in *Critical Race Theory*, edited by Crenshaw, et al., p. 306.
[129] Bell, "Racial Realism," in *Critical Race Theory*, edited by Crenshaw, et al., p. 308.
[130] Kimberle Crenshaw, "Race, Reform, and Retrenchment," in *Critical Race Theory: Cases, Materials, and Problems*, edited by Brown, p. 33.

These views are echoed by still other writers. A University of California at Berkeley professor of African-American studies, June Jordan, wrote regularly in *The Progressive* for 7 years. One of her many columns included this reflection on the contemporary situation faced by blacks in the United States:

> Where I live now makes me wonder if Nazi Germany's night skies ever beheld a really big moon – a heavenly light that failed to dispel the cold and bitter winds tormenting the darkness of earth below.
> Where I live now there is just such a moon tonight – a useless, huge light above our perishing reasons for hope.[131]

Law professor Dorothy E. Roberts also asserts that "Despite decades devoted to civil rights protest and litigation based on constitutional fidelity, the economic and political condition of the majority of blacks has worsened."[132] Other articles with titles like "Whiteness as Property"[133] repeat the same themes.

The message of all of this, from both white and black leaders and scholars, could hardly be clearer. Racial oppression and victimization are the permanent lot of African-Americans. The heavy hand of history and of the pervasive and debilitating racism of contemporary whites constitute a near-permanent block to African-American progress. Handicapped by history and contemporary racism, blacks cannot hope to compete as equals. Just as history can never be undone, so too is it impossible for blacks to change white society.

Yet, the contrast between the facts and this pessimistic rhetoric about white attitudes and black reality is stark. Recall how Myrdal described the conditions of life in the South a half century ago. A white, he wrote, could "strike or beat a Negro, steal or destroy his property, cheat him in a transaction and even take his life, without much fear of legal reprisal."[134] Blacks were not allowed to vote, and were effectively excluded from holding political offices. All public accommodations from restaurants and hotels to buses, rest rooms, and water fountains were legally segregated. Interracial marriages were forbidden by both law and custom. A survey taken in 1944 revealed that a majority of whites agreed "white

[131] Quoted in John McWhorter, *Losing the Race* (New York; Harper Collins, 2001), p. 39.
[132] Dorothy E. Roberts, "The Meaning of Blacks' Fidelity to the Constitution," *Fordham Law Review*, Vol. 65, No. 4 (March 1997), p. 1769.
[133] Cheryl I. Harris, "Whiteness as Property," *Harvard Law Review*, Vol. 106 (1993), p. 1707.
[134] Myrdal, *An American Dilemma*, p. 559.

people should have the first chance at any kind of job."[135] But by 1972, the percentage of white Americans saying that blacks should "have as good a chance as white people to get any kind of job" went to 97 percent – virtually everyone. Similarly, by 1972, 84 percent of whites favored integrated schools and 85 percent expressed no reservation about having a black neighbor. Changes since then have continued that trend.[136] The educational and economic position of most blacks has also improved markedly, as we saw.

Even blacks themselves are often misinformed about the success of their own race. A 1991 Gallup Poll revealed that nearly half of African-Americans believe that the percentage of blacks living in a "ghetto" is 75 percent. That is about three times the rate of actual poverty among blacks, and even fewer blacks actually live in ghettos.[137] Significant numbers of blacks also believe racist white doctors intentionally caused AIDS among blacks; and a black member of the U.S. House of Representatives, Maxine Waters, once asked for an investigation into unsubstantiated reports that the CIA sold crack cocaine to blacks to raise money for secret activities in Central America.

Pragmatism's insight

How are we to understand the importance of these ideas, that blacks continue to be prevented from succeeding by the shackles of history and that they must endure pervasive white racism. Why does it matter that these ideas are so widespread? The answer begins with dignity. When I discussed racial equality in Chapter 4, I argued that segregation constituted a direct assault on people's dignity. Dignity includes self-respect and self-esteem, and both are connected with well-being. People who hold these attitudes believe that what they are pursuing is worthwhile, that they possess the capacities necessary to accomplish those worthwhile ends, and that they are not inherently unworthy in virtue of their membership in a racial, cultural, religious, ethnic, or other group. I also suggested there, without elaboration, the important role a sense of one's own dignity plays in encouraging people to pursue worthy ends.

---

[135] Myrdal, *An American Dilemma*, p. 559.

[136] Thernstrom and Thernstrom, *America in Black and White*, pp. 141, 500. (Figures are from various sources.)

[137] *Newsweek*, April 26, 1991, and U.S. Census Data, cited in Thernstrom and Thernstrom, *America in Black and White*, p. 184.

The importance of the historic emphasis on racial inferiority and, more recently, on the shackles of history and the stacked deck of white racism are nicely illustrated in an essay by William James.[138] James was writing about religious faith, but his general concern was the way in which people's beliefs and faith can affect the likelihood that they will succeed. He illustrates this using the example of friendship. Whether "you like me or not" depends on whether

> I am willing to assume that you must like me, and show you trust and expectation. The previous faith on my part in your liking's existence is in such cases what produces your liking. But if I stand aloof, and refuse to budge an inch until I have objective evidence, until you shall have done something apt. . . . ten to one your liking never comes. . . . There are, then, cases where a fact cannot come at all unless a preliminary faith exists in its coming.[139]

He goes on to ask:

> Who gains promotions, boons, appointments, but the man in whose life they seem to play the part of live hypotheses, who . . . sacrifices other things for their sake before they have come, and takes risks for them in advance? His faith acts on the powers above him as a claim, and creates its own verification.[140]

Faith that people in a room will be friendly has an effect first on the person entering who has the faith, and that, in turn, affects others. Optimism can make it more likely that a belief will be true in many contexts. Believing that it is possible to jump a stream or walk on a log can affect people's confidence and with it their likelihood of success, just as believing that one cannot possibly make it can reduce the likelihood of success. Although keeping faith in the absence of evidence may appear naive, James concludes, it is an "insane logic" that would criticize such optimism universally.

This optimistic faith, when turned to one's own self, takes the form of self-respect and the confidence that one's efforts will not be in vain. The belief that we will probably not succeed, on the other hand, can be debilitating. Why bother to pursue objectives when they are beyond our grasp? With that pessimism about the future comes added failure, as

---

[138] William James (1897), "The Will to Believe," *Essays In Pragmatism* (New York: Haffner Publishing Co., 1948), p. 104.

[139] James, "The Will to Believe," p. 104.

[140] James, "The Will to Believe," p. 104.

the cycle continues. Just as successful pursuit of an end engenders self-respect, including the belief in one's capacities to succeed in the future, failure undermines confidence and with it the prospects of future success. Confidence supports and encourages the willingness to try, self-doubt the opposite.

People who have self-respect are more likely to succeed for still another reason. When people fail (as humans inevitably sometimes will), those who enjoy self-respect will tend to think they can eventually succeed and are inclined to work hard in order to avoid failing again. Self-respect encourages the motivation to work hard and improve skills. Those who lack self-respect, already feeling they cannot succeed, will tend to exert less effort to improve their own abilities to succeed in the future.

Besides these philosophical considerations, there is also empirical evidence supporting James' pragmatist position. One form of intelligence, according to psychologist Martin Seligman, is emotional intelligence, and Seligman thinks that optimism is a component of emotional intelligence. Wanting to put his idea into practice, the Metropolitan Life insurance company asked him to develop a test for applicants for sales jobs that would measure the applicant's level of optimism. They then administered the test and used it in making hiring decisions along with the more traditional criteria. The test divided those who qualified as optimists into those ordinarily optimistic and "superoptimists." After one year it was reported that optimists did better than pessimists and that the superoptimists did better still, selling 57 percent more than the pessimists.[141]

The cases William James imagined were ones in which what was believed was based on inadequate evidence or was even believed despite contrary evidence. Even in these situations, as James points out, it may be rational to be optimistic. The attitudes I have described, of the shackles of history and the racially stacked deck, in contrast, encourage a pessimism that is in fact *unwarranted* on the evidence. Rather than erring on the side of optimism, as James argued it is often rational to do, we see a tendency to do the opposite. This is done by ignoring or denigrating black progress, exaggerating the racism that is actually faced by blacks, and inventing analogies suggesting that slavery and segregation have left blacks crippled and unable to compete. If it is an "insane" logic not to be optimistic in the face of insufficient evidence, then it is even more insane to be pessimistic in the face of contrary evidence.

[141] Nancy Gibbs, "The E.Q. Factor," *Time Magazine*, October 2, 1995.

Nothing in what I have said is meant to deny that blacks face special challenges or that racism is sometimes a real impediment. But acknowledging real problems is different from embracing historical determinism and exaggerated pessimism. Rather than having a single cause, poverty results from a web of mutually reinforcing economic and cultural factors. Most directly relevant, culturally, are single-parent families, crime, and poor educational achievement. In the background is the fact that low-skilled manufacturing jobs have declined substantially in the United States, making educational achievement even more important. Those problems were also made worse, ironically, by the emphasis placed on the burdens of history and the racially stacked deck. But I also argued that slavery and racial oppression did have a role, albeit indirect and difficult to specify, in producing the poverty and economic inequality. Some have suggested that justice demands compensation to the victims of slavery and racial oppression, which is the topic of Chapter 6.

6

Compensatory Justice: Restitution, Reparations, and Apologies

WHATEVER THEIR DEFENDERS MAY HAVE THOUGHT, SLAVERY AND other forms of racial oppression are now recognized for the enormous moral evil they were. Many believe that poverty and other problems facing a quarter of today's African-Americans are traceable at least in part to the lingering effects of that shameful history. Vincene Verdun, for instance, writes that differences in the rates of "unemployment, income, mortality rates, substandard housing and education" are the "effects of over 300 years of oppression."[1] Owen Fiss expresses that view beginning with the title of his book: *A Way Out: America's Ghettos and the Legacy of Racism.*[2] I argued in Chapter 5 that although it is controversial and hard to specify with any precision, historic oppression did contribute to the problems facing African-Americans. It did so by encouraging rumors of inferiority and undermining the cultural commitment to educational achievement. In this chapter, I discuss a proposal that has gained considerable support recently. That proposal usually goes under the somewhat misleading title of reparations, though compensatory justice is more accurate since reparations are only one form that compensatory justice can take.

Justice can take many forms; some are backward looking. Compensatory justice is concerned not with improving current institutions and practices to make them more just but rather with compensating victims of past wrongs. Even if current social institutions and laws were perfectly just, it would still be possible that individuals deserve some form of

---

[1] Vincene Verdu, "If the Shoe Fits, Wear It: An Analysis of Reparations to African Americans," *Tulane Law Review*, Vol. 67 (February 1993), p. 664.
[2] Owen Fiss, *A Way Out: America's Ghettos and the Legacy of Racism* (Princeton: Princeton University Press, 2003).

compensation for past wrongs. Historic social injustices might by themselves provide the ground for compensation.

Proposals to provide some form of compensation for U.S. slavery and racial oppression have a long and controversial history. To date, about a dozen major U.S. cities have passed resolutions asking the federal government to study the issue. For many years Representative John Conyers (D-Michigan) has also introduced a bill in Congress calling for a similar study, though the proposal has never gotten out of committee. The academic and popular literature on the subject has also grown.[3]

While the demands to pay compensation for racial oppression go back at least to the post-Civil War era, the issue has been given added urgency by the confluence of three factors. The first is a heightened willingness to confront historical realities, especially the treatment of racial minorities. We can see this across the board, as textbooks and the media have become more willing to look at American history from the perspective of Native Americans and minorities as well as of settlers. A second reason that compensatory justice has found its way onto the agenda is the civil rights movement, which has enabled and encouraged historically disadvantaged groups to pursue redress of grievances. And third, there is a renewed willingness on the part of both governments and corporations to provide compensation for injustices in other contexts. Often it has taken the form of cash payments or other benefits to victims of Nazi and Japanese atrocities during World War II. Some have sought to return land to native peoples, while others have simply offered apologies. Apologies have been offered for a wide range of past injustices done to Jews, Korean women, Native Americans, and South African blacks. The U.S. government apologized for its role in overthrowing the native government in Hawaii and the elected government in Guatemala.

---

[3] Popular works include Randall Robinson, *The Debt: What America Owes to Blacks* (New York: Dutton, 1999), and Charles J. Ogletree, Jr., "The Case for Reparations," *USA Weekend* (August 16–18, 2002), p. 7. Important philosophical work in the area includes Bernard Boxill, "Morality of Reparation," in *Social Theory and Practice*, Vol. 2 (1972), pp. 119–120; George Sher, "Ancient Wrongs and Modern Rights," *Philosophy and Public Affairs*, Vol. 10, No. 1 (1980); pp. 13–17; Jeremy Waldron, "Superseding Historical Injustice," *Ethics*, Vol. 103 (1992), pp. 4–28; George Schedler, *Racist Symbols and Reparations* (Lanham MD: Rowman and Littlefield, 1999); Robert K. Fullinwider, *The Case for Reparations*, Report of the Institute for Philosophy and Public Policy (College Park MD: Maryland School of Public Affairs, Institute for Philosophy and Public Policy, 2000); Janna Thomson, "Historical Injustice and Reparation: Justifying Claims of Descendants," *Ethics*, Vol. 112 (2001), pp. 114–135; and Janna Thomson, *Taking Responsibility for the Past: Reparation and Historical Justice* (Cambridge UK: Polity Press, 2002).

Demands for some form of compensatory justice raise a host of issues, from the rationale for the compensation to the nature of the harm, who should receive the compensation, the form compensation should take, and who (or what) should pay it. I will survey some of the answers often given to these difficult questions and then focus in particular on the "baseline" problem of how harm or damages are to be determined. In the last section of this chapter, I argue for a different but potentially important form of compensatory justice: an apology.

Two forms of compensation: Restitution and reparation

Two forms of compensation that might be given for past injustices are restitution and reparation.[4] *Restitution* occurs when property that has been taken from the owner is returned. *Reparation*, on the other hand, is repair of harms caused by past wrongs done either intentionally or through negligence.[5] The two are easily confused because violations of a right to a piece of property can also cause harm to a person. But restitution and reparation can be separated, and when considering issues of compensatory justice it is helpful to do so.

The distinction between restoring what was taken and repairing harm that has been wrongfully caused has roots in traditional English common law as well as common sense. Traditionally, the common law allowed for two different writs that litigants could request and that would give them the right to bring a lawsuit. One, known as "repleven," is a demand of restitution, that is, for the return of property to its rightful owner. Another, a "writ of trespass on the case," was a request not to sue for the return of a thing but instead to sue for compensation for damages.[6] The

---

[4] The discussions of compensation for past injustices have not paid close attention to this distinction, often using the terms interchangeably. Janna Thomson, for example, speaks of reparations but sometimes is thinking of claims to objects that may survive through time. She uses the analogy of heirlooms that people have a right to pass down to later generations but then later shifts to the harms that were caused by slavery and segregation. See Thomson, "Historical Injustice and Reparation: Justifying Claims of Descendants," and especially *Taking Responsibility for the Past: Reparation and Historical Justice*, pp. 137–140.

[5] Compensation is not always required based on past wrongdoing. A person might be compensated by an insurance company, for instance. But compensatory justice, as I understand it, does assume it is an historic wrong and not just a loss or harm that warrants the compensation. For a discussion of the more expansive view, see Boxill, "The Morality of Reparation."

[6] Technically, these are damages that were the consequence of a wrongful act. This is the predecessor of negligence, nuisance, and other modern bases of tort liability. See *Black's*

point of those origins, however interesting to historians, is not that the demand for restitution and reparations depends on law but rather that both demands are reflected in traditional as well as contemporary legal systems. They are based in moral claims. Arguments over compensatory justice rest on moral and not just on legal grounds.

Restitution often presents an easy case. Something was taken, and it should be returned. Reparations are different; they involve wrongful actions that *cause harm* and require a different form of compensation. Because reparations do not simply seek return of something to its rightful owner, there does not need to be any specific thing that was taken. In modern times, tort law regulates private relations among citizens and requires repair of damages caused by the person who was at fault.[7] This "repair" generally takes the form of payment for business losses, property damages, medical expenses, lost wages, and "pain and suffering" of the victim, which can also include loss of ability to use part of one's body, loss of a spouse's companionship, and much more. Compensation is required whether the harm was intentional or accidental.

Reparation differs from restitution. Suppose someone breaks a friend's dinner plate. *Restitution* might be achieved by repairing that very plate or buying another one like it. If there is no possibility of returning the original and there is no identical replacement, then restitution could be provided in some other way, for example, money. The question whether the person owed restitution was *harmed* by the loss of the object is not the focus of restitution. The victim may have lots of plates remaining and did not even notice or care about the one that was broken. She may even be glad the plate is gone, having inherited it from a despised relative. The point is that the object belonged to someone, who is entitled to its return. The actual harm done to the victim by the breaking of the plate is not the focus.

Some claims made for compensatory justice are based on restitution. Native people's arguments that their land be returned are an example of this because the object in dispute is the property that was taken and the remedy demanded is its return. Victims of Nazis have also claimed restitution, arguing that their property that was seized should be returned

---

Law Dictionary, 7th ed., edited by B. H. Garner. (St. Paul: West Publishing Co., 1999), p. 1509.

[7] One exception to this occurs when a government is sued for negligence by a private citizen seeking compensation for damages caused by the government official in his or her official capacity.

to them. Some have also suggested that slavery created an obligation to pay restitution to the descendants of slaves.

Note that restitution involves more straightforward issues than reparations. There is no need to determine whether a wrongful act caused damages and, if so, what the remedy should be. Is restitution a proper response to slavery?

Restitution and slavery

The idea that slavery took something from slaves that should be returned may seem to follow naturally from the nature of slavery itself. Ownership of slaves meant masters exerted extraordinary (if not absolute) power over them. Restitution might therefore lie in returning what was lost in consequence of the denial of the slaves' rights and opportunities to control their labor. Bernard Boxill, for example, argues that it is the stolen labor of slaves that ought to be returned.[8] By denying slaves the right to work for themselves, the owners, in effect, appropriated their labor power for themselves. Because the *labor itself* obviously can't be returned, the argument concludes, the best that can be done is to return the *value* of that labor to the descendants of those from whom it was wrongly taken. This seems to be what Randall Robinson famously proposed when he claimed that cash payments to the descendants of slaves should make up for lost wages, which he thinks would total "perhaps a trillion and a half."[9]

One way to object to restitution would be to deny the premise that people have a moral right to have their property returned. If property is a purely conventional or legal right, and can be ignored unless society has established an expectation that people can give their property to their heirs, then, some have argued, there is no property right. If that view of property rights as conventions is accepted, then the possibility of restitution would not even arise in a situation such as slavery where there is no right established by law to inherit property.[10] I will assume, however, that restitution cannot be dismissed so easily, and that it may be owed for violations of property rights. The question is how we are to understand

---

[8] Boxill, "Morality of Reparation."

[9] Quoted in Newburger, "Breaking the Chain," p. 21.

[10] That is argued explicitly by David Haslett, "Is Inheritance Justified?" *Philosophy and Public Affairs*, Vol. 15, No. 2 (1986), p. 122. See also, Liam Murphy and Thomas Nagel, *The Myth of Ownership* (New York: Oxford University Press, 2002).

the demand that restitution be paid for slavery or other distant wrongs. What was taken that needs to be returned?

Perhaps we should treat the value of slaves' labor *as if* it were an heirloom that would have been passed down through the generations. But because we are not simply restoring *physical property* to the original owners or even to their descendants, this requires calculating the value of the slaves' labor in money terms. How could that be done?

Some of the problems associated with restitution for lost labor are practical. We would first have to determine the value of the labor power *at the time*. Feeding, housing, and caring for slaves took a substantial proportion of what slaves produced, but the issue is controversial. By one estimate, only 12 percent of the value of slaves' labor was appropriated by their masters, while 88 percent went to support the slaves.[11] Others disagree, of course. But suppose that we have settled on that or some other percentage, and are now agreed that slaves produced more value, *V*, than they were given in payment for their labor. Should we then return *V*?

Since we must determine what should be given now, to their descendants, it seems that we decide on the *current value* of *V*, many generations later. That poses what has to many seemed an insurmountable problem. How can we decide the current value of something when all we could know (at most) is what it was worth generations ago? History matters in that calculation. Suppose we wanted to compensate an original owner for the theft of a picture of Bill Clinton kissing Hillary Rodham in 1970 when they were students. At the time the photo was taken, the price of the photo might have been next to nothing, but today it would presumably be worth far more. The question of its present value cannot be answered without assuming whether or not history would unfold as it did, making them a famous couple and their picture more valuable. Because this picture was worth nothing at that time, is it reasonable to look backward and say, today, that it was worth more at that time because it is worth more now?

As often occurs with compensatory justice, it is not clear how to answer the photo question. It may be even more difficult when we think of the value of labor, and in a more troubling way. That is because we cannot possibly know what all those many intervening generations would have done with the labor power had they inherited it from the slaves. We have

---

[11] Robert William Fogel and Stanley L. Engerman, *Time on the Cross* (New York: Little, Brown and Co., 1974), p. 109.

no idea if the next generations would have spent it, invested it, lost it, or given it away. We don't even know if *any* of value would still be left to inherit. Should we assume the value of the labor went up slowly with inflation, went up rapidly, was entirely wasted, or given away to charities? Any assignment of some present value to *V* that we might make seems arbitrary.

Because what *V* would be worth now depends on choices people would have made, but didn't, it may even seem that there is no truth of the matter to be known.[12] The value of the inheritance today depends crucially on *free choices* people would have made but didn't. Suppose we ask how much money would be left over at the end of a single person's life had that person (call her Possible Inheritor I) been give a million dollars at birth. Because there was no inheritance, there was no opportunity for Possible Inheritor I to make any of the choices that would have produced the outcome. Jeremy Waldron thinks that this shows not just that the answer is impossible to know but that there is nothing there to be known – no fact to be learned. The value of an inheritance today depends on free *choices people might have* made but didn't. It is like asking how many jellybeans are in an imaginary jar of indeterminate size. Waldron concludes that restitution should be rejected. "My *guess*" about what might have happened, he writes, "has no normative authority whatsoever" about what might have happened had people made different choices about their property.[13] If we know Possible Inheritor I to be frugal, generous, or wasteful, then we might be able to make a reasonable prediction of what she would have chosen.

But we do not have any such information about the immediate descendants of slaves, let alone the many other generations. What those generations (Possible Inheritors II, III, IV, etc.) would have done with the inheritance is impossible to know. We not only lack information about their psychology but also about what options those later generations would have confronted. Their choices would have depended on what they inherited, which would in turn have depended on choices Possible Inheritors before them would have made. Yet, we have virtually no information on which to rely in making that decision.

We might think that the right answer, given our lack of knowledge, would be to assume the choices the descendants would have made are

---

[12] See Waldron, "Superseding Historical Injustice." For the reasons that follow, I think his claim that there is no fact to be known is mistaken in one important respect.

[13] Waldron, "Superseding Historical Injustice," p. 10.

the ones a *typical or ordinary person* in those circumstances would make. But why assume that, unless there is evidence that they are typical? The reason might be that we are always entitled to assume, absent further information to the contrary, that a person is like others.[14] People often generalize about what others will do, based on little available evidence. Why not do the same here and simply assume the descendants of slaves would have behaved like people on average behave with an inheritance? If we do that, and if we assume that the average person would have saved or invested in ways that preserved a certain amount of the value of the labor as an inheritance, then are not descendants entitled to receive that inheritance?

Even granting what has been said, other objections remain against restitution. For one thing, the potential recipients of that inheritance will not be the same people who are often assumed to be the ones entitled to restitution, that is, those African-Americans who are now the poorest and most in need.[15] Poverty would have little or nothing to do with it. Nor would the beneficiaries be the "black community" in general, as is also suggested.[16] The recipients would be the descendants of slaves, and only them. They would exclude immigrant blacks and their descendants who came after emancipation. Indeed, some of the actual descendants of slaves would be very wealthy. (The late Alex Haley, the author of *Roots*, comes to mind.) Yet, it seems odd, at least, to ignore the neediest and most disadvantaged and provide compensation for slavery to the wealthy.

Another potentially troubling question is who owes the debt. The answer to that would depend on who now owns or at least who benefits from the value of the labor that was taken. It is far from clear that, framed that way, there is even an answer to the question. It is not an object after all, but the value of labor that was taken – taken originally by the owners of the slaves. Who now owns or benefits from that unjust taking?

We know that in fact the Civil War virtually destroyed the South economically, including the wealth of the former slaveowners. Sixty percent of *all* the wealth of the South was lost during the War, and one quarter of white males of military age were killed. That loss is proportionally more

---

[14] Defenders of compensatory justice often assume the problem of indeterminacy is weighty, if not conclusive. See, for example, Thompson, *Taking Responsibility for the Past.* These concerns, she writes, put "substantial moral barriers" to restitution (p. 112).

[15] Ogletree, "The Case for Reparations," p. 7.

[16] Joe R. Feagin, *Racist America* (New York: Routledge, 2000), p. 266.

than in any country in World War I.[17] So it seems likely that much or perhaps all the value of the labor that was taken from slaves by slaveowners was destroyed along with the lives and other property of those who benefitted from it at the time. Indeed, it can be argued that not only did the descendants of slaveowners not benefit financially from slavery, but they actually suffered from its presence in U.S. history. Abraham Lincoln eloquently described the cost to the South of eliminating slavery in his Second Inaugural Address:

> Fondly do we hope, fervently do we pray, that this mighty scourge of war may speedily pass away. Yet, if God wills that it continue until all the wealth piled by the bondsman's two hundred and fifty years of unrequited toil shall be sunk, and until every drop of blood drawn with the lash shall be paid by another drawn with the swords, as was said three thousand years ago, so still it must be said "the judgments of the Lord are true and righteous altogether."[18]

Some critics of restitution also claim that the debt has already been paid by other means. One writer calculates that the effect of welfare payments and progressive taxation means there is a net transfer of roughly 75 billion dollars to African-Americans every year, which is the equivalent of a Marshall Plan for blacks every 3 years.[19] It has also been suggested that the debt was paid by the blood of Union soldiers in the Civil War, where more than 350,000 soldiers died.[20]

The argument that slavery created a debt of restitution is rarely distinguished from the idea that *reparations* are owed. Yet, the two are very different. Restitution requires a showing that *something* was taken of value, and that it should be returned to the descendant of its original owner who would otherwise be entitled to it. Each of those claims supporting restitution is problematic, and so it is perhaps understandable that much of the discussion has focused on reparations and the lingering harms of racial oppression rather than on the property that was taken.

---

[17] James M. McPherson, *Abraham Lincoln and the Second American Revolution* (New York: Oxford University Press, 1991), p. 38.

[18] Abraham Lincoln, "Second Inaugural Address," March 4, 1865. http://www. bartleby.com/124/pres32.html.

[19] Michael Levin, *Why Race Matters* (Westport CT: Praeger, 1997), p. 259.

[20] McPherson, *Abraham Lincoln*, p. 37.

Some puzzles about reparations

Reparation rather than restitution has dominated discussions of compensatory justice. A leading public exponent of compensating for slavery, Randall Robinson, clearly thinks in terms of reparations rather than restitution. The argument, according to Robinson, rests on the fact that slavery was "a human rights crime without parallel in the modern world" that "produces its victims, *ad infinitum,* long after the active stage of the crime has ended." The goal, he says, is "repairing the victim" and making the victim "whole."[21] Robinson is thinking not of returning lost property but of reparation for the lingering effects of slavery. In the abstract, the issues here are similar to those raised by restitution: who owes the debt, why is it owed, and to whom should it be paid? But the difference is crucial. Restitution means *returning* property that was wrongfully taken. Reparation means *repairing* the damage caused by a past wrong.

The first objection, then, to demands for reparations for slavery and other historic injustices is the conceptual challenge that nothing can be done today about injustices done to long-dead slaves and other victims of past discrimination. Past wrongs, it is sometimes thought, cannot be repaired so why not focus on current problems instead? Yet, in law, the duty to pay reparations often extends well beyond immediate victims and their contemporaries. A doctor who commits malpractice on a pregnant woman, and environmental polluters whose acts harm future generations, can be morally (and legally) liable for those distant consequences as well as more immediate ones.[22] In law, the famous DES cases illustrate this. Women took the drug, supposedly to prevent miscarriages. The unfortunate effect of the mothers' taking the drug was that their daughters often eventually developed cancer as a result of the DES. Despite the distance in time, the manufacturers of DES were held liable for cancers in the children of women who took it.[23]

Another objection that is sometimes raised against reparations is that nobody living today was responsible for slavery. Why should those innocent people be held to account for the wrongs of others? But again this misses the mark. When the government of Germany paid reparations to

[21] Robinson, *The Debt: What America Owes Blacks,* pp. 19, 21.
[22] For obvious reasons, law does not attempt to compensate all those who have been harmed, however remote. But our concern here is with political morality. Whether it is practical, or wise, as a policy matter to pay reparations for slavery is a question I will touch on in later sections.
[23] *Sindell v. Abbott Laboratories,* 26 Cal.3d 588, cert. denied, 449 U.S. 912 (1980).

Jews who suffered in the Holocaust, and the U.S. government compensated Japanese-Americans who had been forced into camps during World War II, there was no suggestion that it was because living persons were responsible for those injustices. The possibility of governments owing the debt will be considered later, but off-hand it does seem reasonable to suppose a government can owe reparations even when no living person does.

Payments of reparations *would* have to take adequate account of the history of the slave trade, including the fact that many other peoples and governments all over the world were deeply involved in slavery and slave trading. As discussed in Chapter 3, African slavery flourished with the creation of Islam and the emergence of the great Arab civilizations, with millions of Africans bought by Muslim traders for sale or use in their own societies as slaves.[24] In the Americas, the colonies that eventually became the United States were a relatively minor player. The European powers, especially Britain, Spain, and Portugal, did take a major role in the trade to America, but trade to the United States was itself a tiny part of the total slave trade. Only about 3 percent of the total number of Africans sold into slavery in the New World were brought to what is now the United States. The vast majority – more than 90 percent – of slaves went to the Caribbean and to Central and South America.

In reality, then, African slavery in the United States was a mutual undertaking among Arabs, Europeans, Africans, South Americans, and North Americans, with Native Americans and even some African-Americans also participating. The debt, if it exists, rests on the shoulders of many, including Arabs and Africans as well as Native Americans, African-Americans, and Europeans. If reparations for slavery in the United States are owed, it is also only a minor part of the total. Again, these may not be insoluble problems, though the historic record does show the complexity and difficulty of addressing the problem.

Nor would the debt necessarily be owed only to African-Americans. Other groups also suffered historic injustices in the United States, including Asians, Native Americans, Mormons, and women, and there is no reason in principle to exclude them. Some of these victims of historic injustices, like women, also suffered at the hands of ancestors of other victimized groups, raising the possibility that some groups

---

[24] Paul Lovejoy, *Transformations in Slavery: A History of Slavery in Africa* (Cambridge UK: Cambridge University Press, 2000) p. 25.

may be owed reparations by other groups that are themselves owed reparations.

Another difficulty that would have to be faced in deciding who is eligible to receive reparations flows from the fact that virtually all African-Americans except new arrivals to the United States are mixed race: they are the descendants of both whites and African slaves. As I discussed in Chapter 2, genetic tests reveal that the typical "black" in the United States is actually mixed race and has on average roughly 17 percent Caucasian ancestry. Many others are biologically only a small part descendant of slaves. Should *all* of the descendants of a slave be given reparations, no matter how distant their relationship is? That would be, in effect, to follow the historic one drop rule. If that policy were adopted, it would mean that many people, who today think of themselves as white, would in fact be entitled to reparations.

Another possibility, allowing individuals who self-identify as black to collect, would create incentives for people to claim reparations who may not be identified, socially, as African-Americans. Another possibility would be to test eligibility by physical appearance, but that too raises a host of problems. How much should a person "look" African-American to qualify? Still another puzzle is what to do about people whose ancestors came to the United States after slavery. Are they all eligible to apply for reparations? If not, then which ones would be excluded?

Responding to these puzzles, one well-known defender of reparations has suggested that reparations should be directed at those who are in the worst position today, rather than successful blacks, such as "the Tiger Woods and Oprah Winfreys."[25] Instead of checks to everyone, he proposes that an independent commission should be set up to distribute funds to the "poorest members of the black community, where damages have been most severe . . . [in order to help] the truly disadvantaged."[26] But while the proposal may be more consistent with the goal of reparations since these people would presumably be the ones who were most burdened by history, the commission would still need to define the "black community." Are members of the black community anyone with one drop of black blood, anyone who appears black, or anyone who self-identifies as African-American? Other defenders of reparations have taken a different approach, suggesting compensation in the form of more broad-based

[25] Ogletree, "The Case for Reparations," p. 7.
[26] Ogletree, "The Case for Reparations," p. 7.

"community investment and institutional rebuilding."[27]   Joe R. Feagin proposes that reparations should be designed to "significantly upgrade major public facilities in all black communities."[28] Again, however, we are not told precisely how we are to define a black community. Are these communities to be overwhelmingly black, or is it enough that a significant minority of the residents are black? Should we distinguish black communities from mixed race and integrated ones?

Although the problems I have been discussing are daunting, the fact that reparations raise difficult issues is not by itself sufficient reason to reject them. Often in law, and in life, we must do the best we can. Juries are frequently asked to assign monetary payments for damages that seem impossible to calculate – death, loss of limb, and even pain and suffering. They do it not because we have a very precise idea about how much each of those is worth in money but because not compensating would be an even greater injustice. So while these practical problems are important, they do not present overwhelming objections to reparations.

Who owes reparations?

The question whom to pay raises another puzzle: who should pay? It is clear that nobody, today, is guilty of the crimes that are being charged. Often that observation is regarded as sufficient to rebut demands of compensation. U.S. Congressman Henry Hyde famously noted, for example, that

> the notion of collective guilt for what people did 200-plus years ago, that this generation should pay a debt for that generation, is an idea whose time has gone. I never owned a slave. I never oppressed anybody. I don't know that I should have to pay for somebody who did generations before I was born.[29]

There is no doubt that Congressman Hyde's premise is correct. He and his audience never owned slaves. A different approach, taken by Mari Matsuda, also plays into the hands of those who emphasize the distance between themselves and slaveowners. She describes the people who owe reparations as "defendants" who are "*current beneficiaries of past injustice.*"[30]

---

[27] Roy L. Brooks, "The Debate Over Slave Reparations," ABCNEWS.com. Accessed on June 16, 2001.

[28] Feagin, *Racist America*, p. 266.

[29] Henry Hyde, quoted in *Reparations for Slavery*, edited by Ronald P. Salberger and Mary C. Turck. (Lanham: Rowman and Littlefield, 2004), p. 142.

[30] Mari J. Matsuda, "Looking to the Bottom: Critical Legal Studies and Reparations," in *Critical Race Theory*, edited by Crenshaw, p. 70 (emphasis added).

Yet this premise, too, seems implausible. Just as people living today are in no way responsible or blameworthy for historic injustices, it is also far from obvious that people today benefit, on balance, from distant wrongs. But why even raise the spectre of people today "benefitting" from past wrongdoing in order to defend reparations? A negligent doctor who removes the wrong kidney and a driver who injures a pedestrian while distracted by a shooting star can owe their victims compensation regardless of whether or not the doctor or driver gained any benefit. The negligence speaks for itself. Why might it be important to insist that people continue to enjoy the benefits of past injustices for which they are in some way blameworthy?

Perhaps the answer is rooted in the difficulties of proving that historic wrongs have, in fact, caused harm to people living today. As I discuss later in this chapter, the link between the wrongful act and the harm is crucial. However, a wrongful act, in itself, is insufficient – merely having been speeding on the road before an accident is insufficient reason to justify compensation. So, instead of showing that the duty to compensate flows from an act that made a person worse off, now some defenders of reparations argue that later generations wrongfully *benefitted* from the injustices of their ancestors. But as I have argued, it is not at all clear that anyone, today, benefitted from slavery.

If it is not those who continue to benefit from slavery (or who were themselves slaveowners) who owe reparations, then who does? When defenders of reparations press their claim in court they often do so against institutions. Sometimes the target is a corporation, as recent suits in New York illustrate. One corporation, FleetBoston Financial Corporation, was the successor to another bank that had loaned money to a major slave trader. The predecessor of another defendant, Aetna, had sold insurance policies to slaveowners insuring against the death of their slaves. The third defendant, CSX, is the successor to various companies that owned railroads that had been constructed in part by slave labor.[31]

This is a familiar picture in law generally because corporations are often held liable despite the fact that none of their current officers or employees was individually negligent or intended to cause harm. Instead, we treat corporations *as if* they were persons, just as I argued we do when

---

[31] *Wall Street Journal,* March 27, 2002, B. 10.

we look for institutional racism by attributing intentions to collective bodies such as legislators or police departments.[32] The question we ask is a hypothetical one: *if a single agent had done what the institution (e.g., a corporation) did*, would that person be held responsible? If the answer is "yes," then we go on to the next stage, and ask what is the correct remedy. It's the institution that is being personified – and therefore held liable – not any person.

Whatever the *legal* merits of these cases,[33] the moral argument that reparations are owed for slavery by successor corporations may seem doubtful. The conduct of the corporations was legal at the time. Nor were those corporations uniquely, or even mainly, responsible for the injustices. It is, therefore, not clear how they failed in their duty toward slaves at the time or why they should be held accountable today.

Governments, however, are a different story, and the argument for holding them responsible is more promising. If a government failed in its duty to protect its citizens against racial oppression, then perhaps it now has a duty to repair the harms it caused by that failure. If governments have responsibilities that private citizens and corporations do not have, then this could be true independent of what might be owed by current citizens or existing corporations.

The argument that governments could owe reparations therefore depends on the idea that government owes citizens many things that we do not owe each other as individuals. Governments owe citizens justice, for example, including a fair trial and, we usually assume, a decent public education. These facts, assuming they are accepted, open up space to argue that a government might also owe another form of justice: compensation for the lingering effects of its historic injustices.

This idea is reinforced by the fact that ignorance on the part of government is no excuse. Whatever officials may have thought in the past, *we know today* that slavery violated equality and denied the basic rights of slaves. For that reason, we might reasonably conclude, compensation is owed by *government* for the lingering effects of the injustices the government perpetuated. As when corporations are held liable, we would then go on and ask at the next stage how such compensation is to be paid. Those answers might vary, just as governments can fulfill their duties

---

[32] Treating corporations "as if" they were persons is described by Ronald Dworkin in *Law's Empire*, pp. 167–175.

[33] One major hurdle is the fact that statutes of limitations protect against lawsuits over events that happened so many years ago.

to provide public education in different ways. From the perspective of justice and what government owes, however, that issue is of secondary importance. Paying the debt of compensation is what matters most.

It is interesting that this argument has not gotten attention, while others that depend on individuals' benefitting have. The reason may be that so much of the discussion of reparations has been framed by lawyers who, quite naturally, want to make a legal argument. Because governments' legal liabilities under tort law are limited by sovereign immunity to those causes of action the government itself authorizes, and suits for reparations have not been explicitly authorized, there is little prospect of winning in court on these grounds. My concern here is not with law, however, but with justice, and the fact that governments have not allowed reparations as a tort claim does not rebut the arguments considered here.

The advantage of this approach for defenders of reparations is that it does not depend on showing that somebody today is benefitting from slavery or that anyone living today was morally blameworthy for having slaves or for segregation. Nor does it assume someone possesses something slaves' descendants are legitimately entitled to have returned to them, as with restitution. The fact that no *persons* living today could have caused the harm is irrelevant. Governments can be held responsible for the lingering effects of historic injustices they caused generations ago, because governments transcend the generations. So Matsuda may have been right in thinking that those who owe reparations are "perpetrators." Her mistake was in thinking that the perpetrators were people (or even institutions) who *benefitted* from the historic injustices, rather than governments.

Which government would owe reparations? It was states, after all, that imposed slavery and passed laws governing how it worked in practice. The national Constitution, on the other hand, was not blameless: it protected slavery until 1808. Congress also supported slavery with fugitive slave laws and allowed slave states into the union, and the national government later allowed segregation and inequality by failing to enforce the Fourteenth Amendment, with its guarantee of equal protection of law, against the states until the latter half of the twentieth century. So although there are questions about who – which government – should pay the reparations, a case can be made that both states and the national government were, in part, responsible.

I believe this is the best argument available to the defender of reparations (it is also relevant to the argument for an apology for slavery, as I argue later in this chapter). It avoids the objection that descendants of long-dead perpetrators of injustice are themselves innocent, did not cause the injustice, and are not benefitting from it. The response to those oft-heard objections is that those individuals are not the ones who owe the debt; it is their government's burden. Governments that created or enabled slavery and segregation were responsible for it and, therefore, have the duty to repair the lingering effects of their past wrongs.

Although this is a good start, the idea that governments might owe reparations does not show they in fact do owe them. Assuming that adequate answers can be found to the puzzles I have just posed we have still not reached the heart of the problem, namely, that the case for reparations assumes that historic injustices continue to harm current generations of African-Americans, and do so in ways that warrant compensation. This, I will argue, is a problem without a solution.

Tracing the effects of ancient wrongs: The problem of the baseline

Defenders of reparations must answer the question of how much, and in what ways, past injustices of slavery and racial oppression harmed not the slaves but their descendants. Without that, the case for reparations collapses. There is nothing now that needs to be repaired. But what test or measure should be used to determine the level of compensation to current descendants of slaves?

The basic answer, as I have suggested, is to repair the harm. John Locke explained that by saying that the "damnified" victim is entitled to receive from the offender "as much as may make satisfaction for the harm."[34] How are we are to understand the idea of providing "satisfaction"? We can look to the law for guidance, where tort law is well-developed. In an important 1880 British case, Lord Blackburn wrote that the goal is to "put the party who was injured, or who has suffered, in that same position as he would have been had he not sustained the wrong for which he is now getting his compensation."[35] This same idea was put in more modern language in a recent New Jersey case involving medical malpractice. The patient's damages are to be decided, said the Court, "by comparing the condition plaintiff would have been in, had the defendants not been negligent, with plaintiff's impaired condition as a result of the

---

[34] John Locke, *Second Treatise of Government* (London: Dent and Sons, 1924), Chapter 2, paragraph 5.
[35] *Livingstone v. Rawyards Coal Co.*, 5 App. Cases 25, 39 (House of Lords) (1880).

negligence."[36] Both of these judges are saying, in effect, that damages depend on comparing the actual world with another, hypothetical one. They are determined by the difference between the condition of the injured person after the injury and the hypothetical condition the person *would have been in* had the injury never occurred.

But how then can that difference between the two worlds, one actual and one hypothetical, be determined? One answer is a subjective test: assess the cost of the injury from the perspective of what the victim would willingly accept as compensation. Suppose the injury is loss of a finger. Deciding whether the victim has been given "satisfaction for the harm" would vary from person to person, depending on how much the person suffered and how important the finger was to the person. Assuming the pain and suffering were the same, the loss of a finger might be much more damaging to a concert violinist than to a mathematician or gardener. *How much* it mattered to each would be decided by the level of compensation required to make the victim indifferent between the actual world and the hypothetical world. Only then can it be said that the victim is in "that same position as he would have been had he not sustained the wrong for which he is now getting his compensation," as Lord Blackburn put it. If the victim prefers the injury-plus-compensation world to the one in which the injury never occurred, then the level of compensation was too high. If the victim still wishes the injury had not occurred despite the compensation, then the victim has not yet been adequately compensated.

This subjective approach captures the intuitive idea behind reparations as a form of compensatory justice. But it also raises immensely difficult questions. For one thing, the amount of compensation demanded could vary depending on when a victim is asked the question. *Before* an injury, a potential victim might well demand more to undergo an injury than that same person would claim after the injury has already happened. If that is true, then the question arises as to which of the two times is the right one to choose. The subjective test does not, by itself, provide an answer.[37]

An alternative "objective" decision procedure would first identify the nature of all the possible harms to people and then assign some level of economic or other compensation for each one. In the example of the lost finger, the damages would presumably include medical bills

---

[36] *Berman v. Allen*, 404 A.2d 8, 12 (1979) (New Jersey Supreme Court).
[37] Robert Nozick raises the question, though without providing an answer. See Nozick, *Anarchy, State, and Utopia*, pp. 152–153.

and lost income as well as pain and suffering. Then, having identified the damages, we could assign a monetary or other value to each of them. This approach is *objective* because we are not deciding the level of compensation based on the victim's own preferences but instead from the outside, so to speak. But subjective and objective tests aim at the same goal, which is to put the injured party into the position she would have been in but for the wrong. We might even expect that much of the time the objective and subjective tests would reach the same conclusion if the particular circumstances of the injured person are considered. I will not pursue these questions further here, however, and simply assume the goal of reparations is to return the injured party to the position she would have been in according to one of those tests. The crucial question on which I want to focus is how we are to decide when that has been achieved in the case of ancient wrongs done by slavery and racial oppression.

Randall Robinson thinks that it is important, as we think about the question of damages, to focus on the loss of African language and culture that took place as a result of slavery. Robinson speaks of how with "sadistic patience" slavery "asphyxiated memory, and smothered cultures, has hulled empty a whole race of people." In doing so, every "artifact of the victims' past cultures, every custom, every ritual, every god, every language, every trace element of a people's whole hereditary identity" was destroyed.[38] Janna Thompson also emphasizes how African-Americans were "deprived by slavery and other injustices of their African heritage."[39] But the question is not whether *slaves* were harmed by slavery but whether their descendants were harmed generations later, by the loss of African culture. It is far from obvious that descendants of slaves were harmed *simply* by slavery's depriving them of their ancestors' cultural heritage. Consider adoption. I have two friends who recently adopted a baby girl who had been abandoned and brought her to the United States from China. Assume that the girl will grow up as an Asian-American, knowing about Chinese culture and language only as an outsider, and only to the extent that she chooses to learn about it. To make the case closely analogous to slavery, we should consider the plight of that adopted daughter's great-, great-, great-grandchild, now fully assimilated but still physically identifiable as Asian-American. Was that descendant of my friends' adopted daughter harmed by the loss of her culture? It seems to me that she was not.

[38] Robinson, *The Debt: What America Owes Blacks*, p. 216.
[39] Thompson, *Taking Responsibility for the Past*, p. 139.

It is not as if she were *without* a culture. What she has is a different one than she would have had but for the adoption. Similarly, it is not as if the descendants of slaves have no culture at all. If that had been the consequence of slavery, there would be little doubt that slavery harmed African-Americans gravely. But African-Americans are the heir to a rich cultural tradition, which is in many ways a fusion of many diverse cultures, including African. They know a great language, English, and have access to rich artistic and cultural traditions in the United States.

Is the real claim, then, that the descendants of slaves where harmed by having a superior African culture replaced with the inferior hybrid American culture? If the point is that being transplanted into another culture is itself a harm, then almost all living Americans were also victims. I could claim reparations against the English for driving my ancestors from Ireland to America, Jews could claim reparations against Cossacks for driving their ancestors from Eastern Europe, and so forth. Indeed, *any* ancestor who decided to leave for America could be said to have "harmed" their descendants by "depriving" them of their "heritage."

Our question, recall, is about damages and requires comparing the hypothetical world in which the ancient wrong did not occur with the actual world in which it did happen in order to decide on the level of compensation that is due. It is often difficult enough to assess damages when the person who was directly injured is the one claiming damages. How could a contemporary African-American begin to think about whether she is owed compensation for being an African-American rather than an African? She would have to imagine herself, literally and culturally, as a different person. It is not clear that the question even makes sense in this context.

This problem, of determining damages, is in fact deeper than I have so far suggested. As I noted, determining compensation proceeds in two stages. Each stage rests on a counterfactual "baseline" that envisions what would have happened in the absence of the injustice. In the first stage, the correct baseline, which describes the hypothetical world in which the wrong did not occur, must be identified. In the injured finger case, we assume the baseline was no loss of the finger. But in the slavery case, I will argue, we cannot simply say that there was no slavery and then leave it at that. Initial identification of the baseline is far more complicated and, indeed, it is not at all clear when looked at carefully that we are able to determine what the correct baseline is.

The second stage requires historical speculation, which raises another problem. In the case of physical injury, we assume that the victim would not have lost his finger in some other accident pending compensation. In the case of ancient injustices done to ancestors, it is much more complicated: we must imagine how the world without slavery would have evolved over the generations, all the way down to the current day. We need, in other words, to bring the hypothetical baseline up to date in order to determine the position the descendants would have been in had that hypothetical baseline been real. However, I will argue that there appears to be no rational basis on which to decide among the possible baselines.

Here are four possible baselines that might be chosen:[40]

1. Compare the current situation with one in which there had never been any migration or slavery and the ancestors of current African-Americans *remained* in Africa and lived typical African lives.
2. Compare the current situation of African-Americans with the baseline of where they would now be had their ancestors been forcibly brought to this country but then treated as free and equal citizens, perhaps after a period of indentured servitude.
3. Compare the current situation with one in which (like other immigrant groups) the slaves were merely *allowed* to come if they could find their own way but then were treated as free and equal citizens once they got here.
4. Compare the current situation with how African-Americans would have fared had somebody *helped* their ancestors to come as citizens by providing free transportation to the African ports and on to America where they were treated as free and equal citizens.

The choice is unavoidable since a decision to select one baseline will determine whether or not there are damages at all, as well as how much compensation is owed. Some baselines might even suggest descendants of slaves actually benefited from the historic injustices imposed on their ancestors.

The question to ask is "why *not* choose the first option," which imagines that there had been no slavery *and* that the ancestors of current African-Americans remained in Africa? We might think the most natural baseline is whatever was most likely to have actually occurred had there been no slavery. But that would be the one in which the slaves remained in Africa

[40] For a discussion of the problem of baselines in the context of original acquisition of unowned property, see John Arthur, "Property Acquisition and Harm," *Canadian Journal of Philosophy*, Vol. 17, No. 2 (1987), pp. 337–348.

since without slavery, there would almost surely not have been massive immigration of Africans to the European colonies of North America. It is even less likely there would have been forced migration, or subsidized migration without slavery. Only by allowing slavery did governments create incentives for the ancestors of living African-Americans to be brought here.

On that assumption, using that baseline, the argument for reparations appears to collapse unless the cultural argument I criticized could somehow be sustained. The average income of a sub-Saharan African today is roughly $745 per year, far below the poverty line in the United States, and the typical life expectancy in Africa is decades shorter than that of contemporary African-Americans. By almost every objective measure, the average African-American is better off. The possible exceptions, namely, those African-Americans living in poverty and in crime-ridden cities, are not in that situation due just to slavery, though slavery may have played a part in causing the problems. As we saw in Chapter 5, the explanation includes family breakdown, crime, and poor educational achievement along with broader economic shifts away from low-skill manufacturing jobs. How it might be possible to argue from that possibility to a specific debt of reparation is far from clear, although I argue in the last section that it is more plausible as the ground for an apology.

Choosing the realistic baseline that might have resulted in Africans coming to North America does not yield the conclusion that reparations should be paid to living descendants of slaves. To get that conclusion the baseline must be one of the others, in which Africans came but were treated as free and equal citizens on arrival or soon thereafter. Yet, none of those were practical since slavery was the financial motive that drove the whole process. The only way to justify reparations, then, is to ignore what was practically possible and imagine a world in which people came on their own or were brought but not as slaves. But why choose those baselines over the historically realistic one? Defenders of reparations cannot say that the *reason* for choosing that baseline is that it is the one that will justify reparations because that would simply beg the question. That is the issue we hope to answer.

But *even if* we were to take that historically unrealistic baseline and assume the Africans got to American soil without slavery, the reparations argument faces other serious obstacles that grow out of the baseline. Presumably, the level of contribution to payment of reparations would reasonably be based on the relative importance of each negligent actor or its contribution to the injury. Yet the contribution of the U.S. national and state governments to slavery was only a fraction of the total. As I noted earlier, African slavetraders, European merchants, and European governments either actively helped capture and trade the slaves or enabled the slave trade to North America to continue. Indeed, without so much assistance by other people and governments, American slavery would likely not have happened. U.S. laws permitting slavery were only a part of the story. That means, in turn, that even if we had reason to think slavery harmed the distant descendants of slaves, the compensation owed by the governments of the United States might be a very small part of the whole.

Additionally the baseline must be brought up to date. In other words, to determine whether or not the living descendants of slaves are entitled to reparations, we must do more than identify the correct baseline. We need to describe it in enough detail to determine the difference between what would have happened and what did. Only then could we hope to say, with any degree of confidence, what needs to be done to repair the harms caused by slavery. I want to make two points about such speculations. One is practical, the other moral.

To see the practical point, recall the difference between restitution and reparation. If we were restoring a particular object, such as an heirloom, to its owner then we can feel confident that it – the heirloom – should be returned. The descendant would have had it but for the theft. But justifying restitution for the value of the exploited labor power, we saw, is much more speculative. In the case we are now considering, reparation for damages, the injustices slaves suffered were mainly denials of powers, specifically *liberty, rights, and opportunities* rather than theft of property.[41] This was the major wrong done to slaves and this, we are assuming, somehow harmed future generations. We therefore need to imagine what would have happened to the slaves had they been given the rights and opportunities that others enjoyed, and then what would have happened throughout all the subsequent generations right down to the present. Do we know whether those people, now assumed not to be slaves, would have taken advantage of those rights and opportunities, and if so how? Would they have worked hard or chosen leisure? Would they have succeeded on a par with the average of other groups, have done better, or have done worse? It is impossible even to get a grip on how we should answer these questions.

---

[41] As I discussed above, slavery essentially involves the denial of the powers slaves are entitled to exercise.

The moral point concerns not the practical impossibility of tracing what would have happened under the chosen baseline, but the baseline itself. Slavery was unjust primarily because it was slavery. It denied people the power to control their own lives by denying rights and opportunities they should have been given. Reparations for slavery therefore differ from the return of an inheritance or some other form of restitution. The inherited item simply passes from the original owner to the new one. But rights to work, own property, and other opportunities are not like that. They are not a right to receive any given amount of money or property, but are instead the *right to an opportunity* to work and earn. The fact that a person did not *actually do* the work is relevant to the claim that the person should receive what could only have come as a result of actually having worked. Insofar as we believe that income is deserved in virtue of having actually earned it, there is a gap between the denial of the *opportunity* to work and the right to the product of the work. We do not punish people until they have actually done something wrong because they don't deserve it. Why should we reward people or compensate their heirs for work that was not done but might have been? My point is not that violating rights, liberties, and so forth is inconsequential, or even that it cannot deserve compensation. Rather, the question that must be answered is *how much* compensation is owed for the denial of the *rights or opportunities to work and earn*. This compounds even further the problem faced by anyone who claims reparations for historic injustices. Any baseline must respect the fact that people do not deserve income simply because they did not have the opportunity to work for it.

As I have suggested, the proposal to pay reparations raises problems without solutions. Defenders of reparations confront serious problems and objections of many different varieties. Most importantly, we cannot identify a uniquely correct baseline, cannot describe its course through history with sufficient specificity, and cannot deal adequately with the fact that slavery's injustice was mainly that it denied liberties, rights, and opportunities to slaves.

That does not, however, settle the question of the debt that slavery and segregation have left. Slavery was an injustice of enormous proportions. Although providing restitution or reparation poses insuperable problems, that does not exhaust the possible responses. What it does, though, is to suggest that the question needs to be refocused. If we reject restitution and reparations, then what *is* to be done? Should the history of slavery and racial oppression be simply ignored?

Apologies, guilt, and remorse

Restitution and reparation each provides compensation: *restitution* by returning what was owed; *reparation* by making the victim whole for a past wrong. Neither of those, I argued, is the right response to slavery. Apologies are also a response to past wrongdoing, though they do not involve compensation. For that reason, apologies do not make the same demands. Although an apology is owed, there is no necessity to identify property that was taken or the lingering effects of an ancient wrong. But that does not mean that apologies are insignificant.

Between 1931 and 1945, the Japanese Empire used Korean women as sex slaves for their military. Called "comfort women," up to 200,000 were forced to work at "comfort stations" for soldiers fighting in China. In 1995, the Japanese government agreed, as part of a commemoration of the end of World War II, to support the Asian Women's Fund and offer $9,000 to each of the living victims. The government also agreed to attach to the payment a private letter from the Prime Minister apologizing for what the Japanese government had done. Despite the fact that many of the women were poor, the vast majority rejected the money because the apology was not officially offered by the government. (Japan has still not officially apologized to the women.) It was significant to those women that the government refused to apologize.

Both institutions and persons can apologize. Why, first, would it matter if a *person* apologizes? Apologies do not provide compensations in the literal sense. No apology could possibly have compensated the women for what was done to them in the sense of making them "whole." Perhaps nothing could. What an apology does do, however, is to "address" the wrong first by simply recognizing that it took place.[42] One cannot apologize sincerely without acknowledging the past action was done and that it was wrong. An apology is not merely an expression of regret for another's suffering or even for *another's having been wronged*. It is an expression of *guilt for having done the wrong*.

Apologies are also expressions of remorse as well as acknowledgments of guilt. Both of these are *moral* emotions, which distinguishes them

---

[42] My discussion of apologies is indebted to Kathleen Gill, "The Moral Functions of an Apology," in *Philosophical Forum*, Vol. 31, No. 1 (Spring 2000), pp. 11–27; Rodney Roberts, *Injustice and Rectification* (New York: Peter Lang, 2005); John Rawls, A *Theory of Justice, Revised Edition*; and Trudy Govier, *Forgiveness and Revenge* (London: Routledge, 2002).

from other feelings such as anger or grief.[43] Anger and grief are typically associated with physical sensations such as trembling, tightness in the stomach, inability to speak, and shortness of breath. They are also usually accompanied by behavioral manifestations such as weeping or (in the case of anger) a raised voice.

Guilt and remorse are different, for two reasons. First, they need not be accompanied by physical sensations. Unlike pain or even anger, a guilty or remorseful person will often not feel any associated physical sensations.

Second, these moral feelings demand a moral response. We expect persons who feel guilt and remorse to believe, and when appropriate to admit, that they failed to live up to a moral norm. If the bad feelings about what was done are not moral but instead limited to fear of punishment or some other undesired consequence, then the person does not feel genuine guilt or remorse. The person might *regret* what was done, but regret is not a moral emotion. We can regret having made the wrong purchase or having made a wrong turn, as well as having done something wrong. We can also regret mistakes we made or even the harms we might have caused unintentionally, by accident. Remorse and guilt are different from regret. We feel remorse because we believe what we did is properly judged wrong and we are blameworthy for having done it. In that way, guilt and remorse ride piggyback on standards of right and wrong. An amoral person would feel neither guilt nor remorse.

If that is correct, and guilt and remorse are moral feelings, then how can an institution such as a government or nation be said to "feel" anything like guilt or remorse? In considering that question, it is important to notice that while it makes sense to say that a person is *in fact* guilty but does not feel guilty, it is not possible for a person to be remorseful without the accompanying emotion. In other words, a person can be guilty without the moral feeling often associated with guilt, but cannot be remorseful without feeling remorse.

That suggests that a government might in fact *be* guilty, even though it cannot feel guilt. The reason goes back to what I have said about attributing responsibility to collective bodies such as corporations and governments. I argued that we can attribute institutional racism to legislative bodies, for example, by treating the legislature as if what it did were done by a single person. I argued that it is part of our legal and

<hr>

[43] My discussion of moral emotions is indebted to John Rawls, *A Theory of Justice, Revised Edition.*

political practice to "personify" institutions in that way. We do that even though we are not (necessarily) convinced that any single individual is guilty personally.

So although it is common to think of corporations and governments as being guilty for their past wrongdoings, we need not also assume that the government has any of the feelings that are usually associated with guilt in persons. Remorse is different; it is more closely tied to persons because it must include feelings. As I said, one cannot be remorseful yet not feel remorse. That does not mean, however, that remorse plays no role in understanding past injustices and how people should respond to them. As I emphasized in Chapter 4, members of groups, whether familial, religious, civic, racial, or ethnic, often identify with their group. That means, in turn, that when people do belong to a nation and they identify with it, it may be reasonable for them to feel remorse and guilt at what the nation's government has done in the past. Although people today may not even have been alive when the injustice was done, it was done by their government, and in that sense, it was done in their name. The point, then, is that when members of a nation identify with the group and their government has done an injustice, then it is both possible and reasonable for them to feel remorse. Though they are not individually guilty or blameworthy, and do not have personal feelings of guilt for what was done, moral feeling for what was collectively done in their name can be appropriate.

Finally, though it is true that an institution cannot literally *feel* remorse, we might think that an institution such as a government could *express* remorse, just as it could express racism. That is possible for the same reason we can hold a corporation or government guilty: we can treat it as if it were a person. So, not only might individuals feel remorse for what their nation did in their name, but the institution that represents the people – the government – can be guilty and can express remorse. In saying that, we are again treating the government as if it were a person, just as we often do with institutions. We can also reasonably say, in the same spirit, that a government that has not acknowledged its guilt by expressing its remorse, say with an apology, has not yet fulfilled its responsibility to acknowledge its past wrongdoing. It should express such remorse, and the victims are entitled to an apology.

Given that it is both possible and often reasonable for governments to apologize, the next question is why it might be important. Why do apologies matter? Assuming that the victims feel resentment at the wrong they suffered, the first thing to say is that the apology will tend to reduce such feelings and possibly even lead to reconciliation.[44] The fact of the victims' having been wronged will not be forgotten or erased, of course. That is impossible, as critics of apologies often stress. But insofar as the moral emotion of resentment is based on the lack of respect and concern that was manifested by the wrong, an apology can "balance" that by showing respect for the victims now. In that sense, the Japanese government's refusal to apologize publicly may have been experienced by the Korean women as a continuing refusal to show them respect as equals or as persons, just as it had refused to do 50 years earlier when it enslaved them as "comfort women." That fact may partly explain why so many women rejected the apology that was offered.

In acknowledging the wrong and expressing remorse, the apology also does something else. It formally recognizes the perspective of the victims and acknowledges the validity or merit in that perspective. If the victims were chosen on the basis of their membership in racial, ethnic, or other groups with which the victims identify, as persons, then the apology affirms the validity of their perspective not just as individuals but as members of that group. By apologizing, the apologizer confirms the value of who they are as members of the group to which the apology is given.

An official apology for slavery would be both an acknowledgment of guilt by the government and an expression of remorse for what the government and what its people, as a nation, did. There are precedents for such actions by the U.S. government. The United States apologized for internment of Japanese Americans, and, in 1993, the U.S. Congress passed a resolution acknowledging the "overthrow of the Kingdom of Hawaii" 100 years earlier. The resolution went on to say that Congress offered "an apology on behalf of the United States" for the overthrow."[45] More recently, the United States Senate apologized for its failure to enact antilynching laws. It is important that these apologies were not offered on behalf of any individual persons, living or dead. It was the United States that owed the apology, as a nation represented by its government.

Although an apology for slavery would do nothing to compensate for or undo past injustices or change the material or other conditions of slaves' descendants, it would change the moral relationship. The government

---

[44] Trudy Govier has a helpful discussion of these issues in *Forgiveness and Revenge*, especially in Chapter 8.
[45] U.S. Public Law 103–150.

would have acknowledged its wrong and affirmed the perspective of the victims of slavery. It is also an expression of the remorse felt by members of the community at its historic moral failings.

Furthermore, in making the apology, as Govier notes, the "wrongdoer provides the victim with reasons to forgive."[46] Such an apology can benefit the victim, the offender, and their relationship.

> The *victim* benefits because she is replacing negative emotions of anger and resentment with more positive emotions and escaping a fixation with the past and potentially obsessive desires for revenge. The *offender* benefits because he is assisted to make a fresh start, released from the stigma of negative labels and assured that he is no longer an object of moral hatred. Clearly their *relationship* will improve as anger, resentment, and distrust are replaced with acceptance and growing understanding.[47]

This assumes, of course, that the apology is accepted, enabling the moral relationship to be altered between the victim and the offender. *Accepting* an apology is a form of forgiveness, signifying that the moral ledger has been brought back into balance. Whether significant numbers of black citizens and leaders would accept such an apology would probably depend on many factors, including who does it and how it is done. Sincerity would be vital.

There is one further important implication of such an apology for slavery that I want to emphasize. Roughly, it can be expressed with the thought that offering an apology puts the apologizer in the "debt" of the victim. Having expressed guilt and remorse, it is reasonable to expect that the offender will take additional appropriate actions in light of the new moral relationship that now exists between the victim and offender. If appropriate actions do follow, that will tend to confirm the apologizer's sincerity. If they do not, then the supposed expression of remorse may be reasonably interpreted as a sham.

Thus, the apologizer can be expected to pay special heed in the future to avoid wronging the victim. ("You said you were sorry, yet you did *this* to me!" is a serious charge.) The apologizer might also be expected to review carefully other aspects of the relationship to be sure that there are no additional moral failings that have gone unnoticed.

It is important also to note that an apology may provide much, if not all, of what many who demand reparations seek. Janna Thompson, for

[46] Govier, *Forgiveness and Revenge*, p. 48.
[47] Govier, *Forgiveness and Revenge*, p. 48.

example, claims that reparations should take the form of "special consideration" given to the plight of black families. Reparative considerations, she writes, "give us grounds for giving priority to black Americans over people whose disadvantages do not stem from injustices."[48] It seems to me, however, that the argument for this need not rely, as she and so many others say, on repairing the harms to living descendants of slaves or on returning their property. An apology, together with an appropriate sense of remorse and commitment to justice and equality for descendants of slaves, may also require what she and other defenders of reparations want. Certainly an apology and appropriate remorse for slavery could at least suggest that "special consideration" be given the descendants of slaves as Thomson recommends.

[48] Thomson, *Taking Responsibility for the Past*, p. 143.

7

Merit and Race

THE PHRASE "AFFIRMATIVE ACTION" CAME TO PUBLIC USE IN 1961 when President John Kennedy issued *Executive Order 10925* requiring that contractors working for the federal government take "affirmative action to ensure that applicants are hired without regard to their race, creed, color, or national origin." That original meaning evolved, however. In 1965, President Johnson's Secretary of Labor issued affirmative action guidelines for federal contractors that included "goals" as well as "timetables" for increasing minority employment. Although it is rare to find an explicit quota today, affirmative action, as currently understood, requires more than making certain that minorities are recruited and that there is no discrimination or bias on the part of those making the decisions. Affirmative action today refers to policies and individual decisions in which a person's race is used as a reason to justify employment in a position, an award of a contract, or admission to an institution. It is distinguished from ordinary racial discrimination because its goal is to help minorities or otherwise disadvantaged groups.[1]

Affirmative action raises a host of important and controversial questions, which I take up in this chapter and in Chapter 8. At the root of many objections to affirmative action is the claim that it entails disregard of merit, which is the focus of this chapter. First, I will consider the nature of merit: what it is, and why it matters. I also discuss its connection with institutional purposes and why it is often important to put people in positions based on merit. Next, I look at a position that is familiar among defenders of affirmative action, that merit is a "myth" which serves only to exclude some classes of people from desirable positions. I conclude this

---

[1] Thus, in Great Britain, it is often referred to as "positive" discrimination.

chapter by asking whether race could, in some circumstances, constitute a form of merit.

What is merit?

The most important objection to racial preferences in hiring and admissions is often thought to be that they ignore merit. But some defenders of affirmative action respond that in fact race can constitute a form of merit. Ronald Dworkin defended that idea in discussing the case in which the U.S. Supreme Court upheld affirmative action in medical school admissions while it rejected explicit quotas.[2] Although a white candidate, Allan Bakke, had presented much higher test scores and grades, Dworkin nonetheless claimed he was rightfully passed over. Meriting a place in medical school, according to Dworkin, is based on the idea that "a medical school should choose candidates that it supposes will make the most useful doctors," and, therefore, if black skin will "as a regrettable fact, enable another doctor to do a different medical job better, then that black skin is by the same token 'merit' as well."[3] Because Alan Bakke was not black, and having black doctors serves a useful social purpose, Bakke lacked merit for the position.

Other defenders of affirmative action have sometimes taken the opposite tack, claiming that merit is a "myth" and should be ignored in hiring and admissions. Catharine A. MacKinnon, for instance, writes that "Any society's elite class will deem what they do well as constitutive of merit, thus assuring their own positions become even more secure."[4] Another law professor, Duncan Kennedy, is also skeptical about merit. He does not believe, he writes, that "it is real 'merit' that institutions measure, anywhere in the system."[5] All of which raises, but does not answer, the central issue: what, exactly, is merit?

I will begin with the question of how merit and desert are related, since it is sometimes said not just that decisions about hiring and admission

---

[2] *Regents of the University of California v. Bakke,* 438 U.S. 265 (1978).

[3] Ronald Dworkin, "Why Bakke Has No Case," *New York Review of Books,* November 10, 1977. Reprinted in *Morality and Moral Controversies,* 7th ed., edited by John Arthur (Upper Saddle River NJ: Prentice Hall, 2004), p. 634.

[4] Catharine A. MacKinnon, "Reflections on Sex Equality under Law," *Yale Law Journal,* Vol. 100 (1990), p. 1281.

[5] Duncan Kennedy, "Affirmative Action," in *Sexy Dressing Etc.* (Cambridge MA: Harvard University Press, 1993), p. 36.

should be based on "merit" but also that a person who merits a position also "deserves" it. Desert is a broad concept: people are often said to deserve everything from prizes and awards, punishment, positions of honor, raises, and second chances to a better lawyer, a decent school, an apology, and even simply better luck than in the past. What all of those desert claims have in common is the idea that something about a person is a reason for someone else to do something with respect to that person. John Kleinig expressed the idea formally: "[person] M deserves X for A."[6] The reasons for the desert A vary widely. Some of the desert claims are morality-based, arising from a person's past actions. But others are based on reasons such as that a person is better able to perform a job, that a better lawyer is necessary for a fair trial, or that somebody was insulted and therefore deserves an apology.

In what follows, I want to distinguish desert broadly understood, as in these many diverse senses, from the more central concept of desert and also from merit. The central concept of desert involves people deserving something because they have *done something* in the past that constitutes the ground of the desert. Deserved punishment and rewards belong to this category, since both focus either on a wrong the person did (for which punishment is deserved) or on an act that was admirable (such as hard work or other accomplishments for which praise, promotions, or prizes might be deserved).

This core meaning of desert is also clear when we imagine a person claiming something is *not* deserved. John Rawls famously says that we "do not deserve our place in the distribution of native endowments, any more than we deserve our initial starting place in society."[7] The reason for this, Rawls assumes, is that people are simply born into their socioeconomic class with whatever natural talents or handicaps they happen to have. They have done nothing to get them, and therefore do not deserve them. It's just a matter of luck who our parents are and whether we are born handicapped or healthy. These are, as Rawls puts it, "morally arbitrary" facts about people.

So the clearest examples of desert – the paradigm cases – arise because of a person's past actions for which the person can be held responsible. If we say a person does not deserve punishment, we normally mean

---

[6] John Kleinig, *Punishment and Desert* (The Hague: Martinus Nijoff, 1973), Chapter 3, quoted in George Sher, *Desert* (Princeton: Princeton University Press, 1987), p. 7.

[7] Rawls, *A Theory of Justice, Revised Edition*, p. 89.

that what happened was not within her control. The point of saying the person does not deserve punishment is rooted in the ideas of control and responsibility. Similarly, when we say people deserve praise, thanks, or a reward, the reason is generally that the person has done something that justifies the praise, thanks, or reward. Even character traits, when deserved, follow this pattern. When someone deserves praise for being an honest person, for instance, the suggestion is that the honesty is to some extent within the person's control. If the person had merely been born honest, like people are born female or black, then the claim to deserve praise for being honest is dubious at best. Desert in that core sense is backward looking.[8]

Is a person *meriting* a job or other position an example of desert, or is it something different? George Sher thinks that merit is one of the grounds or bases of desert, though he claims that merit comes in two forms: nonmoral and moral. Nonmoral merit justifies desert when people "compete or perform with unusual skill or give an indication of the ability to do so," while moral merit is shown when people "display virtuous character or perform specific acts of courage, thoughtfulness, or generosity."[9]

If what I have said is right, however, Sher's is a misleading way of thinking about the issue. Cases where people's accomplishments or excellence have nothing to do with any choices they have made (and are for that reason "morally arbitrary") are not paradigm instances of desert even if they do "perform with unusual skill" or "display virtuous character." A person who accomplishes something because of luck, or even because of a natural trait like being taller or smarter, may be said not to be deserving for exactly those reasons. Desert is undermined when luck or other factors beyond one's control play a crucial role. Responsibility and past actions, as I said, are the core of desert. Merit is therefore different from desert since, as I will discuss, merit does not depend on past actions. We often distinguish the question who might *deserve* the position most (because the person worked hard in school, for instance) from who should get the position based purely on *merit.* Desert, then, is a moral notion at its core. Merit, however, is different.

---

[8] While this is the core idea of desert, I do not want to deny that we sometimes think of desert in the other, broader ways that I mentioned. Readers who are unhappy with that narrowing may think of my proposal as a stipulative definition, although it is clear that the definition is not at odds with at least one of the core meanings of desert.

[9] Sher, *Desert,* p. 132.

What does it mean, then, to select a person for a position based on merit?[10] Often the answer is clear enough, at least in broad outline. A 2006 *New York Times* article reported that the Governor of Kentucky was being indicted for "violating civil-service hiring laws by filling rank-and-file state jobs based on political leanings of applicants *rather than merit*."[11] The Governor faced a year in prison and a $500 fine. Although the article did not explain the meaning of "merit," I suspect few readers, or the Governor, were much in doubt what the law required. Clearly, a person's political leanings should be distinguished from genuine merit. But what, more precisely, would it mean to hire or admit a person to a position based on merit?

Often when we ask who merits being hired, we are thinking in relative terms, comparing one person with another. But what are we comparing? Matt Cavanaugh discusses but ultimately rejects both a "broad" and a "narrow" conception of merit.[12] The too-broad view of merit, he suggests, means nothing more than that people are hired on "reasonable" grounds, that is, that there is a sound reason to hire the person. But as Cavanaugh himself points out, in this case hiring a relative (or someone based solely on politics) would be an instance of hiring based on merit, since wanting to reward or even just help the person would presumably count as "reasonable." Understanding merit in terms of having reasonable grounds, Cavanaugh concludes, is too broad.

Cavanaugh links merit to the purposes of institutions and the goals of society. For that reason, he concludes that those who think that a decision to admit a person to medical school who will go on to practice medicine in poorer communities is not based on merit are also mistaken. That, he says, would be "too narrow an understanding of 'merit.'" Anyone who does not see that usefulness to society and merit are linked has "lost sight of the purpose of medical schools, which is not to create the best doctors just for the sake of it, but to train doctors on the explicit understanding they will make themselves useful to society."[13] In the end, however, Cavanaugh is uncertain how broadly or narrowly merit should

---

[10] In what follows, I will limit my discussion of merit to cases in which persons are being considered for jobs or for admission to schools or universities.

[11] Ian Urbina, "Indictment for Governor of Kentucky," *New York Times*, May 12, 2006, p. 23 (emphasis added).

[12] Matt Cavanaugh, *Against Equality of Opportunity* (Oxford: Oxford University Press, 2002).

[13] Cavanaugh, *Against Equality of Opportunity*, p. 47.

be understood, although he thinks it does extend to "usefulness in some wider sense, as in the medical school example."[14]

As we saw, Dworkin also emphasizes that link between merit and institutional purposes, as do Fullinwider and Lichtenberg. According to them, universities have various missions: liberal education, vocational education, civic education, and research being the primary ones, though there are others as well. Admitting students and hiring teachers based on merit therefore means choosing people who will further those purposes. They also give the familiar example of an institution committed to improving medical care for African-Americans as an example of why race can constitute merit.[15]

J. R. Lucas has a more individualistic and less institutional understanding of merit. He thinks merit is rooted in attributes people *have*, rather than what they *do*.[16] Leslie Jacobs disagrees, however, holding that merit in a competitive process includes a "combination" of both abilities people have and also effort.[17]

But how then *are* we to understand merit? What is the connection between merit and institutional purposes? Is it, as some suggest, simply that merit-based decisions just are ones that will further an institution's purposes? Or are merit and institutional purposes distinct? I suggest that we should take a step back from the institutional question and begin with the thought that a person merits a job or admission to the extent that the person can perform well in the role. As I noted, the natural home of the concept of merit is in the context of hiring, promotions, and admissions in which we are making implicit or even explicit comparisons among different persons. The error in hiring a person for political reasons rather than merit, as the Governor allegedly did, is that these were jobs for which political leanings were irrelevant and that others could perform better. So, what is essential to understanding the concept of merit is the underlying idea of roles that can be performed well. Without that idea as background we cannot understand what it means to select people for positions on the basis of merit.

There is nothing particularly mysterious about the idea of roles. Societies construct them, and people are presented by their society with an

[14] Cavanaugh, *Against Equality of Opportunity*, p. 48.

[15] Robert Fullinwider and Judith Lichtenberg, *Leveling the Playing Field: Justice, Politics, and College Admissions* (Oxford: Rowman and Littlefield Publishers, Inc., 2004), pp. 54–57.

[16] J. R. Lucas, *Responsibility* (Oxford: Oxford University Press, 1993).

[17] Leslie Jacobs, *Pursuing Equal Opportunities* (Cambridge UK: Cambridge University Press, 2004), p. 88.

array of preexisting social roles. Indeed the roles that are available to members or groups of persons is in some measure a defining feature of a society, distinguishing it from other societies that provide a different set of roles. A society with only a handful of specifically defined roles would be in important respects a different society from another that had either a wider range of roles or a different set.

Unlike many older or simpler societies, in ours the number and variety of roles is vast – ranging from actors, bakers and baseball players to Zen Buddhist monks and zookeepers. Those social roles share a number of important characteristics that distinguish them first, as roles, and second, from each other. Roles are defined by norms that specify how they are to be performed. Without those norms we would have no idea even what it means to be a doctor, lawyer, professor, juror, cook, or friend. Social roles are created by the socially accepted norms and forms of behavior that define them. That means, in turn, that roles exist in a larger social context of institutions and practices. The existence of basketball players depends on the fact that the game is practiced; the role of miners exists because mining is practiced. Students and teachers are possible because we have educational institutions in which they function. (I will have more to say about the relationship between roles and institutional goals.)

Because they are constructed, social roles also differ through time as well as from society to society. Doctors in the twenty-first century share something in common with earlier generations of doctors though the role has also changed dramatically. Roles can also be characterized in general terms as well as more specifically. Within the role of doctor are brain surgeons and family practitioners; soldiers include tank commanders, gunners, and mechanics; baseball players include hitters, pitchers, catchers, and first basemen. Because roles are defined by norms, they can be performed well or poorly. But sometimes the performance is so poor that the role is not just performed poorly; it is not performed at all. It would be misleading, at best, to describe a person as a doctor who knows nothing about biology or medicine. Such a person is more like a child who is "playing doctor."

The idea of putting people into a role "based on merit" therefore depends on the nature of the role and the fact that roles are defined by social norms. Basing a decision to put one person rather than another into a position based on merit *just is* choosing the person who will perform better in that role. As I suggested earlier, *deserving* a position (perhaps because of past hard work or political support) and *meriting* it are distinct ideas.

More broadly, merit is a form of goodness. A thing is good, I assume, when it has the properties to a relatively high degree that it is rational to want in a thing of that sort. A good lawnmower has properties it is rational to want in a lawnmower (cuts grass efficiently and safely, inexpensive to run), while a good plumber has the characteristics it is rational to want in a plumber (knowledge of plumbing and skill with tools, mainly).

But while it is a form of goodness, merit is not a form of *moral* goodness. Merit is simply the possession of necessary qualifications to perform a role, and it is always a further question whether it is a *morally good* role for anyone to play. It is also a further issue whether the person is *worthy of moral praise* for having traits that enable the effective performance. Cold-bloodedness and indifference to suffering may be qualifications for being a good torturer or terrorist, for instance, but that hardly means cold-bloodedness is a moral virtue or that performance of those roles makes someone a morally good person. To say a person merits a job or some other role is not necessarily to praise her morally; it means only that the person will perform the role effectively.

Thus, qualifications and merit are closely related. In the broadest sense, to be "well-qualified" for a role just is to merit it, that is, to have traits that will make a person effective in its performance. Merit, therefore, does not exist in the air, so to speak, independent of roles that people will be performing; people must be qualified *for* something. The related concepts of *merit* and *qualifications* ride piggyback on two assumptions: (1) that different social roles exist and (2) that some people have traits or skills that make them likely to perform those roles more effectively than others. Without those background assumptions about roles and qualifications, we would never be able to say that the practices of excluding people from university positions based on race, posting signs saying "No Irish Need Apply" at a construction site, or using a political test in hiring a government worker were based on factors other than on merit.

Because a role can change through time, qualifications also change. Good doctors in the nineteenth century, when there was little to be known about treatment of diseases, had only some traits in common with good modern doctors. The qualifications to be a medieval knight on horseback would not necessarily put one in a good position to be an effective fighter pilot today, and vice versa. Many roles are also complex: they require different skills and attributes to meet different aspects of the role. Doctors, baseball players, and even friends can require different characteristics that make a person good at the role, which means in turn that people will often present a different mix of those qualifications. A given doctor may be a better diagnostician or surgeon; a baseball player may be a better fielder or base runner; a friend may be more loyal or more enjoyable to be with.

This complexity of roles is often a source of uncertainty and sometimes disagreement about different candidates. We might easily agree that the qualifications of a brain surgeon in a hospital include being knowledgeable about diseases of the brain and skilled at surgery, and that those traits are not qualifications for basketball players or airline pilots. But other times, as we think in more detail about a complex role, we may find ourselves perplexed about how to assess the relative qualifications of different people. Because complex roles often require different skills and characteristics, different candidates often present a different mix of those traits. One brain surgeon might be better at diagnosing diseases, while another might be better in the operating room and a third better at helping patients deal emotionally with the trauma of surgery. The role of a professor is also complex, and includes teaching, doing research, and university service. The same point can be made about firefighters, secretaries, soldiers, and political leaders.

Different aspects of a role, and the different qualifications people present to perform it, must be weighed against each other in order to make an overall assessment of merit. This judgment can be difficult and controversial. How important is bedside manner in doctors, compared with other traits? How much weight should be given to teaching in choosing college professors? How much to stage presence or appearance in a concert soloist? Even with perfect information about how well the person will do at each of the different aspects of a complex role, those differing features of a role are sometimes given different weight, with the result that different overall judgments of merit are reached.

But we rarely if ever have perfect information, raising another source of uncertainty and disagreement about merit. Test scores, for example, are only imperfect indicators of academic merit. Perhaps the applicant had a bad day when the test was taken. Tests themselves are also imperfect. The Scholastic Aptitude Test (SAT) is a useful but far from perfect measure of academic aptitude, just as past grades are also only an indication of an applicant's willingness to work and academic ability. (I will return to this issue in Chapter 8.) Such indicators are fallible, and so it is no surprise that controversies arise when decisions are made about merit and the relative qualifications of different people.

Merit and institutional goals

As I have noted, merit is sometimes thought to be simply the ability to further an institution's goals. Ronald Dworkin, for instance, claims universities should "try to choose a student body that, as a whole, will make the greatest future contribution to the legitimate goals their institution has defined. . . . [Universities] have public responsibilities: they must choose goals to benefit a much wider community than their own faculty and students." He goes on to list the two important goals that racial preferences serve. It is crucial, he writes, "that blacks and whites come to know each other better" and also that society become "more just and harmonious." If done "in pursuit of either or both of those twin goals of student diversity and social justice," affirmative action "in no way compromises the principle that student places should be awarded only on the basis of legitimate and appropriate qualifications."[18] A similar point is emphasized by Fullinwider and Lichtenberg, who claim that affirmative action rests on the claim that decisions should reflect "judgments about the extent to which students will serve the institution's larger purposes. These purposes are multiple and diverse."[19] Besides education and research, the authors also point to improving medical care for African-Americans as a legitimate goal of an institution that should shape its admission policies.[20] Bernard Boxill also claims people can be "worthy" of a position because they can help the institution achieve its purposes.[21] But is this right? What is the connection between serving institutional purposes and merit?

We do sometimes think of a person as "deserving" or "meriting" a position in an institution because the person will further goals that the institution has set for itself. But stated baldly, the view that merit is found in whatever characteristics will further an institution's goals seems wrong. It would follow that an institutional commitment to winning at sports would mean that admitting a good athlete, while turning away a much better scholar, could be an example of admitting the person to the university based on merit. If we are comparing two players and select the better

[18] Ronald Dworkin, *Sovereign Virtue* (Cambridge MA: Harvard University Press, 2000), pp. 403–404.
[19] Fullinwider and Lichtenberg, *Leveling the Playing Field: Justice, Politics, and College Admissions*, p. 55.
[20] Fullinwider and Lichtenberg, *Leveling the Playing Field: Justice, Politics, and College Admissions*, p. 56.
[21] Bernard Boxill, *Blacks and Social Justice, Revised Edition* (Lanham MD: Rowman and Littlefield, 1992), pp. 202–203.

player, then that would be a decision based on merit. But it is only merit relative to the sport, based on the player's ability to perform the role of baseball player. What about the larger question, of whether the decision to admit the person to the university itself, based on athletic ability, was based on merit because the institution had a goal to win?

Those who defend the institutional purpose account of merit seem committed to answering "yes." But intuitively that seems incorrect. The institutional commitment to winning in sports does not define the role of student, or make a good athlete also a good student. Indeed, when Fullinwider and Lichtenberg consider the question of sports and merit they argue that *in fact* athletics do not help universities achieve their financial or other goals. They were driven to that conclusion in order to avoid either giving up their institutional purpose conception of merit or agreeing that admitting a good athlete is, by itself, a merit-based decision.[22] The implication (although they never explicitly say it) is that if athletes did *in fact* help universities achieve their goals, then admitting a good athlete *would* constitute a merit-based admission decision.[23] An applicant to a university who has no prospect of academic success at all (suppose the student is foreign and can't speak a word of English) could nonetheless "merit" admission solely based on basketball skills. The response to that cannot be that athletics serve no legitimate institutional purpose; they clearly can. Rather, meriting admission to a university is not shown simply by the applicant serving an important institutional purpose.

Staying with the example of universities, athletes are not even the most difficult case for this institutional purpose conception of merit. Universities have a wide variety of goals, including raising money, recruiting future students, increasing their stature among other universities, gaining support among powerful legislators, and pleasing alumni. So not only could athletes be thought to merit admission by helping to win athletic competitions, but so too could the children of the rich if admitting them will lead their parents to contribute to the university. Admitting the child of a powerful politician who can be counted on to vote for a new campus building would also have to be understood as a decision based on merit,

---

[22] This suggests that, for them at least, merit depends on whether a person will contribute to *justified* or *legitimate* goals and not merely to whatever goals or mission an institution may set for itself. In what follows, I assume that the distinction is irrelevant, and that the goals are legitimate one for the institution to pursue.

[23] Fullinwider and Lichtenberg, *Leveling the Playing Field: Justice, Politics, and College Admissions*, pp. 32–38.

as would admitting a well-known celebrity whose presence would increase applications or raise the public profile of the institution. Even a university committed to increasing its tuition income would be using merit when it admitted students from neighboring states over instate residents because they would be paying more. Merely serving an institutional purpose is not enough to allow us to understand merit.

The history of discrimination raises another important objection to the institutional purpose view of merit. For many years, elite U.S. universities, such as Harvard, Yale, Princeton, and Columbia, had an institutional goal of limiting the number of Jews among their student bodies.[24] While some pursued that end using explicitly ethnic or religious criteria, others used surrogate criteria by limiting the number of applicants from cities like New York and Philadelphia, which had large Jewish populations. Other times the institutions achieved that purpose by giving preference to athletes, alumni children, and graduates of private secondary schools which themselves had a limited number of Jewish students. Yet, in these cases, there was a clear understanding that such decisions, while they served an institutional purpose, were not based on merit; quite the opposite. When a group of Jewish faculty confronted Harvard's director of admission with the fact that so few highly qualified students were admitted from predominantly Jewish suburbs of New York City, he at least replied truthfully that "they would dominate the college if admissions were to be made on the basis of academic merit, without regard to geographical and sociological diversity."[25]

Understanding merit-based decisions as ones that further the goals of an institution is equally implausible in cases involving hiring and promoting people in jobs. Suppose a baseball team has a goal of attracting more Latino fans. In that case being a Latino player could represent a form of merit, just as hiring a white might constitute merit if the player would help the team become more profitable by attracting more white fans in a predominantly white city. Or suppose a restaurant owner hires her incompetent brother as a chef, having announced that one goal of the restaurant is to help the family.

Something has clearly gone wrong here: whatever else we may want to say about these decisions, it is obvious that they are not ones based

[24] For an excellent account of the events described in this paragraph, see Jerome Karabel, *The Chosen: The Hidden History of Admission and Exclusion at Harvard, Yale and Princeton* (New York: Houghton Mifflin, 2005).

[25] Nathan Glazer, "Late Admissions," *New Republic*, December 26, 2005–January 9, 2005, p. 36.

on merit. The "institutional benefit" view of merit is too broad. But what, then, *is* the relationship between institutional purposes and merit? Answering that question will require a closer look at the nature of roles themselves, at why merit is important, and at roles' relationships to institutions and to the larger society.

How merit matters

"Why hire or admit people based on merit?" is a slightly odd question. A natural response could be to remind the questioner that merit *just is* the ability to perform well. The reason hiring, promoting, and admitting based on merit are important therefore begins with the fact that different social roles need to be filled. If we did not accept the fact that society presents people with different social roles, and that they can be performed relatively better or worse, we would have no purchase on the idea of merit.

Role-differentiation is important: it is a marker of specialization and of social progress. Even a relatively simple hunter-gatherer society would need to think about merit by asking whether speed, skill, and strength are helpful in the role of hunter, for instance. Otherwise it could be just as rational to select a hunting party that included the elderly, the infirm, and very young children. Similarly, women who are able to breast feed are better able to care for infants, which was a reason for men to perform the role of hunter while they did what they were qualified to do. Any society that refused to assign roles based on merit would find it difficult to compete with ones where merit is used in selection of roles. Merit emerges and is important because societies need to accomplish different tasks and people are not all equally good at doing everything. What then is the connection between merit and institutional purpose if it is not the simple one suggested by Dworkin and Cavanaugh?

As I noted, institutions, social practices, and roles all exist in the context of a larger society; they depend for their existence on social norms, standards, and rules.[26] Some social practices like informal games, etiquette, natural languages, and even markets function without a formal institutional structure and are not the result of any individual's purposive decisions. Lacking a structure of authority governing them, they do not serve any purpose that can be altered by a person's decision and often have multiple purposes. Sometimes the purposes are open to dispute. On

---

[26] Thanks to Steve Scalet for helping clarify my thinking on these issues.

the other hand, institutions such as hospitals, universities, governments, and corporations have goals which are to some extent set by the institution – but only to an extent. The limits are conceptual in nature. Were a person to gain control of a hospital, for example, and over time remake it into an institution that promotes the arts or makes war on another group, then the institution would have been transformed from a hospital to something else. An institution cannot be a hospital without having as one of its purposes promoting health and fighting disease. But that still leaves considerable latitude for institutions to pursue various objectives.

Both social practices and institutions can shape and even create different roles. Some roles owe their existence to the institutions that created and sustain them. Bombardiers exist only because the role was created by military institutions; CEOs because there are businesses; and presidents because there are governments and other organizations. Outfielders, on the other hand, exist independent of any formal institution, relying instead on the fact that there is a social practice called the game of baseball. So although some roles are created and defined institutionally, many other roles exist independent of and prior to formal institutions.

That said, however, the institutional purpose theory of merit is correct in noting that many roles are performed within formal social institutions, and that those institutions serve different purposes. Universities, fire departments, and orchestras serve different functions from each other and from armies and hospitals. And because they have different purposes, some final and some instrumental, the institutions need people who perform different roles. To function well, hospitals must employ not only doctors and nurses but also orderlies, administrators, accountants, cleaners, plumbers, painters, and electricians – to name only the most obvious. The same is true of most other large institutions, which require that different roles be filled in order that they can achieve their objectives.

Because institutions have different and sometimes incompatible objectives, they are sometimes forced to choose between different forms of merit. For example, one of the Oxford colleges originally admitted students into its medical program based solely on applicants' academic merit, which it measured using scores on admission examinations and recommendations of teachers. But although those admissions criteria functioned quite well in identifying applicants who would be good medical students, they were not adequate at identifying applicants who would be good in the role of doctor after they graduated. For that the college needed to consider other qualifications. Weight was then given to factors like the applicants' personality. *Academic* merit was therefore sacrificed,

to some extent, for merit of another sort. But because the purposes of
the college included producing good doctors (and not just educating
good students), it changed its admission criteria to serve that purpose
better.

Institutions often face these kinds of trade-offs, in which different
types of merit are in competition. I already described another source of
such conflict, which arises because a particular position may be complex.
College professors often serve as both teachers and researchers. A student
applicant to a college might eventually play the roles of a musician in the
orchestra and athlete as well as student. Though roles are often complex
and open to interpretation, they can all be filled by people who are
more or less qualified. And unless roles are filled by qualified people,
the institution will not flourish; it will become less effective in achieving
its objectives. In that sense, roles, merit, and institutional purpose are
related.

Although it is true that institutional purposes are furthered by selecting
based on merit, and sometimes roles are created to further institutional
purposes, it does not follow that meriting a position is *the same as* serving some institutional purposes. Using merit to make decisions clearly
benefits institutions, but doing what will benefit an institution is not
necessarily hiring or admitting a person based on merit. Merit is not
simply the ability to serve an institution's purposes. Merit exists against
a backdrop of different social roles and is best understood as the ability
to perform a role well. Filling roles with qualified people who will then
perform them well is vital to an institution's success. Merit is therefore
tied to institutional purposes, albeit indirectly through the roles various
people play within institutions.

But it does not follow, nor is it true, that having people who perform
roles well is the *only* way to benefit an institution, let alone society at
large. Merit is one of the different reasons to hire, promote, and admit
people. What then can be said of a more general nature about those
other, nonmerit-based reasons? What are they, and when might it be
reasonable to sacrifice merit in order to further these other ends?

Recall the example of a person who has applied to a university and
is from a rich family that will give generously if the person is admitted.
Suppose there is another applicant who has better grades, test scores,
and other indicators of academic merit. The admission committee faces
a choice between admitting based on academic merit and serving the
institution's financial and other goals. Or suppose that a professional
sports team is choosing between two players. One is a better athlete and

will do more for the team in competitions, but another is able to bring in more fans and increase revenue. Again there is a conflict between choosing a player based on merit and choosing someone who can benefit the institution in other ways. While merit is *a* reason to select a person, it is not the *only* reason.

There is thus an important distinction between merit and the various other institutional advantages that might follow from the decision to admit or hire a person. Merit does benefit institutions in one way, but people can bring all kinds of other advantages to an institution besides performing a role well. How important merit is to the institution as compared with these other advantages it might get by sacrificing merit will depend on the particular case. It is simple dogma to suppose that the dominant reason to put people into roles is always merit.

In addition to those two types of reasons for putting people in positions – merit and institutional advantage – there are two other types of reasons that might justify placing a particular person in a role.

The third type of reasons appeals to a variety of broader social values that might be furthered, and again the category is wide. These can include both moral values and reasons of public policy. An employer might have reason to hire a particular individual for a job simply because the person desperately needs the income, for example. Such a decision might fly in the face of both merit and the goals of the company. Another example might be gratitude; perhaps the applicant deserves the job or promotion because of past service on behalf of the institution. Or maybe a veteran is hired out of gratitude for service to the nation. Again, however, if gratitude is the reason, then the decision rests on neither merit nor institutional interests but instead on the moral ideal of rewarding the person deserving our gratitude for their service. Or suppose, as I suggested earlier, that a restaurant owner has a relative who is an incompetent cook but who needs a job. The owner, we might think, has a reason to hire the relative as a chef though the reason, commitment or duty to the relative, has nothing to do with merit as a cook and will not benefit the restaurant as an institution. Public policy can also serve as a similar sort of reason. Perhaps hiring veterans will encourage others to serve, for instance, or hiring the needy will reduce welfare rolls. There is therefore a wide variety of reasons grounded in morality and public policy that could justify admission and hiring decisions, sometimes at the expense of merit or institutional goals.

The fourth, and final, category of reasons to place people in positions rests on the personal interests and desires of the individual making the decision. This could happen, for example, if promoting, hiring, or admitting a particular person would advance the hiring officer's career by winning the approval of his or her superiors. Or perhaps the person making the decision would be happy to work with the person. Bribery is another example, but bribery is different from situations where, I assume, the person did have morally legitimate reason to make the decision. The crucial point, however, is that these are examples in which the reason to put the person in the position does not rest on merit, institutional purpose, moral duty, or public policy.

There are, therefore, four broad categories of reasons that institutions and individuals can have for placing people in roles. One is merit: the person is better qualified and will perform the role well. Other reasons appeal directly to interests of the institution; to larger social values and public policy considerations such as fairness, need, or gratitude; and finally to the personal interests of those making the decisions. So although merit is one of the reasons for selecting a person for a role, it is not the only one. And there is no reason to assume, a priori, that merit is the most important reason to be considered. Everything depends on the particulars of the case. That said, however, it is nevertheless true that merit matters, often greatly, because performing roles well matters. Before turning to the important question of whether, and in what ways, race might constitute a form of merit, I want to look briefly at the arguments that have been advanced by some of the skeptics of merit in general.

The "myth" of merit?

Merit is often contentious because we do not have perfect predictors of qualifications and, more fundamentally, because roles can be complex and invite different judgments about the relative importance of the applicant's skills and qualifications. But some skeptics have claimed not just that there is controversy over qualifications and merit but, more radically, that merit does not exist and that it should be abandoned. Iris Marion Young, for example, titled a section of a book "The Myth of Merit,"[27] while Patricia Williams describes qualifications as a "con word"

---

[27] Iris Marion Young, *Justice and the Politics of Difference* (Princeton: Princeton University Press, 1990), p. 200.

that works to "dazzle the eye."[28] Yet, both Young and Williams are professors who (I presume) would give thought to their hiring choices of professors in their universities, of doctors for themselves, and of teachers for their children. Do skeptics really believe that merit is a myth and a con word? If they do not believe that every person can perform every role equally well, then what *might* it mean to say that merit is a myth?

One possibility is that skeptics about merit want to stress a point I made earlier, that merit and moral goodness are distinct and that merit is not a moral virtue. Insofar as that is the claim, then their skepticism is warranted. But it is misleading to put their point that way, in terms suggesting that merit is a myth. What other sense might be given to the skeptic's position?

In discussing "The Myth of Merit," Young writes that "normatively and culturally neutral measures of individual performance do not exist," implying, perhaps, that judgments about merit are a myth because they are relative to cultures and depend on values.[29] In a similar vein she later points out that those being evaluated for a job are often expected to behave according to what she terms "certain social norms," such as factory workers who "are often evaluated for their punctuality, obedience, loyalty, and positive attitude." But Young then concludes that "using criteria such as these is not necessarily inappropriate; the point is that they are normative and cultural rather than neutral and scientific."[30] Clearly, Young is correct when she says that merit depends on both culture and value judgments. Being a good ball player or symphony violist doesn't even make sense independent of the rules of baseball and the skills needed to play the instrument, any more than the merits of a lawyer could be assessed without reference to the socially constructed role of lawyers in the institutions and practices of law. Lawyers in an Anglo-Saxon adversarial legal system might need different qualifications from lawyers working in a European or other inquisitorial system. None of that is controversial, but neither does it justify skepticism about merit in general or the conclusion it is a myth.

Nor is assessment of merit value "neutral," as Young also points out. Merit marks the difference between those who are or will be good in a position – who will perform a role well – and those who will not. The

---

[28] Patricia J. Williams, *The Alchemy of Race and Rights: Diary of a Law Professor* (Cambridge MA: Harvard University Press, 1991), p. 103.
[29] Young, *Justice and the Politics of Difference*, p. 202.
[30] Young, *Justice and the Politics of Difference*, p. 204.

fact that merit is not normatively neutral is not a reason to conclude it is a myth unless it is assumed that *all* evaluative judgments are in some sense myths. Yet, that sort of global skepticism is far from what critics of merit seem to have in mind. Their own criticisms of merit are themselves normative.

Other critics of merit take a different tack. Richard Delgado describes merit as "that which I use to judge you, the Other. The criteria I use sound suspiciously like a description of me and the place where I stand."[31] Stanley Fish makes a similar point with an *ad hominem*. Merit, he writes, is "continually in the mouths of our up-to-date, newly respectable bigots who have learned that they need not put on white hoods or bar access to the ballot box in order to secure their ends."[32] The suggestion here is that the accepted measures and tests used to assess merit are tilted in favor of one group, or else are simply not accurate. Such critics might think that roles are defined too narrowly, for example, so that some important feature of a role (such as providing a racial role model) is ignored. Or they might have in mind that tests and grades are not good predictors of success. But neither of those establishes the conclusion that merit itself is a myth, and in fact they assume just the opposite. The claim that different measures that are more accurate predictors of merit should be used assumes there exists a different view of what merit is. Their argument is with the details, not with merit itself. (The fact that judgments of merit are not "neutral and scientific" is also, as I have stressed, neither here nor there.)

Young further contends that merit is a myth because in complex societies in which people work cooperatively it is often "not possible to identify the contribution that each individual makes, precisely, because workers cooperate in producing the outcome or product."[33] But that again misses the mark. The fact that each individual's merit cannot be measured "precisely" by looking at past contribution to a joint enterprise does nothing to establish that merit is a myth. Sally may merit a place on the basketball team because of her superior rebounding and passing skills. Yet, at the same time, it might be impossible to identify with any precision how much she contributed to the team's success in the last game, as compared with others on the team. The fact we can't say she was

---

[31] Richard Delgado, "Brewer's Plea: Critical Thoughts on Common Cause," *Vanderbilt Law Review*, Vol. 44 (1991), p. 9.

[32] Stanley Fish, *There's No Such Thing as Free Speech and It's a Good Thing, Too* (New York: Oxford University Press, 1994), p. 68.

[33] Young, *Justice and the Politics of Difference*, p. 202.

responsible for precisely 30 percent of the team's success is no indication that merit is meaningless. Similarly, we may be confident that a worker is good at a role in a company despite our inability to measure precisely how much that worker contributes to the company's overall success.

Robert Gordon is also impressed by the fact that merit cannot be "measured." He imagines that a black applicant to a professional school

> whose test scores are lower than those of a competing white applicant asks for admission based on "affirmative action." Everybody in that interaction (including the applicant) momentarily submits to the spell of the world view promoted in that discourse that the scores measure an "objective" merit (though nobody really has the foggiest idea what they measure besides standardized test-taking ability) that would have to be set aside to let him in.[34]

Gordon assumes that for merit to be meaningful or "objective" it is essential to know that test scores measure something and to know what that something is. But of course the defender of merit need not accept the misleading metaphor of "measuring," as if merit were like flour or sugar that could be weighed. In fact merit assumes only that there are skills and abilities that make people better at performing a role and that we have available reasonably good (though imperfect) indicators to tell when those skills and abilities are present. Whether test scores, grades, or recommendations are useful indicators of academic merit is a separate question from what, if anything, they might "measure." So although grades and test scores can be measured (a 3.8 grade point average is higher than a 2.0 grade point average), those are related to merit only to the extent, if any, that they predict academic success.

The skeptics about merit have provoked a counter-attack of a different sort from the position I have offered here. Rather than defending the concept of merit against these skeptics, as I have done, these writers attack the motives of its critics. In a book criticizing the "radical assault on truth in American law," Daniel Farber and Suzanna Sherry ask, "Is the Critique of Merit Anti-Semitic?" Their answer is that it is.[35] Jews, they note, not only earn significantly more money than other U.S. groups but are also better educated. Though only 3 percent of the population, Jews are heavily represented among the professions and on university faculties. In

---

[34] Robert W. Gordon, "Law and Ideology," *Tikkun*, Vol. 3, No. 1 (January/February 1988), pp. 14–18, 83–86, reprinted in *Readings in the Philosophy of Law*, 4th ed., edited by John Arthur and William H. Shaw (Upper Saddle River NJ: Prentice-Hall, 2006), p. 214.

[35] Farber and Sherry, *Beyond All Reason: The Radical Assault on Truth in American Law*.

1975, Jews represented 10 percent of all university faculties (20 percent at the best universities) and a quarter of the faculty at law schools. Some estimates suggest the figure is even higher today.[36] Denying that Jewish success reflects genuine merit, Farber and Sherry point out, suggests there must be another explanation for Jews' unusual success; but what? They answer that "if merit can be structured either to 'like' or 'dislike' any particular group, one wonders how it came to be structured to prefer Jews and Asians to white gentiles while those in power – themselves white and gentile – allowed it to remain so structured."[37] The natural and perhaps inevitable explanation of Jewish success, they conclude, is the familiar anti-Semitic claim of a "Jewish conspiracy." The reliance on "qualifications" and "merit" – if these in fact do not exist – must be the result of Jews' inordinate power, exercised in secret.

The idea that the attack on merit is antisemitic gains additional support from the fact that critics of merit sometimes explicitly treat those who succeed and meet the qualifications as oppressors. Richard Delgado describes merit as "white people's affirmative action" and as a form of "racism."[38] Attacking those who defend merit as racists is a familiar tactic. As we saw in Chapter 1, Eduardo Bonilla-Silva describes the "ideology" of meritocracy as "colorblind racism."[39] He also characterizes qualifications as a way to defend "white privilege."[40] Derrick Bell is more explicit, and speaks specifically of Jews. He writes that Jewish law school faculty members "do not recognize that the rigid adherence to standards that now favor them" are in fact "discriminatory to others."[41] To these writers, Jews are oppressors as well as conspirators.

Yet, however familiar such attacks on opponents' motives may be, in this and other contexts involving race, such claims are irrelevant to the real issue as well as often beside the point. It is not racist to question merit. As I stressed in Chapter 1, racism is an attitude of racial contempt;

[36] Figures from Farber and Sherry, *Beyond All Reason: The Radical Assault on Truth in American Law*, pp. 57–58.

[37] Farber and Sherry, *Beyond All Reason: The Radical Assault on Truth in American Law*, p. 60.

[38] Richard Delgado, "Rodrigo's Tenth Chronicle: Merit and Affirmative Action," *Georgia Law Journal*, Vol. 83 (1995), p. 1719.

[39] Eduardo Bonilla-Silva, *Racism without Racists: Color-Blind Racism and the Persistence of Racial Inequality in the United States*, pp. 25–34.

[40] Eduardo Bonilla-Silva, *Racism without Racists: Color-Blind Racism and the Persistence of Racial Inequality in the United States*, p. 32.

[41] Derrick A. Bell, Jr., *Confronting Authority: Reflections of an Ardent Protester* (Boston: Beacon Press, 1994), pp. 76–77. Quoted in Farber and Suzanna Sherry, *Beyond All Reason: The Radical Assault on Truth in American Law*, pp. 58–59.

it is not a belief. To believe that merit should be abolished, even when doing so would, for instance, harm Jews more than other groups, does not constitute antisemitism. Furthermore, attacking critics of merit as antisemitic, *even if* the charge were true, is no defense of merit.

When is race a qualification?

For many roles, the race of the persons performing them will have nothing to do with qualifications. From plumbers and secretaries to lawyers and accountants, doing well is almost always unaffected by race. Yet while that is true of many roles, there is nothing *in principle* to prevent race from being a qualification – perhaps even a critically important one. Everything depends on the nature of the role.

There are some easy cases. A black person may be needed to play a particular acting role, for example. The play may just not work if Othello or Martin Luther King is not a black person. Race would also be a qualification for choosing a police officer whose assignment is to infiltrate a gang, if the gang is made up exclusively of a single race. In these cases, race is so important that people of another race would not normally be considered. Race is not just one qualification, but an essential one. But for many other roles, including ones where race may be a qualification, the situation is much more complicated.

Three questions are relevant in deciding whether to put a person into a position in part or in whole based on race. The first is whether race is *generally* a qualification for the particular role. A second question is whether race will in fact mean better performance by this particular individual. It is possible that, although race *often* makes people better able to perform a role, that is not true for this person. This could be true, for example, if race were thought important because of the experiences people of that race typically have, though this candidate has not had them. The third question arises from the fact that race will often be a qualification for only one aspect of a complex role. It is then important to assess how important that aspect is, for which race is a qualification, when compared with other aspects of the role for which race is not a qualification. Although race is sometimes either a qualification or an indicator of a qualification, the question whether or not, in fact, a person's race is a form of merit in a particular case is often not easily answered.

Turning to particulars, it is sometimes claimed that affirmative action would provide role models, encouraging blacks and others who are "underrepresented" to feel more inclined or able to pursue a career. If being good in the role includes providing a role model, as it might, say, for teachers, then race could be thought of as a qualification for teaching. But whether the role of teachers includes providing role models for others, in addition to helping students learn, is controversial. Being a good role model is at most only one of many aspects of the role of teacher.

One instance when race can be an important qualification is in policing. Suppose we agree that an important aspect of being a good officer is to be able to be trusted by the community. If being black is a trait that makes it more likely that the officer will be trusted, then race is an indicator that the person will fulfill the role more effectively. It is, however, only an indicator that the person will be able to win the trust of the community, which is itself only part of the role. It is possible that another person, of a different race, might be better at other aspects of the role, or even (perhaps) at winning trust. That said, however, the point is that hiring based (partly) on race does not always mean sacrificing merit.

In the policing case, race is a qualification only by accident of history: it is because of the racial and historical context in which the officer works that race matters for job performance. In a different historical context, where people paid no attention to race, it would be as irrelevant for policing as having attached ear lobes. Does it matter, for purposes of thinking about merit, that race is only contingently related to good policing? Not that many years ago, it might not have mattered if a police officer was computer literate or perhaps even literate at all; now it does. In the future, good eyesight and other skills necessary to fire a weapon may not be a qualification, as was true in England a few decades ago when officers were not armed. So the fact that race may not be a permanent qualification for the role of policing does nothing to undermine the fact that it can now be a qualification.

A similar argument is sometimes made in the context of the military, where having both black and white officers is sometimes said to be important for recruitment.[42] This falls under the second of the four types of reasons to put people in positions that I distinguished. It is an institutional reason to hire based on race, not a reason based on merit. Another institutional reason is that morale would be better among the troops if

---

[42] This line of argument influenced the Supreme Court's recent ruling upholding affirmative action, *Grutter v. Bollinger*, 539 U.S. 306 (2003).

the officer corps is racially mixed. Neither of these is a merit-based reason, however, because there is no thought that race would make the person a better *officer*.

That raises perhaps the most popular argument for racial preferences in admissions to educational institutions: that it is educationally important to have a racially diverse faculty and student body. Justice O'Connor said in *Grutter v. Bollinger* that diversity is valuable educationally. It might also be said, elaborating on that idea, that diversity reflects merit because it is important to have teachers and students with different backgrounds to bring to the classroom. In the case of African-Americans, the argument is that because of slavery and racial oppression, being black in this country means having not only a distinct history from other groups but also living in a different social world. Insofar as this is true, and historical or social background is a qualification, then race could be said to be a qualification. But race is only one aspect of a person's background that might be relevant in deciding who is best qualified to teach. It sits alongside many other possible factors including earlier job experiences, religion, family history, and many other facts about people that can sometimes contribute to their teaching. Although such background and experiences may be of value for teaching, their importance is obviously limited. For some subjects such as math and science they may have no importance at all.

It is also worth noting that using race as a criterion for hiring faculty can work against intellectual diversity as well as support it. For one thing, intellectual diversity is a broader concept that political affiliation. But even here, a recent study of the political views of law school faculty concluded that at the elite universities, which have often been supportive of the diversity argument, more than 90 percent of the faculty contributed to the Democratic Party.[43] Because African-Americans are also overwhelmingly Democratic, hiring them would likely lessen intellectual diversity in the political sense even as it increased racial diversity. Nonetheless, law schools continue to use race an important factor in hiring. A study of hiring practices concluded that minorities who participate in the American Association of Law School's hiring process are about twice as likely to get a position teaching in a law school as whites.[44]

---

[43] "If the Law is an Ass, the Law Professor is a Donkey," *New York Times*, August 28, 2005, p. wk. 5.

[44] Richard A. White, "Statistical Report on the Gender and Minority Composition of New Law Teachers and AALS Faculty Appointments," *Journal of Legal Education*, Vol. 44 (1994), pp. 429–430.

For students, the situation is similar. Academic merit is the ability to perform well as a student. It refers to those with the talents and the motivation that makes them good learners. Past grades, test scores, and recommendations are standard indicators of academic merit. The race of a student may seem to have nothing to do with academic merit and qualifications. But again the situation is more complicated. Although academic merit in the sense of ability to learn is the central aspect of the role of student, it might be argued that being a good student includes more. Good students can also contribute to the overall learning environment by participating in classes and bringing a fresh perspective to the discussion. Insofar as that is part of the role of student *and* race is an indicator that a person will be able to perform that aspect of the role of student well, then it is possible that race is also an academic qualification. Admitting students whose background will enhance the intellectual life of the institution therefore need not be incompatible with merit. So although the ability and motivation to learn is the core of academic merit, it is arguably not the entire story.

Many of the other reasons used to justify racial preferences have nothing to do with merit. Some of the reasons fall into the second category I mentioned: institutional advantages. National rankings matter greatly to universities and professional schools, for instance, just as good public relations is vital for corporations. Laws giving corporations that hire minorities advantages in competing for government contracts can also provide institutional reasons to sacrifice merit and hire based on race, just as accrediting bodies or other groups that assess universities and programs sometimes provide institutional advantages for having a racially diverse student body. Still another institutional advantage for private employers is to avoid antidiscrimination lawsuits.

Other reasons for affirmative action depend on the third category of reasons: social advantages based on moral values and public policy. James Rachels, for example, has suggested that race can serve as an indicator that a person has suffered social, economic, or other hardships and that the person therefore "deserves" admission.[45] Other reasons appeal to larger public policy goals. As we saw, Dworkin claims that affirmative action promotes good race relations in society generally, and many universities have offered that as one of their institutional purposes.

---

[45] James Rachels (1978), "What People Deserve," in *Justice and Economic Distribution*, 2nd ed., edited by John Arthur and William H. Shaw (Englewood Cliffs NJ: Prentice-Hall, 1991), p. 136.

Others believe that affirmative action provides role models and educates leaders for the minority community. Insofar as this reasoning is accepted, it too falls into the third category, rather than the categories of either merit or institutional advantage.

The fourth category of reasons for putting people into a role are ones that appeal to the interests of the individuals making the decision, and again these reasons can be powerful in the case of race. (Often, too, these personal reasons will overlap with institutional purposes.) Promotion and raises within an institution may depend, for example, on a manager's success in achieving racial diversity. This is especially important for affirmative action officers and others specifically charged with increasing the numbers. People may also have other personal reasons, including feeling more comfortable politically or otherwise with people of a particular race.

Given these distinctions, the nature of the argument over whether Bakke was denied admission to medical school despite his greater merit is much clearer. The argument that he lacked the "racial merit" of being black rested on either of two ideas: that Bakke would be less useful to society than another applicant who was willing to serve a particular race or location, or that it is important for racial harmony that medical and other high-status, high-paying jobs are integrated. But if what I have argued is correct, then neither of those reasons – however weighty they may be – shows merit for the role of a medical student. Those who were admitted with lower academic qualifications and worse interview scores than Bakke were not admitted based on merit. The justifications given for rejecting Bakke in favor of the black applicants belong to the third category – moral and policy reasons – rather than merit. In other words, although the evidence suggested Bakke would have been both a better medical student and a better doctor, it also suggested he might be *less socially useful as a doctor.*

There is another, perhaps more worrisome sense in which race could enable a person to be a better doctor. Insofar as being a good doctor requires having the trust of patients, and being of a particular race enables a person to achieve that trust and openness from patients, then race would be a form of merit. In that sense, race is like gender. If people are more open or trusting because of the gender of their doctor, then gender may be a qualification that enables a person to perform the role well. But it is also worth noting that this same argument would apply to men as well as women and to whites as well as blacks. Being male or white could also constitute merit as a doctor, given the attitudes of the patients. Insofar as that argument is worthwhile, it would give some sense to the claim that Bakke was less qualified because of his race. Rather than claiming he would not be as willing to serve in the role of a doctor for blacks, the new argument is that he would not be as good in the role as he would have been had he been black.[46]

The argument is worrisome for the reason that it has so often been used to exclude people from positions and to defend the status quo. Hiring whites and non-Jews in law firms and elsewhere was defended in similar terms on the grounds that clients or customers might feel more comfortable and making them comfortable is part of the job. Hiring attractive stewardesses was justified because (male) passengers would also be more comfortable. But it is not clear that such arguments have much weight. For one thing, it seems more important that patients be comfortable with doctors, whose role is often more intimate and private, than with lawyers and stewardesses. And even if that claim is accepted, and making people comfortable is a qualification for the roles, it does not follow that other nonmerit-based reasons cannot also be considered. Merit, as I have stressed, is only one reason to put people in positions. If emphasizing merit leads to social or economic injustices, then perhaps merit should be rejected in favor of those other considerations.

If my account of merit and other reasons is correct, then what have we achieved? We know what merit is, why it is important, and that merit is only one of the possible reasons to put people in positions. We also see that it is a mistake to equate meriting a position with being able to help an institution meet its goals, though merit and institutional goals are related. Often a role can only be understood in terms of institutional purposes. And although having people in roles they can perform well does benefit institutions, there are other cases in which an institutional goal can be furthered by ignoring merit. And as I said at the outset, merit does not require ignoring race in all cases. Sometimes race is important or even vital to performing a role well. So, it does not follow that merit should be used exclusively in making hiring and admissions decisions, or that it demands ignoring race. Even when they do conflict, perhaps race should

---

[46] I do have some weak, anecdotal evidence suggesting that it is not true, and, indeed, that the opposite may be the case. On two different occasions in my teaching at an historically black university, black students have said, in class, that their families mistrust black doctors' qualifications. None of the other black students contradicted their assertions. I will return to this issue in Chapter 8.

be given more weight than merit either because of the other institutional advantages or the social good that it would bring. Although merit and related issues are very important in thinking about affirmative action, other factors are also important. In particular, what other purposes does affirmative action serve, and how effective is it in achieving those goals? The next chapter focuses on that question, and on what should be done to address the problems I have been discussing if affirmative action is to be reduced or eliminated.

8

Affirmative Action and Equal Opportunity

IN DISTINGUISHING MERIT FROM OTHER REASONS FOR PLACING PEOPLE in roles, I addressed one of the key objections to affirmative action. Although merit is important, race can sometimes be a qualification for a position. Affirmative action is therefore often, but not always, in opposition to merit. I have said little, however, about either the other reasons supporting affirmative action or about how those reasons are to be weighed against its supposed disadvantages. Those questions are the focus of the first half of this chapter. I assess the arguments that are relied on by affirmative action's defenders, and also recent work calling into question whether it does, in fact, benefit blacks.

But whatever conclusions are reached about affirmative action, another related question needs to be considered to complete the picture of racism, justice, and equality. Some argue that justice demands that everyone be provided with equal opportunities, while others believe that something less is required. Few deny that society owes those who cannot provide for themselves at least some opportunities – a decent public education, for example. This issue raises a host of problems, including the nature of the opportunities that are to be provided as well as their extent. If we support providing everyone with at least a minimum level of opportunities, what are the opportunities *for*? Answering that requires considering the nature of a successful life, as well as how opportunities to achieve it might be improved. I conclude this chapter by looking at some proposals that have been made to improve opportunities that are available to African-Americans, and how my earlier discussions of poverty and race are relevant to those suggestions.

Debating affirmative action

Giving preference to people for positions because of their race is rarely without controversy. Whether in employment or education, it often occasions deep disagreements about justice and equality as well as about the wisdom and utility of such policies. Sometimes considering race is sufficiently uncontroversial that people may not even think of it as affirmative action, for instance when race is clearly a form of merit. But those cases aside, the fact remains that racial preferences are deeply divisive. Before looking at the issue itself, I want to say something very briefly about the constitutionality of affirmative action.

That legal question depends on whether or not affirmative action violates anyone's constitutional rights, and it is not at all clear that it does. The argument is usually put in terms of the rights of those who are not admitted or hired because of preferences. Bakke, for instance, claimed that quotas setting aside places for minority students at the Medical School of the University of California at Davis violated his rights under the Fourteenth Amendment's requirement that governments not deprive people of the "equal protection of the laws."[1]

First, it is clear from what I have said earlier that racism or racial oppression are not the motivation of those who adopt affirmative action policies. It would be difficult, to say the least, to show that policies giving preferences to African-Americans are examples of institutional racism. In that sense, they need to be distinguished from other race-based policies such as segregated education, bans on interracial marriages, and voting requirements aimed at disenfranchising blacks. Insofar as I am correct, and the Equal Protection Clause is designed to "smoke out" institutional racism, it is not violated by affirmative action. To suggest that it is motivated by a legislature's racial contempt for whites is implausible, given the make-up of legislatures.

Nor, second, does anything in the U.S. Constitution explicitly require that race be ignored by policymakers. A prison guard would violate nobody's rights if he were to temporarily segregate inmates by race in order to avoid a riot. Government is not prevented from inquiring about race on forms in order to track educational progress. Neither does the Constitution *mandate* that people should be admitted or hired based exclusively on merit. Governmental institutions are free to consider a

---

[1] Bakke won on the quota question, although a badly divided Supreme Court also held that race could be used as one among the many factors the medical school used in admissions. *Regents of the University of California v. Bakke*, 438 U.S. 265 (1978).

wide range of possible justifications in making their decisions, and there is no reason why using race to further legitimate social goals could not count among those justifications. Even if using race as a reason means that decisions are subject to special judicial scrutiny by the courts, this in itself does not resolve the issue, if racial preference serves important social, or other, purposes. That is, in effect, what the U.S. Supreme Court has said in upholding affirmative action policies.

That said, however, the fact that affirmative action is consistent with the Constitution and with Equal Protection leaves open the question whether such policies are justified. Many unwise decisions by legislators and other government officials are nevertheless constitutional. That question, of the value and consequences of racial preferences, remains open.

It is very important, in thinking about affirmative action, to decouple two questions that sometimes cloud the discussion. One question is the *economic advantages* that people should enjoy and that should be attached to different positions and jobs. That is the question of distributive justice, and should be distinguished from the reasons – merit-based or otherwise – for placing people in a given role. Reasons for admitting people to medical school, of whatever race, are independent of the question whether doctors should earn several times as much as nurses.[2] Attacking economic injustices or inequalities by insisting on proportional representation of racial or ethnic groups in high paying positions has social costs that could be avoided by changing the tax policies instead. Egalitarians can therefore argue that justice requires more redistribution of income and improved working conditions and also support using merit to decide who occupies different roles. They would secure the social advantages of merit-based hiring without sacrificing the larger goal of economic justice. In my discussion of affirmative action, I will therefore leave aside considerations of economic justice, although I return to that issue in the last sections of this chapter.

The justifications of affirmative action have evolved through time, along with its meaning. It was originally assumed to represent a form of compensatory justice whose purpose was to redress the lingering effects of discrimination and racial oppression.[3] That theme dominated

---

[2] One further complication is that some jobs are more dangerous, unpleasant, and of lower status than others. But this again raises the further problem of the *rewards* people should get from doing different jobs, not whether jobs should be assigned on the basis of who can best perform them.

[3] See, for example, *Equality and Preferential Treatment*, edited by Marshall Cohen, Thomas Nagel, and Thomas Scanlon (Princeton: Princeton University Press, 1977); especially

the early academic defenses of affirmative action, which assumed that blacks' relative inability to compete for positions was explained by historic oppression. Many assumed that affirmative action would last only for a generation, as the effects of history gave way and blacks moved into the mainstream. The ground has since shifted away from compensation, although compensatory justice may still be part of the (unstated) background of the arguments. Affirmative action is now generally understood as part of a larger commitment to some other end, whether integration, battling current discrimination, or diversity.

This move away from compensatory justice in law and in public debate occurred for different reasons, but one was probably the influence of the much discussed and important *Bakke* decision. Justice Powell, who provided the deciding vote in favor of affirmative action, put heavy emphasis in his opinion on the social good that could come from using race as a factor in university admissions decisions. Another reason that compensatory justice is no longer stressed, perhaps, is that the beneficiaries of racial preferences are often not those who are likely to be suffering the lingering effects of past injustices. One author recently concluded that the beneficiaries of racial "set-asides" for minority businesses were not only wealthier than the average person of their race but also better-off than the average of Americans of all races.[4] The economic effect of affirmative action policies was therefore to transfer wealth from the poorer to the wealthier in society. (The same phenomenon has been observed in other countries that practice affirmative action, such as India, Malasia, and Sri Lanka, where the poorest do not in general benefit from racial preferences.[5]) The same pattern is present where racial preferences are used in admissions and hiring in universities. Beneficiaries of racial preferences are often drawn from already relatively advantaged professional and middle classes.

Affirmative action is controversial in part because of problems of implementation. Some of its critics emphasize the difficulty in deciding which groups and individuals are entitled to preferences. The answer will depend, of course, on the purposes that the preferences are designed to serve. Are we to include groups that have been historically discriminated

---

Thomas Nagel's influential opening essay: "Equal Treatment and Compensatory Discrimination."

[4] Sowell, *Affirmative Action around the World: An Empirical Study*, p. 13.

[5] Sowell, *Affirmative Action around the World: An Empirical Study*, pp. 12–13, quoting various studies.

against, or only ones that are now proportionally underrepresented? Is
it relevant that some groups came to the United States in chains, others
to avoid famines and political or religious persecutions, and still others
merely seeking better lives?

Other practical issues must also be faced after the groups to be given
preferences have been identified. If it is a racial group, which members
are to count? A student of mine recently had an admission decision
to a law school changed in her favor when it was learned she had one
Hispanic parent. And as I argued in Chapter 2, there are two different
conceptions of race: the socially constructed one and the natural one. If
we choose the natural one, then there is no clear boundary between the
races, and many will be of mixed race. But even if the socially constructed
conception is chosen, with its background assumption of racial "taint,"
we would face a similar problem of whom to include. Does a person
who has only 1/16th or 1/32rd African ancestry qualify? A recent article
in the *New York Times* reported that an adopted child of white parents,
who had always thought of himself as white, learned using a DNA test
that his "tan-tinted" skin reflected the fact he was 11 percent African.
Unfortunately for him, the father reported, that information came "too
late for the admission process."[6]

These questions have emerged with particular force in the case of
Native Americans. For instance, one person in California who was only
1/64th Native American qualified for a minority business set-aside.[7]
In a much better known case, charges were brought against a University of Colorado professor of Ethnic Studies named Ward Churchill.
Churchill was hired at the university on the basis of his claim that he was
Native American. It later emerged that there are no known Native Americans anywhere in his family tree. Charges were then brought against
Churchill for "fraudulent misrepresentation by misrepresenting himself
as a Native American" in order to gain employment. The University found
that Churchill had indeed identified himself as Native American in his
application for employment and in his professional writings after Indian
leaders complained to the University that he had lied on his application. Churchill is not, in fact, a member of any tribe, though he claimed

[6] Amy Harmon, "Seeking Ancestry in DNA Ties Uncovered by Tests," *New York Times*, April
12, 2006. http://www.nytimes.com/2006/04/12/us/12genes.html.
[7] Bob Zelnick, *Backfire: A Reporter's Look at Affirmative Action* (Washington DC: Regnery
Publishing, 1996), p. 301.

to be at least "1/16th" Indian.[8] He is instead an "associate member" of the United Keetoowah Band of Cherokee Indians, which the University noted is different from actual membership. In its report to the Board of Regents,[9] the University found that "self-identification" was sufficient to qualify as Native American and declined to take action against him. At the University of Colorado, at least, no biological or ancestral connection is necessary to qualify for preferences as a Native American.[10] (The University also noted in its Report that according to the U.S. Equal Employment Opportunity Commission "observation and self-identification are the most reliable indicators of ethnicity," apparently confusing mere appearance of ethnicity with ethnicity itself.)

Although such questions will inevitably arise in its implementation, they do not constitute insurmountable objections to affirmative action. Often laws or policies require what may in fact be somewhat arbitrary decisions (why allow people to drink at age 21 and not at 20?). If affirmative action really is important to maintain, then those practical problems will simply need to be resolved.

Another argument that has been offered in favor of affirmative action is the importance of role models. Seeing teachers or other professionals who look like themselves working in a field, it is claimed, will encourage people to think that they, too, can succeed. This argument faces two problems, however. First, not all role models are positive. As I will discuss, affirmative action runs the danger of putting people in place who are, on average, less qualified. Having a person who is less qualified than others may actually be worse than having no role model at all.

A recent study also raises doubts about the importance of role models, at least in education. The authors concluded that, "Having a professor as a role model makes a small but significant difference in the decision to become a college professor." But it also turns out that the role model's *race* was irrelevant. "For students in all ethnic groups," they wrote, "it makes no difference whether the role model is of the same gender, the

---

[8] Kevin Flynn, "Special Report: The Churchill Files," *Rocky Mountain News,* June 8, 2005. http://www.rockymountainnews.com/drmn/local/article/0,1299,DRMN_15_3841949, oo.html. Accessed on March 20, 2007.

[9] "Report on Conclusion of Preliminary Review in the Matter of Professor Ward Churchill," transmitted to the Board of Regents on March 24, 2005. http://www.colorado.edu/news/reports/churchill/report.html. Accessed on March 20, 2007.

[10] "Report on Conclusion of Preliminary Review in the Matter of Professor Ward Churchill."

same race, or the same gender and race."[11] They conclude that all faculty members, regardless of race, can serve as mentors and role models for students of any race and can have a significant impact on students by spending time with them outside the classroom. Far from being essential for success, role models of the same race provide no real advantages. Japanese-Americans flourished after World War II despite the almost complete absence of role models in the professions.

Another argument for affirmative action has far more current appeal, and is referred to in recent Supreme Court decisions. It is that racial preferences level the field by reducing the effects of *current* biases in admissions and hiring processes.[12] The idea is that as a result of procedural defects in the hiring or admission process blacks are being passed over. Affirmative action therefore serves to level the playing field by securing what is in effect a more fair opportunity to compete for positions. Rather than skepticism about merit, this argument assumes its importance. One oft-quoted study, for example, sent equally qualified white and black applicants to apply for jobs. The result was that blacks received job offers only one third as frequently as identically qualified white applicants.[13] Other studies have also uncovered racial bias in different areas, such as rental housing.[14]

The main objection to this as a defense of racial preferences is that affirmative action seems to be the wrong tool for the job. Insofar as these are serious problems, discrimination in the workplace and admissions is better addressed directly, with laws that effectively discourage it and allow victims to sue when it has occurred. If admission tests are biased or are not useful predictors of academic success, then the tests should be

---

[11] Stephen Cole and Elinor Barber, *Increasing Faculty Diversity: The Occupational Choices of High-Achieving Minority Students* (Cambridge MA: Harvard University Press, 2003), p. 247.

[12] Bernard Boxill, *Blacks and Social Justice* (New York: Rowman and Littlefield, 1992), pp. 147–172, defends this position. See also Luke Charles Harris and Uma Narayan, "Affirmative Action as Equalizing Opportunity: Challenging the Myth of 'Preferential Treatment,'" in *Ethics in Practice*, edited by LaFollette, pp. 451–463.

[13] Margery Austin Turner, Michael Fix, and Raymond J. Struyk, *Opportunities Denied, Opportunities Diminished: Racial Discrimination in Hiring*, Urban Institute Report 91–9 (Washington DC: Urban Institute Press, 1991).

[14] In one study, more than half of African-Americans wanting to buy or rent houses were treated unfavorably. Margery Austin Turner, Raymond J. Struyk, and John Yinger, *Housing Discrimination Study: Synthesis* (Washington DC: U. S. Department of Housing and Urban Development, 1991), pp. i–vii.

revised or eliminated.[15] If employers do not give blacks equal opportunities for jobs, then the remedy should be more effective enforcement of antidiscrimination laws.

A second objection to this defense of affirmative action is that it may not address the most serious problems when they do occur. Institutions and individuals who are drawn to affirmative action policies are precisely the ones *least* likely to show bias in assessing people's qualifications. Much of the time affirmative action would not be used when it is most needed, and would be employed when decisions are already being made without prejudice.

The most common defense of affirmative action in the context of admission to colleges and universities is probably the importance of diversity. The Chancellor of the University of California at Berkeley, for instance, wrote that students on campuses that lack diversity

> can gain just a limited, theoretical understanding of the challenges and opportunities in a highly diverse nation. . . . Every time I walk across campus I am impressed by the vibrant spirit of our diverse community. . . . Young people from barrios, comfortable suburbs, farm towns, and the inner city come together at Berkeley to live and study side by side. Not surprisingly, they find first-time interactions with students of different backgrounds occasionally fraught with misunderstanding and tension.[16]

Lee Bollinger, the President of the University of Michigan, thinks that educational diversity among students "is as essential as the study of the Middle Ages, of international politics and of Shakespeare." The reason, he thinks, is that

> For our students to better understand the diverse country and world they inhabit, they must be immersed in a campus culture that allows them to study with, argue with and become friends with students who may be different from them. It broadens the mind and the intellect – essential goals of education.[17]

---

[15] As I indicated when I discussed black underachievement in Chapter 5, SAT and other tests are not statistically biased against African-Americans. If anything these tests are biased against other groups by overstating black students' predicted academic success.

[16] Chang-Lin Tien, "In Defense of Affirmative Action," in *Sex, Race, and Merit: Debating Affirmative Action in Education and Employment*, edited by Faye J. Crosby, and Cheryl Van De Veer (Ann Arbor: University of Michigan Press, 2000), pp. 36–37.

[17] Quoted in Stanley Rothman, Seymour Martin Lipset, and Neil Nevitte, "Racial Diversity Reconsidered," *The Public Interest*, No. 151 (Spring 2003), p. 34.

The Supreme Court has also stressed the educational value of diversity in its recent Michigan decision. Justice O'Connor explained that affirmative action would provide a "mix of students with varying backgrounds and experiences who will respect and learn from each other . . . contribute to the learning of those around them . . . [and] enrich everyone's education."[18]

But some have doubted whether increased racial diversity on college campuses will by itself further important educational objectives. When discussing merit, I allowed for the possibility that given a broad enough understanding of the role of student, race might constitute one aspect of academic merit. The reason was that students of different racial, ethnic, or religious backgrounds can contribute to one another's educational development. In the statement just quoted earlier, University of Michigan President Bollinger claimed that a racially diverse student body is necessary so that students "better understand the diverse country and world they inhabit." But in what sense is it "essential" for students to work and live in a diverse environment?

The typical answer is that diversity is a valuable part of a liberal education. Confronting alternative values and ways of life is integral to the liberating and critical function of universities; that much is given. But it is less clear what diversity on campuses means, exactly, and whether its impact on students is positive or perhaps even negative.

In a study titled "The Compelling Need for Diversity in Higher Education," University of Michigan psychology professor Patricia Gurin made the case for diversity in the Michigan affirmative action cases.[19] She found a wide variety of educational advantages to affirmative action based on the educational value of diversity. "The vitality, stimulation, and educational potential of a college," said the report, "is, quite obviously, directly related to the makeup of its student body." The result of the study, she concluded, is that "diversity is a critically important factor in creating a richly varied educational experience that helps students learn and prepares them for participation in a democracy that is characterized by diversity."[20] Gurin found that students who attend a "structurally" diverse college (one with

---

[18] *Grutter v. Bollinger*, 539 U.S. 306, 314–315 (2003).

[19] *Gratz et al. v. Bollinger et al.*, No. 97–75321 (E. D. Michigan) and *Grutter et al. v. Bollinger et al.*, No.97–75928 (E. D. Michigan).

[20] "The Compelling Need for Diversity in Higher Education, Expert Report of Patricia Gurin," section V. A., pp. 1–2. http://www.vpcomm.umich.edu/admissions/research/expert/gurintoc.html. Accessed on March 23, 2007.

a diverse student body), take diversity classes (courses in ethnic studies), and enjoy friendships with students of a different race score higher across a wide range of educational measures. These include not only "racial understanding" and "cultural awareness" but also "ability to think clearly" and even "foreign language skills."[21]

But while for most colleges cultural differences, competing values, and other differences of opinion and values are important, it is less clear that the traditional indicators of race employed in implementing policies of affirmative action are good predictors of such intellectual and cultural diversity. Although being Asian, Hispanic, and black are not culturally insignificant in themselves, they are, at most, only an indication of somewhat different values, backgrounds, and cultures. Other indicators, such as being born and raised in a different culture and language, in a deeply religious household, or in extreme poverty, seem equally if not more important. Thus, some members of racial groups may have significantly different values from the typical white student, but many will not – especially those who attended predominantly white schools before entering college, as most minority students admitted to the University of Michigan had done. The connection between race and genuine intellectual or cultural diversity is in that way quite tenuous.

The nature of "diversity" on campus raises another problem: how is a "diversity" educational experience to be identified and measured in order to know if students benefited? In her study Gurin relied on enrollment in ethnic studies classes and on two survey questions given to Michigan University graduating seniors. One asked students the extent to which they were exposed to classes that dealt with issues of race and the other the extent that they feel they were "influenced" by those classes.[22] Even assuming no significant reporting errors, it seems likely that students who took and later reported they were "influenced" by diversity classes could also tend to be students who would be expected to report greater "acceptance" of persons of different cultures and greater "cultural awareness." Gurin also included "informal" measures of "diversity" such as friendships and forms of socializing, and again it seems likely that those students who already enjoyed friendships and socialized with students of another race

---

[21] "The Compelling Need for Diversity in Higher Education, Expert Report of Patricia Gurin," table D1.

[22] "The Compelling Need for Diversity in Higher Education, Expert Report of Patricia Gurin," section IV. D., p. 3

would be more likely to report greater acceptance and cultural awareness later on.

Given its controversial and sometimes questionable findings, it is not surprising that Gurin's argument has been extensively criticized.[23] Alexander Astin studied the same data as Gurin but concluded that the data showed increased diversity on campus (as measured by the numbers of minority students) did not in fact produce educational benefits and that increased numbers of "diversity activities" actually increased racial tensions.[24] Another recent critique of Gurin reached the conclusion that "Astin's interpretations of the existing data are generally reasonable, but Gurin's are not.[25] Gurin, in turn, has responded to those criticisms.[26]

Some other studies have concluded that affirmative action actually has a negative impact on education in general. The consequences of affirmative action were tested in a recent survey of students, faculty, and administrators at 140 colleges and universities.[27] The researchers asked students how satisfied they were with their educational experience, asked each of the three groups how well the school educates students and how hard students work, and asked faculty and administrators how well prepared students are academically. With regard to students' own assessments of their educational experience, not only were the benefits of diversity absent but greater affirmative action produced less satisfaction among students. The same pattern emerged with respect to the quality of education students said they received and the work ethic of fellow students. Faculty and administrators responded in similar ways, again indicating negative effects of diversity and noting the lessened quality of education and poorer prepared students. These results continued after other variables were taken into account among individuals (such as race,

---

[23] See, for example, Robert Lerner and Althea K. Nagai, *A Critique of the Expert Report of Patricia Gurin in Gratz v. Bollinger* (Washington DC: Center for Equal Opportunity, no date). pdf available at http://www.ceousa.org/pdfs/Gurin1.pdf along with other reports discussed in the text. Accessed on March 23, 2007.

[24] Alexander Astin, *What Matters in College?: Four Critical Years Revisited* (San Francisco: Jossey Bass, 1993). Discussed in Thomas E. Wood and Malcolm J. Sherman, *Supplement to Race and Higher Education: Why Justice Powell's Diversity Rationale for Racial Preferences in Higher Education Must be Rejected* (Washington DC: National Association of Scholars, 2003). http://www.nas.org/rhe2.pdf. Accessed on March 23, 2007.

[25] Wood and Sherman, *Supplement to Race and Higher Education*, p. 2.

[26] Patricia Gurin, *Response to the Continuing Critique by the National Association of Scholars of the Expert Witness Report of Patricia Gurin in Gratz et al. v. Bollinger et al. and Grutter v. Bollinger et al.* http://www.vpcomm.umich.edu/admissions/research/pgurin-nas.html. Accessed on March 23, 2007.

[27] Rothman, Lipset, and Nevitte, "Racial Diversity Reconsidered."

gender, age, parents' educational levels) and among institutions (selectivity, student/faculty ratio, student majors, and available disciplines).

These researchers also found widespread, if largely silent, opposition to affirmative action. Eighty-five percent of students said they oppose "racial preferences" and three quarters opposed lowering academic standards in order to achieve racial diversity. Interestingly, those figures also held for minority students themselves: 71 percent opposed racial preferences and 62 percent opposed lowering standards to achieve diversity. Of those administrators who thought affirmative action had an impact on academic standards, the ones who thought the effect was negative outnumbered those who thought it was positive by 15 to 1. Nearly half of all administrators opposed racial preferences in admissions, though far fewer would say so in public.[28]

It is important to note, however, that Gurin herself does not argue that *merely* admitting a racially diverse student body is sufficient to achieve the benefits. She also thinks it is important to "provide stimulating courses" covering cultural and racial issues and to provide an environment that creates "expectations for student to interact across racial and other divides."[29] Her argument is therefore strictly speaking not a defense of racial preferences in admissions alone, but rather of a much larger commitment to realizing the advantages of a diverse student body that requires more than simple numbers of students.

Others have emphasized possible negative consequences of policies that emphasize the value of diversity and tell black and other students in effect that they are there in order to provide different perspectives from others. Richard Ford, for example, writes that the emphasis on diversity

> pushed institutions that wished to engage in affirmative action *and* minority groups themselves to *emphasize* cultural difference. Only by highlighting the stark differences in perspectives, norms and experiences marked by race could universities justify affirmative action . . . [T]his rationale effectively requires universities to incorporate a substantive theory of racial difference into their admissions processes – the post-*Bakke* universities and their minority applicants needed not only to assert that racial minorities would bring distinctive ideas and perspectives to the seminar table . . . A more subtle and much more pernicious implication [was that] only by highlighting their

---

[28] Rothman, Lipset, and Nevitte, "Racial Diversity Reconsidered," p. 7.
[29] "The Compelling Need for Diversity in Higher Education, Expert Report of Patricia Gurin," section V. C., p. 2.

own distinctiveness could minority students justify their presence in the universities.[30]

The consequence of this, according to Ford, has been "an exclusive focus on culture, a (tactical) exaggeration of cultural difference and denial of commonality, and a subsequent inattention to economic inequality and political oppression."[31] Students arrive on campuses supposedly belonging to predefined racial and ethnic categories, are confronted with formal and informal social groups that reflect those categories, and so the emphasis on group differences spreads throughout the institution.

The extent to which racial preferences in admission encourage genuine intellectual diversity or serve other important goals is an open and much disputed question, as are the potential disadvantages of such policies. The controversial nature of these issues is confirmed by the fact that the University of Michigan maintains a large website dedicated to responses to criticisms of its studies supporting diversity and affirmative action.[32] To say there is a lively debate about these issues would be an understatement. What does seem clear, however, is that conclusions people reach about the benefits or costs of affirmative action are often affected by preconceived views and personal interest.[33] Liberal scholars and affirmative action officers tend to believe studies that support diversity while conservatives such as the National Association of Scholars are often the most vocal skeptics.

This debate about the value of diversity may obscure a more important question: is improving the education of (mainly white) students through increased "diversity" really the prime motivation for affirmative action? I suspect that it is not. Writing for blackenterprise.com, Madison Grey quoted an NAACP official who said that arguments about diversity were "missing the point." "From our [the NAACP] perspective, there is a serious gap in educational attainment," the official said. He went on to say that "when you begin to take tools away to address the gap it undermines the ability to have a comprehensive solution. The country can't go on

[30] Richard Thomson Ford, *Racial Culture: A Critique* (Princeton NJ: Princeton University Press, 2005), p. 46 (emphasis in original).
[31] Ford, *Racial Culture: A Critique*, pp. 54–55.
[32] http://www.vpcomm.umich.edu/admissions/research/. Accessed on March 23, 2007.
[33] Gurin's work grew out of work at the University of Michigan's affirmative action and diversity office while critics often represent the National Association of Scholars.

with these vast gaps between blacks and whites."[34] That suggests that whatever the merits of "diversity" as a justification for affirmative action, the arguments go much deeper. Diversity is merely a "tool" – a rationalization – that is useful to address the real concern, which is the "gap" in income as well as in professional and other positions. Insofar as that gap is a result of history, affirmative action can be seen as a (perhaps ineffective) type of reparation. I will suggest, in the last part of this chapter, a more radical (and more costly and difficult) solution.

That leads to another argument that is sometimes given, more in line with the comment about the gaps between blacks and whites, which is the importance of affirmative action to integration. In their oft-quoted book defending affirmative action, *The Shape of the River*, Bowen and Bok stress the social importance of integrating various fields in the face of the "relative scarcity of talented black professionals." Society, they write,

> needs the high-achieving black graduates who will provide leadership in every walk of life. This is the position of many top officials concerned with filling key positions in government, of CEOs . . . and of bar associations, medical associations, and other professional organizations.[35]

Elizabeth Anderson also supports the argument for integration, though she sees the goals of integration more broadly. Not only will it benefit blacks, she concludes, but the lack of integration

> [I]s a loss suffered by the American public at large in its failure to realize civil society – extensive social spaces in which citizens from all origins exchange ideas and cooperate on terms of equality – which is the indispensable social condition of democracy itself. . . . It is high time [to defend] this ideal in its own right, and that the Supreme Court recognize integration as a compelling interest.[36]

A number of points are important in weighing the appeal to integration. It is entirely possible to accept the conclusion – that integration of professions and other positions is an important goal – without endorsing affirmative action as the only or even the best solution.[37] As I suggest

---

[34] Madison J. Gray, "College Diversity Downsizing," at blackenterprise.com. http://www.blackenterprise.com/ExclusivesekOpen.asp?id=1562. Accessed on March 20, 2006.

[35] Bowen and Bok, *The Shape of the River* (Princeton: Princeton University Press, 1998), p. 283.

[36] Elizabeth S. Anderson, "Integration, Affirmative Action, and Strict Scrutiny," *New York University Law Review*, Vol. 77 (November 2002), pp. 1270–1271.

[37] I discuss alternative strategies later in this chapter.

later in this chapter, other approaches to the problem are available that do not rely on racial preferences but instead rely on justice.

Part of the problem with integration as an argument *for affirmative action* is that advantages of admitting and hiring based on merit are clear and significant. Relying on qualifications to make hiring and admissions decisions means putting into the right positions people who will perform the roles well. And while in some contexts race can be a form of merit, that racial qualification is often of secondary importance as we look at the mix of traits that complex roles require. Using race in hiring police officers, for instance, relies on the idea that because of race the person will be better at *only part* of the many-faceted role of a police officer, for instance winning the trust and support of the community. Policing involves many skills that are unaffected by race, however, such as testifying in court and pursuing criminals. The same can be said of other cases where race is a qualification. Even where race is a factor that helps a person do a better job, emphasizing race too much can often result in placing people in roles for which they are not well-qualified.

There is some evidence to reinforce this worry. It is sometimes assumed that race is used as little more than a tie-breaker between equally qualified people, but there is evidence that this is often not the case. The figures for university admissions, for example, are striking. In its *Bakke* decision, the Supreme Court reported that although Alan Bakke had scored in the 97th percentile on the medical school aptitude test, the average of the minority students admitted that same year was only the 30th percentile, far below the average for all test takers, let alone the other students who were admitted. The Court also noted that Bakke's grade average was 3.44, while the average grades for minority students who were admitted was more than a full grade-point lower, 2.42.

The U.C. Davis medical program was not unique in the extent to which it emphasized race rather than academic merit as traditionally understood. Large differences in the academic qualifications of those admitted across the range of programs have been confirmed repeatedly in other studies. Release of figures at Georgetown Law School created a furor when it was learned that the *median* score of black students was lower than *any* white student who had been admitted.[38] A major 1991 study of entering law students concluded that only 24 black students

---

[38] Robin Wilson, "Article Critical of Black Students' Qualifications Roils Georgetown U. Law Center," *The Chronicle of Higher Education*, April 24, 1991, pp. A. 33, A. 35.

would have been admitted to the top eighteen law schools if only grades and LSAT test score were considered, yet 420 black students did get in.[39]

Defenders of affirmative action like Bowen and Bok themselves often acknowledge that there are significant gaps in SAT scores and other measures of academic merit, and that those differences have an impact on students' performance. The average class rank of white students in their study was, as expected, very near the middle at the 53nd percentile. The average black student's grades were below the bottom quarter, at the 23rd percentile.[40] The impact of affirmative action is even greater at less elite universities. At the University of Colorado at Boulder, racial preferences have meant that black students who attend the university averaged more than 200 points below whites on the SAT test. One study found that less than 40 percent of blacks graduated from University of Colorado at Boulder within 6 years while 72 percent of whites did so.[41]

In response to these concerns, Bowen and Bok point to relatively high rates of black graduates' participation in professional and graduate schools to show that beneficiaries of racial preferences are professionally successful. Yet, that may still overlook the depth of the problem. Although it is undoubtedly important to integrate the professions with well-qualified people of all races, their argument overlooks the fact that affirmative action continues beyond admission to schools and universities until after the students graduate and apply for further education or for jobs. In his opinion in the Michigan affirmative action cases, concurring in part and dissenting in part, Justice Clarence Thomas points out that according to the *Michigan Law School Handbook*, affirmative action policies extend to choosing students for the law review, hiring by law firms, and judicial clerkships.[42] It is, therefore, difficult to infer very much about the qualifications of graduates when race continues to be used in the

---

[39] Stephen Thernstrom and Abigail Thernstrom, "Reflections on the Shape of the River," *UCLA Law Review*, Vol. 46 (1995), p. 1610.

[40] Bowen and Bok, *The Shape of the River*, p. 77. Figures are for students entering college in 1989. The authors emphasize, however, that blacks do not suffer from significantly lower graduation rates at these schools. But that fact is almost surely a reflection of the small size of the study sample, and other perhaps unknown factors, because it is not the pattern observed at other universities.

[41] Robert Lerner and Althea K. Nagai, *Racial Preferences in Colorado Higher Education: Racial Preferences in Undergraduate Admissions at the Public Colleges and Universities in Colorado* (Washington DC: Center for Equal Opportunity, no date), pp. 6, 11. Quoted in Sowell, *Affirmative Action around the World: An Empirical Study*, p. 155.

[42] Justice Clarence Thomas, concurring in part and dissenting in part in *Grutter v. Bollinger*, 539 U.S. at 372.

later decisions. The fact that affirmative-action graduates get positions later on, in an environment where race is again given significant weight in the decision-making process, does little to support the claim that they were as qualified as others who were admitted to the university based on academic merit.

Performance on tests after graduation confirms this worry. When the race of any individual test taker is unknown, the aggregate data present a disturbing and in some ways tragic picture. In 1988, more than four times as many blacks as whites failed Part I of the National Board of Medical Examiners examination (51.1 percent versus 12.3 percent). The same pattern is seen in law. Although 63 percent of blacks who took the New York State Bar Examination in 1992 failed it, only 18 percent of whites did not pass.[43] More recent studies confirm these earlier findings.[44]

The evidence on both sides of the argument over affirmative action is mixed, especially in education. Yet, in other contexts, such as the police and the military, I suggested that the balance of reasons would seem to be clearly on the side of considering race. Sometimes, as I argued, race may actually be a qualification for such roles. Other cases are more difficult. Are having more black doctors, government workers, teachers, and lawyers important enough to compensate for their relatively lower skills in the aggregate? Does the hostility generated when racial preferences replace merit outweigh its benefits? These questions cannot be easily answered, and may vary from context to context. Rather than pursuing these issues here, however, I want to look at racial preferences from another, more troubling angle. The question is whether racial preferences really are in the long-term interests of the people who are supposed to benefit from them.

Is affirmative action self-defeating to blacks?

Defenders often claim that affirmative action benefits the larger society in many different ways, ranging from improved race relations to improved educational experiences. Critics of affirmative action deny those claims and emphasize the various costs of affirmative action, including the costs to society of sacrificing merit and competence and of increased racial or ethnic divisions.

---

[43] Thernstrom and Thernstrom, "Reflections on the Shape of the River," p. 1612.
[44] I discuss the effects of affirmative action on academic performance and examinations in detail in the next section.

Common defenses of racial preferences in higher education also emphasize the benefits to blacks themselves. It is thought important for blacks to move into the professions and other high positions, which requires having the opportunity to get an education at the country's "elite" institutions. Jeffrey Rosen has defended racial preferences along those lines in the *New York Times*,[45] and the argument is also explicit in the Bowen and Bok study. The reason blacks should be educated at their sorts of elite institutions, the authors write, is that it would provide "far larger numbers of black graduates in the top ranks of the business, professional, governmental, and not-for-profit institutions that shape our society."[46] Their assumption, then, is that to be a leader in government, business, and elsewhere an education at a more competitive, elite institution is a significant advantage. Not only that, but attending more competitive institutions is of *so much greater value* that it justifies admitting students who, by the institutions' own predictions, will be well below average in their performance at the university and graduate at or near the bottom of the class. But is it really such a great advantage to attend those elite, competitive institutions? And what are the effects of affirmative action on historically black and other nonelite institutions?

First, there is evidence that students who are admitted into institutions using racial preferences in admissions do less well academically than they would have done at an institution that did not use affirmative action. Graduation rates and class rank are both lower for black students than whites where racial preferences play a large role in admission decisions. The situation is different, however, at institutions where affirmative action is not emphasized. One study compared two campuses of University of Colorado. The main campus at Boulder relied heavily on racial preferences for admissions, but the Denver campus did not. At the Denver campus, there was only a small difference of 30 points in SAT scores of blacks and whites as compared with a difference of more than 200 at Boulder.[47] Black graduation rates at Boulder were well below white students. Black students at the Denver campus, however, actually had a slightly *higher* graduation rate than white students. Studies of the performance of students attending predominantly black colleges suggest similar effects. Again, various studies have concluded that black students attending black colleges have higher levels of academic achievement

---

[45] Jeffrey Rosen, "How I Learned to Love Quotas," *New York Times*, June 1, 2003.
[46] Bowen and Bok, *The Shape of the River*, p. 285.
[47] Lerner and Nagai, *Racial Preferences in Colorado Higher Education*, pp. 6, 11.

than ones attending white institutions, and that their educational development is often impaired when they are put into an environment where racial preferences are the norm.[48]

It is sometimes thought that this is explained either by the fact that these students are in the majority or else by racial discrimination at the predominantly white institution. But the evidence again suggests otherwise. A major recent study was concerned to find ways to improve the proportions of blacks on the faculties of colleges and universities.[49] Among the conclusions was one that "the proportion of [African-American] graduates of non-elite schools who want to be college professors is 50 percent greater than the proportion of African-American graduates of the elite schools."[50] "[H]igh achieving African-Americans," the study found, "are much more likely to persist with academic aspirations if they go either to a state university or an HBCU [historically black colleges and universities] than if they go to either one of our elite groups of schools."[51]

The explanation for this, the study concluded, is affirmative action.[52] Because of racial preferences, the highest scoring African-American students "are admitted to schools where, on average, white students' scores are substantially higher, exceeding those of African Americans by about 200 points or more."[53] Since they are more competitive, elite schools must put more weight on race in their admissions process than other schools in order to achieve "diversity." As a result, the black students at elite schools do even less well academically, relative to their peers, than blacks at nonelite schools. "African-Americans and Latinos," the study found,

---

[48] Walter R. Allen, "The Color of Success: African-American College Student Outcomes at Predominantly White and Historically Black Public Colleges and Universities," *Harvard Educational Review*, Vol. 62 (Spring 1992), p. 26; Lamont Flowers and Ernest Pascerella, "Cognitive Effects of College Racial Composition on African American Students after 3 Years of College," *Journal of College Student Development*, Vol. 40 (1999), p. 669.

[49] Cole and Barber, *Increasing Faculty Diversity: The Occupational Choices of High-Achieving Minority Students*.

[50] Cole and Barber, *Increasing Faculty Diversity: The Occupational Choices of High-Achieving Minority Students*, p. 189.

[51] Cole and Barber, *Increasing Faculty Diversity: The Occupational Choices of High-Achieving Minority Students*, p. 208.

[52] Cole and Barber say it is "in part" due to affirmative action, although their study does not suggest that there is anything else that might also contribute to the loss of interest. Their study shows that the absence of role models of the same race is not, in fact, a factor (p. 247).

[53] Cole and Barber, *Increasing Faculty Diversity: The Occupational Choices of High-Achieving Minority Students*, p. 124.

underperform white students. Even when SAT scores (used as a measure of academic preparation) are controlled, these groups get lower grades. African Americans who attend HBCUs, however, do not underperform significantly; and African Americans who attend elite schools are much more likely to underperform than African Americans who attend non-elite schools.[54]

I will have more to say about why black students might perform less well due to affirmative action shortly, but first I want to look at another study of the educational impact of affirmative action, this time on legal education.

Richard Sander, a law professor at the University of California at Los Angeles, used data from the Law School Admission Council (LSAC) that tracked the performance of 27,000 law students and graduates from more than 160 participating law schools (95 percent of the total) as well as gathering data from most of the state bar examiners.[55] The information collected includes race, scores on the LSAT (the law school aptitude test), undergraduate grade point averages, law school performance (GPA), and bar examination pass rates. Sander showed first that there was a very large difference in the academic qualifications of blacks as compared with other groups who are admitted to law schools. Using a combined indicator of GPA and LSAT scores that placed students on a scale of 1 to 1000, he concluded that the typical black students in a given law school scored from 165 to 202 points lower than other students in that school.[56] The reason for this is a "cascade effect." Because there are not nearly enough black students to fill what is in effect a rough quota at the most competitive law schools, they admit students who without affirmative action would have attended a school in the next tier down. Schools in that tier are then forced, given that they too do not want to exclude black students, to accept students who would otherwise attend a still lower-tier school. This goes all the way down, forcing the lowest-tier schools to either have virtually no black students or to accept many students who are below average or who would otherwise not have gone to law school at all.

---

[54] Cole and Barber, *Increasing Faculty Diversity: The Occupational Choices of High–Achieving Minority Students*, p. 138.

[55] Linda F. Wightman, *LSAC National Longitudinal Bar Passage Study* (Newton PA: Law School Admissions Council, 1998). Available at http://www.lsacnet.org/lsac/research-reports/NLBPS.pdf. Accessed on March 23, 2007.

[56] Richard H. Sander, "A Systemic Analysis of Affirmative Action in American Law Schools," *Stanford Law Review*, Vol. 57, No. 2 (2005), p. 416.

The effects of this cascade effect, he argued, are profound. The combined LSAT–GPA Sanders used as an academic index is an excellent predictor of success in law school. Although individual cases will of course vary, for a group of 100 students the correlation between the academic index and law school grades is nearly perfect: 96.[57] Students who scored as little as one point higher on the academic index are still likely to have higher grades than those who scored a point below. No other factors were even remotely close to this one in their ability to predict success, including how much people study, participate in class, and use study groups.

Those academic qualifications predict success for all students in all racial groups, with the result that the overwhelming majority of black students receive lower grades and graduate at or near the bottom of their class at each tier. More than half of blacks graduate in the bottom 10 percent, 70 percent graduate in the bottom 20 percent of the class, and 92 percent graduate in the bottom half. Whites are ten times more likely than blacks to be in the top tenth of their class.[58] The effect is also continuous throughout law school, from the first year to graduation.

Sander then argues that this fact – that blacks do much worse in law school – has an impact on both graduation rates and bar exam pass rates. Low grades in law school are "by far the principal determinant of whether a student in the LSAC-BPS study failed to graduate."[59] Race, however, is irrelevant. Blacks with the *same* academic qualifications as whites are no more likely to drop out or fail out than white students.

The figures show that the effect of grades in law school extends beyond graduation rates to passage rates on the bar examination. "The overwhelming determinant of success" on the bar examination, Sander writes, is "one's law school gpa."[60] The failure rate for blacks on the bar exam after five attempts is six times that of whites,[61] and almost half of all blacks with very low law school grades never pass the bar examination at all.[62] And again, being black or Hispanic *by itself* has no effect. "Members of

---

[57] Sander, "A Systemic Analysis of Affirmative Action in American Law Schools," p. 422.
[58] Sander, "A Systemic Analysis of Affirmative Action in American Law Schools," pp. 426–427.
[59] Sander, "A Systemic Analysis of Affirmative Action in American Law Schools," p. 440.
[60] Sander, "A Systemic Analysis of Affirmative Action in American Law Schools," p. 443.
[61] Sander, "A Systemic Analysis of Affirmative Action in American Law Schools," p. 443.
[62] Sander, "A Systemic Analysis of Affirmative Action in American Law Schools," p. 447.

those groups [who have the same law school grades] do no worse on the bar than anyone else."[63]

Sander concludes that affirmative action has two significant effects. One is the "boosting of blacks from schools where they would have had average grades (and graduated) to schools where they have very poor grades"[64] and may not graduate. The second harmful effect of racial preferences flows from the cascade effect in which more competitive schools admit less qualified students so that the effect cascades down to less competitive schools: "Lower-tier schools admit blacks who would not be admitted to any school in the absence of preferences."[65] The result is that attrition rates of people in this group range from 33 percent to 40 percent,[66] imposing a significant cost on a large group of blacks, both in the financial burden of attending and the emotional cost of failure. Because of the cascade effect, blacks are from 10 to 12 percent more likely to fail to graduate than if there had been no affirmative action.[67]

Like the studies on the advantages and costs of diversity, Sander's article has been criticized on a variety of levels.[68] Of particular interest is his conclusion that eliminating affirmative action would actually *increase* the number of black law school graduates (although he recognized it would also mean they would graduate from less-prestigious law schools). One study critical of Sander's conclusions questioned whether black students really would do better at less competitive law schools. The reason cited is that students who attended their second choice law school (but were also admitted to their first choice) did no better academically and did not pass the bar exam more frequently.[69] Other critics emphasize that Sander ignored the fact that blacks do somewhat less well even when they have the same academic qualifications, so that even without affirmative action blacks would still tend to graduate in a lower position than others.[70]

---

[63] Sander, "A Systemic Analysis of Affirmative Action in American Law Schools," p. 445.

[64] Sander, "A Systemic Analysis of Affirmative Action in American Law Schools," p. 447.

[65] Sander, "A Systemic Analysis of Affirmative Action in American Law Schools," p. 441.

[66] Sander, "A Systemic Analysis of Affirmative Action in American Law Schools," pp. 440–441.

[67] Sander, "A Systemic Analysis of Affirmative Action in American Law Schools," pp. 440–441.

[68] For example, a more recent edition of the *Stanford Law Review* was dedicated to criticisms of Sander's article. See *Stanford Law Review*, Vol. 57, No. 6 (2005).

[69] Ian Ayres and Richard Brooks, "Does Affirmative Action Reduce the Number of Black Lawyers?" *Stanford Law Review*, Vol. 57, No. 6 (2005), pp. 1807–1854.

[70] David Chambers, et al., "The Real Impact of Eliminating Affirmative Action in American Law Schools: An Empirical Critique of Richard Sander's Study," *Stanford Law Review*, Vol. 57, No. 6 (2005), pp. 1855–1898.

Sander's conclusions about the effects of racial preferences on class rank, graduation rates, and postgraduation success are far from resolved to everyone's satisfaction. Rather than attempting to resolve these issues, however, I want to look briefly at a question that lies behind these statistical arguments over the consequences of racial preferences. What other reasons might we have for thinking that disparities in academic merit could actually have an adverse effect on those who supposedly benefit from them?

As early as the 1970s, well before the Sander study, concern was expressed about the academic "mismatch" in the abilities of students created by affirmative action.[71] But why should such an academic mismatch lead to poorer performance even *after* graduation? One suggestion is greater *stress* caused by having to compete with people who have significantly better academic qualifications.[72] Another possibility, proposed by Cole and Barber, is that the academic mismatch reduces black students' *self-confidence*, which, they conclude, explains black students' lack of interest in academic careers. Because of the mismatch, "white students are most likely to see themselves in the top 10 percent [*both* compared with others in their school and people *their own age in general*] and least likely to see themselves as being average or below. Next came Asians – followed by Latinos – with African Americans having the lowest levels of academic self-confidence."[73]

Both increased stress and lack of academic self-confidence might well contribute to black students' poorer performance, but I want to suggest another factor that may also harm students who are academically mismatched. It has to do with how teachers teach. It is an academic commonplace that teachers "teach to the mean." In my own experience, teachers do pay attention to the abilities of the students they have in class and adapt their teaching accordingly. Within a year, I taught at Harvard, where students are among the most academically qualified, and at Tennessee State, where students were nearer the other end of the spectrum. It was completely clear to me that if I was to be successful I had to modify significantly both my teaching and my expectations to fit the students, which I did. If I had not taught the students as I found them, either those

---

[71] Clyde Summers, "Preferential Admissions: An Unreal Solution to the Real Problem," *University of Toledo Law Review* (Spring/Summer 1970), p. 393.

[72] For example, B. A. Glesner, "Fear and Loathing in the Law Schools," *Connecticut Law Review*, Vol. 23 (1991), p. 627.

[73] Cole and Barber, *Increasing Faculty Diversity: The Occupational Choices of High-Achieving Minority Students*, pp. 117–118.

students who were well-prepared and academically able would be bored with the pace and difficulty of the material, or those students whose academic ability and motivation are substantially lower would have been lost and learned very little. That could also affect their motivation because working hard for them may mean barely passing or failing completely. This phenomenon might help explain why academically mismatched students would suffer educationally.

Whether cased by stress, loss of self-confidence, or the level of teaching, once it is realized that there may be a price to be paid for the academic mismatch, the issue of racial preferences becomes more complicated. More than a third of blacks entering law schools never pass, and (if Sander is correct) the others will do less well on professional examinations. This is by itself a reason to be concerned about affirmative action even if the majority do eventually pass.

The Bowen and Bok study expressed concern that the elimination of racial preferences would reduce substantially the number of blacks occupying important positions in society. But as Sander noted there is some evidence that the effects of reducing or eliminating affirmative action on the total numbers who work in various professions may not be large. Although racial preferences do result in a larger number of black students attending more competitive, elite universities, the experience in California and Texas also tends to suggest that eliminating racial preferences need not have a significant effect on overall enrollment. When California abolished affirmative action in public universities, black enrollment at the most competitive campuses, Berkeley and UCLA, went down substantially. This also happened in Austin at the most competitive campus in the Texas system when that state did the same.[74] But at the same time the *overall enrollment* of blacks in the two systems actually increased (albeit after a brief decline in California). Rather than attending Berkeley, where they were often academically mismatched, blacks enrolled in other colleges and universities where their skills and academic preparation were more similar to other students. So, unless it is assumed that attending a more competitive, elite university is in itself a large advantage, the demise of affirmative action might not impose the costs on blacks that are sometimes suggested.

[74] Peter Schmidt, "University of California Ends Affirmative Action," *The Chronicle of Higher Education*, May 25, 2001, p. A. 24. *See also*, Sowell, *Affirmative Action around the World*, pp. 159–161.

But is it true that attending an elite school itself is a significant advantage? It is important to note that although students who graduate from elite universities do tend to excel in later life, at least part of the explanation of that is the students themselves rather than where they received their education. Graduates of those institutions are people who are most likely to succeed *no matter what institution they attend.* Economist Paul Samuelson summarized the results of studies of the advantages of attending elite universities with the observation that "Graduates of those schools generally do well. But they do well because they're talented. Had they chosen colleges with lesser nameplates, they would (on average) have done just as well."[75] Without further evidence we cannot assume that the success of students who graduate from elite institutions is due to the fact they attended those institutions. The key questions therefore remain: what effect do racial preferences have on those who attend elite universities, and on those who attend other institutions?

Graduates from elite institutions do earn more, on average, than people who graduate from less competitive institutions. The Sanders study considered income levels and concluded that in the case of lawyers income is affected by three different factors. The location of the law firm in a big city is the most important variable. And while the second factor, the status of the law school from which the lawyer graduated, is somewhat important, the third factor, class rank, is significantly *more important* than the academic rank and competitiveness of the law school.[76] Assuming that is right, eliminating or reducing racial preferences would have both a positive and negative impact on income of black graduates. Because people would graduate higher in their classes than if they had attended more elite institutions, the loss in income that comes from an elite degree would be offset. If Sander is correct, salaries might even increase. Whether or not there would be other effects is also an open question. Bowen and Bok seem to assume that black leaders are well served if they graduate from elite, predominantly white institutions, although I know from my own experience that people at historically black colleges and elsewhere would disagree. Do we really know that graduating at the *bottom* of the law school class at Harvard is better than graduating at the *top* of the class at a less elite university?

Racial preferences can have other disadvantages for blacks as well. First, they can reduce the value of their academic and other qualifications

[75] Robert J. Samuelson, "The Worthless Ivy League?" *Newsweek* (November 1, 1999).
[76] Sander, "A Systemic Analysis of Affirmative Action in American Law Schools," p. 459.

generally. In a classic article discussing markets and the effect of "lemons," Nobel Prize-winning economist George A. Akerlof writes that employers who refuse to hire minorities may do so for reasons of profit maximization rather than prejudice. Race, he writes,

> may serve as a good *statistic* for the applicant's social background, quality of schooling, and general job capabilities. Good quality schooling could serve as a substitute for this statistic; by grading students the schooling system can give a better indicator of quality than other more superficial characteristics. . . . The certifying establishment, however, must be credible. The unreliability of slum schools decreases the economic possibilities of their students. This lack [of reliable indicator of qualifications] may be particularly disadvantageous to members of already disadvantaged minority groups.[77]

Under a regime where racial preferences override merit, being black may become an indicator that a person is probably less qualified than others. And this is true *whether it applies in an individual case or not.* As Akerlof emphasizes, employers and others constantly face the need to make decisions in conditions of uncertainty, without complete knowledge. When qualifications are replaced by racial preferences, the ability of the "schooling system" to provide evidence of an applicant's qualifications is compromised.

This problem can be further exacerbated by grading policies. In a competitive institution where affirmative action is the norm, black students will, on average, perform less well. Desiring not to fail significant numbers of black students, teachers may inflate grades either for black students or, perhaps more likely, for the entire class. What would normally be a reliable indicator of qualifications – grades – then can become less reliable as grade inflation moves everyone up the scale. As racial preferences become more entrenched and stereotypes are confirmed, the danger is that the ongoing cycle may continue. There are also studies suggesting that affirmative action works to undermine support for blacks and for policies that would otherwise benefit them. It may even encourage racism. Racial preferences are widely believed to be unfair. As I have noted, one study involving 140 universities and colleges found that 85 percent of students and about half of faculty and administrators rejected racial preferences. A *Newsweek* magazine poll done in January 2003 found even stronger opposition among the population as a whole. Although

---

[77] George A. Akerlof, "The Market for 'Lemons': Quality, Uncertainty and the Market Mechanism," *Quarterly Journal of Economics*, Vol. 84, No. 3 (1970), pp. 494–495 (emphasis in original).

67 percent of adults opposed preferential admissions to universities, 56 percent of all minorities also rejected racial or gender preferences for blacks and 71 percent of minorities rejected racial preferences in general.[78]

There is evidence that this hostility toward affirmative action policies translates into general negative attitudes toward blacks. Two researchers gave white subjects a series of questions designed to assess their attitudes about race. Sometimes the series of questions mentioned affirmative action and other times it did not. They then compared the responses by those who took the test without the affirmative action issue having been raised previously with ones where it had been mentioned earlier. They concluded that the "mere mention" of affirmative action and racial preferences affected responses by whites to blacks generally. For example, there were significant differences in the percentages of whites who agreed that blacks are "lazy" or "irresponsible" after racial preferences were mentioned during interviews.[79] When there had been no prior mention of racial preferences or affirmative action, attitudes toward blacks were more positive. Besides encouraging racial animosities, racial preferences may actually undermine support for programs designed to benefit African-Americans.

Finally, there is another possible cost to blacks of affirmative action. This can be even more difficult to measure than the effects I have been describing, though it may be more important. In his discussion of "subconscious" racism, Charles Lawrence (not thinking about racial preferences) wrote that we must

> evaluate governmental conduct to see if it conveys a symbolic message to which the culture attaches racial significance. . . . actions that have racial meaning within the culture are also those actions that carry a stigma for which we should have special concern. . . . And stigma that has racial meaning burdens all blacks and adds to the pervasive, cumulative and mutually reinforcing system of racial discrimination.[80]

I believe that Lawrence is right about racial segregation, but we also need to consider the messages that affirmative action sends to both African-Americans and others. In Chapter 4, I described the possible negative effects of being treated as if shackled by history and facing a racially

---

[78] Figures quoted in Rothman, Lipset, and Nevitte, "Racial Diversity Reconsidered," p. 33.

[79] Sniderman and Piazza, *The Scar of Race*, pp. 102–104.

[80] Lawrence, "The Id, the Ego, and Equal Protection," pp. 356, 358.

stacked deck. Affirmative action policies risk carrying the same message, with the same effect. Unable to compete on the basis of merit, blacks are assumed to need special advantages.

A few years ago, I had an African-American student who strongly opposed affirmative action and had refused to identify herself racially when she applied to colleges. Since arriving at my university she had shown herself to be among the very best students. After she received a prestigious academic award, she and I were discussing affirmative action (which I then actively supported). She responded by describing how her fellow students had reacted to her winning the award as well as to her other academic successes. She said they often said to her, as she put it to me, that they were "surprised I'm black."

In his opinion in a recent affirmative action case, the Supreme Court's only black member, Justice Clarence Thomas, also suggested that the University of Michigan Law School's policy of admitting students based on race was stigmatizing. The majority of blacks, he wrote, are admitted to the law school only because of race, and

> because of this policy all are tarred. . . . When blacks take positions in the highest places of government, industry, or academia, it is an open question today whether their skin color played a part in their advancement. The question itself is the stigma – because either racial discrimination [i.e. racial preferences] did play a role, in which case the person may be deemed "otherwise unqualified," or it did not, in which case asking the question itself unfairly marks those who would succeed without discrimination.[81]

Justice Thomas expressed sentiments that my former student would have well understood.

Replacing merit-based decisions in admissions and hiring in favor of race-based ones can also undermine self-respect. The Cole and Barber study described one way that this can happen, by the academic mismatch of students. But affirmative action can undermine self-respect in another way as well. Successful, happy human lives depend on people's ability to achieve their ends, and to work hard, people need confidence that they are capable of succeeding. Perhaps the most important way that people can gain confidence and self-respect is by *actually succeeding* in a task or role. Some ways of succeeding are not likely to produce self-respect and confidence: succeeding on an examination or winning a game by cheating, for example, cannot be a source of genuine self-respect. The

---

[81] Justice Clarence Thomas, concurring in part and dissenting in part in *Grutter v. Bollinger*. 539 U.S. at 373.

cheater did not earn the grade or the award, and the fact of having won
it does not warrant self-respect.

Racial preferences can work both to support and to undermine the
sense of achievement and the self-respect that often accompanies such
success. To graduate from a prestigious university or be given an important job can often add to self-respect. But to be admitted or promoted
based on race rather than merit can work in the opposite direction: it
is similar to being admitted based on parents' willingness to contribute
money to the institution rather than merit. Indeed, racial preferences
have a potentially even more damaging message than other non-merit
based preferences such as legacies. Children of alumni are not easily
identifiable by other students. Their lives in the institutions are not colored by the knowledge that others may suspect, rightly or wrongly, that
they are there despite their lack of merit.

Affirmative action can also affect self-esteem, as well as self-respect. I
said that self-esteem is the sense that membership in one's racial, ethnic, religious, or other group is a source of pride and is not a badge of
inferiority. There is therefore a danger that race-based affirmative action
might produce the same effect that Justice Thurgood Marshall attached
to racial segregation when writing in Brown v. Board of Education: members of minority groups come to see their membership in the group as
a sign of inferiority. A well-known African-American critic of affirmative
action, John McWhorter, imagined Jews' reaction to preferences that
might have been given to them in an effort to help new immigrants during the first half of the twentieth century. He describes them as "chafing
under the condescension inherent in affirmative action."[82] Affirmative
action, he concludes, "reveals nothing less than a concept of black people as essentially less than whole."[83] So besides attacking the ground
of self-respect – pride in accomplishment – affirmative action can also
undermine self-esteem while at the same time feeding residual fears of
inferiority. Even Bowen and Bok, who apparently put virtually no weight
on these concerns, quote a student who was admitted based on race as
asking "Will I be the dumbest here?"[84]

Finally, affirmative action has a larger political consequence that may
not be appreciated by its supporters. It tends to hide from public view
the true nature and extent of various social injustices that are endured

[82] McWhorter, *Losing the Race*, p. 240.
[83] McWhorter, *Losing the Race*, p. 240.
[84] Bowen and Bok, *The Shape of the River*, pp. 82–83.

disproportionately by blacks (as well as others). Racial preferences in admissions and in hiring make invisible the differences in qualifications that now exist but that *would be evident* if decisions were based on merit. Without racial preferences the failures of the educational system, in particular, would be even more in evidence because the gaps in academic achievement and qualifications would be apparent for all to see. The effect of racial preferences is therefore that parents, teachers, educational institutions, communities, political leaders, in fact, everyone who shares responsibility for insuring that black children have the qualifications necessary to succeed will appear more effective than they really are. Social institutions charged with providing opportunities for black children appear to be better than they are. The ultimate victims of the failures of society, hidden by affirmative action, are those who are inadequately educated and unprepared to compete. This is the most radical of the criticism of racial preferences. Affirmative action makes society appear more just than it is and therefore makes it perhaps even less likely to move toward what justice requires.

It does not follow from the arguments against reparations and affirmative action offered here, nor do I believe it is true, that *simply* rejecting reparations and cutting back racial preferences is an adequate solution. When I discussed compensatory justice, I argued that the history of slavery and racial oppression should not go unacknowledged and that an apology is warranted. I also argued that apologies should have consequences: when a person or government apologizes, then the recipient of the apology can reasonably expect a renewed commitment to avoiding similar errors in the future. Slavery and its aftermath matter, and merely apologizing for that and other forms of racism and racial oppression, without more, is not enough. The remorse that apologies express requires a further commitment to insuring that racial equality and justice are not hollow ideals. The history of African-Americans is unique: no other group was brought to the country as slaves and then subjected to the same degree of racial oppression. But if reparations and affirmative action are not the solution, then what should be put in their place?

Successful lives

I suggested earlier in this chapter that those who argue for affirmative action based on the importance of integrating society are onto something important. My objection was to using racial preferences to achieve the goal. But the goal, expressed in that way, can also be questioned.

Should we be concerned about the outcome of laws and social practices, or with equality in the processes, law, and procedures themselves? Thinking in terms of affirmative action invites the former, outcome-oriented approach, by seeing the problem as simply too few people in various roles. But there is another approach to the problems of poverty and race that does not aspire to equality of outcome but instead to equality of opportunity. While it may not guarantee equal outcomes, it also avoids the problems I have described with affirmative action. At the same time, it will also require far more radical and potentially costly steps in its implementation.

Frederick Douglass, himself a former slave, expressed views well over a century ago that resonate with the argument that I now want to consider. "The American people," he wrote,

> have always been anxious to know what they shall do with us. . . . Do nothing with us! . . . If the negro cannot stand on his own legs, let him fall also. All I ask is, give him a chance to stand on his own legs! Let him alone! . . . Your interference is doing him positive injury.[85]

Douglass's proposal to society is simply this: "What I ask for the negro is not benevolence, not pity, not sympathy, but simply *justice*."[86] But what does justice require, in this context?

I noted in Chapter 4 that most agree that one of the requirements of justice is to provide opportunities for a decent education for everyone.[87] A just society would not leave some without a reasonable chance for a decent life.

It is natural, when thinking about the poverty facing many African-Americans, to suppose that the solution should be economic: people have too little money, so we should give them more. But is the greatest problem facing African-Americans really lack of income? Chapter 5 began with that familiar idea, but as the argument proceeded, other,

---

[85] Frederick Douglass, "What the Black Man Wants," a speech delivered in Boston Massachusetts, January 26, 1865. Reprinted in *Frederick Douglass Papers*, Vol. 4, edited by J. Blassingame and J. McKivigan (New Haven: Yale University Press, 1991), p. 68.

[86] Douglass, "What the Black Man Wants," p. 59.

[87] I believe *distributive justice* includes seeing that those who cannot work are provided for. Others, I said, think distributive justice demands much more, including provisions for decent medical care or economic equality in general. This is not a book about distributive justice, and so I want to set those issues aside and assume that it is more or less agreed that justice at least requires paying serious attention to the opportunities people are able to enjoy.

deeper problems emerged as causes of poverty: unemployment, family breakdown, crime, and perhaps most importantly, poor educational achievement. Educational underachievement is fed, in turn, by a variety of cultural factors with roots extending into the family, culture, and even the history of slavery. So it is not at all clear that the deepest problem really is lack of money. Lack of income is a problem, to be sure, but the causes and significance of poverty are deeper.

The question, put simply, is whether it is worse for a person to be poor without those other problems or to be better off economically but still have to deal with crime, family breakdown, and poor educational achievement. For most of us,[88] income levels have little to do with how happy we are or how satisfied we are with our lives. Kwang Ng summarized the research on this subject with the observation that in economically advanced societies "money does not buy happiness, or at least not much."[89] So not only are those social and cultural problems the explanation of poverty but they are also in many ways themselves the real heart of the complex web of problems that we call poverty.

Rather than focusing exclusively – or even primarily – on income levels, we should instead think in terms of providing the cultural, social, and economic conditions that will enable people to have successful lives. Before asking what those further conditions might be, I want to say something, again very briefly, about what I mean by a successful life.

I understand a successful life to be a life that is spent in the *successful pursuit of valuable activities or ends*.[90] As background, I assume that there is a wide range of valuable activities and ends that any given person can successfully pursue and that would secure for the person a successful life. One way a life may not go well is for a person to fail at his or her most important goal. But most people, fortunately, are not so invested in a single aim that the failure to achieve it would cast a shadow over our entire lives. Yet, failure is worse than success, and the more we fail in our pursuits the less well our lives have gone. Furthermore, it is not as if people choose a single life-plan. Goals are embedded in one another,

---

[88] Except those, for example, who voluntarily choose a religious vocation and a life of relative poverty.

[89] Kwang Ng, "A Case for Happiness, Cardinalism, and Interpersonal Comparability," *Economics Journal*, Vol. 107 (1997), p. 1849.

[90] For a defense of this idea, see Joseph Raz, *Ethics in the Public Domain*. Readers familiar with Raz's work will see that it has had a significant influence on my own thinking about these issues, though I disagree with him at various points as well.

and often change over time. There is no single valuable life, appropriate for everyone. People's talents, tastes, and circumstances vary greatly.

Merely achieving one's ends, whatever they might be, is not sufficient unless the ends are themselves valuable, that is, worthy of pursuing. A life dominated by the desperate pursuit of drugs and crime, even if the person achieves those ends, is not worthwhile. The reason is that those are not valuable pursuits. Nor is a life filled with obsessive concern for money and power valuable, or one dominated by envy or petty vindictiveness. The evil person's successful pursuit of injustice and immorality for their own sake, or the otherwise useless pursuit of recognition or money, are not enough to claim a successful life, except in the trivial sense that the person got what was wanted. We want not to get whatever we want, but for our wants or desires to be based on good reasons. That said, there is nonetheless a vast range of worthwhile pursuits and ends that are normally open to people, from forming loving family, friendships, and other social relationships, to working at useful careers and jobs, to participating in the arts or athletics, to simply appreciating life and enjoying art or nature.

A skeptic may doubt whether there really is a distinction between valuable activities and ones that are not worth pursuing, but there are two answers to such skepticism. One is to appeal to specific cases, as I did earlier, and ask if the skeptic really does believe that anyone who achieves their ends, *whatever the ends may be*, has thereby enjoyed a successful life.

The second response is to note that the skeptic, like the rest of us, assumes that we can make mistakes and choose what is not worth pursuing. We (and the skeptic) assume that some choices are more valuable than others when we deliberate about careers and other major lifetime goals. It's not just a matter of whether we will be good at something (though that is obviously one issue we consider). We also reflect on whether we will find the course we are contemplating rewarding and be confident that it is not something we will regret having chosen because we find that the goals are not worthwhile even if they can be achieved.

Most of us have worried, at least on occasion, that we might reach a point when we believe that our own life has been on the wrong course or, worse, that it was wasted. That attitude may sometimes rest on the fact that we have not succeeded to the extent we hoped; but other times the concern may reach deeper, to the value of whatever goals or successes we have had.

So, skepticism about the claim that some pursuits are valuable and others are less valuable to the extent of lacking value altogether seems difficult to square with familiar facts about our lives. If all activities and ends really were equally valuable (or equally without value) and all people could do is make an arbitrary choice, then what sense would it make for people to deliberate about which goals are worth pursuing in the future or to be concerned that they might waste their lives by making bad choices?

Another feature of a successful life is that people cannot *make* another person's life a success. We can, if circumstances are fortunate, shape our own lives into something successful by pursuing what is worthwhile and within our reach. But we face serious limits if we try to do that to or for someone else. This is true for at least three reasons. First, a successful life requires acting; it involves the successful *pursuit* of valuable activities and ends. Forcing people (against their will) to pursue one end rather than another makes it far less likely that their half-hearted efforts will succeed.

Second, as John Stuart Mill famously emphasized, people are generally in a better position to judge which pursuits will make their lives a success than are strangers. Not only do they tend to be better informed about their own interests and talents, but they also are more concerned about their own success than others are likely to be.

Finally, and I think most importantly, having had ends chosen for us rather than choosing them ourselves means there is an important sense in which they are not our own. That means, in turn, that our *life* will not be our own. Since part of a successful (human) life includes exercising autonomy and deciding for one's self which activities and ends to pursue, a life that has not been freely chosen from among a (reasonably broad) range of options is to that extent less successful. In other words, even if the goals are worthy it is also important that people be allowed to make the choice to pursue them freely, for themselves, if the life is to be judged a success.

That is not to say people cannot help enhance (or limit) others' prospects for achieving a successful life. While successful lives do require meeting and overcoming challenges, other people can assist by providing the background conditions that will enable a person to have a success-ful life. Indeed, some conditions make success extremely difficult if not impossible. Debilitating pain, constant humiliation before others in soci-ety, and severe mental or physical handicaps can make it difficult or impossible to pursue valuable activities and ends with much prospect of success. Some of these conditions society can help overcome; others are beyond anyone's control.

But even people in less dire straits can be helped by improving background conditions. People also need, as a rule, at least a modicum of self-respect and self-esteem. Living in a society that encourages self-respect and self-esteem can be important, especially for those with few other sources of such attitudes. Providing unemployment insurance, basic medical care, and a satisfactory economic minimum for those who cannot support themselves are things society can do to make it more likely that people will have successful lives. It's not that *nobody* who lacks those advantages or who suffers from continuous pain, lack of self-respect, and the rest could succeed. Some no doubt could. The point, rather, is that only the strongest and most tenacious would be able to do so. These extraordinary characteristics cannot be required. Others should help.

Basic provisions for a decent economic minimum, health care, and unemployment insurance are important background conditions; but education and training are equally important. That is because, as I have emphasized, successful lives require active pursuit of valuable activities and ends. Successfully pursuing a valuable career or job (whether inside or outside the home) is among the most important of these activities, not only because productive occupations are themselves worthwhile, but also because they are a source of self-respect. Being handed the means to live is not, *in itself*, a component of a successful life. People who are given such advantages must look elsewhere for success.

This brings me to the remaining issue I want to discuss: equality of opportunity. I suggested earlier that while the problems of race and poverty are real, and demand a solution, the right answer can be found in Douglass's emphasis on social justice and not in affirmative action or reparations. Rather than equality of outcome, as defenders of affirmative action often assume is the ideal, I want to suggest a different conception of justice based on equality of opportunity.

Equal opportunities

It is sometimes said by people of various political persuasions that everybody should have an "equal starting place," or that we want everyone to have a "fair chance at the starting gate." The idea of "no child left behind" also relies on the same, familiar analogy of life as a race that can be fair or unfair. Each of those oft-heard expressions is a way of expressing the ideal of equality of opportunity. But what does it mean for everyone to have a fair chance at the starting gate, understood as equal opportunity?

"Formal" equality of opportunity requires making certain that there are no artificial legal or similar barriers to groups of people as they seek admission and employment. Laws banning women from practicing law violated formal equality of opportunity, as did laws making it impossible for women and others to run for elected office. But there can be other informal but sometimes no less rigid barriers that can prevent people from successfully pursuing valuable activities and ends. For that reason, formal equality of opportunity often needs to be supplemented by anti-discrimination laws that prevent employers and others from denying opportunities to people based on racial or other arbitrary characteristics.

Education and training, along with basic necessities, are another important background condition that shape people's prospects for a successful life. *Fair* equality of opportunity is more than formal equality. James Nickel considered the various conditions that would be necessary to achieve equality of opportunity, including those that go beyond the absence of formal legal obstacles and include the means to succeed. He describes equality of opportunity as circumstances that "combine the absence of insuperable obstacles with the presence of means – internal or external – that give one a chance of overcoming the obstacles that remain."[91] A legal right to pursue a career or other endeavor is important but not sufficient for a person to have genuinely equal opportunities. Rawls characterized the ideal of fair equality of opportunity as the requirement that any two people with the same natural talents also have the same likelihood of succeeding regardless of socioeconomic class.[92] That would mean, in practice, that it would be impossible to predict on the basis of race and social or economic background where any two newborn babies might end up in life. Nothing about their race, culture, or social class would make it more likely that one would succeed than the other.

Still, fair equality of opportunity would not guarantee people equal success in life in their economic pursuits, let alone in the way that matters most: their life as a whole. How people fare in life would still be affected by at least three factors: (1) the *choices they make* about what to do with the opportunities they have been given; (2) their *level of natural abilities*; and (3) *luck*. Some people may choose to work hard, while others put forth less

[91] James Nickel, "Equal Opportunity in a Pluralist Society," in *Equal Opportunity*, edited by Ellen Frankel, et al. (Oxford: Blackwell, 1988), p. 110.

[92] John Rawls distinguishes fair and formal equality of opportunity, defining the former as meaning that "those with similar abilities and skills should have similar life chances . . . regardless of their initial place in the social system." John Rawls, *A Theory of Justice, Revised Edition*, p. 63.

effort; some will decide to take risks while others are more conservative. But beyond the choices that are in people's control, luck will also play a role. Some risky choices will pay off while others do not, just as some people are born with talents that give them advantages others lack. Some will get injured or fall ill. Insurance, medical care, and so on can only mitigate the effects of natural abilities and of bad luck, not eliminate them. Inequalities that result from good and bad luck as well as from people's decisions to work and develop talents and from their differing natural talents are all compatible with fair equality of opportunity.

"Luck egalitarians" would go much further than fair equality of opportunity requires. Because natural talents are undeserved, they argue, society should compensate those who are less advantaged in what Rawls terms the morally arbitrary "natural lottery" of talents.[93] Although I do not want to argue against luck egalitarians in detail, note that three problems face those who seek to go beyond fair equality of opportunity and eliminate all "moral arbitrariness" in people's lives. The first problem is that there is a question whether natural talents really are morally arbitrary. Even though they may be "undeserved," and in that sense arbitrary, natural talents do enable some people to make greater contributions to society than others. So while a naturally talented person may not "deserve" her natural gifts, it is not obvious why the fact that natural talents are undeserved means they can play no role in justifying inequalities. Greater reward may not be morally arbitrary if the talent is used to make a larger social contribution, even if the talent itself is undeserved.

Another problem facing those who would go beyond fair equality of opportunity and seek to eliminate the effects of natural talents flows from the fact that talents must be developed if they are to be of any value. Some people will work harder than others to develop their intellectual, physical, or other abilities. It is *in fact* impossible to disentangle people's "natural" talents from their effort to develop them, and therefore impossible in practice to identify those elements of talents and skills that are "natural" and those that are the product of the choices whether or not to develop them.

A third problem arises for egalitarians who want to eliminate the really serious bad luck some people experience, such as severe handicaps at

---

[93] Rawls, *A Theory of Justice, Revised Edition*, p. 64. Rawls argues that fair equality of opportunity is "unstable" because socioeconomic class is no less morally arbitrary than inherited natural assets. But, as I indicate in the next few paragraphs, there is doubt whether that argument goes as far as Rawls supposes.

birth, catastrophic accidents, or debilitating long-term illnesses. To eliminate those differences and thereby provide all people with the same
opportunities to achieve a successful life might simply be too costly. But
provisions of basic medical care and a minimum of income will not
compensate fully for that truly bad luck. That goal, in other words, is
impossible.

Even the lesser commitment to providing fair equality of opportunity
and eliminating the effects of socioeconomic class must still confront
important limits. None of them is fatal, though they are significant and
need to be taken into account. Families, for example, are an important
stumbling block in any attempt to realize fair equality of opportunity in
full.[94] Families not only differ in the economic resources and talents in
raising and educating children that they are *able* to provide for their children, but also in the sacrifices that parents and others are *willing to make*
for them. Yet, how could government policies eliminate those advantages, without undermining or destroying the institution of the family
itself? Encouraging (or requiring) children to work hard or to enjoy
leisure time is but one of the ways families influence the development of
children's talents.

Equal opportunity also cannot realistically mean that there will be no
affect of family on the occupations, values, and roles children choose.
We know and expect that children raised in devoutly religious homes are
more likely to be religious than ones raised by equally adamant atheists,
for example. Catholic families that encourage their children to become
priests and nuns or to go into teaching or public service will have an
impact on the choices of those children and therefore on their income.
Their children may be very different from ones from families that stress
the importance of economic success, for example, or political office.
Children whose parents emphasize the value of outdoor activities will
be more likely to end up as park rangers, while studious, academically
oriented parents may be expected to produce children whose career
choices reflect *their* values. It seems clear, then, that if we are to sustain
the institution of the family and the right of parents to tend to the
interests of their children as they see fit, then the ideal of fair equality of
opportunity must be compromised.

Besides living in families, children also function in a cultural environment, and those different environments also affect the economic and
other prospects of their members. Like families, different subcultures

---

[94] As Rawls himself acknowledges. See John Rawls, *A Theory of Justice, Revised Edition*, p. 448.

promote different values and goals. Some emphasize academic, artistic, or literary achievement over personal happiness; others emphasize status or financial success. If children are active members of a cultural group, joining in its various practices and developing their major bonds with others in their group, then that too will make fair equality of opportunity difficult to achieve without undermining the cultures themselves.

None of that is to deny that fair equality of opportunity is a worthy goal in its own right. Rather, the lesson is that it cannot be fully achieved in practice without running afoul of other important values. But that is not at all surprising: having to compromise one value in the name of others is a staple of our political and moral lives. Rights, for example, are often compromised in the name of other rights: free speech is limited in order to secure a fair trial, to protect military secrets, or to preserve others' right to speak itself through various rules of order in public meetings. I do not mean to suggest by these remarks that fair equality of opportunity is unworthy as a goal, or that we should not strive to achieve it consistent with protecting other values and the limits they impose on its realization. To the contrary.

What, then, do we want fair equality of opportunity to provide people with? When has the goal been achieved? The answer draws on earlier remarks about a successful life. Fair equality of opportunity is one component of a larger social commitment, required by justice, to provide the social and economic conditions that will enable people to pursue successful lives, insofar as it is possible (that is, consistent with other values such as protecting the family and subcultures, respecting the fact that people must make their own decisions, and acknowledging the inevitable role of natural talents and luck).

In short, the background conditions that government creates should, insofar as possible, give each person the same opportunity to achieve a successful life. I have stressed, however, the sharp limits on the extent to which governments, or anyone for that matter, can achieve even this equality of opportunity, let alone the ideal of everyone's life being *equally* successful. Nobody can make another's life a success, and even the attempt to provide the conditions that will enable people to succeed on their own are limited. Other values come into play, for the many reasons I have mentioned. Nor can background conditions such as educational opportunities, a social minimum, or unemployment and health insurance make people choose wisely or work hard. A reasonable commitment to reducing the effects of socioeconomic class through fair equality of opportunity would therefore not produce equality of result or make everyone's life a success. Equality of outcome cannot be achieved because of variations in luck and skill. Full equality of opportunity could not be achieved if it meant providing people with the same abilities, training, and education to use whatever skills they possess and engendering the same inclination to work hard. We don't want to pursue full equality of opportunity singlemindedly because doing so would compromise other values such as family and culture and would undermine people's free choices.

That said, we nonetheless remain far from doing what we could reasonably do in providing fair equality of opportunity and eliminating the effects of socioeconomic class on people's prospects for a successful life. To put our current situation in perspective, it is helpful to compare fair equality of opportunity with a much weaker ideal. What I have in mind is the minimalist ideal that *all persons should have a realistic opportunity to achieve at least one successful life.* There are three important ideas here, and I will say something about each.

First, by a *"successful"* life I again mean a life that is freely chosen and marked by the successful pursuit of valuable activities or ends. As I noted, for almost everyone there is a range of possible such lives because societies almost invariably provide a variety of different careers, cultural practices, and other roles.

Second, this ideal seeks only to provide the *opportunity* for a successful life. It does not seek what is impossible: to *insure* that anyone's life is successful. Its ambition is only that the background conditions are ones which, insofar as background social and economic conditions can do so, give everyone a reasonable prospect of having at least one realistic option. This need not make it realistic for everyone to succeed at the sort of life that is most preferred or most valuable – only that there is a realistic chance to achieve at least one that is successful.

Finally, a *"realistic"* opportunity to achieve "at least one" successful life means that social and economic circumstances do not make it unreasonably difficult for a person to succeed at everything worth pursuing. Nobody would be allowed to live in an environment (whether socioeconomic, cultural, or educational) in which a person could not achieve at least one valuable life among the many options available in society. This is therefore not an ideal of equality of opportunity, but rather an ideal of *some* opportunity.

Securing a realistic opportunity to achieve at least one successful life therefore falls well short of what many think is required if society is to approach anything like justice. It does nothing to see that opportunities are equal, and it would not require taking any steps to create conditions that minimize the effects of differences in socioeconomic class on people's prospects for a successful life. But what is striking is that even this ideal, however limited and inadequate, goes unmet. Many children growing up in our worst inner-city slums lack a realistic opportunity to achieve *any* valuable life, let alone an opportunity that is equal to others. That is not to say that a few will not succeed. However, it is unrealistic to expect those who are only average in natural ability or inherent motivation, or who are not unusually lucky in natural endowments or other ways, to succeed at anything. Achieving miminal opportunities would at least mean that no children are condemned to leading lives that are a failure, without any realistic prospect of success. Its target is what Jonathan Kozol rightly termed the "savage" inequalities that face the least advantaged in the society.[95]

While a significant proportion of African-American and other children are in desperate need of support at home and better opportunities to learn at school, it is clearly not the children's fault that others have failed them. Parental neglect is no better justification for inaction than educational failures. *Neither* is it an excuse for society to abandon children or for their schools to fail to provide a decent opportunity for them to develop their talents. However irresponsible the parents, officials, and others in authority may be, the children are innocent victims. Surrounded by violence, failing schools, drugs, crime, and (too often) a dysfunctional or abusive home life, there is no reasonable prospect that those children can grow up to have anything resembling a successful life.

My point in mentioning this minimal ideal was to emphasize the depth of our failure to live up to equality of opportunity. Fair equality of opportunity, insofar as it can be realized in light of other values, should remain our ideal. Yet, not only do we fail to provide fair equality of opportunity, we fail even to provide everyone with a reasonable prospect of achieving *any* valuable life. But even providing minimal opportunity for everyone would require sustained effort, significant costs, and potentially radical policy changes.

The way forward

Where, then, do we go from here? The answer to that depends, as I have stressed, on where we think we are now. The burden of the argument I

---

[95] Jonathan Kozol, *Savage Inequalities: Children in America's Schools* (New York: Crown Publishers, Inc., 1991).

made in Chapter 5 was that the explanation of African-American poverty is really a complex web that includes economic shifts, crime, family breakdown, and, perhaps most importantly, poor educational achievement. But the story did not end there. While poor educational achievement is in part an outgrowth of deep-seated cultural attitudes and intellectual insecurities that emerged out of slavery and racial oppression, starting in the 1960s those cultural attitudes were fueled by social and economic policies whose supporters hoped to alleviate the problem. Yet, those policies, and the public justifications on which they rest, have often been a two-edged sword. They emphasized African-Americans' disabilities and the futility of sustained effort, at the cost of emphasizing equal opportunities and the self-respect and self-esteem needed to take advantage of them.

Insofar as that is right, the current problems of poverty, crime, family breakdown, and poor educational achievement must be addressed at the cultural level as well as the economic. People must gain academic confidence and shed rumors of inferiority. Policies must enable people to acquire competence, and with it, self-respect. Policies that undermine self-respect and self-esteem must be replaced with ones that encourage them. Whether affirmative action remains or goes, a hugely expanded effort needs to be made to improve the lives of people living in places where drugs, crime, poverty, and poor educational achievement are a way of life.

Designing specific policies and programs that would move us closer to realizing equality of opportunity for African-Americans is a vexing problem that is well beyond the scope of this book. There are many ideas on the table, and more can be proposed and evaluated. It is important, however, that these discussions begin by recalling the nature of the problem. The natural place to begin is therefore with the two institutions that most affect the prospects of children: schools and families.

One simple suggestion is to improve schools by paying teachers who work in inner-city areas enough to attract and keep the most qualified rather than the least.[96] As things now stand there is a huge turnover in those schools, and the reasons are not hard to see. Those teachers often earn significantly less than teachers in more affluent areas, teach students who are less prepared educationally both because of poor parenting and past educational experiences, and work in environments that are less safe, less physically attractive, and enjoy fewer resources. That situation should be replaced by one in which pay scales are at least comparable to the

---

[96] Suggested by Matt Miller, "Honor Thy Teacher," *New York Times*, May 28, 2005, p. A. 23.

salaries of the far more privileged professors in state universities, which often start at nearly twice what those teachers earn and can easily reach $150,000 or more. Such a change would cost an added $7 billion dollars, roughly 7 percent of total spending on K–12.[97] But to work effectively and to win public support, those increases should be accompanied by other important reforms such as merit pay, higher standards for teachers, and easier procedures for dismissing incompetents. The goal of such changes would be to no longer rely so heavily on the good will and idealism of those teaching our least advantaged. Teaching in those schools should be competitive financially with other and in some respects much easier professions, such as law and college teaching.

There are many other reforms that could be tried, all aimed at addressing the underlying causes of the problem. These include programs that provide early intervention, such as better prenatal care for mothers and improved early-education development for children. Examples include Head Start, the Perry Preschool Project, and the Elmira Project.[98] In many cases, these programs have proven to work and to be cost effective.[99] KIPP Academies have also had remarkable success in improving poor African-American and Hispanic students' reading and mathematical skills.[100] In Texas, for example, students who passed tests for grade level only 33 to 66 percent of the time achieved 90 percent pass rates after one year and almost 100 percent after two years. Similar results were achieved in New York. The success is attributed to an extended school day (including Saturday and summer school), greater involvement of parents, small size of the schools, and high levels of commitment and professional development by teachers.[101] Other policy innovations might

---

[97] This figure comes from Miller, "Honor Thy Teacher."

[98] See, for example, Ellen Fish, "The Benefits of Early Intervention," *Stronger Families Learning Exchange* Bulletin No. 2 (Spring/Summer 2002), pp. 8–11, summarizing the literature outlining the potential advantages of these and other programs.

[99] See, for example, *Costs and Benefits of Preventing Crime*, edited by Brandon C. Welsh, David P. Farrington, and Lawrence W Sherman. (Boulder: Westview Press, 2001), which discusses a variety of programs and their long-term financial benefits. These benefits included fewer emergency room visits, greater participation in the workforce, and reductions in food stamps and Medicaid.

[100] KIPP Academies enroll randomly selected poor minority students, more than 95 percent of whom are eligible for federal breakfast and lunch programs. Grades go from fifth to ninth.

[101] For a summary of the results, see Donna Walker James, Sonia Jurich, and Steve Estes, "KIPP Academies," *Raising Minority Academic Achievement: A Compendium of Education Programs and Practices* (Washington DC: American Youth Policy Forum, 2002), pp. 143–146.

include experiments with educational vouchers and freedom of choice in preuniversity education; holding parents accountable when children fail due to negligent parenting practices; and abolition of "legacy" preferences in college admissions for children of former students. The aim of these and other proposals and experiments would be to see that every child *at least* has a realistic opportunity to achieve a valuable life and, eventually, to come as close to fair equality of opportunity as is feasible.

The advantages of emphasizing equality of opportunity would be significant. Because it does not demand equality of outcome, the principle may be able to gain relatively wide support. It reflects, and also publicly affirms, the idea that government's role is not to take over the responsibility people have for their own lives but instead to be sure that all people who are responsible can succeed. It is an ideal that rewards work and encourages the growth of the work ethic whose lack, I have argued, is a significant part of the explanation of poor educational achievement. Unlike redistributive welfare and other policies of the past that are sometimes counterproductive, these proposals would address the underlying educational, cultural, and social factors at the heart of the problem.

Emphasizing equality of opportunity rather than affirmative action and reparations would bring other advantages as well. First, the focus would shift from race to skills and training. All groups, majority and minority, have members who suffer educationally and are in poverty. People's racial or ethnic background therefore becomes less important, and the fact that they were not given equal opportunities to develop their talents becomes central. For that reason, unlike racial preferences and reparations, equality of opportunity does not pit one group against another. This is important since, as we have seen, the "mere mention" of affirmative action in a survey of racial attitudes reduced the level of concern about blacks.

Emphasizing equality of opportunity rather than equality of outcome also leaves room for the idea that people who have worked hard and made significant contributions to society deserve their positions. It creates greater space for individual responsibility. Equality of opportunity also makes injustice more transparent than affirmative action does, which is itself an advantage. As I noted earlier, affirmative action hides the extent to which society is failing to realize the idea of equal opportunity. Hiring and admitting under policies that give preference based on race rather than merit may leave the impression of greater equality of opportunity than is in fact present for African-Americans.

It is also important to emphasize that the value of an education extends well beyond economic rewards. Though I have stressed the importance of reducing poverty, and equal educational opportunities would undoubtedly advance that goal, education is important for other reasons having to do with the underlying goal of enabling people to achieve a valuable life understood as the successful pursuit of valuable activities and ends. One reason is that education enables people to participate fully in the cultural life of their community as well as in its political and civic institutions. Though perhaps not strictly necessary for a valuable life, both of those are among the most familiar paths.

But education is linked, in turn, with another important theme I have emphasized: self-respect. Lack of education can be a source of self-doubt and even humiliation. It undermines people's sense that their goals are worthy and that they have a reasonable prospect of achieving them. When it is also associated with race and ethnicity, given the burdens of history and rumors of inferiority I have described, lack of educational achievement also erodes self-esteem. Both self-respect and self-esteem are eroded in seeing others hold us in contempt – or even express pity – for lack of education, either as an individual or as a member of a group.

Equality of opportunity can promote self-respect and self-esteem in still another, broadly political way. People often take seriously and sometimes internalize the implicit and explicit attitudes toward them that are conveyed in law and public policy. That was perhaps the most important message of the U.S. Supreme Court's ruling in *Brown v. Board of Education* when it overturned *Plessy v. Ferguson*. The Court said in *Brown* that it had erred in *Plessy* by underestimating the impact of legal segregation on people's sense of their own worth given the message that segregation sent about their status as citizens. A genuine commitment to equality of opportunity would convey the idea that all persons are equally worthy of respect, including those whose situation makes it difficult or impossible to get a good education.

I said earlier that, according to the defenders of affirmative action, the problem that needs to be addressed is inequality of outcome (too few people in particular positions). While I agreed that integration of society is an important ideal, the question is how integration is to be achieved if reparations and affirmative action are rejected. I have argued that justice in the form of equal opportunity, and not preferences, is a better approach. So despite my criticisms of affirmative action programs and of reparations, mine is far from a recommendation of complacency or inaction. To the contrary: an apology by government for institutional racism and its effects is owed and should be given. But that is only a first, tiny step. Apologies and expressions of guilt and remorse bring the further responsibility to pay special heed to injustices. Racial preferences should be cut back or replaced with a serious commitment to secure the background conditions which, insofar as possible, enable everyone to have a successful life. One pillar of that goal is equality of opportunity.

Pursuing that ambition would be far more intellectually and politically challenging, and potentially costly, than continuing with affirmative action policies, but its advantages could also be more substantial. I have raised serious questions about not only reparations but also racial preferences. Turning away from both could bring advantages, whatever else is done. I have hinted here at some of the other proposals that should be pursued, and clearly much needs to be done. The arguments I have given against reparations and racial preferences should not be the end of the story.

Whether equality of outcome would follow greater equality of opportunity, in which all racial and ethnic groups would eventually be proportionally represented in universities, professions, and other positions, is an open question. We cannot know what the long-term effects of such a change in direction might be and where equality of opportunity would lead. But were we to achieve something close to genuinely equal opportunity, then at least we might hope that whatever cultural or group-based differences remain could be accepted by society in good conscience; but certainly, not until then.

Bibliography

Akerlof, George A. (1970). "The Market for 'Lemons': Quality, Uncertainty, and the Market Mechanism." *Quarterly Journal of Economics, 84, 3,* 488–500.

Alcoff, Linda Martin. (2002). "Philosophy and Racial Identity." In *Philosophies of Race and Identity.* Edited by Peter Osborne and Stella Stanford. London: Continuum, p. 15.

Allen, Walter R. (1992). "The Color of Success: African-American College Student Outcomes at Predominantly White and Historically Black Public Colleges and Universities." *Harvard Educational Review, 62* (Spring), 26–44.

Anderson, Elizabeth S. (2002). "Integration, Affirmative Action, and Strict Scrutiny." *New York University Law Review, 77, 5* (November), 1195–1271.

Antony, Louise M. (1993). "Quine as Feminist." In *A Mind of One's Own: Feminist Essays on Reason and Objectivity.* Edited by Louise M. Antony and Charlotte Witt. Boulder: Westview Press, p. 217.

Antony, Louise M., and Charlotte Witt (Eds.). (1993). *A Mind of One's Own: Feminist Essays on Reason and Objectivity.* Boulder: Westview Press.

Appiah, K. Anthony. (1996). "Race, Culture, Identity." In *Color Conscious: The Political Morality of Race.* Edited by K. Anthony Appiah and Amy Gutmann. Princeton: Princeton University Press, pp. 30–105.

Appiah, K. Anthony, and Amy Gutmann (Eds.). (1996). *Color Conscious: The Political Morality of Race.* Princton: Princeton University Press.

Aptheker, Herbert. (1992). *Anti-Racism in U.S. History.* Westport CT: Greenwood Press.

Arrow, Kenneth, Samuel Bowles, and Steven Durlauf (Eds.). (2000). *Meritocracy and Economic Inequality.* Princeton: Princeton University Press.

Arthur, John (Ed.). (2005). *Morality and Moral Controversies* (7th ed.). Upper Saddle River NJ: Prentice Hall.

Arthur, John. (2004). "Institutional Racism and Equal Protection." *American Philosophical Association Newsletter on Philosophy of Law, 4, 1.*

Arthur, John. (2003). "Multiculturalism." In *The Oxford Handbook of Practical Ethics.* Edited by Hugh LaFollette. Oxford: Oxford University Press, pp. 413–432.

Arthur, John (Ed.). (2002). *Morality and Moral Controversies* (6th ed.). Upper Saddle River NJ: Prentice Hall.

Arthur, John. (2002). "Racism and Reparations." In *Morality and Moral Contro-versies* (6th ed.). Edited by John Arthur. Upper Saddle River NJ: Prentice Hall, pp. 534–550.

Arthur, John. (2002). "Sticks and Stones." In *Practical Ethics* (2nd ed.). Edited by Hugh LaFollette. Oxford: Blackwell Publishers, pp. 356–364.

Arthur, John. (2000). "Critical Race Theory: A Critique." In *Reflections: An Anthology of African-American Philosophy*. Edited by James Montmarquet and William Hardy. Belmont CA: Wadsworth, pp. 330–340.

Arthur, John. (1992). *Words That Bind: Judicial Review and the Grounds of Modern Constitutional Theory*. Boulder: Westview Press.

Arthur, John. (1987). "Property Acquisition and Harm." *Canadian Journal of Philosophy, 17, 2,* 337–348.

Arthur, John, and Amy Shapiro (Eds.). (1996). *Color Class Identity: The New Politics of Race*. Boulder: Westview Press.

Arthur, John, and William H. Shaw (Eds.). (2006). *Readings in the Philosophy of Law.* (4th ed.). Upper Saddle River NJ: Prentice-Hall.

Arthur, John, and William H. Shaw (Eds.). (1991). *Justice and Economic Distribution* (2nd ed.). Englewood Cliffs NJ: Prentice Hall.

Astin, Alexander. (1993). *What Matters in College?: Four Critical Years Revisited.* San Francisco: Jossey Bass.

Austin Turner, Margery, Michael Fix, and Raymond J. Struyk. (1991). *Opportu-nities Denied, Opportunities Diminished: Racial Discrimination in Hiring*, Urban Institute Report 91–9. Washington DC: Urban Institute Press.

Austin Turner, Margery, Raymond J. Struyk, and John Yinger. (1991). *Housing Discrimination Study: Synthesis*. Washington DC: U.S. Department of Housing and Urban Development.

Ayres, Ian, and Richard Brooks. (2005). "Does Affirmative Action Reduce the Number of Black Lawyers?" *Stanford Law Review, 57, 6,* 1807–1854.

Baer, Judith. (1983). *Equality Under the Constitution: Reclaiming the Fourteenth Amendmeent.* Ithaca: Cornell University Press.

Banfield, Edward. (1974). *The Unheavenly City Revisited.* Boston: Little Brown.

Banton, Michael, and Jonathan Harwood. (1975). *The Race Concept.* New York: Praeger.

Beachey, R. W. (1976). *The Slave Trade in Eastern Africa.* New York: Harper and Row.

Bell, Jr., Derrick A. (1994). *Confronting Authority: Reflections of an Ardent Protester.* Boston: Beacon Press.

Bell, Jr., Derrick A. (1992). "Racial Realism." In *Critical Race Theory: The Key Writings that Formed The Movement.* Edited by Kimberle Crenshaw, et al. New York: New Press, 1995, p. 308.

Bell, Jr., Derrick A. (1987). *And We Are Not Saved: The Elusive Quest for Racial Justice.* New York: Basic Books.

Berger, Peter L., and Thomas Luckmann. (1966). *The Social Construction of Reality: A Treatise in the Sociology of Knowledge.* Garden City NJ: Doubleday Pub. Co.

Block, Ned. (1995). "How Heritability Misleads about Race." *Cognition, 56,* 99–128.

Blum, Lawrence. (2002). *"I'm not a Racist, but. . . ." The Moral Quandary of Race.* Ithaca: Cornell University Press.

Bonilla-Silva, Eduardo. (2003). *Racism without Racists: Color-Blind Racism and the Persistence of Racial Inequality in the United States.* Lanham MD: Rowman and Littlefield.

Bouchard, T. J., et al. (1990). "Sources of Human Psychological Differences: The Minnesota Study of Twins Reared Apart." *Science, 250* (October), 223–228.

Bowen, William G., and Derek Bok. (1998). *The Shape of the River.* Princeton: Princeton University Press.

Bowie, Norman E. (Ed.). (1988). *Equal Opportunity.* Boulder: Westview Press.

Boxill, Bernard. (Ed). (2001). *Race and Racism.* Oxford: Oxford University Press.

Boxill, Bernard. (1992). *Blacks and Social Justice, Revised Edition.* Lanham MD: Rowman and Littlefield.

Boxill, Bernard. (1972). "Morality of Reparation." *Social Theory and Practice, 2,* 119.

Brandt, Joseph. (1991). *Dismantling Racism: The Continuing Challenge to White America.* Minneapolis: Augsburg Fortress, Publishers.

Brown, Dorothy A. (2003). *Critical Race Theory: Cases, Materials, and Problems.* St. Paul MN: West Publishing.

Bullock, Allan. (1962). *Hitler: A Study in Tyranny.* New York: Harper and Row.

Cahill, Thomas. (1995). *How the Irish Saved Civilization.* New York: Random House.

Calhoun, John C. (1837). "Speech on the Reception of Abolition Petitions Delivered in the Senate, February 6th, 1837." In *Slavery Defended: The Views of the Old South.* Edited by Eric McKitrick. Englewood Cliffs NJ: Prentice Hall, 1963, pp. 12–16.

Carmichael, Stokeley, and Charles Hamilton. (1967). *Black Power.* New York: Vintage Press.

Cartwright, Samuel A. (1851). "Report on the Diseases and Physical Peculiarities of the Negro Race." *New Orleans Medical and Surgical Journal, 7,* 691.

Cavanaugh, Matt. (2002). *Against Equality of Opportunity.* Oxford: Oxford University Press.

Chambers, David, et al. (2005). "The Real Impact of Eliminating Affirmative Action in American Law Schools: An Empirical Critique of Richard Sander's Study." *Stanford Law Review, 57,* 6, 1855–1898.

Chomsky, Noam (Ed.). (1973). *For Reasons of State.* New York: Vintage Press.

Chomsky, Noam. (1973). "Psychology and Ideology." In *For Reasons of State.* Edited by Noam Chomsky. New York: Vintage Press, p. 363.

Cobb, Thomas R. R. (1858). "An Inquiry into the Law of Negro Slavery." In *Defending Slavery: Proslavery Thought in the Old South.* Edited by Paul Finkelman. Boston: Bedford/St. Martins, 2003, pp. 143–156.

Cohen, G. A. (2000/1978). *Marx's Theory of History: A Defense, Expanded Edition.* Princeton: Princeton University Press.

Cohen, Joshua. (1997). "The Arc of the Moral Universe." *Philosophy and Public Affairs, 26,* 2, 91–134.

Cohen, Marshall, Thomas Nagel, and Thomas Scanlon (Eds). (1977). *Equality and Preferential Treatment.* Princeton: Princeton University Press.

Cole, Stephen, and Elinor Barber. (2003). *Increasing Faculty Diversity: The Occupational Choices of High-Achieving Minority Students.* Cambridge MA: Harvard University Press.

College Board. (1999). *Reaching the Top: A Report of the National Task Force on Minority High Achievement.* New York: College Board Publications.

Coulter, Jeff. (1979). *The Social Construction of Mind: Studies in Ethnomethodology and Linguistic Philosophy.* Totawa NJ: Rowman and Littlefield.

Crenshaw, Kimberle, et al. (Eds.). (1995). *Critical Race Theory: The Key Writings that Formed The Movement.* New York: New Press.

Crenshaw, Kimberle. (1988). "Race, Reform, and Retrenchment: Transformation and Legitimation of Antidiscrimination Law." In *Critical Race Theory: The Key Writings that Formed The Movement.* Edited by Kimberle Crenshaw, et al. New York: New Press (1995), pp. 103–122.

Crosby, Faye J., and Cheryl Van De Veer (Eds.). (2000). *Sex, Race, and Merit: Debating Affirmative Action in Education and Employment.* Ann Arbor: University of Michigan Press.

D'Souza, Dinesh. (1996). *The End of Racism: Principles for a Multiracial Society.* New York: Simon & Schuster, Ltd.

Dalaker, Joseph. (2001). *Poverty in the United States: 2000*, Current Population Reports, Series P60–214. Washington DC: U.S. Census Bureau.

Davis, Angela. (1998). *The Angela Y. Davis Reader.* Edited by Joy James. Malden MA: Blackwell.

Davis, Angela. (1998). "Prisons, Reparations, and Resistance." In *The Angela Y. Davis Reader.* Edited by Joy James. Malden MA: Blackwell Publishers, pp. 3–109.

Davis, David Brion. (1975). *The Problem of Slavery in the Age of Revolution, 1770–1823.* New York: Oxford University Press.

Day, Jennifer Cheeseman, and Eric C. Newburger. (2002). *The Big Payoff: Educational Attainment and Synthetic Estimates of Work-Life Earnings*, Current Population Reports, P23-210. Washington DC: U.S. Census Bureau.

Deglar, Carl N. (1976). "The Irony of American Negro Slavery." In *Perspectives and Irony in American Negro Slavery.* Edited by Harry P. Owens. Jackson: University of Mississippi Press, p. 19.

Deigh, John. (1983). "Shame and Self-Esteem." *Ethics 93*, 2 (January), 225–245.

Delgado, Richard. (1995). "Rodrigo's Tenth Chronicle: Merit and Affirmative Action." *Georgia Law Journal, 83*, 1711–1748.

Delgado, Richard. (1991). "Brewer's Plea: Critical Thoughts on Common Cause." *Vanderbilt Law Review, 44*, 1–14.

de Tocqueville, Alexis. (1835). *Democracy in America.* New York: Alfred A Knopf, 1945.

Dornbusch, Sanford M., and Myra H. Strober (Eds.). (1988). *Feminism, Children and the New Families.* New York: Guilford Press.

Dorschel, Andreas. (2000). *Rethinking Prejudice.* Aldershot UK: Ashgate.

Douglass, Frederick. *The Frederick Douglass Papers, Series 1, Speeches, Debates, and Interviews* (Vol. 2). Edited by John W. Blasingame and John R. McKivigan. New Haven: Yale University Press, 1982.

Douglass, Frederick. *The Frederick Douglass Papers* (Vol. 4). Edited by J. Blassingame and J. McKivigan. New Haven: Yale University Press, 1991.

Du Bois, W. E. B. (1899). *The Philadelphia Negro: A Social Study*. New York: Schocken Books, 1970.

Dworkin, Ronald. (2000). *Sovereign Virtue*. Cambridge MA: Harvard University Press.

Dworkin, Ronald. (1986). *Law's Empire*. Cambridge MA: Harvard University Press.

Dworkin, Ronald. (1977). "Why Bakke Has No Case." *New York Review of Books*, November 10, 1977. In *Morality and Moral Controversies* (7th Ed.). Edited by John Arthur. Upper Saddle River NJ: Prentice Hall, 2004, pp. 630–637.

"Race." (1969). *Encyclopedia Britannica, 18*. Chicago: William Bentor Pub.

Eder, Klaus. (1996). *The Social Construction of Nature*. Translated by Mark Ritter. London: Sage Publishing Co.

Elder, Larry. (2000). *The Ten Things You Can't Say in America*. New York: St. Martin's Press.

Eltis, David Eltis. (1993). "Europeans and the Rise and Fall of African Slavery in the Americas: An Interpretation." *American Historical Review, 98*, 5, 1399–1423.

Ely, John Hart. (1980). *Democracy and Distrust: A Theory of Judicial Review*. Cambridge MA: Harvard University Press.

Emery, George Neil. (1993). *The Facts of Life: The Social Construction of Vital Statistics, Ontario, 1859–1952*. Montreal: McGill-Queens University Press.

Eze, Emmanuel Chukwudi (Ed.). (1998). *African Philosophy*. Malden MA: Blackwell.

Eze, Emmanuel Chukwudi. (1997). "The Color of Reason." In *Post Colonial African Philosophy: A Critical Reader*. Edited by Emmanuel Chukwudi Eze. Oxford: Blackwell, p. 129.

Eze, Emmanuel Chukwudi (Ed.). (1997). *Postcolonial African Philosophy: A Critical Reader*. Oxford: Blackwell.

Ezorsky, Gertrude. (1991). *Racism and Justice: The Case for Affirmative Action*. Ithaca NY: Cornell University Press.

Farber, Daniel, and Suzanna Sherry. (1997). *Beyond All Reason: The Radical Assault on Truth in American Law*. New York: Oxford University Press.

Farkas, George, and Kevin Vicknair. (1996). "Appropriate Tests of Racial Wage Discrimination Require Controls for Cognitive Skills." *American Sociological Review, 61*, 557–560.

Feagin, Joe R. (2000). *Racist America*. New York: Routledge.

Feagin, Joe R., Hernan Vera, and Pinar Batur. (2001). *White Racism* (2nd ed.). New York: Routledge.

Feinberg, Joel. (1970). "The Nature and Value of Rights." *Journal of Value Inquiry, 4* (Winter).

Ferguson, Ronald. (1998). "Teachers' Expectations and the Test Score Gap." In *The Black-White Test Score Gap*. Edited by Christopher Jencks and Meredith Phillips. Washington DC: Brookings Institution Press, pp. 273–317.

Finkelman, Paul (Ed.). (2003). *Defending Slavery: Proslavery Thought in the Old South*. Boston: Bedford/St. Martins.

Finkelman, Paul. (1996). "The Rise of the New Racism." *Yale Law and Policy Review,* 15, *1,* 245–282.

Finkelman, Paul. (1993). "The Centrality of the Peculiar Institution in American Development." *Chicago-Kent Law Review, 68,* 1009–1033.

Finkelman, Paul (Ed.). (1986). *Law of Freedom and Bondage: A Casebook* (New York University School of Law Series in Legal and Constitutional History). New York: Oceana Publications.

Fischer, Claude, et al. (Eds.). (1996). *Inequality by Design: Cracking the Myth of the Bell Curve.* Princeton: Princeton University Press.

Fish, Ellen. (2002). "The Benefits of Early Intervention." *Stronger Families Learning Exchange, 2* (Spring/Summer), 8–11.

Fish, Stanley. (1994). *There's No Such Thing as Free Speech and It's a Good Thing, Too.* New York: Oxford University Press.

Fiske, Susan T. (1998). "Stereotyping, Prejudice, and Discrimination." In *Handbook of Social Psychology.* Edited by Daniel T. Gilbert, Susan T. Fiske, and Gardner Lendzey. New York: McGraw-Hill, p. 391.

Fiss, Owen. (2003). *A Way Out: America's Ghettos and the Legacy of Racism.* Princeton: Princeton University Press.

Fitzhugh, George. (1857). "Sociology for the South: Or the Failure of Free Society." In *Defending Slavery: Proslavery Thought in the Old South.* Edited by Paul Finkelman. Boston: Bedford/St. Martins, 2003, pp. 187–198.

Flew, Anthony. (1985). *Thinking about Social Thinking.* Oxford: Blackwell.

Flowers, Lamont, and Ernest Pascerella. (1999). "Cognitive Effects of College Racial Composition on African American Students after 3 Years of College." *Journal of College Student Development, 40* (November/December), 669.

Flynn, James. (2000). "I.Q. Trends over Time: Intelligence, Race, and Meritocracy." In *Meritocracy and Economic Inequality.* Edited by Kenneth Arrow, Samuel Bowles, and Steven Durlauf. Princeton: Princeton University Press, p. 40, figure 3.2.

Fogel, Robert William, and Stanley L. Engerman. (1974). *Time on the Cross.* New York: Little, Brown and Co.

Folsom, Moses, and J. D. O'Connor. (1879). *Treasuries of Science, History, and Culture.* Chicago: Moses Warren Publishing Company.

Ford, Richard Thomas. (2005). *Racial Culture: A Critique.* Princeton: Princeton University Press.

Fordham, Signithia, and John U. Ogbu. (1986)."Black Students' School Success: Coping with the Burden of Acting White." *Urban Review, 18, 3* (September), 177.

Frank, Robert H. (2004). *What Price the Moral High Ground?* Princeton: Princeton University Press.

Frankel, Ellen, et al. (Eds.). (1998). *Equal Opportunity.* Oxford: Blackwell.

Franklin, John Hope, and Alfred A. Moss, Jr. (1994). *From Slavery to Freedom: A History of African Americans* (7th ed.). New York: McGraw-Hill.

Frazier, E. Franklin. (1957). *The Negro in the United States, Revised Edition.* New York: Macmillan Co.

Fredrickson, George M. (2002). *Racism.* Princeton: Princeton University Press.

Friedman, Lawrence M. (1973). *A History of American Law.* New York: Simon and Schuster.

Fullindwider, Robert K. (2000). *The Case for Reparations.* Report of the Institute for Philosophy and Public Policy. College Park MD: Maryland School of Public Affairs Institute for Philosophy and Public Policy.

Fullinwider, Robert, and Judith Lichtenberg. (2004). *Leveling the Playing Field: Justice, Politics, and College Admissions.* Oxford: Rowman and Littlefield Publishers, Inc..

Garcia, Jorge L. A. (1996). "The Heart of Racism." *Journal of Social Philosophy,* 27, 1 (Spring).

Garner, B. H. (Ed.). (1999). *Black's Law Dictionary* (7th ed.). St. Paul: West Publishing Co.

Genovese, Eugene. (1974). *Roll, Jordan, Roll.* New York: Pantheon.

Gilbert, Daniel T., Susan T. Fiske, and Gardner Lendzey (Eds.). (1998). *Handbook of Social Psychology.* New York: McGraw-Hill.

Gill, Kathleen. (2000). "The Moral Functions of an Apology." *Philosophical Forum,* 31, 1, 11–27.

Glesner, B. A. (1991). "Fear and Loathing in the Law Schools." *Connecticut Law Review,* 23, 627.

Goldberg, David Theo. (1990) "Racism and Rationality: The Need for a New Critique." In *Racism.* Edited by Leonard Harris. Amherst NY: Humanity Books, pp. 369–397.

Goldin, Claudia Dale. (1973). "The Economics of Emancipation." *Journal of Economic History, 33* (March), 71.

Goldmann, Robert B., and A. Jeyaratnam Wilson (Eds.). (1984). *Independence to Statehood: Managing Ethnic Conflict in Five African and Asian States.* London: Francis Pinter.

Goldwin, Robert A., and Art Kaufman (Eds.). (1988). *Slavery and Its Consequences: The Constitution, Equality and Race.* Washington DC: American Enterprise Institute.

Gordon, Robert W. (1988). "Law and Ideology." *Tikkun,* 3, 1, 14–18, 83–86.

Gossett, Thomas. (1963). *Race: The History of an Idea in America.* Dallas: Southern Methodist University Press.

Gould, Stephen J. (1984). "Human Equality is a Contingent Fact of History." *Natural History,* 93, 11, 26–27.

Govier, Trudy. (2002). *Forgiveness and Revenge.* New York: Routledge.

Grissmer, David, Ann Flanagan, and Stephanie Williamson. (1998). "Why Did The Black-White Score Gap Narrow in the 1970s and 1980s?" In *The Black-White Test Score Gap.* Edited by Christopher Jencks and Meredith Phillips. Washington DC: Brookings Institution Press, pp. 182–226.

Hacking, Ian. (1999). *The Social Construction of What?* Cambridge MA: Harvard University Press.

Hammond, James Henry. (1858). "Speech on the Admission of Kansas, under the Lecompton Constitution, Delivered in the Senate of the United States, March 4, 1858." In *Defending Slavery: Proslavery Thought in the Old South.* Edited by Paul Finkelman. Boston: Bedford/St. Martins, 2003, pp. 80–88.

Harrington, Michael. (1984). *The New American Poverty.* New York: Holt, Rinehart, and Winston.

Harris, Cheryl I. (1993). "Whiteness as Property." *Harvard Law Review, 106,* 1707–1791.

Harris, Leonard. (1999). "What, Then, Is Racism?" In *Racism.* Edited by Leonard Harris. Amherst NY: Humanity Books, p. 437–450.

Harris, Leonard (Ed.). (1999) *Racism.* Amherst NY: Humanity Books.

Harris, Luke Charles, and Uma Narayan. (2002). "Affirmative Action as Equalizing Opportunity: Challenging the Myth of 'Preferential Treatment.'" In *Ethics in Practice* (2nd ed.). Edited by Hugh LaFollette. Oxford: Blackwell Publishers, pp. 451–463.

Harrison, Lawrence E., and Samuel P. Huntington (Eds.). (2000). *Culture Matters: How Values Shape Human Progress.* New York: Basic Books.

Hartley, Gillian M., and Susan Gregory (Eds.). (1991). *Constructing Deafness.* London: Pinter Publications.

Haslanger, Sally. (2000). "Gender and Race: (What) Are They? (What) Do We Want Them to Be?" *Nous 34, 1,* 33.

Haslett, David. (1986). "Is Inheritance Justified?" *Philosophy and Public Affairs,* 15, 2, 122.

Henning, William Waller (Ed.). (1823). *The Statutes at Large: Being a Collection of All the Laws of Virginia, from the First Session of the Legislature, in the Year 1619.* New York: R. & W. & G Bartow.

Hernstein, Richard J., and Charles Murray. (1994). *The Bell Curve: Intelligence and Class Structure in American Life.* New York: Free Press.

Hernstein, Richard, and James Q. Wilson. (1985). *Crime and Human Nature.* New York: Simon and Schuster.

Hirschfeld, Lawrence. (1996). *Race in the Making: Cognition, Culture, and the Child's Construction of Human Kinds.* Cambridge MA: MIT Press.

Hirchfeld, Magnus. (1934). *Racism.* Translated by Eden Paul and Cedar Paul. London: Victor Golancz, Ltd., 1938.

Hochschild, Jennifer L. (1988): "Race, Class, Power, and Equal Opportunity." In *Equal Opportunity.* Edited by Norman E. Bowie. Boulder: Westview Press, pp. 75–111.

Hofstadter, Douglas R. (1985). *Metamagical Themes.* New York: Basic Books.

Honore, Tony. (1995). *About Law: An Introduction.* Oxford: Clarendon Press.

Hume, David. (1751). "An Enquiry Concerning the Principles of Morals." In David Hume, *Enquiries Concerning the Human Understanding and Concerning the Principles of Morals.* Edited by L. A. Selby-Bigge (2nd ed.). Oxford: Clarendon Press, 1902.

Jacobs, Leslie. (2004). *Pursuing Equal Opportunities.* Cambridge UK: Cambridge University Press.

Jacobson, Jonathan, et al. (2001). *Educational Achievement and Black-White Inequality.* National Center for Educational Statistics, NCES 2001–061. Washington DC: U.S. Department of Education.

Jackson, Matthew Frye. (1992). *Whiteness of a Different Color.* Cambridge MA: Harvard University Press.

James, Donna Walker, Sonia Jurich, and Steve Estes. (2002). "KIPP Academies." *Raising Minority Academic Achievement: A Compendium of Education Programs and Practices.* Washington DC: American Youth Policy Forum.

James, William. (1897). "The Will to Believe." *Essays In Pragmatism.* New York: Haffner Publishing Co., 1948.

Jefferson, Thomas. *The Writings of Thomas Jefferson.* Edited by Merrill D. Peterson. New York: Library of America, 1984.

Jencks, Christopher, and Meredith Phillips (Eds.). (1998). *The Black-White Test Score Gap.* Washington DC: Brookings Institution Press.

Johnson, Allan G. (2000). *Blackwell Dictionary of Sociology* (2nd ed.). Malden MA: Blackwell.

Johnson, William R., and Derek Neal. (1998). "Basic Skills and the Black-White Earnings Gap." In *The Black-White Test Score Gap.* Edited by Christopher Jencks and Meredith Phillips. Washington DC: Brookings Institution Press, pp. 480–497.

Jones, James M. (1997). *Prejudice and Racism* (2nd ed.). New York: McGraw Hill.

Jussim, Lee, Jacquelynne Eccles, and Stephanie Madon. (1999). "Social Perception, Social Stereotypes, and Teacher Expectations: Accuracy and the Quest for the Powerful Self-fulfilling Prophecy." *Advances in Experimental Social Psychology,* 28, 350.

Kaiser, Jocelyn. (2003). "African-American Population Biobank Proposed." *Science, 300,* 5625, 1485.

Kant, Immanuel. *Political Writings.* Edited by Hans Reiss. Cambridge UK: Cambridge University Press, 1991.

Karabel, Jerome. (2005). *The Chosen: The Hidden History of Admission and Exclusion at Harvard, Yale and Princeton.* New York: Houghton Mifflin.

Kaufman, Phillip, Martha Naomi Alt, and Christopher D. Chapman. (2001). *Dropout Rates in the United States, 2000.* National Center for Educational Statistics, NCES 2002–114. Washington DC: U.S. Department of Education.

Kelly, Alfred H., Winfred A. Harbison, and Herman Belz. (1991). *The American Constitution, Its Origins and Development* (7th ed.). New York: W. W. Norton and Co.

Kennedy, Duncan. (1993). *Sexy Dressing, Etc.* Cambridge MA: Harvard University Press.

King, Mary-Claire, and Arno G. Motulsky. (2002). "Mapping Human History." *Science, 298,* 5602, 2342.

Kinross, John Balfour. (1977). *The Ottoman Centuries: The Rise and Fall of the Turkish Empire.* New York: William Morrow.

Kirsch, Irwin S., et al. (1993). *Adult Literacy in America: A First Look at the Results of the National Adult Literacy Survey.* National Center for Education Statistics. Washington DC: U.S. Government Printing Office.

Klein, Martin A. (1993). "Introduction: Modern European Expansion and Traditional Servitude in Africa and Asia." In *Breaking the Chains: Slavery, Bondage, and Emancipation in Modern African and Asia.* Edited by Martin A. Klein. Madison: University of Wisconsin Press, pp. 3–36.

Klein, Martin A. (Ed.). (1993). *Breaking the Chains: Slavery, Bondage, and Emancipation in Modern African and Asia.* Madison: University of Wisconsin Press.

Kleinig, John. (1973). *Punishment and Desert*. The Hague: Martinus Nijoff.

Ko, Gwangpyo, Kimberly M. Thompson, and Edward A. Nardell. (1990). "Estimation of Tuberculosis Risk on a Commercial Airliner." *New England Journal of Medicine*, 322, 422.

Kozol, Jonathan. (1991). *Savage Inequalities: Children in America's Schools*. New York: Crown Publishers, Inc.

LaFollette, Hugh. (2003). *The Oxford Handbook of Practical Ethics*. Oxford: Oxford University Press.

LaFollette, Hugh (Ed.). (2002). *Ethics in Practice* (2nd ed.). Oxford: Blackwell Publishers.

Latour, Bruno, and Steve Woolgar. (1979). *Laboratory Life: The Social Construction of Scientific Facts*. Beverly Hills: Sage Publishing Co.

Lawrence, III, Charles R. (1987). "The Id, the Ego, and Equal Protection: Reckoning with Unconscious Racism." *Stanford Law Review*, 39, 317–388.

Lee, Robert E. *Lee's Dispatches*. Edited by Douglas Southall Freeman. New York: G. P. Putnam's Sons, 1957.

Lerman, Robert I. (1989). "Employment Opportunities of Young Men and Family Formation. *American Journal of Economics*, 79, 62–66.

Lever, Annabelle. (2005). "Why Racial Profiling Is Hard to Justify: A Response to Risse and Zeckhauser." *Philosophy and Public Affairs*, 33, 1, 94–110.

Levin, Michael. (1997). *Why Race Matters*. Westport CT: Praeger.

Lewontin, R. C., S. Rose, and L. J. Kamin. (1984). *Not in Our Genes*. New York: Pantheon.

Lewis, Bernard. (1990). *Race and Slavery in the Middle East*. New York: Oxford University Press.

Lichtenberg, Judith. (1992). "Racism in the Head, Racism in the World." *Philosophy and Public Policy*. College Park MD: Newsletter of the Institute for Philosophy and Public Policy, p. 12.

Lipset, Seymour Martin, and Earl Raab. (1995). *Jews and the New American Scene*. Cambridge MA: Harvard University Press.

Locke, John. (1690). *An Essay Concerning Human Understanding*. New York: E. P. Dutton, 1947.

Locke, John. (1690). *Second Treatise of Government*. London: Dent and Sons, 1924.

Loehlin, John, Gardner Lindzey, and J. N. Spuhler. (1975). *Race Differences in Intelligence*. San Francisco: W. H. Freeman Co.

Loury, Glenn C. (2002). *The Anatomy of Racial Inequality*. Cambridge MA: Harvard University Press.

Lovejoy, Paul. (2000). *Transformations in Slavery: A History of Slavery in Africa*. Cambridge UK: Cambridge University Press.

Lucas, J. R. (1993). *Responsibility*. Oxford: Oxford University Press.

Lyons, David (Ed.). (1979). *Rights*. Belmont CA: Wadsworth Publishing Co.

MacKinnon, Catharine A. (1990). "Reflections on Sex Equality under Law." *Yale Law Journal, 100*, 1281.

Madison, James. (1787). "Notes on the Constitutional Convention." In *The Antifederalist Papers and the Constitutional Debates*. Edited by Ralph Ketcham. New York: Signet Classics, 2003.

Madison, James. (1788). *The Federalist Number 54. In The Federalist Papers.* Edited by Clinton Rossitor. New York: Mentor, 1999, p. 337.

Mannheim, Karl. (1952). *Essays on the Sociology of Knowledge.* London: Routledge and Kegan Paul.

Matsuda, Mari J. (1995). "Looking to the Bottom: Critical Legal Studies and Reparations." In *Critical Race Theory.* Edited by Kimberle Crenshaw, et al. New York: The New Press, pp. 63–79.

Matsuda, Mari J. (1991). "Voices of America: Accent, Antidiscrimination Law, and a Jurisprudence for the Last Reconstruction." *Yale Law Journal, 100,* 1329.

Mautner, Thomas (Ed.). (2000). *The Penguin Dictionary of Philosophy.* London: Penguin.

Mayer, Henry. (1998). *All on Fire: William Lloyd Garrison and the Abolition of Slavery.* New York: St. Martin's Press.

McKitrick, Eric (Ed.). (1963). *Slavery Defended: The Views of the Old South.* Englewood Cliffs NJ: Prentice Hall.

McMurtry, Larry. (1985). *Lonesome Dove.* New York: Simon and Schuster.

McPherson, James M. (1991). *Abraham Lincoln and the Second American Revolution.* New York: Oxford University Press.

McWhiney, Grady. (1988). *Cracker Culture: Celtic Ways in the Old South.* Tuscaloosa: University of Alabama Press.

McWhorter, John. (2001). *Losing the Race.* New York: Harper Collins.

Mill, John Stuart. (1859). *On Liberty.* Edited by Elizabeth Rapaport. Indianapolis: Hackett Publishing Co., 1978.

Miles, Robert. (1989). *Racism.* London: Routledge.

Mill, John Stuart. (1862). "The Contest in America." In *Collected Works of John Stuart Mill, Vol. XXI: Essays on Equality, Law, and Education.* Edited by John M. Robinson. Toronto: University of Toronto Press, 1984, p. 127.

Miller, Randall M., and John David Smith (Eds). (1988). *Dictionary of Afro-American Slavery.* Westport CT: Greenwood Press, Inc.

Miller, Scott L. (1995). *An American Imperative: Accelerating Minority Educational Advancement.* New Haven: Yale University Press.

Mills, Charles. (1994). "Non-Cartesian Sums: Philosophy and the African-American Experience." *Teaching Philosophy, 17,* 3, 228.

Modood, Tariq. (2001). "'Difference,' Cultural Racism and Anti-Racism." In *Race and Racism.* Edited by Bernard Boxill. Oxford: Oxford University Press, p. 238.

Montmarquet, James, and William Hardy (Eds.). (2000). *Reflections: An Anthology of African-American Philosophy.* Belmont CA: Wadsworth Pub. Co.

Montmarquet, James. (1992). "Epistemic Virtue and Doxastic Responsibility." *American Philosophical Quarterly, 29, 4,* 331.

Moore, Elsie G. J. (1986). "Family Socialization and the I.Q. Test Performance of Traditionally and Transracially Adopted Black Children." *Developmental Psychology, 22,* 317–326.

Murphy, Liam, and Thomas Nagel. (2002). *The Myth of Ownership.* New York: Oxford University Press.

Myrdal, Gunnar. (1944). *The American Dilemma: The Negro Problem and American Democracy.* New York: Harper and Row.

Nash, A. E. Deir. (1970). "A More Equitable Past? Southern Supreme Courts and the Protection of the Antebellum Negro." *North Carolina Law Review*, 48, 197.

Ng, Kwang. (1997). "A Case for Happiness, Cardinalism, and Interpersonal Comparability." *Economic Journal, 107*, 1849.

Nickel, James. (1988). "Equal Opportunity in a Pluralist Society." In *Equal Opportunity*. Edited by Ellen Frankel, et al. Oxford: Blackwell, p. 110.

Nozick, Robert. (1974). *Anarchy, State, and Utopia*. Cambridge MA: Harvard University Press.

Oaks, James. (1982). *The Ruling Race: A History of American Slaveholders*. New York: Knopf.

Ogbu, John. (1994). "Racial Stratification in the United States: Why Inequality Persists." *Teachers College Record, 96*, 2, 154.

Omi, Michael, and Howard Winant. (1994). *Racial Formation in the United States: From the 1960s to the 1990s*. New York: Routledge.

Osborne, Peter, and Stella Standford (Eds.). (2002). *Philosophies of Race and Identity*. London: Continuum.

Owens, Harry P. (Ed.). (1976). *Perspectives and Irony in American Negro Slavery*. Jackson: University of Mississippi Press.

Oxford English Dictionary (2nd Ed.). (1989). Oxford: Oxford University Press, 15.

Parfit, Derek. (1984). *Reasons and Persons*. Oxford: Oxford University Press.

Patterson, Orlando. (2000). "Taking Culture Seriously: A Framework and Afro-American Illustration." In *Culture Matters: How Values Shape Human Progress*. Edited by Lawrence E. Harris and Samuel P. Huntington. New York: Basic Books, pp. 202–218.

Patterson, Orlando. (1995). "The Paradox of Integration." *New Republic* (Nov. 6). In *Color Class Identity: The New Politics of Race*. Edited by John Arthur and Amy Shapiro. Boulder: Westview Press, 1996, pp. 65–72.

Patterson, Orlando. (1987). *Slavery and Social Death: A Comparative Study*. Cambridge MA: Harvard University Press.

Peeples, F., and R. Loeber. (1994). "Do Individual Factors and Neighborhood Context Explain Ethnic Differences in Juvenile Delinquency?" *Journal of Quantitative Criminology, 10*, 2, 141–157.

Perdue, Theda. (1988). *Slavery and the Evolution of Cherokee Society*. Knoxville TN: University of Tennessee Press.

Phillips, Meredith, et al. (1998). "Family Background, Parenting, Practices, and Black-White Test Score Gap." *The Black-White Test Score Gap*. Washington DC: Brookings Institution Press, pp. 103–145.

Pope, Carl, and William Feyerherm. (1995). *Minorities and the Juvenile Justice System: Research Summary*. Washington DC: Office of Juvenile Justice and Delinquency Prevention, U.S. Department of Justice.

Rachels, James. (1978). "What People Deserve." In *Justice and Economic Distribution* (2nd ed.). Edited by John Arthur and William H. Shaw. Englewood Cliffs NJ: Prentice-Hall (1991), pp. 136–148.

Ramist, Leonard, and Solomon Arbeiter. (1986). *Profiles, College-Bound Seniors, 1985*. New York: College Entrance Examination Board.

Rawls, John. (1999). *A Theory of Justice, Revised Edition*. Cambridge MA: Harvard University Press.

Raz, Joseph. (1994). *Ethics in the Public Domain: Essays in the Morality of Law and Politics.* Oxford: Oxford University Press.

Reiss, Hans (Ed.). (1991). *Political Writings.* Cambridge UK: Cambridge University Press.

Ridley, Matt. (2003). "Genes Are So Liberating." *New Scientist,* May 17, 38.

Robinson, Randall. (1999). *The Debt: What America Owes to Blacks.* New York: Dutton.

Roberts, Dorothy E. (1997). "The Meaning of Blacks' Fidelity to the Constitution." *Fordham Law Review, 65, 4,* 1761–1771.

Roberts, Rodney. (2005). *Injustice and Rectification.* New York: Peter Lang.

Rosenberg, Noah A., et al. (2002). "Genetic Structure of Human Populations." *Science, 298,* 5602, 2381.

Rossiter, Clinton (Ed.). (1999). *The Federalist Papers.* New York: Mentor.

Rothman, Stanley, Seymour Martin Lipset, and Neil Nevitte. (2003). "Racial Diversity Reconsidered." *The Public Interest, 151,* 25–38.

Ruffin, Edmund. (1853). *The Political Economy of Slavery; or, the Institution Considered in Regard to Its Influence on Public Wealth and the General Welfare.* In *Defending Slavery: Proslavery Thought in the Old South.* Edited by Paul Finkelman. Boston: Bedford/St. Martin, 2003.

Salberger, Ronald P., and Mary C. Turck (Eds.). (2004). *Reparations for Slavery.* Lanham: Rowman and Littlefield.

Sander, Richard H. (2005). "A Systemic Analysis of Affirmative Action in American Law Schools." *Stanford Law Review, 57,* 2, 367–484.

Scanlon, Thomas. (2003). *The Difficulty of Tolerance.* Cambridge UK: Cambridge University Press.

Scanlon, T. M. (1998). *What We Owe Each Other.* Cambridge MA: Harvard University Press.

Schaefer, Richard. (1990). *Racial and Ethnic Groups* (4th ed.). Glenview IL: Scott Foresman.

Schauer, Frederick. (2003). *Profiles, Probabilities and Stereotypes.* Cambridge MA: Harvard University Press.

Schedler, George. (1999). *Racist Symbols and Reparations.* Lanham: Rowman and Littlefield.

Schlesinger, Arthur M., Jr. (1992). *The Disuniting of America: Reflections on a Multicultural Society.* New York: W. W. Norton Co.

Schweninger, Loren. (1988). "Slaveholders, Black." In *Dictionary of Afro-American Slavery.* Edited by Randall M. Miller and John David Smith. Westport CT: Greenwood Press, Inc., p. 665.

Sher, George. (1987). *Desert.* Princeton: Princeton University Press.

Sher, George. (1980). "Ancient Wrongs and Modern Rights." *Philosophy and Public Affairs, 10, 1,* 3–17.

Sills, David L. (Ed.). (1968). *International Encyclopedia of the Social Sciences, 13,* 265.

Singer, Peter. (1993). *Practical Ethics* (2nd ed.). Cambridge UK: Cambridge University Press.

Singer, Peter. (1975). "All Animals Are Equal." In *Animal Liberation.* Edited by Peter Singer. New York: Avon Books, pp. 1–26.

Singer, Peter (Ed.). (1975). *Animal Liberation.* New York: Avon Books.

Skillen, Anthony. (1993). "Racism: Flew's Three Concepts of Racism." *Journal of Applied Philosophy, 10*, 73–89.

Sniderman, Paul M., and Thomas Piazza. (1993). *The Scar of Race.* Cambridge MA: Harvard University Press.

Snyder, Thomas, and Linda Shafer. (1996). *Youth Indicators 1996: Trends in the Well-Being of American Youth.* Washington DC: U.S. Department of Education.

Sowell, Thomas. (2005). *Black Rednecks and White Liberals.* San Francisco: Encounter Books.

Sowell, Thomas. (2004). *Affirmative Action around the World: An Empirical Study.* New Haven CT: Yale University Press.

Sowell, Thomas. (1995). *The Vision of the Anointed: Self-Congratulation as a Basis for Social Policy.* New York: Basic Books.

Sowell, Thomas. (1987). *A Conflict of Visions: Ideological Origins of Political Struggles.* New York: Quill.

Sowell, Thomas. (1981). *Ethnic America: A History.* New York: Basic Books.

Stampp, Kenneth M. (1956). *The Peculiar Institution: Slavery in the Ante-Bellum South.* New York: Vintage Books.

Steele, Claude M., and Joshua Aronson. (1998). "Stereotype Threat and the Test Performance of Academically Successful African Americans." In *The Black-White Test Score Gap.* Edited by Christopher Jencks and Meredith Phillips. Washington DC: Brookings Institution Press, pp. 401–427.

Sternberg, Laurence. (1996). *Beyond the Classroom: Why School Reform Has Failed and What Parents Need to Do.* New York: Simon and Schuster.

Storing, Herbert J. (1988). "Slavery and the Moral Foundations of the American Republic." In *Slavery and Its Consequences: The Constitution, Equality and Race.* Edited by Robert A. Goldwin and Art Kaufman. Washington DC: American Enterprise Institute, p. 48.

Summers, Clyde. (1970). "Preferential Admissions: An Unreal Solution to the Real Problem." *University of Toledo Law Review* (Spring/Summer), 393.

Thernstrom, Abigail, and Stephan Thernstrom. (2003). *No Excuses: Closing the Racial Gap in Learning.* New York: Simon and Schuster.

Thernstrom, Abigail, and Stephan Thernstrom. (1997). *America in Black and White: One Nation, Indivisible.* New York: Simon & Schuster.

Thernstrom, Stephan, and Abigail Thernstron. (1995). "Reflections on the Shape of the River." *UCLA Law Review, 46*, 1583–1631.

Thompson, Janna. (2002). *Taking Responsibility for the Past: Reparation and Historical Justice.* Cambridge UK: Polity Press.

Thompson, Janna. (2001). "Historical Injustice and Reparation: Justifying Claims of Descendants." *Ethics, 112*, 114–135.

Tien, Chang-Lin. (2000). "In Defense of Affirmative Action." In *Sex, Race, and Merit: Debating Affirmative Action in Education and Employment.* Edited by Faye J. Crosby and Cheryl Van De Veer. Ann Arbor: University of Michigan Press.

Tucker, William. (1990). *The Excluded Americans: Homelessness and Housing Policies.* Washington DC: Regnery Gateway.

U.S. Bureau of the Census. (2001). *Black Population in the United States: March 2000,* Series PPL-142 Washington DC: U.S. Government Printing Office.

U.S. Bureau of the Census. (2000)."Poverty in the U.S., 2000." Washington DC: U.S. Government Printing Office.

U.S. Bureau of the Census. (1992). *Current Population Reports*, Series P-20, No. 468. Washington DC: U.S. Government Printing Office.

U.S. Bureau of the Census. (1992). *Current Population Reports*, Series P-23, No. 181. Washington DC: U.S. Government Printing Office.

Van den Berghe, Pierre L. (1995). "Does Race Matter?" *Nations and Nationalism, 1, 3.*

Vars, Fredrick E., and William G. Bowen. (1998). "Scholastic Aptitude Test Scores, Race, and Academic Performance in Selective Colleges and Universities." In *The Black-White Test Score Gap.* Edited by Christopher Jencks and Meredith Phillips. Washington DC: Brookings Institution Press, pp. 457–479

Verdu, Vincene. (1993). "If the Shoe Fits, Wear It: An Analysis of Reparations to African Americans." *Tulane Law Review, 67* (February), 597–668.

Waldron, Jeremy. (1992). "Superseding Historical Injustice." *Ethics, 103* (October), 4–28.

Walker, Henry. (1988). "Black–White Differences in Marriage and Family Patterns." In *Feminism, Children and the New Families.* Edited by Sanford M. Dornbusch and Myra H. Strober. New York: Guilford Press, p. 91.

Wasserstrom, Richard. (1977). "Racism, Sexism, and Preferential Treatment." *UCLA Law Review, 24,* 581–622.

Weiner, Myron. (1984). "The Pursuit of Ethnic Inequalities Through Preferential Policies: A Comparative Public Policy Perspective." In *Independence to Statehood: Managing Ethnic Conflict in Five African and Asian States.* Edited by Robert B. Goldmann and A. Jeyaratnam Wilson. London: Francis Pinter, p. 64.

Wellman, David. (1993). *Portraits of White Racism.* New York: Cambridge University Press.

Welsh, Brandon C., David P. Farrington, and Lawrence W. Sherman (Eds.). (2001). *Costs and Benefits of Preventing Crime.* Boulder: Westview Press.

Western, Bruce. (2005). *Punishment and Inequality in America.* Princeton: Princeton University Press.

White, Richard A. (1994). "Statistical Report on the Gender and Minority Composition of New Law Teachers and AALS Faculty Appointments." *Journal of Legal Education, 44,* 429.

Wiecek, William M. (1977). *The Sources of Antislavery Constitutionalism in America: 1760–1848.* Ithaca: Cornell University Press.

Wightman, Linda F. (1998). *LSAC National Longitudinal Bar Passage Study.* Newton PA: Law School Admissions Council.

Williams, Patricia J. (1991). *The Alchemy of Race and Rights: Diary of a Law Professor.* Cambridge MA: Harvard University Press.

Wills, Gary. (1978). *Inventing America: Jefferson's Declaration of Independence.* Garden City NJ: Doubleday and Company.

Wilson, William Julius. (1987). *The Truly Disadvantaged.* Chicago: University of Chicago Press.

Wilson, William Julius. (1996). *When Work Disappears: The World of the New Urban Poor.* New York: Random House.

Wright, N. M., et al. (2002). "Growth Hormone Secretion and Bone Mineral Density in Prepubertal Black and White Boys." *Calcified Tissue International,* DOI: 10.1007/s00223-001-1068-0. New York: Springer-Verlag New York, Inc.

Young, Iris Marion. (1990). *Justice and the Politics of Difference.* Princeton: Princeton University Press.

Zack, Naomi. (2003). "Race and Racial Discrimination." In *The Oxford Handbook of Practical Ethics.* Edited by Hugh LaFollette. Oxford: Oxford University Press, pp. 245–271.

Zelnick, Bob. (1996). *Backfire: A Reporter's Look at Affirmative Action.* Washington DC: Regnery Publishing.

Table of Cases

Scott v. Sandford, 60 U.S. 393 (1857).

Sindell v. Abbott Laboratories, 26 Cal.3d 588, cert. denied, 449 U.S. 912 (1980).

Somerset v. Stewart, 1 Lofft 1 (1772); 12 Geo. 3 (1772) K. B.

Souther v. Commonwealth, 7 Gratt. (Va.) 672 (1851).

State v. Boon, 1 N.C. 103, Taylor 246 (1801).

State v. Harden, 2 Spears (S. C.) 151 (1832).

State v. Hoover, 4 Dev & Bat (N.C.) 365 (1839).

State v. Jones, I Miss. 83 (1820).

State v. Mann, 2 Dev. (N. C.) 263 (1829).

Strauder v. West Virginia, 100 U.S. 303 (1880).

United States v. Carolene Products, 304 U.S. 144 (1938).

United States v. Reese, 92 U.S. 214 (1875).

Wallace v. Jaffree, 472 U.S. 38 (1985).

Washington v. Davis, 426 U.S. 229 (1976).

Index